D0217930

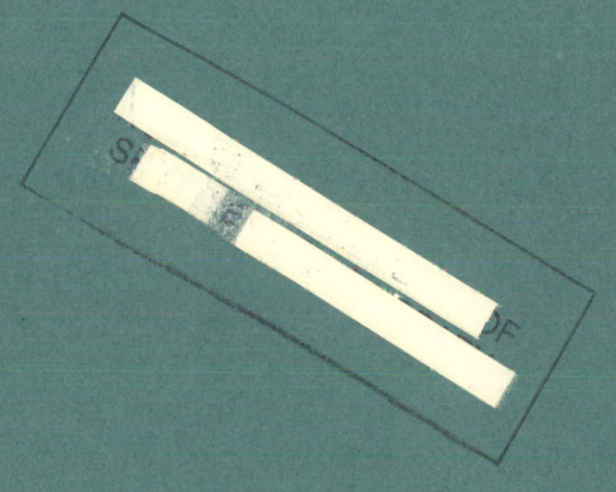

Race, Riots, and Roller Coasters

POLITICS AND CULTURE IN MODERN AMERICA

Series Editors: Margot Canaday, Glenda Gilmore,
Michael Kazin, and Thomas J. Sugrue

Volumes in the series narrate and analyze political and social change in the broadest dimensions from 1865 to the present, including ideas about the ways people have sought and wielded power in the public sphere and the language and institutions of politics at all levels—local, national, and transnational. The series is motivated by a desire to reverse the fragmentation of modern U.S. history and to encourage synthetic perspectives on social movements and the state, on gender, race, and labor, and on intellectual history and popular culture.

Race, Riots, and Roller Coasters

The Struggle over Segregated Recreation in America

VICTORIA W. WOLCOTT

UNIVERSITY OF PENNSYLVANIA PRESS
PHILADELPHIA

Published by
University of Pennsylvania Press
Philadelphia, Pennsylvania 19104-4112
www.upenn.edu/pennpress

Printed in the United States of America
on acid-free paper

2 4 6 8 10 9 7 5 3 1

Library of Congress Cataloging-in-Publication Data

Wolcott, Victoria W.
Race, riots, and roller coasters : the struggle over segregated recreation in America / Victoria W. Wolcott. — 1st ed.
p. cm. — (Politics and culture in modern America)
Includes bibliographical references and index.
ISBN 978-0-8122-4434-2 (hardcover : alk. paper)
1. African Americans—Recreation—United States—History—20th century. 2. African Americans—Segregation—United States—History—20th century. 3. Recreation—Social aspects—United States—History—20th century. 4. African Americans—Civil rights—United States—History—20th century. 5. United States—Race relations—History—20th century. I. Title. II. Series. III. Series: Politics and culture in modern America.
E185.86.W65 2012
323.1196'073—dc23

2012002588

For Erik,
who listens

Contents

Introduction

> When you suddenly find your tongue twisted and your speech stammering as you seek to explain to your six-year-old daughter why she can't go to the public amusement park that has just been advertised on television, and see tears welling up in her eyes when she is told that Funtown is closed to colored children . . . then you will understand why we find it difficult to wait.
>
> —Martin Luther King, Jr., "Letter from Birmingham Jail" (1963)

> I do not know many Negroes who are eager to be "accepted" by white people, still less to be loved by them; they, the blacks, simply don't wish to be beaten over the head by the whites every instant of our brief passage on this planet.
>
> —James Baldwin, *The Fire Next Time* (1963)

WHEN Martin Luther King, Jr.'s daughter Yolanda Denise asked her father why she could not go to Funtown, she touched on a painful reality that has been largely forgotten. Across the country, North and South, young African Americans discovered that time-honored discriminatory practices limited their access to amusement parks and other recreational facilities. And when they did approach these spaces they often confronted the white violence invoked by James Baldwin. Blacks wanted freedom and mobility without being "beaten over the head." They sought to live their lives fully as citizens and consumers without the constraints of segregation. Like King, they wished to protect their children from the reality of racism. Blacks desired not to be "loved" by whites but to coexist with them—and to use the swimming pools, roller-skating rinks, and Funtowns that made urban life in mid-twentieth-century America pleasurable.

The segregated recreation that the King family encountered in Atlanta was present throughout the country. The problem of segregated amusements was national in scope and the solution required a broad-based movement. African Americans in the twentieth century engaged in just such a movement, not simply for integration but for the occupation of public space in American cities. Among the most coveted urban spaces were those that encouraged young men and women to put aside their daily cares, flirt, and play. This potential for romance, and the association of African Americans with dirt and disorder, led to whites' insistence that recreational spaces be racially homogenous. Owners and managers of amusements constantly reassured their white customers that their facilities were clean and safe places to let loose and mix with the opposite sex. The result was an elaborate system of racial segregation in urban recreation. How African Americans challenged this segregation is the subject of this book.

Historians have developed a deep understanding of racial discrimination in housing and labor in mid-twentieth-century cities, yet their understanding of recreation remains shallow. Recreational facilities are public accommodations and can appear marginal compared to economic and political structures.[1] Historians who have challenged the "master narrative" of civil rights by expanding their analyses both chronologically and geographically have promoted the primacy of economic and housing issues in the past decade and moved away from the examination of public accommodations. The long civil rights movement now incorporates the class struggles of the Great Depression and the welfare rights and black power movements of the 1970s. Rather than focusing on the conflict between the southern civil rights movement and whites' massive resistance to integration, historians have reached north and west to examine myriad local struggles for racial equality and freedom. Central to these examinations are economic policies, particularly in works that incorporate labor struggles during the Great Depression and World War II. And the civil rights movement's expansion north and west has shifted our attention to discriminatory housing patterns that segregated American cities.[2]

For historians who focus on political economy, the struggle to open public accommodations is sometimes viewed as legalistic.[3] Some see efforts to desegregate public accommodations as part of an "integrationist framework" that ignores black nationalism and views the 1964 Civil Rights Act as the culmination of the movement.[4] Integration, it has been argued, also undermined black economic power and self-determination.[5] Focusing on public accommodations can also reify the dichotomy of the "innocent" North, where Jim Crow supposedly did not exist, versus the "evil" South, with its system of legal apartheid. Historians of the long civil rights movement reject this dichotomy and demonstrate the culpability of the state in creating and reinforcing patterns of segregation throughout the country. These historians also reject the notion that black power activists' commitment to self-defense undermined nonviolence and interracialism, thus leading to the movement's decline. Instead, they take seriously the broader goals of black nationalism and refuse to elevate nonviolent activists to near saintly positions in the American imagination.

With these important correctives in mind, is it possible to revisit the struggle to open public accommodations while escaping the "integrationist framework"? I believe it is, but historians must recognize that our view of what constituted civil rights activism cannot be a zero-sum game. Desegregating public accommodations was a goal powerfully desired by African Americans throughout the country. Just because white liberals, who saw integration as the primary goal of racial equality, also embraced this objective does not diminish its centrality in the black freedom movement. Liberal interracialism coexisted with radical interracialism promoted by nonviolent pacifists and ordinary black citizens who demanded immediate change, not the gradual process of moral persuasion promoted by racial liberals. These movements are related but should not be conflated. Therefore, writing public accommodations out of the civil rights narrative, or downplaying it, is a mistake. Rather, we need to rethink the struggle for public accommodations with the insights of the long civil rights movement historiography in mind.

One way to broaden our understanding of desegregation is by conceiving of it as part of a broader struggle for control of and access to urban space.[6] The segregation of public accommodations denied African Americans their right to occupy the same spaces as whites. They could not act as consumers on an equal basis, and they could not fully inhabit the cities and towns in which they lived. African Americans' demand for the right to use recreation was not simply about integration and interracial friendship but about power and possession. For this reason the struggle for recreational space was not only the purview of southern nonviolent activists but a national movement that included teenagers, mothers, and ordinary consumers who demanded equal access without having to face racial epithets and daily violence. African

Americans wanted to participate in all the recreation cities had to offer, and they wished to protect their children from white violence. Violence perpetrated by whites, however, has not been widely recognized as a major factor in maintaining segregation.[7] Popular memories of mid-twentieth-century urban amusements are replete with nostalgia and rarely contain references to segregation. This erasure of white violence has led many to blame the decline of urban recreation on "deviant" behavior by African Americans in newly desegregated amusements.

The struggle to desegregate public accommodations in the face of white terror did not begin with Rosa Parks's defiant stance in 1954. Even when identifying only activists who employed nonviolent passive resistance to challenge Jim Crow, one has to look at least a decade before the Montgomery bus boycott. The pioneering members of the Congress of Racial Equality (CORE) carried out a major campaign against Chicago's segregated White City Roller Rink in 1942 and fine-tuned organizing strategies that would prove enormously effective a decade later. And prior to the war years many ordinary African American citizens challenged segregated recreation nationwide, swimming at whites-only beaches, boycotting segregated roller rinks, and picketing Jim Crow amusement parks. For most the goal was desegregation, obtaining the right to occupy recreational space, rather than integration, fully sharing facilities with white neighbors. But motivations for engaging in the struggle over recreation varied. Liberal and radical white supporters of desegregation campaigns—for example, the white members of CORE who put their bodies on the line to fight for racial equality—were more likely to view full integration and interracialism as the goal. Middle-class African Americans often sought the respectability that came with full participation in consumerism. Working-class African Americans frequently conceived of the occupation of public space as a form of community control and a means to protect family members. Together these actors challenged the racial logic that associated white spaces with safety and security.

Moreover, the struggle for desegregated public accommodations was never fully distinct from the struggle for equal access to housing and employment. A local swimming pool or playground was an extension of a neighborhood, and as the racial composition of neighborhoods changed, urban dwellers contested these spaces. Whites who defended their "rights" to all-white workplaces and communities perhaps best understood this connection. Indeed, there is a relationship between what I term "recreation riots," racial conflicts in spaces of leisure, with housing riots in mid-twentieth-century American cities.[8] Historians have documented hundreds of small-scale and large-scale housing riots in the 1940s and 1950s.[9] In most cases, these were precipitated by an African American family's attempt to move into a white neighborhood, only to be met with angry residents who burned crosses, damaged property, and generally terrorized the newcomers. In the summer of 1951 one such riot in Cicero, an all-white suburb of Chicago, gained national attention as thousands of whites firebombed and gutted an apartment building after a middle-class black family moved in.[10] Many miles away that same summer a white guard at Palisades Park, a New Jersey amusement park across the Hudson River from Manhattan, invoked this housing riot to justify his own threat of racial violence. When a black activist, Ulysses Smith, attempted to enter the Palisades Park pool the guard stopped him and asked whether "he wanted to create an incident such as had occurred in Cicero."[11] In this case the Palisades guard used Cicero as a weapon to intimidate black activists and consumers. Violent attempts to forestall housing integration legitimated violent attempts to forestall recreational integration.

Two years before Smith approached the Palisades pool, New Jersey passed the Freeman Civil Rights Act in response to pressure from activists. The act specifically named swimming pools as a public accommodation where discrimination was prohibited.[12] But the legal niceties of civil rights legislation had minimal meaning in such confrontations. Instead, it was Smith's willingness to brave the guards and white crowds at the pool that defined the limits and possibilities of desegregation. The law was a major player in the struggle over recreational segregation, but it did not have the power to enforce equal access to public accommodations. Most northern and border states had both civil rights laws and segregated recreational facilities. Some southern communities had no segregation laws mandating separate facilities, and yet blacks had little access to recreation. This complex story undercuts the simplistic binary of southern de jure segregation versus northern de facto segregation.[13] Despite this, many scholars and observers would agree with Randall Kennedy that "Racial discrimination in places of public accommodation was, for the most part, a peculiar feature of southern folkways."[14] This "southern exceptionalism" pervades discussions of public accommodations and reinforces the myth of an innocent North and guilt-ridden South.[15] But even a cursory review of the evidence demonstrates that recreational segregation and the struggle to dismantle it were both national in scope.

Arguing for a national civil rights narrative and the end to southern exceptionalism does not erase the specific legal and social histories of different localities. White resistance to recreational integration in Birmingham, Alabama, was more profound and violent than white resistance to recreational integration in Buffalo, New York. And specific forms of recreation were more popular in some regions than others. Traditional urban amusement parks, for example, were largely phenomena of the Northeast and Midwest where entrepreneurs built them at the end of trolley lines. Throughout this book I have emphasized the lesser-known stories of northern segregation that have been widely neglected by scholars. To borrow from Jeanne Theoharis, in these cities recreational segregation was "hidden in plain sight."[16] The presence of northern segregation challenges notions of northern innocence and helps us understand the civil rights movement as circulatory, rather than traveling from south to north. Individual activists who led campaigns to open amusement parks in Cleveland and New Jersey during the 1940s and 1950s trained nonviolent activists who challenged segregated accommodations in the South in the early 1960s. In addition, throughout the country ordinary African Americans insisted on their right to access amusements during the postwar period. Some became part of a political movement by filing lawsuits with the National Association for the Advancement of Colored People (NAACP) or joining CORE, but many others engaged in daily forms of civil disobedience that were disconnected from civil rights leadership. When teenagers carried out this disobedience most commentators viewed their occupation of public space as juvenile delinquency or crime rather than a demand for racial equality. Throughout this book my focus will be on uncovering these stories on the local level rather than making broad regional generalities. Together these local stories document a national narrative of a mass movement to open recreational facilities to all Americans.

Although the struggle against segregation was national in scope, African Americans who sought to highlight the pervasiveness of Jim Crow and shame whites who supported it often used the language of regionalism as a tool. For example, in 1921 the African American newspaper *Chicago Defender* editorialized against beach segregation with the statement "This is not the South, and we refuse to be 'jim-crowed.'"[17] In claiming that Chicago was "not the South" Chicago blacks were demanding that white northerners live up to their reputation as moderate on racial issues. Thus the myth of southern exceptionalism was not an invention of white supremacists alone but was mobilized and perpetuated by African Americans to gain racial equality in the North and West. Some whites used this rhetoric of regionalism to justify segregation. The owners of Coney Island Amusement Park in Cincinnati, for example, argued that their park had to be segregated because whites from nearby Kentucky frequented it. Southern exceptionalism may have been a myth, but in the realm of discourse it was a myth that was often deployed as a weapon both for and against segregation. In this way regionalism continued to wield real power throughout the twentieth century.

We cannot accurately map segregation using the southern de jure and northern de facto binary. How, then, was a national system of recreational segregation organized? To a startling extent it was violence—or the fear of violence—that dictated where and to what extent racial mixing could take place. This violence was not regional, located only in the South, but local. When whites beat African Americans seeking leisure at amusement parks or swimming pools, white officials and the mainstream media often viewed them as "hoodlums" causing trouble. But politicians and the courts also routinely used the threat of such incidents as a reason to slow the pace of integration, and owners of recreational facilities invoked the potential for racial conflict as a primary motivation for keeping blacks out. White violence was both physical and performative; white defenders of leisure spaces sought to intimidate African Americans and demonstrate the negative outcome of desegregation.[18] White defenders ensured that recreation riots often followed formal attempts at desegregation. The state used this threat of violence to justify segregation. In the logic of judges and politicians, public space had to be orderly and safe in order to function. Violence resulting from desegregation efforts disrupted this order, and, in a circular argument, segregation needed to be maintained to prevent violence.

Much of that violence took place at amusement parks, swimming pools, and skating rinks—the main foci of this book. By examining these sites, in addition to activists and political organizations, it is possible to uncover broader patterns of struggle. Racial conflict between ordinary black consumers seeking leisure and white defenders of recreational space often lies outside the purview of social movements.[19] African Americans challenged essential racial hierarchies when they occupied the most coveted forms of public space.[20] When blacks destabilized these hierarchies, recreation riots, white resistance, and the denigration of such spaces often ensued. The centrality of controlled, orderly white recreation in urban life is most clearly evidenced by the aftermath of desegregation orders. When the courts declared particular recreational facilities "open," the result was rarely peaceful integration. This fact contradicts the popular understanding of the 1964 Civil Rights Act as solving the problem of public accommodations "virtually overnight."[21] Instead, owners of pools and parks used a variety of subterfuges, particularly privatization, to subvert the law. And many municipalities closed down public facilities rather than comply with the courts. Owners of urban amusement parks that finally admitted black customers allowed their facilities to deteriorate and eventually sold the valuable land to developers. The denigration of urban amusements by the late 1960s created, in Heather Ann Thompson's words, the "criminalization of urban space."[22] For many whites urban pools and parks were no longer sought-after respites but spaces of danger and potential conflict.

Recreation was a central racial battleground during the postwar period in part because leisure and consumerism had become key motifs in American life. The relative prosperity of American families meant they had both more time and more money to travel to an amusement park or frequent a roller-skating rink. The baby boom brought increasing demands for kiddie parks and playgrounds and, by the 1950s, growing ranks of teenagers looking for leisure and escape. Within the African American community, reformers had been leading campaigns for access to recreational facilities at least since the first Great Migration following World War I. By World War II, with a second Great Migration under way, these demands became more pressing. Ordinary African American citizens crowded into parks and beaches to occupy public space while demanding equality and supporting reformers' efforts. Within this wider context, civil rights leaders in the 1950s and 1960s were following the lead of previous generations of activists and black citizens. As Lizabeth Cohen asserts, "Mass consumption begot a mass civil rights movement."[23] Access to equal recreation, then, was a principal demand of both the organized movement and ordinary people. It was also a demand that sympathetic white liberals found relatively unthreatening.

Given liberal support for integration by the 1940s, the duration and strength of white opposition to desegregation are notable. Among public accommodations this opposition was most pronounced in amusement parks, swimming pools, and skating rinks. All of these spaces invited young men and women to mix, raising the specter of interracial romance. They were also sites where hardworking Americans could be free from inhibition and forget the mundane trials of daily life. Recreation had transgressive potential as "liminal" spaces that represented "a liberation from the regimes of normative practices and performance codes of mundane life."[24] This escapism into "imaginary landscapes" could lead to misbehavior, a fact owners and managers of amusement parks have long understood and sought to harness.[25] While marketing thrill rides, illicit pleasures, and physical exertion to a white mass public, they also gated and policed their amusements, banning alcohol and "undesirables." Above all, the sense of safety amid chaos promoted by amusement parks and other recreational facilities was premised on segregation. Because safety and control were racialized categories, desegregation led to fears of violence. And when that violence broke out in the form of recreation riots, the relationship between race and disorder was reinforced.

Of course other forms of public accommodations experienced racial violence during the civil rights era. Lunch counters, department stores, movie theaters, and restaurants all saw white resistance and violence to varying degrees. But the pervasiveness of conflicts in recreational facilities undergoing integration was distinctive. In the case of amusement parks this was, in part, due to their size: they were usually the largest public accommodation in a city. Activists often targeted them for this reason. In Cincinnati, for example, activists chose to desegregate their local amusement park, Coney Island, because, as one protestor noted, "as Coney Island went so went the restaurants, bars, and bowling alleys that catered to the general public."[26]

Despite the optimism of Cincinnati's civil rights workers, amusement parks proved difficult to fully integrate. Some owners leased their swimming pools, dance halls, and skating rinks to private entities to subvert civil rights laws. Therefore, many parks had segregated spaces within formally desegregated landscapes. Even with these steps, meant to reassure white customers, the majority of traditional urban amusement parks closed by the late 1960s and early 1970s, as whites increasingly perceived them as locations of danger rather than pleasure. Many urban swimming pools also closed down or privatized after desegregation. For amusement parks there was also a spatial solution that impacted American culture in profound ways. Starting in 1955 when Disneyland opened in Anaheim, California, theme parks built on earlier amusement park owners' insistence on cleanliness and order. But by locating their parks outside cities, inaccessible by public transportation, theme parks successfully avoided racial conflict. By the late 1970s these parks no longer needed to define themselves explicitly as white spaces; therefore, there was little noticeable conflict at the new theme parks. With high gate fees teenagers could not easily roam the grounds of such parks, and the parks' well-trained staff helped defuse conflicts. This was a public accommodations' version of the "color-blind meritocracy" historians have found in public discourses around housing and education.[27] Those who could afford to go to the theme park in their private cars belonged there. Those who could not were relegated to the city with few recreational options.

* * *

This book begins in Chapter 1 with a brief examination of how segregated recreation was both created and challenged at the turn of the twentieth century. Owners and operators marketed recreational facilities as safe spaces where white families would find cleanliness and order. By excluding African Americans they reinforced associations of disorder with blackness. But blacks continually confronted this segregation, even as it was being implemented. They occupied beaches, filed lawsuits, and boycotted amusement parks throughout the country. Given the weakness of state civil rights laws, those who policed segregation could rely on their institutional policies not to be successfully challenged in the courts. And white defenders of recreational space on Chicago's beaches and elsewhere used their fists to ensure coveted recreational facilities stayed white. By World War II civil rights organizations and liberal whites had begun to join forces with ordinary African Americans to challenge the color line in recreation. Chapter 2 examines this coalition in the 1940s, when racial liberalism dominated political life. For liberals, recreational segregation clearly contradicted the promises of American democracy, particularly during the war years. Radical nonviolent activists also targeted recreational segregation as new civil rights groups, most importantly CORE, developed innovative strategies to open parks and pools. But this idealism often clashed with the reality of white resistance, as attempts by black citizens and interracial activists to occupy recreational space sparked violent recriminations and the privatization of previously public recreation.

The role of radical nonviolence in opening recreation is further explored in Chapter 3 through an examination of the campaign to desegregate Cincinnati's Coney Island. In the early 1950s a group of pacifists led a remarkable series of protests at Coney Island that achieved partial desegregation and provided significant lessons for future campaigns. In 1954 the *Brown v. Board of Education* decision emboldened other activists, in the South as well as the North, to challenge the legal landscape of recreational segregation. Each lawsuit was preceded by an act of courage as African American mothers escorted their children to segregated parks, black teenagers swam at segregated beaches, and black businessmen took their golf clubs to municipal courses. Fear of racial conflict on the part of judges and local officials slowed the pace of desegregation during the *Brown* era, giving many communities time to subvert the law through privatization and closings. Chapter 4 examines how ordinary African Americans, disconnected from formal civil rights organizations, challenged white domination of a Buffalo amusement park, Crystal Beach. In Buffalo the fear of disorder stemmed not from civil rights protests but from the increased presence of black teenagers in the park. City officials and the local white media saw the violence as a problem of juvenile delinquency, unrelated to race. Proponents of Jim Crow in the South viewed the Buffalo riot as evidence of the racial violence that inevitably followed integration. Walt Disney offered a new solution to racial mixing at crowded amusement parks like Crystal Beach when he opened the first theme park in 1955.

Not all teenagers who challenged recreational segregation were dismissed as delinquents. Chapter 5 examines a more politicized group of young people who engaged in widespread protests. In 1960 the student movement focused on integration of public accommodations, including southern parks and pools. The response from southern white officials was swift as they closed public parks in Birmingham and drained pools throughout the region to forestall desegregation. In many northern cities African American activists and ordinary people also challenged recreational segregation. In cities such as Chicago, they faced large crowds of angry whites hurling rocks and racial epithets. Nonviolent activists, meanwhile, attacked racial segregation in a series of amusement parks. They finally opened the pool and dance hall in Cincinnati's Coney Island and made headlines with mass marches at Gwynn Oak in Baltimore.

Chapter 6 explores the impact of the 1964 Civil Rights Act on recreational segregation. Although many view Title II of the act, which called for desegregation of public accommodations, as an unmitigated success, the reality was that white resistance to its full implementation stymied the law's intent. Many African Americans were incensed by the slow pace of change and sought to make full use of amusement parks, beaches, and pools in their cities. But white consumers caught up in a public discourse of law and order increasingly associated urban recreational spaces with black criminality. Traditional amusement parks, in particular, closed in large numbers and were replaced by suburban theme parks that provided safety from black urban crowds.

The history of recreational segregation has been largely lost to the public imagination. There is an enormous amount of nostalgia associated with the urban trolley parks and lavish resort pools of a bygone era, a nostalgia that is explored in the conclusion. But the daily intimidation and violence experienced by African Americans seeking to enjoy urban leisure has not been given its due. Instead, commentators often blamed the racial rebellions and rising crime rate of the late 1960s for the decline of urban amusements. The popular myth of a golden age of urban recreation does not include the reality of white violence and black exclusion. Nostalgia for a lost past distorts this history and lays the blame for urban amusements' decline on African Americans' criminality in spaces of leisure after desegregation. However, childhood experiences of amusement parks and roller-skating rinks also point to a more complicated past and promising future. Combing the sources I have identified hundreds of racial incidents in recreational spaces to piece together the narrative presented here. But the facilities that saw little or no conflict, and welcomed black children to swim and play, are largely absent from the historical record. That history of interracial peace is also part of our past, present, and future. But in order to fully realize the promise of desegregation, we need to understand the struggle to achieve it.

CHAPTER 1

A Tarnished Golden Age: Race and Recreation Before World War II

IN 1924, when the educator and social activist Dorothy Height was twelve years old, she decided to learn how to swim. Height and a few friends traveled to Pittsburgh's downtown YWCA and approached the front desk. The receptionist told them simply, "Negro girls [cannot] swim in the YWCA pool." "The YWCA's discrimination seemed small and petty," remembered Height, "but it struck a painful chord that reverberated in each of us long afterward." She never did learn to swim, but she later worked to desegregate all YWCA facilities nationwide and in 1965 ran their newly established Office of Racial Justice.[1] Countless activists across the country echo Height's early experience of recreational segregation. A young Livingston Johnson, who was a leading activist in 1960s Pittsburgh, recalled being thrown out of a local roller-skating rink in the 1930s. "The ticket taker told me, 'get out of here; these people will kill you.' I got out."[2] Johnson identified this incident as the inspiration for his later civil rights work in the city. As these anecdotes suggest, recreational segregation was particularly cruel to children, who would harbor the memories of exclusion throughout their lives. As these children grew up, many used such memories to fuel their passion for racial justice. The experiences of Height and Johnson in prewar Pittsburgh also illustrate the kinds of racial barriers erected by recreational facilities, from the YWCA's institutional policy of exclusion to the violence meted out by rowdy whites at a local skating rink.

A utopian vision of urban life might center on public amusements. Crowds of immigrants and native-born Americans, men and women, working and middle classes, young and old, cavorting together at an amusement park or beach suggests democratic promise and urban vitality. Nostalgia for such scenes is prevalent in the twenty-first-century reality of privatized leisure and urban decline. Boarded-up and abandoned amusement parks and boardwalks in Atlantic City, Coney Island, and countless other resorts have become central images in our national declension narrative of neglected cities. But what we have lost was always an illusion; democracy was premised on racial exclusion. The amusement park was never, as suggested by the historian Judith Adams, "a perfect embodiment of the American spirit."[3] Nevertheless, the allure of public leisure was understood by all Americans, across racial and class lines. African Americans, believing in the promise of democratic space, resisted their exclusion from recreation. It was this resistance, rather than the illusory idea of a vibrant and open recreational culture, that might define the early twentieth century as a "golden age" of public leisure. But it was a golden age that was tarnished because white violence and institutional policies supporting recreational segregation undercut black resistance.[4] White owners and customers believed recreation could be kept virtuous and safe by excluding African Americans and promoting a sanitized vision of white leisure.

In the late nineteenth century modest picnic grounds and religious camps on the outskirts of major northern cities proved irresistible to entrepreneurs seeking to capitalize on the success of the Chicago World's Fair and Coney Island—pioneers in the area of commercial recreation. Private companies running electric trolley lines built amusement parks around these picnic grounds to lure riders and increase profits. Steamboat operators on the Great Lakes and Midwest rivers also capitalized on the new fascination for parks, beaches, and boardwalks.[5] Cincinnati now had its own Coney Island, Cleveland had Euclid Beach, New Jersey had Palisades Park, Youngstown had Idora Park, and Pittsburgh had Kennywood Park. Most major northern cities boasted large trolley parks by 1910, and a handful of southern cities, such as Ashland, West Virginia, where Camden Park was located, followed suit. Americans, blessed with increased leisure time, now routinely traveled by trolley, train, or boat to swim, dance, and risk the new mechanical rides. But this physical movement immediately raised issues of exclusion. Indeed, the legal foundation of segregation, the 1896 Supreme Court decision *Plessy v. Ferguson*, emerged from white resentment of elite Louisiana blacks who regularly traveled by train from New Orleans to Gulf Coast resorts.[6] In this decision the relationship between segregation and violence emerged as a central tenet of the "separate but equal" doctrine.

While the majority of the justices argued that segregation would maintain social order, Justice John Marshall Harlan, in the lone dissent, wrote that segregation "can have no other result than to render permanent peace impossible, and to keep alive a conflict of races, the continuance of which must do harm to all concerned."[7] For Harlan, segregation incited violence rather than preventing it, but this argument would find little support in legal circles until after World War II. By the 1940s the question of whether individual rights usurped the quest for public order was at the center of legal struggles over segregation. Did preventing violence require the separation of the races? Many lawyers and judges suggested it did. Arguing before the Maryland court in 1952 that Baltimore's beaches and swimming pools should remain segregated, the city solicitor stated, "I think one of the greatest objectives is to keep order and prevent riots. It is better for public safety in any activity involving physical contact that the races be separated."[8] But this widely held belief that segregation in public accommodations was necessary for public order was not inevitable or maintained equally across the nation. Nevertheless, by the mid-twentieth century, the threat of violence shaped arguments both for and against segregated recreation.

Patterns of racial segregation in parks, beaches, and roller rinks were more complex and less bounded by law than most Americans recognize. The 1875 Civil Rights Act included a provision requiring equal access to public accommodations, but the *Civil Rights Cases* in 1883 undermined the ability of courts to force private individuals or businesses to end discrimination. Such forms of discrimination, the court ruled, were not "state action" covered by the Fourteenth Amendment. In response, eighteen northern and border states passed civil rights laws that banned racial discrimination in public amusements.[9] Meanwhile the *Civil Rights Cases* and the *Plessy* decision unleashed a torrent of southern legislation explicitly segregating public accommodations. These laws suggest a strict binary—southern codification of segregation versus northern informal practices of segregation—most commonly referred to as de jure versus de facto segregation. This dichotomy has oversimplified our geographic and chronological understanding of recreational segregation from its outset.

Prior to the codification of segregation in the 1890s the South and North practiced very similar forms of de facto segregation in places of amusement. Starting with C. Vann Woodward's foundational 1955 work, *The Strange Career of Jim Crow*, numerous scholars have detailed how segregation was not the "natural" outcome of previous racial practices but a campaign of white supremacy and terror that reached its height at the turn of the twentieth century.[10] Howard Rabinowitz's revision of Woodward's thesis—that segregation replaced total exclusion from some public accommodations and therefore represented an incremental improvement for southern blacks—is particularly persuasive in the area of urban recreation. City officials often excluded blacks from parks and pools, sites fraught with tension, prior to the 1890s. Leon Litwack argues, "The expansion of recreation in the late nineteenth century mandated exclusion of blacks from most amusement parks, roller skating rinks, bowling alleys, swimming pools, and tennis courts."[11] In addition, these sites of commercial recreation were usually heterosocial, where men and women met for leisure and relaxation. This gender mixing immediately raised the specter of miscegenation, as leisure suggested physical intimacy. As Edward Ayers points out, "the history of segregation shows a clear connection to gender: the more closely linked to sexuality, the more likely was a place to be segregated."[12] Therefore, even before codification of Jim Crow in the 1890s, whites were more likely to enforce racial separation in recreational spaces than anywhere else.

Unlike public parks and picnic grounds, which had existed for decades and where there was some interracial mixing in the Reconstruction period, commercial recreation reached its height at the same time as statutory Jim Crow. Therefore, there was no historical memory of interracial contact in skating rinks and amusement parks. Like segregation itself, commercial amusements were modern institutions that came of age in the 1890s.[13] Because they were concentrated in towns and cities, they also reflected a reorganization of urban space, a geography of leisure. Central to this geography was consumption, and in sites where leisure was consumed actively and men and women mixed, segregation invariably followed. In the South this practice was more immediately evident, with "Whites Only" signs and state laws underlying the racialization of space. Nevertheless, in the urban North, where commercial recreation was exploding in popularity by 1900, civil rights laws were generally unenforced before the 1940s. State legislatures passed these statutes to appease black voters, but white opinion was deeply opposed to "social equality."[14] Even when civil rights laws were enforced, penalties for violating them were minimal. In 1885 a series of cases won by African Americans protesting racial discrimination in roller-skating rinks in Cleveland, for example, resulted in awards ranging from one cent to fifty cents.[15] More typical was the lawsuit filed in 1900 by an African American man denied entry into a dancing pavilion at Idora Park in Youngstown, Ohio. In this case the Court of Common Pleas ruled that it was not a "public resort" and therefore not subject to civil rights statutes.[16] On the issue of recreation the nation was relatively united at the turn of the century. Racial mixing at amusement parks, beaches, roller rinks, and swimming pools proclaimed full social equality. And a white public newly entranced by commercial amusements would not tolerate the presence of African Americans in these spaces.

African American sociologists and scholars writing about black life in the first half of the twentieth century noted the pervasiveness of recreational segregation. Particularly in the era of the first Great Migration, during the late 1910s and into the 1920s, black scholars and migrants catalogued regional differences around segregation. For them the simplistic de jure versus de facto dichotomy never fully described either southern or northern urban life. Rather, the lived experience of mobility, violence, and the elusive term "freedom" mapped their world. The integrated train and streetcar became a central image of a loosening of segregation's ties in the urban North. The segregated amusement park and swimming pool, in contrast, reflected segregation's persistence. Forrester B. Washington, a prominent reformer in the National Urban League, was typical in his focus on the "problem" of recreation for racial uplift ideologues concerned about the respectability of migrants. Washington lamented that the migrant has "found the wholesome agencies of recreation either closed or closing to him, while at the same time the agencies of commercialized vice have welcomed him with open arms."[17] Ordinary migrants were less concerned with the dangers of vice but were equally incensed by the pervasiveness of segregated recreation documented by Washington. In seventeen southern cities Washington found there was "complete segregation" of all playgrounds, parks, bathing beaches, and swimming pools. Of the forty remaining cities in his study, all segregated their bathing beaches and only three reported no segregation in swimming pools. Playgrounds and parks, in contrast, were not formally segregated in the North. Commercial recreation followed a similar pattern: southern cities segregated amusement parks and movie theaters entirely, while owners of private amusements in other cities dictated some segregation.[18]

The difference was one of degree. A swimming pool in Richmond, private or public, was a whites-only facility. A similar pool in Pittsburgh might allow African Americans to enter on allotted times or days, often a Monday. In the case of amusement parks, the policies in cities throughout the country were similar. Park owners gave African Americans the opportunity to use the park on "off days," often at the beginning or end of the season when the weather was less agreeable. In some cases this was only once a year, as in Lakewood Park in Atlanta or Idora Park in Youngstown.[19] In other cases it was once a week, as in Bob-Lo Island outside Detroit, or on alternate days, as in Hot Springs, Arkansas.[20] Parallel policies existed for golf courses, bowling alleys, and roller rinks—few were entirely integrated, but on particular days African Americans could gain entrance. In response some African American entrepreneurs opened black-only amusement parks, rinks, or pools. Norfolk, Virginia, alone boasted two black parks in the 1920s, and black-owned and -managed amusement parks were located in Joplin, Missouri, Lexington, Kentucky, Washington, D.C., Baltimore, Birmingham, Atlanta, and Macon, Georgia.[21] In Nashville, Tennessee Preston Taylor, a wealthy funeral director, opened Greenwood Park for local blacks, complete with a skating rink and amusement hall.[22] And in Kansas City, Missouri, African Americans opened Lincoln Electric Park as an alternative to the segregated Electric Park.[23] These were often precarious enterprises, but they offered safe spaces for black consumers to picnic, dance, and play without fear of confrontation with white customers or hired guards. They also demonstrated African Americans' full engagement with the world of commercial amusements that defined urban America in the early twentieth century. The creation of separate spaces was

Figure 1. African Americans strolling in Suburban Gardens. This black park offered African Americans rides, picnic grounds, and other amenities denied to them in white facilities. William H. Jones, *Recreation and Amusement Among Negroes in Washington, D.C.* (Washington, D.C.: Howard University Press, 1927), 101.

a strategy of resistance that refuted white assumptions that blacks were not worthy of such amusements.

The landscape of segregated amusements in the North and South did reflect the regions' different legal structures. Rather than a "Whites Only" sign, the universal symbol of Jim Crow, a northern migrant would often encounter a "Members Only" sign.[24] In order to circumvent the civil rights laws of the late nineteenth century and prevent lawsuits from black consumers, white owners created fictitious "clubs" at their pools, rinks, and parks. These policies marked the recreational landscape of the urban North and West as profoundly as the apartheid system in the urban South. Indeed, many of the legal struggles in midcentury to open segregated recreation focused on revealing private clubs as public accommodations. At the same time these clubs reinforced white notions of privilege and encouraged white consumers to defend "their" facilities from outsiders. The private club also shifted the focus away from race as the primary motivation for exclusion. In 1944 the sociologist Charles S. Johnson noted, "Northern proprietors have used numerous devices for effecting exclusion of Negroes while still remaining just within the letter of the law. For example, accommodations may be refused Negroes on 'purely personal grounds' rather than on account of color."[25] Excluding black customers on "personal grounds" looked outwardly distinct from the "Whites Only" signs of the South. But the distinction was semantic at best. Linking "Club Members Only" and "Whites Only" signs was the enforcement of recreational segregation through discriminatory policies, privatization, policing, and violence.

Policing Parks

The disjuncture between civil rights laws and the reality of segregation was particularly stark in Ohio. In 1894 an African American state legislator from Cleveland, Harry C. Smith, introduced a law barring discrimination in housing, employment, and public accommodations. Five years later the inventor of kettle corn, Dudley Sherman Humphrey, bought Euclid Beach Park on the southern shore of Lake Erie at the end of Cleveland's trolley line. His first priority was to establish the park as an "open and clean business," which meant eliminating the beer garden and freak shows and aggressively ejecting any customers he and his managers deemed "undesirable."[26] To bolster his marketing of a clean, family-friendly park, Humphrey openly refused to comply with Ohio's civil rights statutes, banning entrance to African American customers. To enforce this mandate he hired a private police force, analogous to the Pinkertons that American industrialists used to attack striking workers. Because the park had an open-gate policy, charging only for specific concessions, by the 1930s some African Americans began to gain entrance into the grounds. However, once inside the park they could not enter eating establishments, the bathhouse, the roller-skating rink, or the dance pavilion. This internal segregation was common among northern amusement parks that contained a variety of concessions. Whites perceived activities that promoted heterosocial mixing—swimming and dancing in particular—as sacrosanct. Disease was also a primary concern in restaurants and swimming pools; therefore, white stereotypes of African Americans as unclean disease carriers helped justify their exclusion from these facilities. And if owners did allow blacks entrance, white violence would be the result; thus the potential for disorder necessitated segregation.

Like Humphrey, amusement park owners throughout the country marketed their parks as clean, safe, and moral. They were striving to counteract negative perceptions of amusement parks as overcrowded spaces where immorality and criminality thrived. Owners sought to simultaneously harness the transgressive power of amusement parks and appease a white public eagerly seeking out commercial recreation. Within parks individuals could move outside their ordinary social sphere, reinvent themselves, and create new identities.[27] The historian John Kasson describes a Coney Island that "plunged visitors in to a powerful kinesthetic experience that, like the surf itself, overturned conventional restraints, washed away everyday concerns, buoyed and buffeted participants as they submitted to its sway."[28] In a 1930s study of amusement parks, a fifty-five-year-old steelworker remarked, "The bunch comes to raise a little hell when we are in the mood. We sort of let loose and all act like a lot of kids."[29] Owners and managers of amusement parks designed rides and spectacles to effectively market this potential to a mass public. Young women's skirts flew up with jets of hot air at the fun house, exotic dancers performed for crowds in "Little Egypt," and all decorum was lost on the roller coaster. But the potential for transgression led most parks to prohibit alcohol and gambling, hire private police forces, and aggressively eject "undesirable" customers.[30] Prohibiting African Americans was an integral part of this marketing tactic. The amusement parks of the early twentieth century were white spaces that signaled their purity and safety through racial exclusion.

Humphrey's policy of segregation and employing a police force, then, was typical of the policies at other early twentieth-century trolley and steamboat parks. Another midwestern park, Coney Island in Cincinnati, employed a similar strategy. In the 1880s Coney Island was a picnic ground nestled in an apple orchard and accessible from Cincinnati only by boat. An enterprising steamboat captain, William F. McIntyre, bought the land in 1886 and added a dance pavilion and a few rides, calling his new park "Ohio Grove, the Coney Island of the West." By the end of the first season most Cincinnatians simply referred to the park as Coney Island. As soon as the park opened McIntyre wanted to assure potential customers of its safety and respectability. One of the park's officers stated, "We intend that everything be first class. All ladies and children will be just as safe here as at home. We are determined to protect them, and all bad characters will be made to keep straight or be excluded from the grounds."[31] Although the park opened only two years after passage of the Ohio civil rights law, the "bad characters" included African American customers. In the case of Coney Island, as in most traditional amusement parks, order and safety were dependent on the exclusion of blacks. Thus white consumers associated disorder with the presence of African Americans, an association that would have profound consequences when these racial barriers finally fell.

Idora Park in Youngstown, Ohio, similarly focused on creating an "aura of respectability" for the working-class crowds of the rapidly industrializing city. In 1902 the park owner, Robert T. Ivory, told the public, "the morals of the park are to be maintained with more regard for propriety then [*sic*] ever and that means that women and children can go there without a particle of fear of being offended."[32] He posted signs throughout the park that read, "This is a private park. The management reserves the right to exclude any person from the grounds."[33] As in Euclid Beach and Cincinnati's Coney Island, a private police force ensured that the park excluded African Americans. The park had two "colored days" per year, one for the black Masons and the second for all African Americans on a Monday near the end of the season. On the day the Masons held their annual picnic, the Homestead Grays, one of the premier Negro League baseball teams, played an exhibition game and major African American performers put on shows that drew thousands of paying customers.[34] But even on these days black customers did not have full use of the park. "Closed for repairs" signs appeared on the swimming pool, and the more exclusive restaurants closed down.[35] Clearly park managers feared their while customers would perceive the "contamination" of black bodies in the water and eating establishments, even after African Americans had left the park. And these signs signaled to African Americans the limits of their inclusion at the park.

Preventing racial mixing was the primary concern of amusement parks seeking to market family-friendly, safe, clean recreation. However, they also worried about competing ethnic groups in growing industrial cities. "Sponsor days" became an efficient means of controlling the mixing of working-class crowds of all ethnicities and races. This policy was popular among both the owners and managers of parks and the companies and social groups that visited the parks. Sponsor days also provided a ready defense for owners charged with violating civil rights laws. Sponsors temporarily transformed parks into private "clubs" and justified the exclusion of others, at the managers' discretion. In many cities ethnic organizations sponsored picnics for their particular nationality. At Idora Park in Youngstown, for example, the Ancient Order of Hibernians sponsored Irish Day. Beginning in the late nineteenth century the Irish of Tammany Hall ran free excursions to New York's Coney Island. Donna DeBlasio notes that by the mid-1930s sixteen ethnic groups, "ranging from the Croatians and the Ukrainians to the Greeks and Hungarians," sponsored days highlighted by large picnics, speeches, music, and full use of the grounds at Idora.[36] On the one hand ethnic festivals at Idora Park and elsewhere "commodified group identity, defining it as something to be celebrated and displayed in a commercial setting, rather than in free public spaces such as churches and neighborhoods."[37] But this privatization of ethnic pride also could prevent violence between ethnic neighborhood gangs in public spaces. Italian Americans or Irish Americans could celebrate their heritage without fear of harassment or clashes among youth gangs.

By the 1920s corporations also began to take advantage of sponsor days as part of their growing commitment to welfare capitalism. Company unions from steel mills and automobile factories held large picnics at amusement parks. The Ford Motor Company, the Shin Company, and the Motorola Company, for example, held annual outings at Riverview Park in Chicago. On Youngstown Sheet and Tube Day over twenty thousand steel workers visited Idora Park.[38] These events occasionally brought black workers to parks, but until the 1930s, when industrial unions actively recruited African Americans, segregated recreation was not often challenged during sponsor days.[39] Instead, black workers would simply be excluded from such excursions or barred from swimming pools and dance halls at large picnic grounds or amusement parks. In the case of the Ford Motor Company, the corporation built a separate large athletic park with playing fields, playgrounds, and a bandstand for their workers.[40] But black industrial workers in urban America generally found little integration outside the factory floor in the 1920s. Commercial recreation outside their communities was largely closed to them, and even entering public parks and playgrounds risked potential violence.

African American urban migrants in the first half of the twentieth century constantly negotiated an urban terrain where segregation was carefully policed in some forms of recreation and not in others. "In amusement places such as roller-skating rinks, bowling alleys, and public dance halls there is a rigid line," note St. Clair Drake and Horace Cayton describing Chicago in the 1920s. "All these are recreational situations that emphasize active participation rather than merely looking on, and in which men and women participate together."[41] Spectatorship, for Drake and Cayton, did not require segregation; the intimacy of eating, dancing, or playing together violated social norms. Gunnar Myrdal, in his seminal work *An American Dilemma*, suggests that there were different motivations for recreational segregation in the North and South: "It would seem much more reasonable in the North than in the South to accept the belief that Negroes are dirty as the main reason why they are not liked on the same bathing beaches. This belief is more natural for Northerners, since there is quite a bit of physical touch contact between Negroes and whites in the South and little in the North. Southerners tie up the bathing prohibition to the sexual prohibition—which Northerners less frequently do."[42] Both of these theories are undermined by the facts. For example, many northern theaters—clearly sites of spectatorship—were segregated until the postwar period. And northerners were particularly sensitive to the threat of miscegenation implied by interracial dancing and skating—two of the most commonly segregated activities. But these authors, and indeed all commentators on the issue of recreation, agreed on one pattern. It was interracial swimming that inspired the most condemnation and violence. In the water fears of contagion and interracial sexuality made for a treacherous mix.

Before the first Great Migration one can find instances of interracial swimming on beaches and in pools. Bryant Simon notes that in Atlantic City, for example, city beaches were open to blacks before 1920. After hotel owners complained that their customers "positively will not stand rubbing elbows with colored bathers" the city created a black beach, known as Chicken Bone Beach, and police routinely ejected African Americans who ventured onto "white" beaches.[43] Another famous New Jersey resort town, Asbury Park, segregated its beaches significantly earlier. By 1885 a small Methodist camp founded by James A. Bradley had become a full-fledged resort complete with a boardwalk and an explosion of new hotels. African American residents who worked in the hotels and restaurants often intermingled with white guests on the beach. Business owners and their white customers objected to this presence, claiming it was a "white people's resort and it derives its entire support from white people."[44] Bradley argued he "owned" the beach and therefore had the right to exclude blacks, much as an amusement park owner controlled who could enter his park. An 1885 *New York Times* article on the controversy claimed that African Americans were "overstepping all bounds, intruding themselves in places where common sense should tell them not to go, and monopolizing public privileges to the exclusion of whites."[45] Southern papers began to cover the story, reveling in the hypocrisy of Methodists' "liberal racial attitude" and their discomfort with the social equality of blacks on the bathing beaches.[46] Indeed, the southern press often covered racial conflict over recreation in the North to justify southern segregation practices. Southern papers expressed regional pride in their ability to maintain order, in contrast to a disorderly and potentially violent North. Local blacks in Asbury Park vociferously protested the emerging policy of exclusion with one local minister declaring, "Mr. Bradley might as well try to hang his handkerchief on the horns of the moon as to keep the colored people off God's beach."[47] But it was also Bradley's beach and he had the power to keep social equality at bay.

Most urban beaches, in the North and the South, separated black and white bathers by the 1920s, and many did so much earlier. In contrast, swimming pools present a more complicated history of racial exclusion. The historian Jeff Wiltse argues that municipal swimming pools in the urban North began in the late nineteenth century as spaces where working-class boys, usually immigrants and African Americans, swam together. These gender-segregated facilities did not raise major alarms about social equality. By the late 1910s and accelerating into the 1920s, major cities began to build "resort" pools, large and lavish facilities that often included sandy beaches, waterfalls, and changing facilities. Women and girls were invited to join in the fun, and racial segregation became the norm. Mixed-gender swimming in an era of shrinking bathing suits and a sexual revolution brought fears of racial miscegenation to the fore.[48] Resort pools, in contrast to earlier modest facilities, were also more coveted spaces among middle-class urban whites. Although they were built with tax dollars, these facilities became whites-only spaces because of their desirability. Racial homogeneity, whether in a residential neighborhood or a swimming pool, maintained the value of a particular space for many whites. Therefore, by the 1920s most bodies of water, both contained and natural, were subject to Jim Crow.

Resistance and Recreation Riots

Segregated swimming may have been ubiquitous by the 1920s, but so was African American resistance to that segregation. Across the country blacks protested, petitioned, filed lawsuits, and violated the barriers raised by white owners and mangers of pools and beaches. The result was continual conflict and, as predicted by Justice Harlan in 1896, escalating violence. African Americans in Omaha, Nebraska, for example, protested when the city proposed segregating the local pool in McKinley Park, offering to build separate "Jim Crow" pools in the black neighborhood. On a hot night in July fistfights at the pool between white and black swimmers broke out. Police quickly intervened with nightsticks and ordered the pool drained.[49] In Omaha, as in cities across the country, the transition to segregated swimming did not go smoothly. African Americans vociferously protested their exclusion from many resort pools that invited white women and girls in and kept all blacks out. The first large resort pool to promote mixed-gender play, Fairground Park Pool in St. Louis, opened in 1913 as a segregated facility. The city responded to protests by blacks by building a ten-foot-high fence around the pool to prevent incursions by black swimmers and stationing police officers to supplement the pool guards. African American activists protested segregation in Los Angeles pools in the 1920s as they were being built. In the face of growing anger, the city's recreation department allowed blacks into the pools on the days before they were cleaned. Southern California blacks were also incensed by their total exclusion from beaches, with the exception of Ink Well and Bruce's Beach, two small areas reserved for African Americans.[50] When Congress authorized segregated beaches and pools in Washington, D.C., in the early twentieth century, the sociologist William H. Jones noted, "The Negro population strenuously objected to the segregated beaches or pools and sought to have the bill stripped of all adjectives that bespoke segregation."[51] These protests failed to stem the tide of segregated swimming and might be dismissed as ineffectual. But segregated beaches also lay at the heart of one of the most notorious race riots of the first Great Migration, one that dramatically shaped interwar race relations.

Chicago's 1919 race riot was the bloodiest of the red summer that followed World War I. After seven days of rioting, twenty-three blacks and fifteen whites lay dead on Chicago's streets. Scores more were injured. The riot began when a fourteen-year-old African American boy, who had been riding on a makeshift raft with a group of friends, drifted over to the white beach on the other side of a dividing line at 29th Street. Seeing the boy swimming in the water, a white man threw rocks at his head, drowning him. His friends raced to get help, and soon a crowd of blacks congregated at the white beach. When the police refused to arrest the perpetrator the crowd grew angry and a black man, James Crawford, shot into a group of police officers. An African American cop fired back, killing Crawford and signaling the beginning of a full-scale riot.[52] Much of the fighting took place along the border of the black belt and the West Side immigrant neighborhood, with Wentworth Avenue as the dividing line. Other fights broke out at the stockyards where black workers had to pass through gangs of white youths to reach home. In nearly all the historical literature on the 1919 riot, two factors stand out as the primary causes of the violence: housing and labor. During World War I industries hired African Americans, many of them recent migrants, to replace enlisted workers and act as strikebreakers. Meanwhile a growing tide of black migrants began to put pressure on the limited housing available in

Figure 2. A crowd congregates at the Twenty-Ninth Street Beach after the drowning of Eugene Williams. Chicago Commission on Race Relations, *The Negro in Chicago: A Study of Race Relations and a Race Riot* (Chicago: University of Chicago Press, 1922), ii.

the expanding black belt.[53] Although clearly labor competition and struggles over housing were major factors in producing racial tension, historians have largely overlooked the fight over recreational space and the anger over segregation of beaches as causes of the riot rather than mere context.[54]

The 1919 conflagration on Chicago's streets was a recreation riot. It followed years of anger and fighting over recreational space, particularly parks and beaches, and foreshadowed many more decades of skirmishes. For example, in 1912 a white mob attacked an African American child who attempted to bathe at the 39th Street Beach.[55] The largely Irish working-class teenagers who carried out many of the attacks on blacks in streetcars and at the gate of the stockyards were the same teens who had skirmished over parks, playgrounds, beaches, and ballparks in the years prior to the 1919 riot. The authors of *The Negro in Chicago*, commissioned by the city to study the riot, argued that "gangs and hoodlums" were the primary perpetrators of the violence, Ragen's Colts being the most notorious. "Molestation of Negroes by hoodlums," they argued, "had been prevalent in the vicinity of parks and playgrounds and at bathing-beaches."[56] Many were members of "athletic clubs," youth gangs that made use of the scant recreational facilities in the city. As one Chicago official reported, "I think they are athletic only with their fists and brass knuckles and guns."[57] According to an African American playground director, black boys knew not to go to 38th Street Beach because "They rock you if you go in." In the wake of the riot, the authors of *The Negro in Chicago* noted that African Americans could safely use only one of the eight available bathing beaches in the city, the one on 26th Street.[58]

The young black teenagers on the makeshift raft were not the only ones violating the Jim Crow line at the 29th Street Beach that hot summer day in 1919. Earlier that afternoon a group of African American adults purposely crossed over into the white beach until they were driven back when pelted with stones and insults from white bathers.[59] This type of spontaneous protest was common as segregated leisure increasingly defined everyday life in both the North and the South. For disappointed and disheartened urban migrants, such racial divisions were particularly difficult to stomach. Nevertheless, to label the 1919 riot a recreation riot is not to suggest that it was not part of a larger struggle over labor and housing. Indeed the bombings of private homes, restrictive covenants, and housing riots that marked Chicago through the first half of the twentieth century defined the neighborhood lines that also shaped struggles over parks and pools. Anger over strikebreaking black workers and economic competition certainly fueled white hostility at the time of the riot. But the murder at the 29th Street Beach was not merely a spark for the riot. Chicago's black community was claiming their right to occupy and enjoy recreational space, and the riot was a direct result of this demand.

The 1919 riot did not end the struggle over Chicago's beaches. Just two years later the *Chicago Defender* declared, "We are going to use every beach along the shores of Lake Michigan and if our white brothers and sisters fear that the waters that we splash around in are contaminated we have not the slightest objection in the world to their continuing the use of their old reliable bath tub every Saturday night."[60] Despite this bravado, or rather because of it, there was intermittent fighting on Chicago's beaches throughout the 1920s, culminating in a call by the city's black leaders for improved police protection. But the police did not adequately protect the civil rights of black bathers and would not for more than a generation. Indeed, park police routinely turned away black swimmers in a system that paralleled the private armed guards patrolling many amusement parks. And they often turned a blind eye when white beachgoers attacked African Americans seeking respite from the city's heat. Jackson Park Beach, south of 57th Street, was a focal point of repeated incidents of violence. In 1925 whites chased a young black couple off the beach, yelling at them and beating them with sticks. When they turned to a policeman for assistance he told them, "This beach is for white people only. Come on and get out of here and go to your own beach: that's where you belong."[61] The couple complained their "own" beach had no bathhouse or shower and was frequented by rats.[62] In 1929 a white gang threw stones at a group of twenty-three African American Girl Scouts, driving them from the beach.[63] Noting the growing tension, the *Chicago Tribune* editorialized:

> We should be doing no service to the Negroes if we did not point out that to a very large section of the white population the presence of a Negro, however well behaved, among white bathers is an irritation. This may be a regrettable fact to the Negroes, but it is nevertheless a fact, and must be reckoned with. Moreover, it is a fact which has frequently contributed to disorders, and notably to the race riots of a decade ago. Under the circumstances it would seem that the Negroes could make a definite contribution to good race relationship by remaining away from beaches where their presence is resented.[64]

In fact, African Americans did not challenge beach segregation throughout the city, but Jackson Park Beach was close and convenient for a large percentage of Chicago's black community, and they persisted in their attempts to make full use of it.

In 1931 a black newspaper reported that on South Side beaches, "groups of colored bathers have been insulted, molested, or threatened by bands of white hoodlums who resented their presence at the public recreation places."[65] Perhaps fearing an escalation of violence leading to another 1919 riot, the city raised a powerful symbol of northern Jim Crow at Jackson Park Beach soon thereafter: a fence dividing white and black swimming areas. This fence became a symbol of recreational segregation in Chicago: one Chicago black politician swore he would "tear it down with his own hands," numerous African Americans faced violence and arrest by jumping the fence, and a group of white students from the University of Chicago denounced it in 1935.[66] After a particularly vicious heat wave in 1937 the *Chicago Defender* noted that the "historic fence that separates the 'browns' from the 'tans' still remains, despite the efforts of civic, religious, political, and recreational representatives' pleas for its removal."[67] Even with these challenges the Jackson Park fence remained in place until at least 1940.[68] African Americans' pleas fell on the deaf ears of city officials and the police department who, like their compatriots in the South, mistakenly believed racial separation would lead to racial peace.

Even before World War II using segregation as a means of riot prevention was clearly ineffective. Small- and large-scale racial conflict over recreation prevailed in Chicago throughout the 1930s. Daily harassment of blacks who attempted to use public facilities was common. When a pool attendant denied a black mother and her four daughters a locker at a public pool, white children cut up their clothes while they swam. Some African Americans avoided swimming altogether to protect themselves and their families. As the sociologists Drake and Cayton remarked, "most Negroes do not wish to risk drowning at the hands of an unfriendly gang."[69] The violence perpetuated by Chicago's white youth gangs and beachgoers was effective in limiting the recreational spaces African Americans could safely and freely use. Violating racial lines, whether actual fences or imaginary boundaries, could mean serious injury and arrest. Given that daily reality, the frequency with which ordinary African Americans risked violence to exercise their rights is remarkable, particularly in an era when neither government nor powerful organizations were coming to their aid.

Resisting recreational segregation in an era in which racial peace was valued above racial justice often took the form of individual or group protests outside traditional racial reform organizations. Although the NAACP did attempt to prosecute segregated recreation cases in the North during the interwar period, their lawyers were largely unsuccessful in courts willing to ignore late nineteenth-century civil rights laws. The Urban League was primarily engaged in creating alternative "respectable" recreational facilities for African Americans rather than challenging segregated facilities. Urban League officials routinely sponsored supervised dances, picnics, and ball games that reformers deemed both respectable and safe from white violence. Black nationalist organizations, such as Marcus Garvey's United Negro Improvement Association (UNIA), were similarly focused on developing separate facilities rather than encouraging blacks to face the humiliation and violence of white-dominated spaces. Yet individual African Americans continued to protest segregated facilities. In 1927, for example, Roberta W. Booker wrote a letter to the editor of the *Pittsburgh Courier* complaining about Idora Park. Booker pointed out that on August 22, the designated day for blacks, "twelve thousand Negroes from Pittsburgh and nearby towns flocked to Youngstown's beautiful Idora Park." Calling for a boycott of the park, Booker asked, "Is it ignorance, indifference, lack of race pride, the inferiority complex, or just what, that makes our folks submit to such humiliations?"[70] Eight years later Booker's call for a boycott was spectacularly successful when African Americans refused to attend the All-American Colored Day in favor of nearby Craig Beach, where Chick Carter, a well-known jazz musician, performed for over a thousand.[71] Although Youngstown's black community had not convinced the owners of Idora Park to integrate, they had demonstrated their economic power and withdrawn their support for an openly racist institution.

Euclid Beach Park in Cleveland, in contrast to Idora Park, did allow African Americans to walk the grounds and try out the mechanical rides. On a few specifically allotted days the Humphrey family would open the dance hall or roller-skating rink to African American customers. But in these spaces of greater intimacy racial mixing was not permissible, and by 1934 some racial liberals in Cleveland had begun to protest this policy. When the park banned African American schoolchildren from the dance hall during a series of school picnics, the Cleveland School Board passed a resolution whereby schools would not use the park until "all the children" were "accorded the full and equal enjoyment of the accommodations."[72] The following year two black high school students filed lawsuits when they were denied entry into the dance hall. At this point the Humphrey family set up a fund of ten thousand dollars to settle these cases, and others they anticipated would follow, out of court.[73] Their legal fund soon came in handy when nine members of the NAACP Youth Council filed suit against the Humphrey Company in 1943 and received a generous settlement.[74] The Humphreys' main weapon in maintaining racial segregation, however, was the threat of violence. In 1938 the private security force brutally beat Joe Gray, a young African American man, for violating racial norms. Soon after, a young black couple also charged that park guards attacked them in an "unprovoked assault."[75]

Hiring private police forces and setting up legal funds to fend off lawsuits were necessary because of the constant pressure put on segregated facilities by frustrated black consumers. Amusement park owners and managers were continually fending off attempts to violate their whites-only policies, often by violence. Clashes between black customers and the Pinkerton-like private police helped forge the white popular opinion that racial segregation equaled racial peace. A black presence at a beach or a pool was threatening because blacks themselves embodied the possibility of disorder, even when they were not responsible for the violence that followed. In addition to the potential for violence, racial mixing also suggested the potential for interracial romance and disease to a white public. Two sets of consumers of recreational space, white and black, were each expressing their "right" to an orderly, clean, safe place to play. These incompatible demands spawned recreation riots. From the beaches of Chicago in 1919 to the midways of Cleveland in the 1930s, the racial struggle over recreation was a significant part of urban life in the first decades of the twentieth century. And those who supported segregation could rely on weak civil rights laws to ensure that institutional policies would not be successfully challenged in the courts.

Recreational Segregation in Depression-Era Cities

The role of the state in creating and sustaining segregated recreation was heightened during the 1930s. Urban historians have exposed the culpability of the state in segregating American housing during and after Roosevelt's New Deal.[76] Less well understood is the culpability of the state in segregating other urban spaces during the Depression. This history further undermines the de jure–de facto dichotomy, suggesting that the government did more to unite regions around racial segregation than it did to divide them. By the 1930s recreational segregation was beginning to gain some notice, in part because African American activists had been calling attention to the woefully lacking recreational facilities and discriminatory policies since the early twentieth century. Concerns about juvenile delinquency as a cause of recreation riots also led to increased sensitivity on the part of city officials. After 1929 recreation was a favorite topic of social scientists and government officials faced with a nation of unemployed workers saddled with unwanted leisure time. Louis Walker, in his 1931 book *Distributed Leisure: An Approach to the Problem of Overproduction and Unemployment*, called for a federal "Division of Leisure" that would parallel the work of the Labor Department.[77] Although this did not come to pass, Roosevelt's New Deal agencies funneled funds to local communities to run recreation programs, build swimming pools and other facilities, and promote wholesome alternatives to commercial vice. These funds both bolstered segregated recreation and helped foster the interracial institutions and alliances that would challenge it.

One might suspect that the depths of the Great Depression would bring recreation to a standstill. The opposite proved to be true. Although Americans had less money, they had more leisure time and spent scarce resources on movies, amusement park visits, and excursions to bowling alleys and roller rinks. More than any other urban institution, the local swimming pool became a central part of American lives. Municipalities had built pools in the 1920s, the resort pools that carefully excluded black swimmers, but in the 1930s the federal government took the lead role in building more pools. Initially the Civil Works Administration (CWA) took on the task of building pools during the first New Deal between 1933 and 1935. After 1935 the Works Progress Administration (WPA) continued the massive building projects that constructed post offices, libraries, schools, and swimming pools. Jeff Wiltse estimates that between 1933 and 1938 the federal government built "nearly 750 pools and remodeled hundreds more."[78] These public pools were similar to other New Deal programs in conforming to segregation practices in local communities. Cities routinely prevented African Americans from swimming in New Deal pools that, as taxpayers, they had helped fund. In Ironton, Ohio, for example, WPA funds built a swimming pool at the local high school that blacks could use for only four hours on Thursdays.[79] Like the segregated public housing built during the New Deal, segregated pools inscribed racial lines legitimated by the federal government.

Black citizens responded to government-sanctioned segregation with a rising tide of anger and protest. Exclusion from New Deal pools was particularly painful in communities that were developing a new relationship with the federal government—a relationship that was based on promises of representation and aid in return for electoral support. African Americans also had a keen sense of their consumer rights and demanded access to recreation even at the risk of white violence. When the city of Pittsburgh built the lavish Highland Park pool in 1931, for example, attendants asked for health certificates from blacks who approached the gates and then turned them away regardless. In the years that followed whites viciously beat young black swimmers who managed to gain entry into the pool, but blacks continued to protest unequal treatment. In the summer of 1934 the black newspaper the *Pittsburgh Courier* editorialized against the "whitewashed" Highland Park pool, calling for continued action until "some city official with a bit of backbone comes forth with the courage and the intestinal stamina to take a stand against this vicious practice of segregation in city pools which Negroes pay taxes to support."[80] Their taxes had paid for the pool and yet blacks had to risk hospitalization to use it. By World War II a rcinvigorated NAACP would follow the lead of Pittsburgh's blacks and file lawsuits to desegregate federally funded recreational facilities. But during the Great Depression African Americans faced angry white mobs with little legal backing.

Whites were also sensitive to the potential use of federal dollars to build recreational facilities that might promote racial mixing or invite blacks into coveted facilities. During the New Deal, Miami was surrounded by exquisite beaches completely closed to blacks and offered twenty pools to whites exclusively. When the segregated Civilian Conservation Corps (CCC) proposed an African American work camp at the Matheson Hammock Park in Miami, the county rejected it based on complaints from whites who were frightened that black workers "would come constantly in contact with people enjoying park facilities."[81] Similarly a city proposal for a segregated public housing project in Liberty City, complete with a pool, sparked a white backlash. According to the architectural historian John A. Stuart, "For many white citizens, the pool was simply too much of an improvement in the condition of the black residents and threatened to open up too many new opportunities for parities in leisure between black and white residents of the city."[82] The city built the Liberty City project with no pool, and it was not until 1945 that local blacks managed to obtain a swimming beach at Virginia Key, a small island between Key Biscayne and Miami.[83] The white power structure successfully ensured that the influx of federal money would not open recreational opportunities to black residents. African Americans noted this failure, and Miami became a central southern site of recreational struggles after World War II.

In the 1930s the power of the black "citizen consumer" was manifested in

"Don't Buy Where You Can't Work" campaigns, cooperatives, and economic nationalism. These movements shaped urban African Americans' perception that consumerism was a route to political as well as economic power.[84] "By mobilizing as consumers," argues Lizabeth Cohen, "African Americans participated in a broader political culture of dissent where 'the consumer' became viewed as a legitimate and effective agent of protest, particularly for women and blacks who were marginalized from the mainstream of politics and the labor movement."[85] Demanding access to recreation, a much-prized commodity, was an assertion of consumer rights and, in an era when government money was funneled to recreation, an assertion of citizenship rights. African American urban reformers argued that denied these rights, young blacks would turn to illicit activity and become more vulnerable to juvenile delinquency. By the late 1930s some interracial organizations devoted to providing wholesome recreation to young Americans, particularly the YWCA, YMCA, Scouting groups, and schools, began to challenge segregated recreation in a limited way. Preventing delinquency by providing recreation to urban youth was a wedge that activists used to promote integration and confront Jim Crow.

Writing in 1940, E. B. Henderson, a prominent educator who is credited with popularizing basketball among African Americans, argued, "to a larger degree than other youth, Negro youth have suffered much in the attainment of many social objectives under policies of segregation." This was, he argued, "as true for recreation as it is true of segregated systems of education."[86] Although Henderson noted that local government, using federal funds, had built new playgrounds and some recreational buildings designated for blacks during the 1930s, there were almost no public facilities for bowling, golf, ice-skating, or swimming. This was problematic because commercial roller rinks, pools, and golf courses almost entirely banned African Americans.[87] Large urban schools in particular struggled with these policies when planning excursions. Although residential segregation and carefully drawn district lines limited their diversity, majority-white high schools in the North and West usually had a few black students who could not enter pools, rinks, or parks. In 1933, for example, George Prioleau, a black student at Los Angeles's Polytechnic High School, accompanied his classmates on an excursion to the Rollerdome skating rink. The rink refused entry to the handful of black students. Prioleau, with the help of his mother, contacted the NAACP and convinced them to file a lawsuit. Meanwhile the school district agreed to no longer hold school trips there.[88] Such excursions educated public officials about the pervasiveness of segregation in commercial recreation.

The Los Angeles school district, like the Cleveland school district that banned excursions to Euclid Beach Park, had to respond to the increasingly angry demands of their young students and their parents. Other youth organizations faced similar dilemmas. By the 1930s Cincinnati's Coney Island was running under the ownership of Edward Schott, who continued the park's policy of complete segregation when he took over the park. "Today the idea of a real park is one that provides wholesome, clean, invigorating rest, recreation and amusement," Schott assured white patrons.[89] For Schott and many whites in Cincinnati, keeping Coney Island "wholesome" and "clean" required the exclusion of black residents. Virginia Wilson Coffey was one of the first to directly challenge this assertion. An African American activist, Coffey came to Cincinnati in 1932 where she directed the all-black West End YWCA. By the late 1930s she was asked by the Cincinnati Girl Scouts to be a field director for the African American Scouts, a position she took on with the goal of eliminating all forms of segregation within the Scouts in five years. Each year Cincinnati Girl Scouts rode the lavish steamboat *Island Queen* to Coney Island on a much-anticipated excursion, but as the park historian Charles Jacques points out, "the *Island Queen* was segregated as was the park, and no African Americans were permitted as passengers."[90] With the formation of a black troop this trip was in jeopardy. The troop directors suggested that an alternate trip be planned for the African American girls but Coffey refused. "If it's a Girl Scout program that all Girl Scouts are going to Coney Island, then we should all go or none of us should," Coffey declared. Coffey convinced the Scouts to cancel Coney Island day and hold a picnic in its place, angering many white parents. Because of Coney's intransigence the Cincinnati Girl Scouts did not return, and the Cincinnati Scouts did integrate within Coffey's five-year time frame. In the end Coffey integrated the Scouts but not Coney Island.[91]

Farther south, the Scouting movement maintained segregation until after World War II and was not at the forefront of interracialism. In Galveston, Texas, Eldrewey Stearns remembered growing up in the segregated Scouts during the 1930s. When he was thirteen Stearns' black troop camped north of Galveston on land owned by a white philanthropist. Walking with his troop leader, he came upon an adjoining camp for white Scouts. There, Boy Scouts enjoyed a large swimming pool and mess hall: "It was a small paradise in the woods. I remember . . . wondering why we couldn't have something like that—the swimming pool and all the luxuries."[92] Scouting in the South was a white activity, virtually unknown to blacks before 1926. Even then, allowing African American boys to wear the uniform in segregated units was deeply contested. In Richmond, Virginia, Boy Scout officials promised a public burning of Scout uniforms if forced to allow African American Scouts to wear them. Northern states also had very small proportions of black Scouts, and when troop leaders recruited larger numbers of African American boys they were usually segregated into separate troops. In Camden, New Jersey, for example, local Scouting officials were alarmed to note that a full fifth of local Boy Scouts were black. They quickly responded by dividing the county into ten districts, reserving one for blacks only.[93] This parallel to school redistricting in the urban North is apt, as segregated Scouting often followed the lines of segregated schools.

Segregated YMCAs and YWCAs were marginally more progressive than the Scouts, as some local branches pressured their communities to cease building separate recreational facilities. While in the early 1920s support from white philanthropists and the needs of urban black residents often led African American reformers to acquiesce to segregation, by the end of the decade African Americans saw separate facilities as a barrier to future reform. In 1929, for example, a local white reformer offered to build a pool for the black residents of Orange, New Jersey. The local African American secretary of the segregated YWCA protested, saying she "felt that such a segregated pool would retard the day when the white and Negro groups would use the same facilities."[94] Despite her protests the pool was built. By the outbreak of World War II the "separate but equal" policies of the Y movement were unsustainable during the fight for democracy abroad. White association leaders, however, insisted on waiting until the war's end to abolish racial designations. Only with the growing calls for interracialism in the 1940s would the YWCA and YMCA implement full desegregation of its facilities and governance in 1946. Even after 1946 local associations resisted desegregation, particularly of swimming pools and other coveted recreational facilities.[95] As late as 1953 a branch of the Manhattan YMCA, near Pennsylvania Station, continued to bar black members, sending black railroad workers up to the Harlem branch of the Y.[96]

A generation of urban blacks like Dorothy Height had searing memories of exclusion from youth programs in local Ys and schools. This exclusion sometimes led them to seek out more radical alternatives that allowed for interracial recreation. In 1939 Nelson Peery was a teenager and avid athlete growing up in Minneapolis who decided to try out for his high school's swim team. He made the team, the first black student to swim for a public high school in the city, but soon discovered the practices and competitions were at the white YMCA. Incensed, Peery remembers telling the Y director, "I'm going to make you stop saying Christian when you mean white." School officials convinced Peery and his friends to form an alternate black recreation club, but two years later the Minneapolis YMCA had still failed to integrate its facilities. Enormously frustrated and feeling complicit in furthering Jim Crow, Peery began to attend meetings of the Communist Party.[97] For Peery, as for many others, the radicalism of the Communist and Socialist parties was a welcome respite from the more moderate NAACP and Urban League affiliates. Particularly during the Popular Front, when the Communist Party reached out to more moderate allies in the struggle against fascism, activists on the left advocated interracialism, while respecting black self-determination. Demanding integration of recreation was consistent with this politics and began to shape a new set of tactics and priorities by the late 1930s. Public accommodations were powerful targets for radicals intent on displaying their political power.

In 1938 the *Daily Worker*, the Communist Party newspaper, received a letter protesting the discriminatory policies of the Brooklyn roller-skating rink. When a reporter from the paper interviewed the owners, they protested that there was no formal discrimination but that whites "objected to Negroes" and routinely beat them when they tried to skate. The local Communist Party organized a test case: two black couples went to the rink to skate. Employing a typical tactic, the owners charged the couples extra for their skates. A group of whites, unaffiliated with the formal protest, intervened, protested that they had been charged nothing for their skates, and threatened to leave. Management backed down and the couples proceeded to skate unmolested.[98] In these cases one can see slow but steady growth in interracial efforts to address segregated recreation. Among more conservative groups, like the Scouts or Ys, the efforts were intermittent, but among leftist groups interracial organizing made segregated recreation an anathema. Blacks and whites who could march and demonstrate together should also skate, swim, or ride a roller coaster together.

The contrast between integrated politics during the Great Depression and segregated recreation was particularly stark in the growing industrial unions. The "culture of unity" that came with mass unionization during the 1930s challenged segregated recreation more forcefully than had earlier company unions that scheduled the occasional outing to a local park.[99] Organizers in the Congress of Industrial Organizations (CIO) attempted to build cultural as well as class bridges to reach out to black workers. They organized picnics, sporting teams, and bowling leagues, but these efforts collided with the reality of segregated leisure. Bowling, enormously popular among working-class city dwellers, was among the most segregated forms of commercial recreation. The American Bowling Congress (ABC) barred African Americans entirely until 1951, and in 1939 black players formed their own National Negro Bowling Association. Black bowlers typically had to wait until closing time when bowling alleys would place a "closed for private party" sign on the door and open the alleys to black players. This practice did not violate the bylaws of the ABC and allowed lanes to maintain their certification. Organized labor was crucial to the eventual desegregation of bowling. In 1947, the same year Jackie Robinson desegregated baseball, the United Autoworkers (UAW) threatened to withdraw their sponsorship of bowling leagues unless the ABC opened their competition to all. It took three more years of threats and litigation before the ABC relented, and even then many lanes refused to admit black bowlers well into the 1960s. The CIO's culture of unity was not a panacea for segregated recreation, but it did highlight the contradictions between interracial organizing and segregated leisure.[100]

Some unions had more immediate results than the UAW when they confronted segregated recreation. In the spring of 1939, white members of a cafeteria employees union in New York City vigorously protested when the Mecca Roller Skating Palace refused to sell tickets to their black members. After being threatened with a lawsuit, the rink's owners allowed the interracial group to skate together.[101] Similarly, when the CIO in Lancaster, Pennsylvania, sponsored a Labor Day picnic at Rocky Springs Park, guards barred black members from the swimming pool. The union promptly had the park's owner and son arrested for violating the state's 1939 antidiscrimination act.[102] In these cases the culture of unity did prompt immediate change. But overall, the increased interracial activism of the New Deal era was undermined by recreational segregation of public works projects and unenforced civil rights statutes in the North. Institutional integration of local Ys, Scouts, and schools was incremental at best. And when segregation was challenged it was most often ordinary black consumers who took the lead, such as the two black women who filed a lawsuit against Cleveland's Skateland rink in 1939.[103] These women, and hundreds like them, challenged the racial disparities among citizen consumers. Ordinary African American men and women trying out for swim teams, attending company picnics, and taking their families out for a weekend visit to the amusement park regularly faced barriers to their full inclusion in recreational life. By the eve of World War II, civil rights organizations began to vigorously respond to their calls for justice.

Opening Public Accommodations in the Prewar Years

Historians writing about the long civil rights movement focus on the 1930s and early 1940s as a period that placed labor activism at the center of the freedom struggle. These historians argue for the "lost promise" of civil rights that united class and racial interests, in contrast to what they perceive as a less radical focus on public accommodations in the postwar years.[104] Although there is no doubt that the struggle for economic rights had its heyday in this pre–cold war period, the desegregation of public accommodations was a demand promoted by radical organizations and mainstream civil rights organizations before the onset of war. Nelson Peery, for example, was drawn to the Communist Party as a direct result of his exclusion from a segregated pool. And demands for access to recreation and other public accommodations inundated NAACP offices and other centers of political activity in the late 1930s and early 1940s. This was not unrelated to labor activism, as black and white workers experienced the limits of brotherhood in their leisure time. Black urban workers wanted access to the same recreational experiences their white counterparts had, and notions of citizenship and consumerism were deeply intertwined. Rather than a separate or less significant demand, access to recreation was linked to workers' rights, demands for equal housing, and voting rights. And recreation, unlike unionization of adult workers, impacted all community members—men, women, and children—who sought access to leisure in the midst of economic despair.

By the end of the 1930s local NAACP chapters were putting increasing pressure on the national office to file lawsuits challenging segregated recreation. In July 1941 Thurgood Marshall, then special counsel to the NAACP, received a letter from Marie G. Baker, secretary of the Decatur, Illinois, branch. She reported that a group of African Americans had attempted to go to a beach with a well-appointed bathhouse. Two years before the city had built a "colored" bathhouse, which the black community refused to use. Although they were sold tickets to the beach, the two men in the group were immediately confronted by a group of young white men. Neither the police, who had been alerted that there might be a confrontation, nor the ticket seller would help the black men pass. Nor did they intervene when the whites began to savagely beat the black men, who did not resist. Soon after the local branch filed a lawsuit.[105] Because the city was openly violating the civil rights laws of Illinois, a private company did not run the beach, and there was no subterfuge of a "club," the suit was successful. Marshall urged the local branch to "insist on Negroes using the bathhouse in common with any other patrons" during the summer of 1942.[106] Following his advice, a group of young African Americans went to the bathhouse in July, but the concessionaire, C. W. Wintz, told them to go to "their" bathhouse. When the black men returned a few days later, Wintz met them with a police club, striking one young man before being forced to relinquish the weapon.[107] Faced with the determination of black patrons and a civil rights lawsuit, Wintz turned to violence to ensure that the public beach and bathhouses remained segregated.

Violence also dictated the limits of integrated swimming in Philadelphia in the early 1940s. A local reformer noted that "even though geographically available, a recreational facility may be made unavailable to an individual or group by various social devices, among the more obvious of which are threats of violence or actual violence."[108] That reality characterized much of the urban North. In North Philadelphia, the Athletic Recreation Center, a city-owned pool, carefully demarcated when young African Americans and young whites could swim. Because the center was located at the junction of a white neighborhood and a black one, city officials divided use of the pool into hour-and-a-half intervals, reportedly to avoid "racial friction." In the midst of a summer heat wave in 1941, when such friction was at its height, the city hired two black lifeguards. White swimmers continually taunted and threatened the new employees. On July 1 Joseph Aiken, a fourteen-year-old African American boy, was caught in one of the turnovers from white to black swimmers. A group of white youths grabbed him and held him underwater, almost drowning him. A melee ensued that spread to the surrounding streets. It quickly turned into a recreation riot as hundreds of Philadelphia's finest arrived and joined in the battle. Thirty people were injured, and the police arrested nobody, although they used their nightsticks liberally. By all reports the riot was not unexpected, and it served as a harbinger of larger conflagrations over swimming and recreation in Philadelphia for decades to follow.[109]

Youngstown, Ohio, home of Idora Park, witnessed a similar recreation riot in 1940. This case involved an organized protest of a segregated municipal pool on the city's North Side. Youngstown's branch of the Future Outlook League (FOL), founded in Cleveland in 1935 to address issues of unemployed black workers, sought to integrate the pool. On July 19 a group of fourteen blacks managed to enter the pool, but white swimmers began to taunt them with shouts of "niggers" followed by physical blows. The FOL activists were experienced at radical, direct action protests through their boycotts and picketing campaigns of white businesses, but they were not nonviolent pacifists and defended themselves from the abuse of white patrons. The fighting escalated, leading to the near drowning of a young African American woman. When the police arrived they arrested the FOL's militant leader, Bertrand Carlson, and charged him with instigating a riot. The city then closed the pool, but after Carlson was acquitted officials reopened the North Side Municipal Swimming Pool as an integrated facility.[110] While the FOL is known to historians primarily for its labor activism, this desegregation campaign suggests that black activists did not separate economic and civil rights. Like the interracial activists on the left, black radicals in the FOL worked simultaneously to improve the economic conditions of African Americans and demand full access to public accommodations.

The growing radicalism of the 1930s, embodied by the FOL, sensitized African Americans to the similarities between European fascists' racial theories and the justifications for segregation in the United States. Particularly chilling was a 1938 ordinance passed in Long Branch, New Jersey, that forced bathers to wear badges authorizing them to use either the black or white areas on the beach. One year later the Nazis forced Jews in occupied Poland to wear a yellow badge. As had been done in Asbury Park, city officials had segregated Long Branch beaches in the late nineteenth century. The ordinance passed by the city did not explicitly mention race but invoked the most common and powerful justification for segregation—the prevention of violence. It was "for the better protection and safety of patrons on said beaches" that bathers would have to buy badges authorizing them to swim in a particular area of the beach. This would prevent "congestion" and ensure a "proper distribution of patrons."[111] After passage of the ordinance police officers arrested two African American women for bathing without the necessary tags. Incensed by the arrests and the humiliation of the badges, the black community founded a local chapter of the NAACP to eliminate segregation on beaches altogether.[112]

In the early 1940s the NAACP responded to black consumers' anger over swimming pool and beach segregation with a series of lawsuits that began to bear some fruit. An early indication of the coming proliferation of cases played out in Pasadena, California, at Brookside Plunge, the local municipal pool. When Pasadena first opened Brookside Plunge in 1914 a group of African Americans organized the Negro Taxpayers and Voters Association (NTVA) to protest the city policy of opening the pool to blacks only one day per week. The response of the city attorney suggests the deep connection between recreation segregation and education segregation: "If the policy of Separation of the Races for educational purposes is sound," argued attorney John Munger, "that of separating them for bathing purposes would seem to be equally sound and certainly no less desirable."[113] Both policies impacted children, and both drew upon a wider spatial segregation of the races. They would remain intertwined in the legal history of Jim Crow for decades to come. Rather than address the NTVA's complaints, the city decided to ban blacks from the pool altogether. Jackie Robinson, who grew up in Pasadena, remembered, "During hot spells, you waited outside the picket fence and watched the white kids splash around. I honestly think the officials didn't think the Negroes got as warm and uncomfortable as white people during the Pasadena heat."[114]

In 1930 the city reinstated its initial segregation policy by opening its facilities to African Americans one day a week, Tuesday, which was called International Day. At the end of each Tuesday the pool was drained, cleaned, and refilled for use by whites. Blacks protested the policy throughout the 1930s, and in 1939 the NAACP filed a formal lawsuit after six black men were turned away from the pool on a Sunday. The city manager fired Jackie Robinson's brother, Mack, and other black city workers in retaliation for the lawsuit. In addition, elite whites formed the Pasadena Improvement Association in the summer of 1939 to restrict "the use and occupancy of property" to whites only.[115] This was a western version of the southern "massive resistance" to school desegregation that followed the *Brown v. Board of Education* decision. Businesses and political leaders in Pasadena supported the association in the same way that southern business leaders supported citizens' councils in the post-*Brown* South. Despite the Improvement Association's power on the local level, the court ruled in the NAACP's favor and after four years of appeals the city integrated and reopened Brookside Plunge in 1942. But in 1946 they closed it, reopening it again only after the NAACP filed an injunction against the city. A refurbished and integrated Brookside Plunge opened in 1947.[116] Central to the NAACP's case in Pasadena was the fact that black residents had paid to build and maintain Brookside Plunge—a fact recognized by the NTVA, whose name highlighted their role as both taxpayers and voters. When the city of Galveston, Texas, used federal funds to build Pleasure Pier, a small amusement park, black citizens similarly cried foul.[117] Such protests spanned the country, as African Americans demanded access to facilities their tax dollars supported.

City dwellers coveted swimming pools and amusement parks such as Brookside Plunge and Galveston's Pleasure Pier. But the most significant conflicts over racial access to recreation often centered on large urban parks and beaches, as in Chicago's 1919 riot. In 1943 an echo of the 1919 recreation riot exploded in Detroit, Michigan, over the use of public recreational space. Belle Isle was an island park at the center of the Detroit River where white and black Detroiters picnicked, fished, and played baseball. They did so in separate groups, and at times there were fights over the use of an outdoor grill or prime fishing sites. But when the city became desperately overcrowded as the second Great Migration brought more African Americans to the city and workers of all races flocked to join the front line of the war industries, recreational space became increasingly contested and the fights more frequent. As in the years prior to the Chicago riot, Detroit youth gangs were on the front lines of racial discord. One contemporary observer noted that in the months preceding the riot, "groups of Negro zoot suiters were brawling with gangs of young white toughs."[118] Increased racial tension over wartime housing and employment also exacerbated anger in public places, and whites began calling Belle Isle "Nigger Island" as more black migrants used it.[119] Facing these struggles at home, Detroit blacks were also deeply disheartened to hear news of racial oppression in the armed forces and of attacks on black soldiers and sailors at southern military bases.

On a searing hot June day in 1943 thousands of African Americans walked across the bridge to Belle Isle to enjoy the park's amenities. There were minor skirmishes between blacks and whites during the day that culminated in a large group of whites, made up in part of white sailors from a nearby armory, attacking a group of African Americans. One black woman, attempting to leave the park after a day of canoeing, reported that on the bridge a group of whites approached and said, "We don't want any niggers on Belle Isle." She was beaten by a group of white women and hospitalized with serious injuries.[120] Rumors that whites had thrown a mother and her baby into the Detroit River reached Detroit's black East Side, and the riot quickly escalated. By the riot's end thirty-four Detroiters were killed, twenty-five of them black, and over six hundred were injured.[121] The gendered nature of the riot, with a vulnerable mother and child at its center and black men defending their honor, is a significant theme in the history of leisure and recreation.[122] Because children and families were the primary users of recreation areas, their protection was a major motivation for activists and ordinary people who sought equal access to facilities. Emotions ran high when the fate of a child—such as the boy swimming in Lake Michigan in 1919 or a baby (even an imagined one) in the Detroit River in 1943—was at risk. The right of black families to use Belle Isle unmolested was at stake, and the riot was, in part, a claiming of public recreational space in the city. It was also a wake-up call for the nation's cities that the problem of racial coexistence needed to be addressed.

After the riot, an interracial citizens' committee convened to pressure city officials to respond to the conflagration. At their recommendation, Mayor Edward J. Jeffries, Jr., organized a permanent interracial committee to improve race relations in the city. The committee became the model for race relations committees throughout the country that played a key role in negotiating very gradual recreational integration and developing tactics to prevent further racial violence. In a pamphlet analyzing the 1943 riot the journalist Earl Brown suggested that interracial committees should promote common use of recreational spaces. In "public parks and other recreational centers where racial friction often occurs," argued Brown, "city officials and civic leaders of both races should promote public programs in which members of both races could take part. These programs should be held in parks and other public places in order to bring the two races together in a wholesome and constructive way."[123] While interracial committees had some control over public parks and playgrounds, they could act only as advocates and educators in commercial recreation. A 1945 Detroit interracial committee leaflet informed city residents that "Negroes are excluded from most commercial recreational establishments."[124] But blacks were now putting enormous pressure on these establishments to open their doors. How the interracial committees and local governments they advised would respond to this pressure dominated urban agendas in the 1940s and 1950s.

The study of race relations came of age during World War II. Racial conflict in the military, the 1943 Detroit riot, and continuous skirmishes on the home front sharpened the attention of social scientists and government officials. Some, such as Robert C. Weaver, a black economist and New Deal official, saw the interracial committees in the urban North as playing a vital role in transforming the nation's attitudes toward racial segregation. To do this effectively, however, he and others had to ensure the North saw itself in opposition to southern racists. "The acceptance of southern racial patterns in the North," argued Weaver in 1944, "will not lead to racial understanding. These patterns have not succeeded in their native habitat; they cannot succeed elsewhere."[125] The North needed to distinguish itself from southern patterns of segregation rather than imitate them. Such statements underplayed the depth of racial segregation in the North, but Weaver used this rhetoric to appeal to northerners' sense of superiority. Weaver also agreed with Justice Harlan's 1896 dissent that eliminating segregation would prevent violence. "It is up to society to determine whether it will change quickly enough to avert clashes or whether it will delay modifying its institutions, thereby inviting violence."[126] Detroit, like Chicago two decades earlier, was the warning that large-scale violence was always a possibility. Segregated recreation, in Weaver's estimation, would encourage violence, not prevent it. But racial mixing in a public park sparked the Detroit riot, which suggested to others a very different conclusion: integration would inevitably lead to violence. Which interpretation would prevail was unclear in 1943.

* * *

Robert Weaver was not the only observer to view segregation as a national, not a regional, problem. Charles Johnson, an eminent African American sociologist, wrote in 1943: "The ubiquitous color line in the United States thus traces a varied and complex pattern. It is less often seen and defined than discreetly or defiantly sensed by Negroes, and imperiously or indefinitely felt by whites. Irrational or intangible in many relationships, devoid of defensible logic in a theoretically democratic society, it is, nevertheless, one of the most positive realities in American life. It is uniquely, persistently, and universally an American institution."[127] Johnson did not view the problem of segregation as a southern one but as an American one. In the first half of the twentieth century American cities experienced both a dramatic expansion in commercial recreation and the drawing of a color line. Although the means of drawing that line—a "Whites Only" sign, private clubs, or a vicious shove out the door—differed from place to place and from time to time, the reality was that African Americans had limited access to leisure spaces as they migrated in increasing numbers to American cities. This limitation circumscribed their citizenship and consumer rights, and for this reason blacks challenged segregated public accommodations from their very founding. In the first half of the twentieth century ordinary African Americans launched these challenges daily, facing beatings, arrests, and even death. By the 1930s civil rights organizations and sympathetic whites would also take up the cause. Blacks could increasingly turn to the NAACP to seek redress when they were beaten or arrested for violating the color line. And interracial unions and leftist organizations no longer tolerated recreational segregation. While increased concerns over juvenile delinquency and the red scare would shape post–World War II struggles over recreation in new ways, the challenges of ordinary people would remain a constant.

Violent white resistance to black incursions in amusement parks, swimming pools, and roller-skating rinks also continued during and after World War II. Despite black resistance, commercial leisure spaces had become deeply racialized over the course of the first half of the twentieth century. Whites visited places like Euclid Beach Park because they were safe, fun, and clean—which mandated racial exclusion. In 1939 the sociologist John F. Cuber remarked that in amusement parks, "People temporarily set aside taboos, inhibitions, and restraints—are boisterous, immodest, and impulsive—not necessarily immoral in any strict sense, but unconventional enough to be appreciative of the protection provided by the degree of anonymity and conviviality which the institution fosters. There seems to be a tacit understanding among the participants that behavior here somehow 'does not count elsewhere' and will not be 'held against' one even if he is observed by his acquaintances."[128] This permission to be "boisterous" and "impulsive" without the normal constraints of conventional society created an atmosphere of fun and vigilantism. Protecting white spaces of leisure was a form of leisure in itself for some young white men. This pattern ensured that violence would continue to dictate access to recreation.

CHAPTER 2

The Fifth Freedom: Racial Liberalism, Nonviolence, and Recreation Riots in the 1940s

THE noted black sociologists St. Clair Drake and Horace R. Cayton predicted in 1945 that "racial radicalism" of "gigantic proportions" would follow World War II unless the United States made significant racial progress. African Americans "were aware . . . that they were participating in a titanic struggle fought under the banner of the Four Freedoms. They were liberating people from Fascism abroad and they were expecting to be liberated from Jim-Crow at home. For them this was a Fifth Freedom as precious as the other four."[1] Linking racial democracy at home with political democracy abroad was the central unifying theme of African American activism during the 1940s. It was exemplified by the "Double Victory" (or Double V) campaign, launched by the *Pittsburgh Courier* in 1942, that exposed the contradiction of blacks facing racial apartheid in the United States while fighting for democracy overseas. But Double V activism often met with violence from whites whose private motivations for fighting fascism during World War II superseded an inclusive democratic ideal.[2] Albert T. Luster, an African American protestor who was attempting to integrate Cleveland's Euclid Beach Park, was one victim of this brutality. When park police confronted Luster and told him to leave the park, in defiance he sat down on a bench and stated, "This place is getting worse than Nazi Germany." The beating was immediate and severe: Luster ended the day in the hospital with multiple lacerations and bruises on his legs, arms, and the bottoms of his feet.[3] What to Luster seemed an apt comparison was for Euclid's hired guards an abomination. Protecting one's family, for many whites, included protecting recreational spaces from black invasions. Whites met the upsurge in black activism with a strengthened arsenal of legal and extralegal tactics to resist desegregation.

In the 1940s race relations was center stage in American life and politics in ways not seen since Reconstruction. Many social scientists, activists, and politicians viewed race as a national problem, not one limited to a backward South steeped in traditions of Jim Crow. Escalating racial violence during the war years, epitomized by the 1943 Detroit riot, forced states and the nation to confront pervasive racial inequality. A number of trends ensured this greater attention. Two great migrations of African Americans north during the first and second world wars changed the racial makeup of urban America. A New Deal coalition that incorporated black migrant voters changed the political makeup of the Democratic Party. Organized labor incorporated black industrial workers into their rank and file. And, in the years before the cold war, radical organizations actively promoted racial equality. During World War II ordinary African American soldiers and citizens expressed outrage at the discriminatory policies in the segregated military and war industries. They joined the NAACP in unprecedented numbers, demanded a national Fair Employment Practices Committee (FEPC) through threatened mass action, and engaged in countless daily acts of resistance to segregation and discrimination. Whites who felt threatened by black activists and citizens fought back—with their fists and their votes. This resistance to the desegregation of public space slowed the pace of racial progress and highlighted the extent of white resistance to racial equality nationwide.

Racial Liberalism and Racial Violence in the War Years

Directly challenging white violence was not the focus of policymakers sympathetic to the cause of racial equality. Instead they embraced an ideology of racial liberalism—a belief that social scientists, working through the state, could promote racial reform. Racial liberalism was built on the pathbreaking work of the Swedish economist Gunnar Myrdal, whose 1944 study *An American Dilemma* argued, "The American Negro problem is a problem in the heart of the American."[4] This "moral dilemma" was the result of ignorance and could be solved through education and moral persuasion. Much like Progressives early in the twentieth century, racial liberals believed in the power of amassing facts and wielding them to convince policymakers and ordinary Americans to reform their ways. There was, as a result, an explosion of social scientific work on race relations throughout the 1940s. By the end of the decade racial liberalism had infiltrated the executive branch with the publication of President Harry Truman's 1949 report *To Secure These Rights*. Truman also helped craft a relatively strong civil rights platform in the Democratic Party, and after his reelection he used his executive power to desegregate the military.[5]

By the immediate postwar years many African American activists and their white allies moved away from an agenda that promoted economic equality toward a Myrdalian approach to race relations. The lack of attention to economic parity had significant costs for African Americans as they failed to achieve the same level of class mobility and wage increases as their white counterparts. Nevertheless, this shift illuminated the social costs of segregated recreation. Because interracial contact and assimilation were major goals of racial liberalism, public accommodations became a focus for legal strategy and public education on race. For example, a 1947 study of Philadelphia suggested, "From all types of evidence it seems probable that the provision of not only equal but nonsegregated recreation will be a significant contribution to the diminution of racial tensions."[6] And Truman's Committee on Civil Rights recommended the enactment and enforcement of laws guaranteeing "equal access to places of public accommodation," including recreation, to resolve Myrdal's American dilemma.[7] Racial liberalism, then, shone a spotlight on the problem of segregated recreation. But the call for education and enlightenment was not sufficient to end segregation in the country's amusement parks, swimming pools, and roller-skating rinks.

Activists and politicians most frequently deployed racial liberalism at the local and state levels. As communities faced the growing racial conflict of the war years, racial liberals shaped their responses to racial bias and black demands for redress. New York State, for example, created the State Commission Against Discrimination (SCAD) in 1945 to investigate cases of racial discrimination. At the local level cities created interracial commissions to mediate disputes and prevent racial violence. The first such commission emerged from the Chicago Race Riot in 1919, when the mayor appointed prominent scholars and politicians to investigate the causes of the riot. Two decades later the 1943 Detroit riot led that city to appoint a permanent interracial commission that served as a model for dozens of cities and towns nationwide. These commissions exhaustively studied race relations in their communities and set about educating citizens and training police officers in a Myrdalian effort to transform the "hearts and minds" of white Americans. In 1945 approximately three hundred groups dealt with interracial cooperation, and by 1948 that number had grown to over one thousand.[8] But there was a deep disconnect between the work carried out by racial liberals and the actions of radical activists and black consumers. Many liberals cautioned against too rapid change, fearing an increase in racial conflict that would undermine the cause of racial equality. Thus they allowed violence, both potential and real, to dictate the pace of desegregation. In contrast, many ordinary African Americans and some activists sought an immediate end to racial segregation.

Separate public accommodations were the most visible form of segregation. More than employment and housing discrimination, problems hidden from public view, recreational segregation was an observable product of white supremacy. Commentators on race relations understood that conflict over recreational space often led to violence, as it had in Detroit in 1943. Therefore, racial liberals argued for the gradual desegregation of leisure spaces to facilitate racial understanding. By contrast, a new generation of nonviolent radical activists targeted public accommodations as a means of illustrating the disconnect between promises of American democracy and racial apartheid. At the same time, ordinary black consumers barred from recreation because of the color of their skin increasingly challenged prohibitions against play. White owners of amusement parks, swimming pools, and other facilities fought back against these incursions using private police forces and legal subterfuges. They also depended on young white "hoodlums" to force out unwanted customers. This wide-scale resistance to desegregated recreation demonstrated the limits of the Myrdalian paradigm. Many white Americans believed the fight for democracy abroad and racial divisions at home were separate issues.[9] They also did not make a distinction between the gradualism of racial liberals and the immediatism of radical activists. The result was a series of recreation riots in many American cities, events that racial liberalism was ill equipped to handle.

"What the Negro wants," argued Roy Wilkins in a 1944 collection of essays by that title, "is to be able to go to parks, playgrounds, beaches, pools, theatres, restaurants, hotels, taverns, tourist camps, and other places of public amusement and accommodation without proscription and insult." "If the Negro's goal is complete equality," he continued, "complete acceptance as a member of the American public, then he wants access to these accommodations on an equality with other Americans."[10] Belonging required access—to economic equality and the vote, but also physical access to spaces of consumerism and leisure. "However segregation may be rationalized," argued Sterling A. Brown in the same collection, "it is essentially the denial of belonging."[11] Fighting for democracy at home and abroad was a form of belonging that made the exclusion from recreation particularly painful. While some blacks expected participation in the war effort to ease segregation and racial violence, the opposite proved to be true.[12] Surveying race relations in 1943, the sociologist Howard W. Odum noted the "widespread violence of an extraordinary number, range, and variety of incidents" since the outbreak of war.[13] Much of this violence occurred in public spaces—on streetcars, in parks, on playgrounds, in municipal swimming pools, and on city streets north and south. And commercial recreation, such as amusement parks and roller rinks, were deeply contested spaces during the war years as whites and blacks sought leisure in overcrowded cities.

After A. Philip Randolph successfully pressured Franklin Roosevelt to grant blacks greater access to war industries through his March on Washington Movement (MOWM), black workers had more money in their pockets but fewer places to spend it. In the West, a region that experienced tremendous black population growth during World War II, segregation became significantly more pervasive and racial conflict a daily reality. White military personnel were at the forefront of racial violence in public spaces and often instigated conflict. Detroit's 1943 riot and the zoot suit riots in Los Angeles that same year both involved white soldiers. During the zoot suit riots white servicemen infiltrated the working-class spaces of leisure frequented by African American and Mexican American youth, who were easy to spot and abuse in their stylish outfits. At the center of conflicts at military bases were black servicemen who vociferously protested their exclusion from recreation. These protests and the violence they met are too numerous to recount. Many were fleeting, flashes of anger in the face of a segregated USO dance or closed officer's clubs. Others were deadly, as in Fort Dix, New Jersey, in 1942 when a gun battle between white and black soldiers broke out over the use of a telephone in the Military Sports Palace near the barracks. Three soldiers were killed, two of them black, and five black soldiers were wounded.[14] Leading up to the shootout, reported the *Chicago Defender*, "was treatment given Negro soldiers by various recreation and eating place attendants who appeared bent on letting it be known that the soldiers were not wanted."[15] Violence was the most efficient means of letting soldiers know they did not "belong." But it also led to a growing demand for equality of access.

As violence at home-front military bases and surrounding cities reached a peak in 1943, the adjutant general of the army, its chief administrative officer, issued an order that recreational facilities be open to all races. Military leaders noted that soldiers consistently complained about segregated recreation both on and off bases, and addressing this concern could alleviate racial tension. But although the military removed "Whites Only" signs from many camps, in general the segregation policies remained intact. Nevertheless black soldiers, aware of the order, used the policy to demand more access to recreation.[16] They were particularly incensed that German prisoners of war could enter facilities to which African American soldiers were denied access.[17] At Camp Barkeley in Texas, for example, a black soldier reported that latrines in the German prisoner-of-war camp were segregated—one for German prisoners and white soldiers, and a second for African Americans. "It made me feel," he wrote in a letter to the White House, "the tyrant is actually placed over the liberator."[18]

Home-front groups experienced parallel forms of recreational segregation. In Los Angeles in 1943 a group of black and white teenagers, members of a Victory Club supporting home-front activities, attempted to enter Skateland for an evening of roller-skating. When the teens confronted the manager he insisted, "the Negroes only cause fights, and anyway they'd be happier amongst their own people." Insisting that they would protest the discrimination, the Victory Club reported, "We youth of America are fighting not only to smash the axis abroad, but to wipe out those fascist tendencies that exist in our own country." This echoing of Double V rhetoric was common among consumers and activists who confronted Jim Crow in wartime America. The response of the Skateland manager also fit a pattern that would define many of the interactions across the color line in the 1940s. Many believed that integration would lead to violence because blacks "cause fights" and integration would not be beneficial to blacks because they are "happier amongst their own people." This manager was confronted with a peaceful group of interracial teenagers that belied his concerns. As a commentator in the *New York Amsterdam News* noted, "The management of this skating rink, in my opinion, is not really concerned whether the Negro people are 'happy' . . . just as Hitler does not practice his theories for the 'happiness' of the Jews."[19]

The escalation of racial violence during the war years inspired racial liberals to champion programs to educate prejudiced whites and negotiate gradual and peaceful desegregation plans. But the youth in Los Angeles's Victory Club suggested a different trajectory for racial change—direct confrontation and demands for immediate desegregation. In contrast to racial liberals who called for a gradual approach to ending Jim Crow, many ordinary African Americans and radical activists called for freedom now. Fighting a war for democracy facilitated their demands for immediacy, particularly in the North. Indeed, the call for Double V during World War II gave racial struggles an unprecedented moral authority that lasted into the postwar years. Although the rhetoric of Double V did not always win white allies, it built support for interracial commissions on the local level and led to national calls for racial equality. Less organized, but no less powerful, daily challenges to racial segregation in the war years echoed these demands. Ordinary consumers, soldiers, and radical activists found that the very presence of black faces in white spaces was enough to spark violence and create a crisis.

The Radical Response to Recreational Segregation

The most significant innovation in challenging recreational segregation during the 1940s was nonviolent direct action. George Houser, a leading white civil rights activist, defined nonviolent direct action as "group action against injustice by challenging directly the right of that discrimination to exist." He emphasized that it differed from other protest methods by not relying on the state or the courts but on overt challenges to racist policies.[20] This was not an entirely new weapon in the arsenal of protest. In the 1930s the Fellowship of Reconciliation (FOR), a pacifist organization founded in 1914 and dedicated to nonviolence and Gandhian principles of passive resistance, attracted young radicals. The militancy and daring of radical pacifism in FOR and in similar Christian pacifist groups were models for later civil rights activists. Two major movements came out of this early experimentation in passive resistance: A. Philip Randolph's MOWM and the Congress of Racial Equality (CORE). Both targeted public accommodations as a priority for African Americans, and together they pioneered a blueprint for desegregation of recreation that offered an alternative to racial liberals' gradualism.

Although the MOWM is known primarily for A. Philip Randolph's successful campaign to ensure fair treatment of African American employees in war industries, historians have largely overlooked the attention Randolph paid to public accommodations. The MOWM began in 1941 when Randolph called on blacks to join him for a mass march on Washington, D.C., to protest racial discrimination in federal contracts and the military. This work built on Randolph's labor activism as the organizer of the Brotherhood of Sleeping Car Porters and his linking of economic rights to the broader freedom struggle.[21]

It culminated in Roosevelt's issuing of Executive Order 8802, which both forbade discrimination in war industries and established the FEPC to oversee compliance, one week prior to the scheduled march. Randolph's claim that he could rally one hundred thousand African Americans in the nation's capital also had a public accommodations component. When Eleanor Roosevelt asked him where the marchers would sleep and eat, Randolph replied that they would register in hotels and eat in restaurants. This was impossible in segregated Washington, and Randolph's threat suggested the broader goals he envisioned for his movement.[22] Ideally the MOWM would become a mass movement that linked economic freedom to the fifth freedom, desegregation in all spheres of American life.

After canceling the march, Randolph attempted to reinvigorate the movement the following spring by calling for a series of massive rallies around the country to fight for racial democracy at home. During this period the MOWM was intent on promoting nonviolent direct action as a primary means of fighting Jim Crow. Writing in 1943 Randolph proclaimed: "Discriminations against Negroes in restaurants, dance halls, theaters, and other public places of amusement and entertainment above the Mason-Dixon line are alarmingly quite general. But the March on Washington Movement has proclaimed its dedication to and advocacy of non-violent good will direct action as a method of meeting this discrimination."[23] He went on to lay out the steps to address such discrimination, insisting on negotiation with management before any action and a total commitment to nonviolence, "to the extent of not even using violent language against the management or the employees."[24] In the end it was CORE, rather than the MOWM, that carried out this campaign, but Randolph's promotion of radical nonviolence and his singling out of public accommodations reflected a powerful new strategy to address recreational segregation.

Randolph's championing of nonviolence drew from his association with A. J. Muste, the director of FOR. In 1941, as Randolph was launching his MOWM, Muste sent two young black organizers, Bayard Rustin and James Farmer, to work with Randolph on nonviolent strategies.[25] Rustin and Farmer were part of a group of radical pacifists working with FOR who had begun to engage in a form of experimental interracialism—living with white activists and promoting racial egalitarianism. Their commitment to interracialism distinguished them from the MOWM, an all-black movement. Although Randolph was not a nationalist—he was outspoken in his opposition to Marcus Garvey during the 1920s—he felt that an all-black movement would enhance the self-esteem of African Americans. Above all Randolph was trying to launch a mass movement, excluding whites so as to address working-class blacks' perceptions of elitism that were often attached to the interracial NAACP or National Urban League (NUL). Randolph also barred whites from the movement to avoid the factionalism of white communists and socialists, as well as conservative accusations of "red" infiltration.

Randolph's concerns about anticommunism were well founded as accusations of communist associations often followed nonviolent direct action protests. In 1941, for example, a large municipal pool in Garfield Heights, a suburb of Cleveland, became a political as well as racial battleground. Although blacks from Cleveland used the surrounding picnic grove, groups of white youth stymied their attempts to swim by chasing them out of the water. On July 4, 1941, Independence Day, blacks retaliated by taking over the pool using sheer numbers, ignoring the racial epithets of whites. But this was a temporary victory. In August an interracial group, including members of Ahimsa Farm, an experimental pacifist community near Cleveland, and the local chapter of FOR decided to use nonviolent direct action to permanently desegregate the pool. Twelve whites entered the pool with four blacks, intending to form a protective ring around them if white swimmers attacked. When challenged by a group of whites they explained their position and left the pool area. They continued this protest throughout the summer. A local reporter, who worked undercover to "infiltrate" the group, published an article accusing the activists of being communists and deliberately inciting a race riot.[26] It was relatively easy for the local press to smear the activists as "reds" and dismiss their concerns, a fate Randolph hoped to avoid.

Despite such setbacks, by 1942 Randolph's views on how to effectively use nonviolent direct action had shifted to parallel those of Muste, Farmer, Rustin, and other pacifists. Although he continued to favor mass action, he also saw the value in small-scale interracial campaigns to desegregate public accommodations. While the MOWM declined as a result of a lack of funds, CORE took up the mission that Randolph had promoted. After working with the MOWM, Farmer and Rustin moved to Chicago where, along with George Houser and students from the University of Chicago, they met every Saturday afternoon to discuss Gandhian nonviolence, Christian pacifism, and racial discrimination. In 1942 they formed CORE and their first projects were public accommodations—local restaurants and a roller-skating rink aptly named White City.[27] The neighborhood where the rink was located, like many during the second Great Migration, was in a period of rapid racial transition from white to black. But the rink's owner persisted in admitting only white patrons using the "club" method to subvert Illinois's civil rights statute. It was relatively simple for CORE to demonstrate that the "club" was fictitious. White activists gained entrance without joining the "club" or showing membership cards, while the manager informed black customers that they needed to prove membership. When a lawsuit challenging White City's discrimination failed, CORE carried out a four-year nonviolent campaign: they picketed the rink, negotiated with the management, and distributed leaflets around the neighborhood.[28] Frustrated by the lack of progress and appalled by their increasingly heated confrontations with police and white customers, CORE demonstrators innovated a new technique: the "stand-in" or "stand-up," blocking the ticket counter at the rink so no patrons could enter. This method would be emulated in nonviolent demonstrations at amusement parks, pools, and roller-skating rinks nationwide.

Two elements of the final, successful demonstration at White City were notable: the violence it provoked and the role of veterans. In January 1946, on a very cold night, police officers and white soldiers in uniform confronted a group of forty-five picketers including World War II veterans carrying signs reading, "The draft boards did not exclude Negroes." The officers demanded to see the activists' "club cards" and roughly refused them entrance into the rink, shoving the group away from the ticket window. White soldiers knocked a woman to the ground and dragged several demonstrators away from the box office. The protestors blocked the entrance, forcing a crowd of white patrons to wait in the cold despite some calling out that they were willing to skate with African Americans. The rink's manager closed down early, fearful of the "riotous" crowd. Police arrested twelve of the protestors for "disorderly conduct," and two of the black veterans filed a complaint against the rink's owner for violation of their civil rights.[29]

After this confrontation, CORE members gave leaflets to white customers, stating, "We are American citizens who have fought for the preservation of our freedoms."[30] This call for inclusion brought larger crowds to picket lines every weekend through January and February, and CORE organized a mass meeting at the local AME church.[31] In March a local court refused White City's demand for an injunction against the pickets, which by then had cut attendance by 50 percent. Soon after, the rink's management agreed to open White City to blacks, and the court dropped all charges against both the protestors and the rink's owners.[32] The visibility of veterans in the White City fight and the retaliatory violence protestors suffered suggested the war for

Figure 3. Activists, led by the Congress of Racial Equality, picket the White City Roller Rink in 1946. Chicago History Museum, Negative ICHI-17209.

democracy was continuing at home. As one local African American paper stated, "The fight against White City is considered to be the opening gun in a campaign to smash discrimination in all skating rinks and amusement centers in Chicago."[33]

The war against recreational segregation spread to cities across the northern and border states in the 1940s. Randolph encouraged the attack against recreational segregation in what he called "civil rights states" where he endorsed a strategy that would take the "positive form of Negroes exercising their right to make use of agencies and enter places they do not normally make use of, such as going into downtown sections of cities as patrons of the hotels, restaurants and places of entertainment."[34] Civil rights states had statutes outlawing discrimination on the books that were either not enforced or narrowly applied. Ohio was one such state, and the recreational facility most targeted by activists was Cleveland's Euclid Beach Park. By 1946 the park's segregation policies had already been challenged by the local school board and black consumers, but Euclid Beach's private police force had stymied attempts to fully integrate the park. But that year a young African American veteran of the new nonviolent movement, Juanita Morrow, established a new, vibrant chapter of CORE. Morrow's campaign began when an interracial group of activists entered the park on July 21. The group was a coalition of members from the American Youth for Democracy (AYD), affiliated with the Communist Party, the National Negro Congress, a left-wing labor organization, and the United and Allied Veterans of America, an organization of black veterans.

When the coalition of young activists entered Euclid Beach Park police harassed them repeatedly, telling them they could not speak or sit together. When they attempted to enter the dance pavilion they were told to leave the park and were roughly escorted out by the private police force.[35] Working with CORE, the activists immediately filed a lawsuit and began a series of pickets outside the park gates. Morrow increased the pressure on Euclid Beach by leading twelve CORE activists to the park on August 23 to challenge its Jim Crow policies. This time park police did not wait until they attempted to dance or roller skate. Rather, guards confronted the group as they were playing Skee-Ball and forcibly led them out of the park, grabbing their arms and shirt collars as they walked. Guards targeted the white participants; one guard stated, "You've got a lot of nerve hanging around with Niggers. They want to take over the Park." It was during this action that Albert T. Luster was separated from the larger group and badly beaten by park guards. Drawing from a well-used stereotype of aggressive black men, park police later claimed Luster had been "molesting women" in the park.[36]

The August beatings of CORE activists challenged Clevelanders to address the antidemocratic policies of Euclid Beach. In September that challenge was brought to the dance pavilion, the most carefully guarded racialized space in the park. Two off-duty black police officers accompanied two couples, one white and one black, to test segregation at the pavilion. When the park guards barred the couples' entrance, the off-duty police officers attempted to arrest them because they were violating the state's civil rights statute. In the brawl that followed the gun of one of the police officers went off and he was badly wounded in the leg.[37] Fearing an escalation of violence, the mayor ordered Euclid Beach Park shut down a week before its season ended.[38] Seeking a final victory, the activists turned to the city council, asking them to pass a local ordinance requiring that public accommodations' licenses include an antidiscrimination clause. The council resisted for a time, but the executive secretary of the Community Relations Board pointed out to the interracial council that "You City Councilmen could not have an outing at Euclid Beach Park without the danger of having your heads bashed in."[39] Perhaps persuaded by this argument, the council approved the legislation after months of heated debate. The mayor was uneasy with this result, reportedly saying, "I don't like legislation of this type. It tends to disturb passions in men that shouldn't be disturbed."[40] The belief that segregation would leave "passions" undisturbed lay at the heart of the *Plessy* decision. In contrast, a CORE activist wrote to a local paper in the wake of the shooting, "To overlook this open and shot case is to commit a sin of omission; and invite a race riot."[41] Violence could maintain segregation, but it could also beget more violence.

The mayor's unease signaled a way out for Euclid Beach Park. When the new season began in the spring of 1947, the park's management temporarily shuttered the ballroom, skating rink, and bathhouse. These facilities later reopened, but they were run as private clubs exempt from the licensing law, free to discriminate at will.[42] This pattern was repeated in other parks. Idora Park in Youngstown, for example, closed down its elaborate saltwater swimming pool in 1948 rather than face integration. They replaced the pool with the Motor Boat Lagoon ride.[43] Similarly, in 1953 Pittsburgh's Kennywood Park turned its Sunlite Pool into the U-Drivem Boat Concession rather than desegregate the facility.[44] Park owners had free reign to subvert the law and brutalize protesters who challenged their segregationist policies. CORE members and their allies were deeply discouraged by the beatings of nonviolent activists and parks' evasion of civil rights statutes. But they had also discovered how targeting the largest recreational facilities in American cities, urban amusement parks, could galvanize activists and consumers.

The demonstrations at Euclid Beach Park also suggest the significance of radical interracial coalitions that challenged segregation in public accommodations. Such a coalition was central to the eventual success of the CORE campaign against White City in Chicago. Throughout the 1940s fellow travelers on the left, who sometimes went on to spearhead their own campaigns, routinely joined CORE. In 1946 the AYD, which worked with CORE in Cleveland, picketed Woodside Amusement Park in Philadelphia. The park owners had closed their roller rink rather than open it to blacks. They then ensured their pool would remain white by creating a private club, which remained in place, despite repeated protests, until the amusement park closed down in 1955.[45] The AYD's activism, generally overlooked in most civil rights histories, suggest that the early nonviolent movement was closer to a mass movement than often recognized. Although the numbers in CORE were relatively small, their demonstrations involved hundreds of picketers and protesters, and their work was emulated and supported throughout the North and West. Veterans, youth groups, and consumers who had supported Double V during the war saw in segregated parks and pools a challenge to their deepening beliefs in racial democracy. This was not the mass movement that Randolph envisioned, but it presented significant challenges to the racial status quo in midcentury America.

That challenge was perhaps best exemplified in 1940s New York City, a center of racial activism and the headquarters of FOR, MOWM, and a vibrant chapter of CORE. A tempting target for these activists lay just across the river in New Jersey at Palisades Park, an amusement park known for its racial discrimination. In the late 1940s CORE activists targeted segregation at the Palisades Park pool after successfully integrating the dance floor.[46] What followed were several years of violent conflict between activists and park police. On summer Sundays in 1947 CORE members lined up in front of the pool's ticket booth after being refused admission—this was the "stand-in" tactic they had honed at the White City rink in Chicago. After several weeks park guards began to forcefully remove the activists, shoving them to the pavement and punching them in the face. The park's owner, Irving Rosenthal, finally asked local police to intervene—they responded by dragging the activists and blackjacking them. James Peck, a white CORE activist, remembered, "It got so that each Sunday when we went to Palisades, we knew in advance that we would be beaten, arrested or both."[47] Peck noted that Rosenthal used two forms of "club" to defeat the activists, "the membership club and the police club."[48] In the summer of 1947 Peck suffered a fractured rib and broken jaw at the end of a police club. The activists filed a lawsuit in the Newark Federal District Court but lost the case when the judge ruled "a private amusement park is not required by the constitution to admit persons it considers objectionable."[49] This ruling reflected the court's uncertainty as to whether the existing civil rights statute covered commercial amusements. In the meantime, Rosenthal had made it clear that he found the CORE members objectionable and would continue to order their expulsion. "You'll all be dead before I change," Rosenthal declared.[50]

James Peck, who also was beaten in Birmingham in the 1961 Freedom Rides, noted in his 1962 book *Freedom Ride* that Palisades was "a long way from Alabama. Yet, if an observer had stopped off there on certain summer Sundays in 1947 and witnessed the violence to which CORE members were subjected, he would have believed himself transported to the heart of the South."[51] Peck's brutal experiences at Palisades Park gave him and others training in the use of nonviolence and demonstrated the blurring of de facto and de jure lines of segregation—New Jersey and Alabama had something in common.[52] In a pattern that foreshadowed the Student Nonviolent Coordinating Committee (SNCC) campaigns of the early 1960s, the vicious beatings increased public support for the activists and led directly to the passage of the 1949 Freeman Civil Rights Act in New Jersey.[53] Legislators carefully wrote the act to cover all recreational facilities in the state:

> Any tavern, roadhouse, or hotel, whether for entertainment of transient guests or accommodation of those seeking health, recreation or rest; any retail shop or store; any restaurant, eating house, or place where food is sold for consumption on the premises; any place maintained for the sale of ice cream, ice and fruit preparations or their derivatives, soda water or confections, or where any beverages of any kind are retailed for consumption on the premises; any garage, any public conveyance operated on land or water, or in the air, and stations and terminals thereof; any public bathhouse, public boardwalk, public seashore accommodation; any auditorium, meeting place, or public hall; any theater or other place of public amusement, motion-picture house, music hall, roof garden, skating rink, swimming pool, amusement and recreation park, fair, bowling alley, gymnasium, shooting gallery, billiard and pool parlor.[54]

No state had passed a civil rights statute guaranteeing equal access to public accommodations since 1931, and those previous acts relied on individuals to take the initiative to sue for damages or press for criminal prosecution. The Freeman Civil Rights Act marked a break from this practice by creating administrative remedies to violations of the civil rights statute. New Jersey legislators created the Commission on Civil Rights, designed to investigate complaints of racial discrimination and prosecute offenders.[55] This interracial commission was a hallmark of racial liberalism created in the wake of radical nonviolent activism.

The commission was hardly a foolproof system. Olympic Park outside Newark, for example, successfully excluded blacks until the 1960s. And towns transformed municipal swimming pools into private clubs to forestall integration. But in the wake of the passage of the act, the New Jersey

Figure 4. Palisades Park pool, c. 1962. Despite the efforts of CORE activists and passage of the Freeman Civil Rights Act, the pool remained a white space into the 1960s. © Bettmann/CORBIS.

courts forced Palisades Park to desegregate all its facilities in 1951. In practice, however, park management admitted into the pool only African Americans whom they recognized as CORE members likely to complain. Guards told other black customers they had to join a private club, as they had for decades. After rejected black visitors filed series of complaints against Palisades, the owners finally agreed to fully comply in 1952.[56] CORE took steps to publicize the desegregation order, distributing thousands of leaflets throughout Harlem urging blacks and Puerto Ricans (who had also been barred from entry) to patronize Palisades Park.[57] This was in stark contrast to the actions of more conservative civil rights groups, such as the Urban League, which ordinarily negotiated with owners to slowly desegregate by identifying "respectable" black citizens. Instead, true to their principles of creating a racial democracy, CORE members sought to invite everyone into the pool. Stronger enforcement of civil rights laws and the blood spilled by CORE activists were not enough to fully integrate the Palisades Park pool. It was nominally desegregated, but African Americans knew they were unwelcome and would risk racial taunts and violence if they ventured there in large numbers.

Across the country, CORE took the struggle for integrated swimming to a Hollywood resort pool in Los Angeles. Bimini Baths was an elegant pool frequented by Hollywood movie stars and the Los Angeles white elite since the early twentieth century.[58] In 1949 CORE activists, after hearing complaints that Bimini banned African Americans and dark-skinned Mexican Americans, targeted the baths with a series of stand-ins. Pool employees beat the activists, even throwing one through a plate-glass window. On at least two occasions guards turned a fire hose on the group in a scene that predated the infamous civil rights struggles in Birmingham by fourteen years. Bimini Baths' management also drew on two other methods of resisting integration that were specific to the postwar moment. During one protest the manager appeared and invited the entire group of CORE activists inside if they would sign affidavits proclaiming there were not communists. Similarly, the owner of Palisades Park, Irving Rosenthal, had accused CORE activists of being communists, stating that he had seen an FBI report on their activities. In both cases CORE members refused to discuss their affiliations. Trying another tack, the manager of the pool requested that the African American activists show health certificates before admittance. This time the activists produced the required certificates but were still denied admission.[59]

Attacking proponents of desegregation as communists was an increasingly common tactic used by pool owners and managers in the midst of a growing cold war. Assailing them as potential disease carriers had deeper roots in the association of blacks with illness, particularly venereal disease and tuberculosis.[60] By 1949 polio epidemics were peaking in the United States and closing pools to prevent further spread of the disease heightened the association between water and potential disease transmission.[61] Add race into the mix and protecting young children from disease quickly translated into resistance to desegregation. Protecting vulnerable American citizens against communism and disease justified white violence at Palisades and Bimini. To the shock of the Los Angeles picketers, however, when the manager of Bimini approached them in the fall he announced, "How would you all like to go in for a swim?" The reaction was jubilation, but it was short-lived.[62] Within a year Bimini had shut its doors. Looking back on that period, the owner's son, Bud Warick, remembered that "people would not come into the pool if they allowed minorities in there."[63] Rather than fully test this assumption, Bimini Baths' owner ensured that profitable integrated swimming would never succeed by simply closing the pool.

Racial liberals did not condone CORE's remarkable campaigns for recreational integration in Chicago, New Jersey, Cleveland, Los Angeles, and elsewhere. Radical nonviolence through stand-ins and sit-ins created crises and sparked violence that challenged the ability of interracial commissions to foster racial peace. In some cases, as in the Palisades campaign that encouraged lawmakers to craft antidiscrimination legislation in New Jersey, CORE's success was dramatic. In many other cases, such as Euclid Beach and the Bimini Baths, desegregation through the work of direct action did not lead to flourishing integrated spaces but private clubs and closings. But CORE's methods proved to be a vital model for consumers and activists to follow. And they did not act alone. While historians have been somewhat dismissive of CORE's 1940s activism as relatively small in scale, when combined with the array of like-minded protestors and the actions of ordinary consumers, CORE's focus on recreation appears both timely and significant.

George Houser reflected on the contrast between racial liberalism and nonviolent direct action in his 1945 book *Erasing the Color Line*: "Many groups have been organized in this country to pursue this personal and educational approach. Usually these groups sponsor such activities as interracial teas, interracial meetings, and interracial church services. . . . This educational approach is good as far as it goes, but it should not become a fetish with its advocates, excluding other methods. The seriousness of the times would seem to demand more virile action to supplement personal conversion and enlightenment by education."[64] Houser, Rustin, Peck, and their fellow activists carried out such "virile actions" throughout the 1940s. Randolph, who argued in 1942 that it was "not enough to fight isolated instances of injustice, not enough to do research and educational work," also embraced the potential of radical nonviolence and expressed dissatisfaction with racial liberalism.[65] These activists' forms of education and persuasion were more physical and more immediate than the Myrdalian call for education. Ordinary African Americans who were also challenging segregation through action rather than words shared that desire for immediacy. In 1948, for example, a group of African Americans in Indianapolis entered segregated Riverside Amusement Park. A park official, five park police, and a city policeman followed them. When the African Americans asked, "Is there anything wrong with our being here?" the park official replied, "You're not welcome here, not wanted. We won't keep you out, but your lives aren't worth a dime here without police protection."[66] The group refused to leave. Such acts of courage paralleled the more organized attempts of nonviolent activists to challenge racial segregation.

Ordinary consumers' defiance also forced the courts to rule on civil rights cases as the NAACP more aggressively pushed for the enactment of public accommodations laws. Much as the actions of Rosa Parks forced the city of Montgomery, Alabama, to abide by *Brown v. Board of Education* in 1955, a young black woman, Sarah Elizabeth Ray, forced open the gates of an amusement park outside Detroit, Michigan, ten years earlier with an act of daring. Detroit's African Americans had repeatedly attempted to gain access to Bob-Lo Park, located on Bois Blanc Island across the Detroit River in Canada, but the ferry operators that carried passengers to the park and ran the island's concessions turned them away. The Bob-Lo Excursion Company's stated policy was to refuse admission to "negroes and disorderly persons." In 1945 Ray had just graduated from secretarial school. Along with her white classmates she tried to board the ferry to celebrate at Bob-Lo. After guards threw her off the boat, Ray called the local NAACP office and with their assistance filed a criminal complaint against the Bob-Lo Excursion Company. The branch had received other complaints and was eager to help.[67]

The Michigan Supreme Court found Bob-Lo in violation of the state's Civil Rights Act. But in 1948 the company appealed to the U.S. Supreme Court, arguing that the state law did not apply to foreign lands. Noting that the only access to Bois Blanc Island was via Detroit, the justices upheld the Michigan law, ensuring that the amusement park would be forced to welcome blacks in the future.[68] Ray's decision to challenge Bob-Lo's policies set an important legal precedent, but it also demonstrated the kind of "virile action" that Houser was calling for. Like Juanita Morrow, Sarah Elizabeth Ray asserted her power as a consumer and an activist alongside the better-known male leaders of radical pacifism. As a result, the bucolic Bois Blanc Island was now accessible to a postwar generation of urban blacks. Increased activism by local chapters of the NAACP and proponents of radical nonviolence bolstered challenges to recreational segregation. White owners of commercial recreation responded with vigorous legal defenses in the courts and by openly encouraging their young white customers to threaten and assault African American who dared cross the color line.

Opening Rinks and Alleys

Because of their size and popularity, amusement parks and municipal resort pools were popular targets for CORE and other nonviolent activists. Protestors and consumers also targeted two of the most used forms of urban leisure: bowling alleys and roller-skating rinks. On cold winter days in the urban North rinks and alleys were welcome respites of leisure, equally important urban terrains as playgrounds and parks in summer months. Owners limited access to these facilities primarily through membership clubs, asking black customers for cards if they approached and promptly throwing out their membership applications. Urban working-class communities at mid-century had become particularly attached to their local bowling alleys, but the American Bowling Congress (ABC) admitted no black bowlers and there were few alleys where black bowlers could comfortably meet. CORE activists, therefore, often focused on bowling in their campaign to desegregate recreation. In the late 1940s CORE targeted bowling alleys in Minneapolis, slowly gaining community support and opening up one alley after another. This campaign culminated in 1951 at ABC's annual convention in the city when they agreed to allow blacks to become members.[69] A similar pattern of excluding blacks existed in roller rinks, and consumers and activists targeted segregated facilities and demanded inclusion at rinks as well. But roller-skating proved more contentious than bowling.

The 1940s and early 1950s saw repeated skirmishes in roller rinks. These spaces paralleled dance halls as they invited young men and women to intermingle and flirt. Therefore rink owners were more likely to segregate their facilities, fearful of interracial mixing among young men and women. As rinks became increasingly popular venues for black and white teenagers during and after the war years, the racial exclusion practiced by most rinks deeply angered many black families. Capitalizing on this frustration, beginning with the White City campaign in Chicago, activists targeted roller-skating rinks using nonviolent direct action. In the winter of 1943, for example, an early chapter of CORE in Syracuse, New York, attempted to integrate the Alhambra Roller Skating Rink. Despite the manager's insistence that "Negroes are rowdies," activists pointed out that he was losing business to another rink that did allow black skaters. This economic argument, rather than the moral one, gained traction.[70] During the 1940s the NAACP also proved more willing to respond to complaints of discrimination by filing lawsuits against skating rinks in violation of state civil rights laws. In 1943 in St. Paul, Minnesota, for example, pressure from the local NAACP opened up the rink in Harriett Island Park.[71]

The NAACP did not always succeed in its efforts, however. In 1946 Andrew Merriweather, a member of Cincinnati's NAACP Youth Council, led a group of African Americans seeking entrance into Sefferino's Rollerdrome. They were turned away, told that the rink had been engaged for a private party. In this case a local jury acquitted Sefferino of the charge that he had violated the local Equal Rights Law.[72] In Glassboro, New Jersey, when an African American was denied entrance into the Delwood Roller Skating Rink he contacted the local NAACP, which filed a complaint. But despite the Freeman Civil Rights Act, the state did not act on a cease and desist order.[73] Even when such actions failed, the NAACP's newfound commitment to recreational desegregation encouraged African American consumers to turn to civil rights organizations for redress.

It is notable that in many of these cases young men and women led the fight against Jim Crow, seeking leisure in an expanding postwar economy. The City Wide Youth Committee of the Four Freedoms, for example, picketed a Brooklyn rink that barred its black members.[74] This aptly named interracial youth group viewed access to public recreation without fear of violence as a part of the four freedoms, echoing Drake and Cayton's call for a "fifth freedom"—the end of Jim Crow. In the 1940s it was often the Youth Councils of local NAACP chapters that most aggressively challenged racial discrimination.[75] In Flint, Michigan, for example, the NAACP Youth Council instigated a boycott of the Flint Roller Drome in protest of separate skating days for blacks and whites.[76] The physical challenges and group atmosphere of direct action clearly attracted young blacks and whites eager to put their beliefs into practice. But there was also a sense of play in their actions. Drawing from their success at White City, the Chicago CORE chapter began to hold "CORE skating parties" to test rinks around the city. CORE recruited some talented skaters from the black Savoy rink, then engaged in the "tripping game" at the white rinks. When whites attempted to trip the Savoy skaters, the protesters used their well-honed skills to elude them. When management denied

Figure 5. African Americans skating at the Savoy Ballroom in Chicago, 1941. CORE recruited talented young skaters from the Savoy to help desegregate white rinks. Courtesy Library of Congress, Prints & Photographs Division, FSA/OWI Collection.

activists' requests for protection, they would picket, file lawsuits, or simply continue the parties.[77] It often took many years to force managers to comply with civil rights laws and convince them that black customers were neither "rowdy" nor detrimental to their business.

The tenacity of recreational activists is well illustrated by a long campaign against Cleveland's large and very popular Skateland roller rink. The owners of this rink also owned the Play-More rink, where they welcomed African American customers. This "separate but equal" policy was common for both bowling alleys and skating rinks—although the black facilities were rarely equal and when owned by whites allowed white customers to enter at will. In 1944 a group of young Quakers and the NAACP Youth Council decided to take on Skateland using nonviolent direct action. The interracial group of twelve was turned away for not being "members" of the white rink. They then entered into negotiations with the manager, who warned them that "white skaters would use violence in all probability if Negroes entered the rink."[78] In response the activists decided to attempt to desegregate the rink using only young women. Despite George Houser's call for "virile" action, female activists were routinely on the front lines of radical nonviolence. Eventually some female protestors managed to get into the rink, but both management and hostile whites on the skating floor harassed them incessantly. With tensions escalating the manager brought the activists into his office. Outside a crowd of white teenagers gathered, waiting to confront the women. They managed to slip out a side exit and board a streetcar, but the mob spotted their escape and followed in two cars. At a public square the activists got off to confront their pursuers, guessing that the threatened violence was less likely in such a public place. Their ploy worked, but Skateland remained segregated.

It was another young African American woman who would take the most blows from the skaters intent on keeping Skateland white. Eroseanna (Sis) Robinson was a young staff member at a Cleveland community center in 1952. (By 1952 Juanita Morrow had left Cleveland for Cincinnati, where she led another fight against amusement park segregation, and the local CORE chapter was largely defunct.) Robinson, who had attended an interracial workshop sponsored by CORE in 1951, decided to take on the project of desegregating Skateland. One Saturday afternoon she brought three children from the community center, two black and one white, to skate at the rink. After much delay the manager gave them skates, but as soon as they were out on the rink a group of teenage boys repeatedly tripped them. Robinson returned to the rink several days later in the evening, accompanied by a white friend, a male graduate student sympathetic to radical nonviolence. During that visit white customers constantly harassed them, and the rink guards refused to intervene in the escalating threats and violence. The following evening Robinson returned with more friends for support. This time as soon as she skated out on the rink a group of white men assaulted her. Robinson fell and cut her knee badly, but she got up and kept skating. She was tripped again, and again she got up. This continued—not a sit-in or a stand-in but a skate-in that required constant motion and a high tolerance for pain. Robinson had been a track star in college and described herself as a "better than average skater," so she was able to fend off her attackers with her speed and agility for a time. Finally, after a violent shove, Robinson crashed to the floor and broke her arm. Only then did she agree to leave and seek medical attention.[79]

George Houser, who had advised the nonviolent Cleveland activists in 1944, wrote to Robinson after hearing of her injuries: "It will take some pretty strong support to break down Skateland. I know from my own experience there in 1944 that it is a pretty tough proposition and that it will not be any fly-by-night tactic that will change its policy."[80] Robinson had known that Skateland's manager would not intervene as the violence escalated: "He indicated there were 'business reasons' for not offering to protect colored patrons; that other incidents of this kind had occurred, and he stated generally that he had no responsibility for protecting colored skaters from whatever rough treatment befell them."[81] Skateland did not have the hired guards of a large amusement park; it depended on the willingness of white patrons to police the rink. The rink's owner claimed that he "wouldn't mind seeing colored people come to skate so long as they were clean and neat." He went on to suggest, "The people at Play-more Roller Rink were 'better behaved' than his patrons."[82] His patrons were white, rowdy, and uncontrollable, but they were allowed to dominate the rink and drive away any blacks who dared to join them.

Although Skateland's owner suggested that Play-More's black customers had more decorum, there is evidence that blacks at Play-More tripped white patrons who ventured into the rink. In those cases, however, Play-More's white manager chastised his black customers and the practice quickly stopped. This contrast in the disciplining of customers' behavior ensured that only Skateland would remain racially homogenous. African Americans who frequented Play-More were more successful during a spontaneous protest when a white organist was hired for the rink. Black skaters quickly staged a "sit-down strike" and then boycotted the rink until an African American musician replaced the organist.[83] Black consumers wanted to skate at the better-appointed Skateland, but they also defended their rights at Play-More. In the end, Robinson's defiance and substantial injuries did not change the policy of segregation.

Because Play-More was a white-owned business whose proprietor also ran the hated Skateland, there was continual tension in the rink. More popular were black-owned rinks that took advantage of membership clubs to attract African American consumers. In Philadelphia, where only a handful of rinks allowed black skaters, a group of African Americans formed the Penn Rollers in 1946. This group sought to buy their own rink, with the slogan "A Rink Owned and Operated by Colored," but in the meantime they used white rinks on designated days and times. By the early 1950s Philadelphia boasted the Sepia Skating Club, and nearby Chester was home to the Ebony Skating Club.[84] All of these clubs made use of a system similar to that of amusement parks whereby black customers were allowed access on particular days of the week, usually Mondays. In 1953 a coalition of civil rights groups negotiated an agreement with six of Philadelphia's segregated rinks to desegregate. The Commission on Human Relations, an interracial group that reflected the racial liberalism of the time, crafted this agreement. "Armed with complaints from Negro skaters who were denied admittance to the skating rinks because of their color," the commission helped enforce a 1939 law that prohibited discrimination in public accommodations.[85] In Philadelphia blacks employed a variety of resistance strategies to open skating rinks, from creating separate clubs to deploying the negotiating tools of racial liberalism.

But the case of Philadelphia also demonstrated that African American consumers had to remain vigilant if these strategies were to be effective. In 1957, for example, Reverend S. Amos Brackeen, a Baptist minister and social activist, sued Philadelphia's Lexington Skating Palace for noncompliance with the 1939 law and 1953 agreement. The court found that although the "Lexington Skating Club was formed in 1946 for the purpose of keeping out all persons of objectionable character and conduct," it had been proven that it was "used by the defendant to exclude Negroes."[86] The court also found that there were no African Americans among the approximately thirty thousand members. Furthermore, while whites gained entrance even with no membership cards, managers routinely barred blacks from entering. Blacks who did attempt to skate in 1957 were a representative mix of activists and consumers. Joining Reverend Brackeen was the executive secretary of the local NAACP, a local father with two young girls, and two young black men. These individuals, and many like them, continually pressured recreational facilities to abide by the law. After years of litigation, the court finally issued an injunction against the Lexington Skating Palace to end its racial discrimination.[87]

Even without civil rights organizations' support there were moments when black consumers received some justice when mistreated at a local rink. In June 1948 two African American couples attempted to skate at the Skateland Roller Rink in Bridgeport, Connecticut. After a lengthy argument they managed to get in but were then given the wrong size skates. Infuriated by how they had been treated, the couples contacted an attorney. After a long legal battle the court forced Skateland's manager to pay a $100 fine and spend two days in jail for racial discrimination.[88] This punishment of a rink manager was unusual, but the challenges to segregation posed by African Americans and sympathetic whites in Cleveland, Philadelphia, and countless other northern and border cities across the nation had become commonplace by the late 1940s.

Battling Segregated Swimming

In skating rinks, hostile whites tripped and harassed black customers who managed to get by cashiers and managers requesting membership cards. A similar dynamic existed in the nation's swimming pools and beaches: white teenagers routinely harassed and beat blacks who attempted to swim. For example, in 1941 a group of white teenagers chased five African American boys from Cleveland's Woodland Hills Park swimming pool when they attempted to swim there.[89] City officials most often viewed such incidents as juvenile delinquency rather than a serious threat to public order or civil rights violation. But the increasing number of swimming pool and beach riots in the 1940s was an outgrowth of larger challenges to segregated recreation. These riots, both large and small, also reflected the ways in which postwar America's racial anxieties coalesced in the water: fears of disease in the midst of a polio epidemic, concerns over the safety of young children in America's growing families, apprehension about the rapidly changing racial and ethnic makeup of urban neighborhoods, and alarm over the seeming rise of teenage delinquency. Swimming pool demonstrations and conflicts in the late 1940s and early 1950s demarcated racial boundaries in rapidly changing cities and structured the response of state agencies ranging from local recreation boards to the Supreme Court. "When pools have been opened on a nonsegregated basis," noted one legal scholar in 1954, "either under legal compulsion or by voluntary action, disturbances have resulted more frequently than in any other instances of desegregation."[90] There was no urban space as racialized as the local pool.

At the same time CORE activists were targeting the Palisades Park pool, African American teenagers were challenging the persistence of swimming segregation elsewhere in New Jersey. In Summit three African American girls protested the local YMCA's refusal to let them take lessons at the local pool in 1945.[91] The Paterson chapter of AYD targeted their local municipal pool after the cashier turned away the black members of the group, claiming it was a private club. This led to a campaign of picketing and continued nonviolent direct action.[92] Even after the passage of the Freeman Civil Rights Act that explicitly forbid pool segregation, many New Jersey pools openly discriminated. In Asbury Park, for example, a pool operator who continued to flagrantly ignore the newly passed law justified his practice by invoking a black "invasion." When meeting with the NAACP he expressed his apprehension of "Harlem and Philadelphia Negroes coming to his pool by the bus loads."[93] Such fears led many pool operators to further privatize their facilities—charging steeper membership fees and carefully checking membership cards at the gate in an effort to subvert the law. These practices would make swimming in New Jersey a flashpoint of racial violence well into the 1970s. Nearby in New York City, swimming segregation also remained a problem in the 1940s. CORE members actively tested and desegregated numerous pools during this period. In 1947 they held a "beach party" at the St. George Pool in Brooklyn after repeated reports of discrimination. There they "splashed and ducked without discrimination" as the management changed its policies under pressure from consumers and activists.[94]

As local governments yielded to the pressure of nonviolent tactics and repeated lawsuits by opening their municipal pools to blacks in the 1940s, new forms of white resistance to desegregation emerged. Towns closed down pools or privatized their operations. While larger cities could rely, to an extent, on residential segregation to keep recreational facilities separate, towns with only one municipal pool had no such options. In 1947, for example, a local NAACP branch forced the town of York, Pennsylvania, to desegregate its municipal pool after the guard denied entry to two young African American boys.[95] White attendance decreased dramatically, but there were no incidents of violence. The decreased attendance was also difficult to separate from a local polio outbreak that kept children away from the pool. In response to lower numbers of swimmers, York's Director of Parks, who had vociferously opposed desegregation, ordered the pool closed, citing a "lack of income." The city council forced him to reopen the pool for the summer season of 1948; possibly as a result of the controversy a local election brought a new mayor and new members of the city council into office who opposed desegregation. This shift in local political leadership away from a progressive stance on desegregation reflected a national trend of rising conservatism among the nation's mayors by the late 1940s.

After his election, York's new mayor began holding secret meetings with conservative African American leaders in the community and revived a defunct interracial commission. Here was the danger of racial liberalism's emphasis on negotiation and compromise—in the case of York, reactionary city leaders easily manipulated this discourse to, in the words of the local NAACP, "give the appearance of 'good-will.'"[96] The interracial commission proposed either building a separate pool at the Crispus Attucks Center for blacks, a plan opposed by the center's operator, or building a separate pool at a local playground used primarily by blacks. After a mass meeting demonstrated the strength of opposition to the idea of a separate pool, the city council voted to sell the municipal pool. The NAACP filed an injunction to try to stop the sale, noting that it violated Pennsylvania's antidiscrimination laws as well as "the Constitutional rights of Negroes."[97] Despite the injunction the city sold the pool, privatizing its operation and placing it outside the purview of the law.[98]

York was not the only Pennsylvania community to confront a more active and militant local NAACP branch after the war. In Washington, Pennsylvania, the city council met in a special session (at the same time York was selling its pool) to explicitly restrict the Washington Park pool to whites. That had been the practice for some time, but the local NAACP had requested that the city allow blacks to swim, prompting the more explicit (and illegal) policy. The statement of Washington's mayor, Elmer R. Wilson, was grounded in the longstanding defense of segregation as violence prevention: "Of all the possibilities discussed [by city council], the one which was of most concern to us, was the possible problem of maintaining order. We know that the small children would get along fine together. However, older persons who do not possess the same degree of tolerance are more likely to succumb to violent emotions and innocent children suffer serious injury as a result of the conduct of their elders."[99] Wilson's call to protect the town's children from their parents' ignorance echoed the themes of racial liberalism—that racism was a result of a lack of tolerance. In the midst of a postwar baby boom his concern for the city's children most likely struck a chord. And some believed there was increasing evidence that racial mixing in pools could indeed lead to violence. By legislating segregation Wilson was, in his own words, "maintaining order."

While CORE was using nonviolent direct action to protest pool segregation, the NAACP was forcefully attacking pool segregation in the courts. There was a direct relationship between these trends as many legal cases began as either formal or informal protests. As local NAACP branches became increasingly militant during the 1940s, they pushed the Legal Defense Fund to target the recreational segregation that so angered their membership. A case in Warren, Ohio, proved these legal struggles could have real effects. The Warren Pool, located in Packard Park, was built with Works Progress Administration (WPA) funds in 1936 but did not allow blacks to swim until 1946 after a local NAACP campaign to open the pool to all. That year the city lost $3,500 in operating expenses because of declining white attendance at the pool, a significantly larger deficit than in previous years. The city council asked local blacks to agree to swim only one day per week, but when they refused they leased the pool to the Veterans Swim Club to be run as a private facility, citing financial loss. Warren's local NAACP branch was eager to prosecute the case, noting that the lease was clearly an effort to avoid Ohio's civil rights statutes and that black veterans could not receive membership cards. They lost in the lower court but won their appeal.[100] Bowing to legal pressure, the city opened the pool on June 15, 1948, as a desegregated facility. The front page of the local paper featured a picture of children lining up to enter the pool, the last two clearly African American. The caption read, "Last one in the water is a monkey."[101]

By the late 1940s activists and ordinary consumers were putting enormous pressure on city officials to open public waters to blacks. These demonstrations, court cases, and racial clashes came to a head in the summer of 1949. An escalation of racial violence led some to question racial liberals' ability to mediate a transition to fully integrated public spaces. And many African Americans became increasingly frustrated by the ability of white teenagers to forestall desegregation with their fists. Gary, Indiana, exemplified this escalation of youthful clashes over swimming facilities. After the 1943 Detroit riot, city officials in Gary began to discuss the possibility of opening one of the beaches, used only by whites, to blacks in an attempt to forestall rioting in the steel city. Instead they decided to allow African American students to use the pool in the large central high school, the Froebel School, as a compromise. White students responded by walking out of the school and demanding segregated education, as well as segregated recreation.[102] In 1949 a group of protestors, who called themselves Young Citizens for Beachhead Democracy, announced plans to occupy Miller Beach in Marquette Park on Lake Michigan. They were met by forty squad cars and scores of white residents who attacked their cars with baseball bats and lead pipes. Groups of protestors occupied the beach, marking their territory with an American flag planted in the sand. They left peacefully when police told them the beach was closed for the day. The police captain blamed the riot on the protestors, suggesting they were "communist inspired," and the city noted that although there were no segregation ordinances for the beach, "Negroes seldom used it."[103] The reasons why it was seldom used were evident, and beachhead democracy was delayed. The historian Andrew Hurley argues that it was not until the late 1960s "that African Americans felt safe visiting Gary's beaches. Even then, they used the lakefront cautiously, adopting patterns of beach use that minimized conflict."[104] It was the freedom of movement that defined equality for Gary's black citizens in the late 1940s, a freedom that would not be gained until the late twentieth century.

But it was in a border city, St. Louis, Missouri, that a recreation riot gained the most notoriety. St. Louis was home to Fairgrounds Park, a large and luxurious pool with a sandy "beach" and well-appointed changing facilities. The city opened the pool in 1913 as a segregated facility, restricting local blacks to three dilapidated indoor pools run by the Division of Parks and Recreation. In June 1949 the mayor announced that all public recreational facilities would be desegregated, underestimating the amount of press coverage and strong reaction among white city residents that would follow.[105] The day after the mayor's announcement young African Americans flocked to Fairgrounds Park. Inside the pool grounds a group of about fifty blacks was met by 250 whites, some armed with clubs and knives. As the African Americans fled the pool they ran through a mob of several thousand whites who surrounded the park. Battles raged into the evening with at least ten injuries, and the police did not arrive in force until night fell. The following morning the mayor closed both outdoor pools "in the interest of public safety" and rescinded his desegregation order,[106] despite the fact that blacks swam at the other outdoor pool, Marquette pool, with no incidents of violence.[107]

What followed the Fairgrounds unrest became a predictable pattern in postwar recreation riots. City officials and the local press blamed the violence on "juvenile delinquents," thus absolving the city from any responsibility for segregation. When the pool at Fairgrounds Park reopened in 1950 the city defended its segregation policy in the local courts by making the plea that it was trying to avoid more violence and worked to quickly build an outdoor pool for blacks. The "separate but equal" ploy failed when a U.S. District Court forced the city to reopen both the Fairgrounds and Marquette pools on an integrated basis. That summer was tense as black swimmers, according to local reports, "go to and from the pool between two lines of policemen, who face outward, separating the swimmers from a crowd of several hundred white men, women and children. Most of the whites make no secret of their hatred of what they regard as an intrusion." The "intrusion" of black swimmers led to an 80 percent drop in white attendance; in 1956 the city closed Fairgrounds pool for good.[108]

In order to preserve recreational spaces as orderly, whites-only facilities, city officials supported their privatization in the 1940s and 1950s. When that failed, proprietors shut down swimming pools, skating rinks, and amusement parks. To justify their actions officials invoked not the actual violence of white vigilantes but the perceived violence of black criminality that threatened white consumerism. In the end the effect was the same. Violence inscribed racial boundaries that were reinforced by local officials to justify their exclusion policies. In St. Louis, as in so many other cities, riot prevention became the primary justification for maintaining Jim Crow. Recreation riots, however, were also a symptom of a broader youth movement for integrated recreation. The actions of the Young Citizens for Beachhead Democracy and the dozens of African American children who braved the crowds at Fairgrounds Park suggest that the mid- to late 1940s was a period not only of racial liberalism and a growing nonviolent movement but a broad challenge to northern Jim Crow waged largely by young people. A. Philip Randolph, Bayard Rustin, and others tapped into the energy of this movement, and at times guided it, but there was an organic and grassroots opposition to segregated recreation beyond formal organizations. Yet another riot, this time in the nation's capital, further suggests the relationship between a growing civil rights movement and black children's demands for a place to play.

Racial Democracy in Washington, D.C.

The same summer that St. Louis and Gary experienced recreation riots, Anacostia Pool in Washington, D.C., exploded in violence. This recreation riot was particularly controversial because of the capital's symbolic importance in the Double V campaign and civil rights struggles of the 1940s. Racial liberals and radical activists alike targeted segregation in Washington, where Myrdal's "American dilemma"—the contrast between the promises of democracy and the reality of racism—was most evident. The civil rights activist Pauli Murray noted that when she arrived in Washington to study law at Howard University in 1943, "Union Station was the only place in downtown Washington where a Negro could get a meal or use rest room facilities. Although the city had no segregation ordinance requiring separation of the races, Negroes were systematically barred from hotels, restaurants, theaters, movie houses, and other places of public accommodation."[109] The city was a natural target for activists, and its persistent discriminatory practices angered the growing African American community, which led to increased confrontations in spaces of leisure.

A group of strong-minded women, including CORE leader Juanita Morrow, joined Murray at Howard University. These women were instrumental in spearheading the burgeoning nonviolent movement while many of their male compatriots were serving time in jail as conscientious objectors. Indeed, Howard University was a hotbed of tactical experimentation in the wartime civil rights movement. Murray had worked with the MOWM while at law school when A. Philip Randolph began to target segregated public accommodations. There she mentored a group of young undergraduates, all women, who had independently decided to take on segregated restaurants in the nation's capital. A remarkable young freshman, Ruth Powell, had been quietly sitting-in at local restaurants since her arrival at Howard University in 1941. By 1942 Powell was joined by two friends, Marianne Musgrave and Juanita Morrow. When police arrested the three women at the United Cigar Store on Pennsylvania Avenue after they refused to leave the premises when they did not get the hot chocolate they ordered, this galvanized the student body, which organized a Civil Rights Committee under the leadership of Pauli Murray. Over the next year they successfully desegregated several downtown establishments, ending their campaign only when the university (under pressure from Congress) forced them to.[110] While Murray went on to denounce "Jane Crow," Morrow became a prominent activist in CORE and eventually moved to Cleveland to lead the fight to desegregate Euclid Beach Park.

CORE began holding interracial workshops in Washington, D.C., soon after Murray and Morrow's demonstrations in 1944. George Houser and Bayard Rustin led one such workshop, targeting segregated restaurants, in the summer of 1947. By 1949 activists from CORE and the NAACP had begun a wholesale attack on segregated public accommodations in the city. Nonviolent activists targeted the segregated theaters of downtown Washington. They chose the Trans-Lux Theater, timing their stand-in to coincide with the showing of *Home of the Brave*, a film portraying the problem of racism in the military. CORE's leaflet pointed out that the film showed "colored and white fighting together to protect those rights and ideals which are denied them in this theater."[111] Washington's theaters had also been the focus of an ongoing boycott by leading directors, actors, and playwrights who refused to work at segregated stages. In 1948 the National Theater closed its doors rather than allow blacks in its audience.[112] In 1949 the issue of segregation in public accommodations was at the forefront of black and white consciousness in Washington. Typically, it was recreational segregation that would elicit the most violent and passionate responses from whites in the community.

Washington, D.C., a segregated capital in a democratic nation, raised

"IT'S YOUR CAPITAL" —Says the Board of Trade

BUT FOR NEGRO AMERICANS WASHINGTON HAS A MEANING OF ITS OWN

HOTELS
"NO COLORED"

Hotels in the downtown area will not rent rooms to Negroes. This has embarrassed dark-skinned foreign visitors.

RESTAURANTS
"NO COLORED"

In downtown area restaurants will not serve Negroes. At lunch counters Negroes must stand to be served.

THEATERS
"NO COLORED"

Negroes will not be admitted to downtown theaters. Unless they pose as aliens, they are told to go to segregated theaters.

Most white cab drivers pass up Negro patronage in downtown Washington.

In the "best" department stores clerks turn their backs at the approach of a Negro.

CAPITAL GETS WORLD-WIDE PUBLICITY ON SEGREGATION

The Daughters of the American Revolution refused to permit Marian Anderson, Negro, to sing in Constitution Hall.

The National Theater, Capital's only commercial playhouse, is being converted to a movie theater, because of boycott by Actors' Equity for banning Negroes.

Ingrid Bergman, star of "Joan of Lorraine," at Lisner Auditorium, was shocked at the exclusion of Negroes.

Figure 6. Racial liberals produced publications designed to persuade Americans to oppose segregation in the nation's capital. *Segregation in Washington: A Report of the National Committee on Segregation in the Nation's Capital* (1948), 36.

the ire of both racial liberals and their more radical direct action counterparts. The city was a potent symbol of Double V during wartime and a useful propaganda tool to illustrate the limits of American democracy as part of the research efforts and moral suasion campaigns promoted by Myrdal and others. Two publications best illustrate this trend. In 1948 a group of civic leaders formed the National Committee on Segregation in the Nation's Capital. It was an interracial organization that included Eleanor Roosevelt, Walter Reuther, Helen Hayes, and Hubert Humphrey, as well as prominent African American reformers and intellectuals such as Charles H. Houston, Robert C. Weaver, and E. Franklin Frazier. The committee published *Segregation in Washington*, which was based on two years of research. The book continued the themes of Double V for a cold war context by emphasizing the ways communist propaganda exploited America's segregated capital. The authors highlighted the negative treatment dark-skinned diplomats and visitors experienced in Washington. "I would rather be an Untouchable in the Hindu caste system," said one traveler from India in 1948, "than a Negro in Washington."[113] Throughout the study the authors' emphasized the problem of white racism, with no mention of black resistance to segregation. The real danger, concluded the authors, was the "ghettoes of the spirit . . . that cram the soul of the nation in the place of its pride, and lessen the meaning of its life."[114] The meaning of Washington, D.C., could be restored with increased interracial contact and the promise of true democracy.

Harry S. Truman's Committee on Civil Rights took up this theme the following year in its pivotal study *To Secure These Rights*. Like *Segregation in Washington*, this work was deeply influenced by Myrdal's *An American Dilemma* in its presentation of race relations as a moral conflict between American ideals and practices.[115] The committee highlighted segregation in Washington by providing a separate section titled "Civil Rights in the Nation's Capital," which presented the same litany of facts found in the earlier study. The authors emphasized recreational segregation in this section, noting, "In the field of public recreation, compulsory segregation has increased over the past twenty five years. Various public authorities have closed to one race or the other numerous facilities where whites and Negroes once played together harmoniously." But *To Secure These Rights* went further in arguing that the federal government should safeguard civil rights in the District of Columbia, calling for a federal law that would "protect several million people directly, and encourage the states and local communities throughout the country to do likewise."[116] Truman did not follow through on this sweeping recommendation, but the federal government did engage in a struggle with local segregationists to open recreational facilities to all. It was the 1949 Anacostia riot that brought together racial liberals, nonviolent activists, and Washington's African Americans in this common goal.

By 1949 the capital was caught between racial liberals in the Truman administration and the Dixiecrats of the segregationist South. New Deal liberals ran six of the city's swimming pools, including the Anacostia Pool. The Department of the Interior controlled the federally owned land where these pools were located and leased them for daily operations. In the summer of 1949 the assistant secretary of the Department of the Interior declared that the federal government's nonsegregation policy applied to the swimming pools. Shortly after this announcement, fifty African American boys attempted to enter the large Anacostia Pool. The pool's lifeguards, who were employees of the District Recreation Board, which supported segregated facilities, turned the African American youths away with the assistance of several local white boys. In the two days that followed lifeguards admitted a few dozen black swimmers, but they eventually asked to be relieved of their duties, "saying they feared they might not be able to handle disturbances." The first such "disturbance" occurred the day after the announcement that the pool had been desegregated. Two African American boys were "surrounded by a small group of white boys who splashed water into their faces and drove them to the side of the pool." White teenagers splashed and taunted black swimmers as a crowd of "between 700 and 800" whites watched the incidents. By the evening a large crowd of whites and blacks had gathered. By the end of the night whites had injured four African Americans and police had arrested three whites and two blacks.[117] At that point the Department of the Interior shut Anacostia Pool down for the remainder of the summer.

The Anacostia riot was part of a longer struggle between the federal and local governments in Washington. In the summer of 1945 the Washington, D.C., Board of Recreation issued an explicit rule segregating public recreation facilities under its control. Their immediate justification was a complaint by the District playground director that she could "not handle" racially mixed groups who used public recreation centers.[118] The threat of violence induced the board to draw a map that designated recreation areas for blacks and for whites. There was immediate opposition from civil rights organizations under an umbrella group, the Citizens Committee Against Segregation in Recreation, which argued, "Washington, as the Capital of the world's leading democracy, must set an example of democracy and decent living."[119] The

Department of the Interior clearly agreed, as they ensured all the golf courses, tennis courts, and other recreational facilities under their jurisdiction had no racial restrictions. On V-J Day, August 15, 1945, when the Allies celebrated their victory over Japan, several hundred Washington residents protested the fascism of recreational segregation at home.[120] But the Board of Recreation's attempts to spatially segregate the city's leisure spaces were stymied by the reality of demographic change. The racial zoning of recreational spaces was inflexible and could not react quickly to the reality of racial succession. In 1948 the Citizens Committee pointed out, "Because of shifting population several play areas supervised by the Recreation Board are maintained as 'white' yet there are as many if not more colored children in the neighborhood."[121] This limitation also applied to swimming pools in areas that were seeing increasing numbers of black residents. Meanwhile blacks and whites were playing tennis on the mall, picnicking in Rock Creek Park, and playing golf together on federally owned courses.[122]

But they weren't swimming together. Even in the six federally owned pools segregation was the common practice until 1949.[123] Yet the District Recreation Board, with the backing of southern Democrats in Congress, felt the need to ensure segregated swimming was the law, as well as the practice, of the nation's capital. Starting in 1948 southern Democrats introduced congressional bills to transfer control of the six swimming pools from the Department of the Interior to the local Board of Recreation. After the Anacostia riot supporters of the legislation could use the threat of violence to rationalize their request. The board offered a moderate policy of "gradualism" as a compromise, desegregating tennis courts and two playgrounds but holding the line on swimming pools. Desegregation would progress when it was "consistent with the public interest, public order and effective administration."[124] This widely publicized statement suggested that a lack of public order could easily forestall desegregation, a call to arms to whites hoping to keep blacks out of "their" pools. Similarly, the Kiwanis Club, in support of a resolution asking for the reopening of the Anacostia Pool for whites only, argued "there had been no trouble when only white persons used it."[125] Trouble would come only with integration.

Threats of potential rioting also came from southern Democrats in Congress. Representative John Bell Williams of Mississippi most likely referred to St. Louis's Fairgrounds riot when he commented on the secretary of the interior, Julius Albert Krug's desegregation order: "The Secretary . . . had but to look to similar occurrences . . . to know that such an order would bring bloodshed and race riot."[126] Civil rights activists responded by asking President Truman whether closing Anacostia Pool indicated "that a Federal agency can be intimidated by a few teen-age hoodlums, who use the threat of a race riot at a swimming pool."[127] One letter to the editor of the *Washington Post* suggested, "Whenever an 'area' previously segregated is open to all there will always be a group that screams 'there will be riots and bloodshed!'"[128] Could violence or the intimidation of southern Dixiecrats force the administration to backtrack on its civil rights stance? In this instance the answer was no. In early 1950 the new secretary of the interior, Oscar Chapman, announced that all six pools would continue to operate as desegregated facilities.[129] The summer of 1950 would bring swimming to all Washington residents.

With the executive branch holding the line on civil rights, Congress stepped up its activity. A 1950 bill that demanded that all recreational facilities be turned over to the Board of Recreation pitted white southern Democrats against northern liberals, including a young John F. Kennedy.[130] The *Washington Post* supported the Dixiecrat bill to turn over the pools to local control because it "reduces to a minimum the risk of a recurrence of riots such as those which resulted in the closing of the Anacostia Pool last summer."[131] Riot prevention, not racial segregation, was the primary justification for maintaining Jim Crow. A local resident wrote to the *Post* that desegregation at Anacostia would "start race riots, like a match tossed carelessly into a pile of paper." Another suggested, "When the majority says it will not swim with Negroes it is inviting race riots for the Negroes to try to force their will upon the majority."[132] But the promised race riots never materialized; instead, as had happened at Fairgrounds Park, whites abandoned the newly integrated pools. During the summer of 1950 attendance in the Department of the Interior's pools dropped by one-third. The Anacostia and McKinley pools, which had been entirely white before 1949, were now 90 percent black. Francis and Banneker pools had always been African American facilities and remained so. One pool, Takoma, was 98 percent white. True integration occurred only at East Potomac, which was two-thirds white and one-third black.[133] Although it maintained control over the pools, continuing to defeat the Dixiecrat efforts to resegregate them, the Department of the Interior allowed the pools in predominantly black neighborhoods to decline.[134] As in St. Louis and elsewhere the result of desegregation was not the predicted violence but abandonment and neglect.

Threats of violence and fears of race riots structured the response by civil rights activists and city officials to desegregation. These political actors felt that ideally it should happen in a slow, controlled manner and with much supervision to appease opponents. Violence prevention, rather than civil rights or equality, preoccupied those who oversaw desegregation. The Citizens Committee Against Segregation in Recreation took the lead in Washington by constantly reassuring officials and the public that desegregation would be overseen by professional social workers and well-trained police officers. To that end in August 1949 the National Capital Park Service conducted a training program for police officers in "human relations" run by Joseph D. Lohman, a University of Chicago sociologist specializing in race relations. Meanwhile, twenty civic groups, including the Jewish Community Council and the American Veterans Committee, created procedures to help ease the transition to desegregation. This plan, which was adopted by the Department of Interior, called for cooperation on the part of police and the press as the swimming season approached. In addition, "trained and skillful personnel," both white and black, were placed at the desegregated pools to help mediate conflict.[135]

City leaders in St. Louis developed a similar plan in 1949 in response to the Fairgrounds pool riot. After the riot George Schermer, who had guided Detroit's interracial committee after the Motor City's 1943 riot, declared St. Louis as "psychologically unprepared to undertake the adjustments which changing population, economic and social conditions are forcing upon the community."[136] Here Schermer was employing "Myrdalian rhetoric" in asserting that racism was primarily a psychological problem.[137] Convincing white Americans to tolerate the physical presence of blacks, even in the swimming pool, took gentle persuasion. Schermer, for example, suggested that the city conduct a thorough investigation of the "disinfection equipment" of the Fairgrounds pool and reassure whites that the transmission of disease was unlikely.[138] St. Louis's Council on Human Relations suggested after the riot that only two indoor pools be immediately desegregated and all outdoor pools, including Fairgrounds Park, be opened to blacks only after a thorough "educational program." In response the mayor, clearly relieved, stated, "Public safety demands the approach you have outlined."[139] After desegregation, civil rights organizations often handpicked which African Americans would be allowed to use the facilities.[140] This contrasts with CORE's approach at Palisades Park when they encouraged Harlem's blacks and Puerto Ricans to use the pool without any screening process. But in St. Louis and Washington, civil rights leaders employed a politics of civility designed to appeal to liberal whites and to prevent violence. Immediate and full access to recreation was not a demand often voiced by moderate activists, as it would reinforce fears of race riots.

Reformers, politicians, and lawyers repeatedly invoked the Anacostia and Fairgrounds Park recreation riots well into the 1950s. "In Washington, D.C. and in St. Louis, the first efforts to integrate the public swimming pools were met with violence by hoodlums," wrote Sol Rabkin, a lawyer, in 1954. "But intelligent police action and firmness on the part of public authorities resulted in the reestablishment of law and order and in the peaceful operation of the swimming pools on an integrated basis in both these cities."[141] In 1952 John P. Frank, a prominent lawyer, connected the recreation riots to the larger problem of residential segregation: "A dominant fear of those who would restrain legal action to secure equality is that it will cause a reaction of physical violence against the Negro minority. . . . In some particular situations where the abolition of segregation has conflicted with strong local custom, there has in fact been violence. The bombings, North and South, which have accompanied Negro entrance into what had been white housing areas, are generally familiar. The difficulties at the Anacostia swimming pool in Washington and at the municipal pool in St. Louis show the ugly situations which can develop."[142] For Frank, the Department of the Interior's willingness to stand up to the racist Board of Recreation in Washington was a success story to be emulated. "The crowning weakness of the argument that fear of violence should restrain legal action," argued Frank, "is that it is a yielding to lawlessness." Invoking a cold war metaphor, he went on to suggest that yielding to such lawlessness was akin to yielding to communism: "If we stand up to the Communists, we may lose. If we stand up to the hooligans, we may also lose. This is no reason for yielding."[143] Frank had heard this argument repeatedly from judges and lawyers in his work as an adviser for the NAACP. By the late 1940s the threat of juvenile delinquents, "hooligans," was analogous to the threat of communism—both undermined the values and stability of American society. Racial liberals argued that giving in to this threat would endanger rather than protect the American way of life.

In the rhetoric surrounding recreation riots it was clear that racial conflict, both potential and real, provoked white fears of integration. But it is also important to note that in both St. Louis and Washington there were outdoor pools that saw no racial violence at the time of the Fairgrounds and Anacostia riots. In some cases this was because these nominally desegregated pools were not truly racially integrated; they were in racially homogenous neighborhoods or swimmers abided by segregationists' custom. But in other cases there was limited interracial swimming in outdoor pools. Observers, however, rarely noted racial peace. Instead, recreation riots continued to be fodder for both supporters and opponents of segregation. After the 1949 Gary, Indiana, beach riot, for example, a Mississippi newspaper editorialized, "Such incidents are reported with increasing frequency in the North, the Mid-West and the East, even as agitation continues for enactment of federal anti-segregation laws. They support the South's belief and contention that legal segregation, with fair division of public recreation facilities between the races, is fairer, preferable, and more effective than 'practical' segregation unauthorized by law but unofficially enforced."[144] The idea that legal segregation, with separate but equal facilities, was preventing violence more effectively in the South was a fiction. In fact, southern communities did not provide a "fair division of public recreation," and recreational segregation engendered its own violence. But this discourse was a potent weapon in the arsenal of white supremacists. Racial liberals' response—that discrimination reflected the misguided beliefs of individual whites—suggested that education and careful interracial negotiations would end segregation. But these measures proved insufficient. It was only when they were combined with the work of radical activists, a burgeoning youth movement, and ordinary consumers that blacks gained some access to urban recreation in northern and border cities.

* * *

The fifth freedom, liberation from Jim Crow, was not achieved during the war years. And the "racial radicalism" predicted by Drake and Cayton did, indeed, result from the failure of white America to accept African Americans as equal citizens. The right of access to private and public recreational spaces powerfully represented that citizenship. Yet even in states with civil rights laws, the incursion of black bodies into white leisure spaces was a source of escalating friction. Activists recognized the symbolic power of targeting recreational public accommodations in their struggle for full racial equality. And there were tangible successes as a result. When Sarah Elizabeth Ray asked the Detroit NAACP to help her sue Bob-Lo Island, they won a Supreme Court case that forced the state of Michigan to abide by the law. But Luster's violent beating at Euclid Beach and Robinson's failed attempts to skate in Cleveland demonstrated the limits of this activism. As the historian Lisa Levenstein suggests, "postwar racial liberalism" was accompanied by "growing white resistance to African American advancement."[145] And many whites did not differentiate between the interracial commissions that studied race relations and published voluminous reports on discrimination and the radical activists who put their bodies on the line to occupy white spaces. Instead they saw earlier strategies of recreational segregation, like the YMCA's institutional segregation policy and the lack of enforcement of civil rights statutes, as no longer effective under the onslaught of empowered African Americans and an energized NAACP. An increase in racial violence, privatization of public facilities, and the closing down of commercial recreation were the result.

Although many whites did not distinguish between black activism's different strands, there were significant disparities in how African American activists and consumers addressed the problem of recreational segregation. Proponents of radical nonviolence called for an immediate occupation of recreational space and through their own example of interracialism offered a transformative model of race relations. Racial liberals sought gradual desegregation and focused on managing that change so as to mitigate potential violence or conflict. But there was another group that is often overlooked in our understanding of midcentury civil rights: the many children and teenagers who ventured into newly opened pools and parks to demand social equality on their own timeline. In St. Louis and Washington, D.C., it was dozens of young African Americans who tested the waters of desegregation. Some worked with interracial youth organizations, but others sought to possess and use the same spaces of leisure available to urban whites. As postwar prosperity expanded in the early 1950s, these demands for equal access intensified. Coney Island, a popular amusement park in the border city of Cincinnati, soon became a focus of such longings.

CHAPTER 3

"A Northern City with a Southern Exposure": Challenging Recreational Segregation in the 1950s

ON a warm summer day in 1952, Marian Spencer, an African American woman living in Cincinnati, heard one of the ubiquitous radio ads for the city's Coney Island Amusement Park. During the spring and summer "Uncle Al" would lure children to Coney with these words: "Come on, kiddies. Come on out. Meet Uncle Al. Come out to Coney Island!"[1] Spencer called the park to ask if they meant all children were welcome. She was told initially, "Oh, yes, all children." She went on to say, "Ours is a Negro family." The reply was, predictably, "Well now of course, that's not my doing; it's management's decision, but I don't think it means Negro children."[2] Outraged, Spencer turned to a group of radical nonviolent activists to help her young children gain access to the park, and she contacted the NAACP to explore the possibility of filing a lawsuit. Spencer called on the full spectrum of civil rights organizations and was willing to personally challenge Cincinnati's racial status quo by participating in demonstrations against the park. But white Cincinnatians stymied her efforts by brutalizing activists who showed up at Coney's gates and using sympathetic courts to undermine the Ohio's civil rights statute. At Coney Island, and in similar facilities nationwide, the limits of racial liberalism became clear with increased white resistance to desegregation.

White resistance was necessary because by the early 1950s postwar black consumers increasingly demanded full access to recreation, and NAACP lawyers challenged the courts to abide by civil rights laws. During this period of economic prosperity, black consumers were eager to use amusement parks and roller-skating rinks in their communities. These grassroots struggles were buttressed by a growing legal assault on segregation as the NAACP increasingly took on public accommodation cases. As the legal landscape shifted with the 1954 *Brown v. Board of Education* decision, activists became more emboldened to challenge recreational segregation nationally. While CORE and the NAACP had previously targeted facilities in states with existing civil rights laws, by the early 1950s they began to turn their attention to the South, spurred by new legal precedents and the courage of southern blacks who violated Jim Crow. In response to this growing resistance, white proprietors of recreational establishments responded by privatizing or closing their facilities. And white customers who had frequented segregated pools stopped swimming when African Americans finally gained access. But the partial victories activists and African American consumers achieved were possible because of a broad campaign to open the country's parks and pools to all Americans. One battlefront, at Cincinnati's Coney Island, exemplifies the possibilities and limitations of this campaign.

Cincinnati's Coney Island

Cincinnati was located in a state with a strong civil rights law, but it was also firmly on the Mason-Dixon Line. Like Baltimore, Washington, D.C., and other border cities, Cincinnati's struggles over segregated recreation were particularly protracted and often violent. "Cincinnati is a northern city with a southern exposure," explained an African American reformer in 1919, "a gateway between North and South used alike by fugitive slave and freedman of yesterday and migrant of today in their quest of Utopia."[3] For white Cincinnatians, part of that utopia was found at the sprawling and idyllic Coney Island where they had played and picnicked since the late nineteenth century. Coney Island's gates, however, were firmly closed to African Americans prior to 1955. Opening those gates required all the skill and strength that local civil rights organizations, radical nonviolent pacifists, and black consumers in Cincinnati could muster. Even then, their victories were partial and came at significant costs.

Coney Island was similar to many midwestern and northern amusement parks. Founded in the late nineteenth century, the park was linked to the city not by the streetcar but by a steamboat, the *Island Queen*. After faithfully carrying white Cincinnatians to the park for two decades, the original *Island*

Queen burned in 1922, placing the park's viability in jeopardy.[4] At this point two Cincinnati businessmen, Rudolph "Rud" Hynicka and George F. Schott, joined forces to buy the faltering park. Schott's son Edward would become civil rights activists' main adversary when he inherited Coney Island in 1935. When Hynicka and Schott took control of the park they began building an even more lavish *Island Queen*, reportedly the largest and most expensive steamboat in operation.[5] The owners also built the two attractions that would prove most difficult to integrate: Moonlite Gardens, a deluxe dance palace, and the 400-by-200 foot Sunlite Pool.[6] When Hynicka died, Schott took control of the park, promising cleanliness and safety for his white customers. "Today the idea of a real park is one that provides wholesome, clean, invigorating rest, recreation and amusement," assured Schott.[7]

Although Edward Schott continued his father's policy of racial exclusion after 1935, this policy did not go unchallenged. At times parents and teachers escorting mixed groups of schoolchildren tried to gain entrance into Coney Island to no avail. As noted in Chapter 1, Virginia Coffey forced a Girl Scout boycott of the park in the late 1930s. While Coffey instigated a boycott, other black Cincinnatians simply tried to board the *Island Queen* and join the summer fun. These incidents may have been the result of unwitting recent migrants who heard Coney Island's ubiquitous advertisements on the radio and were not aware of the policy of racial segregation, or they may have been deliberately launching a direct challenge to a racist policy. On June 29, 1946, for example, three African Americans visiting Cincinnati attempted to board the *Island Queen* grasping tickets they had purchased in Dayton. Coney Island employees took the tickets from them but refused to allow them to board. They then approached a police officer to intervene on their behalf. The officer claimed he had no jurisdiction over the wharf and told them to talk to the *Island Queen*'s second mate. Meanwhile a young white teenager grabbed their camera and smashed it. When the local NAACP protested to the chief of police, he replied with the statement, "better thinking colored people did not approve of NAACP tactics."[8] In a similar incident the following year, a group of CORE members bought tickets for a ride to the park sponsored by the Gold Star Wives of World War II, but guards refused to allow them to board.[9] In the decades to follow, African Americans attempting to enter the park would repeatedly encounter this combination of police collusion, park employee rudeness, and the physical violence of white youths.

These incidents in the 1940s led the Mayor's Friendly Relations Committee (MFRC) to send its director, Marshall Bragdon, to speak with Schott about desegregating the park. A few months following the devastating 1943 riot in Detroit, Cincinnati's mayor had met with the executive director of the NAACP and the Community Chest's Division of Negro Welfare to form the MFRC. This group was nominally committed to "cultural pluralism" but soon gained a well-earned reputation for championing civil rights and harboring radicals.[10] Although talks with the MFRC came to nothing, by the mid-1940s it was clear to the ownership and management of Coney Island, the police department, and the city that racial segregation was causing growing unrest. Adding to the park's difficulties in maintaining control was a disastrous accident that ended the second *Island Queen*'s run. When the *Island Queen* burned in 1947, careful monitoring of Coney Island's customers became more difficult. After 1947 Schott relied heavily on chartered buses to shuttle groups to the park, but he could not control private automobiles that approached the park gates. In the early 1950s civil rights activists targeted Schott's new private automobile entrance when they began their campaign of nonviolent direct action. In addition, the end of steamboat excursions did not cut off public transportation entirely, as would happen at other urban amusement parks. Cincinnatians could take a trolley to Government Square where they caught a bus to the park.[11] Soon Schott would have to guard all of these entrances from a direct assault by a group of deeply committed activists.

Pacifists and Peacemakers

In the early 1950s a remarkable group of radicals coalesced in Cincinnati. Juanita Morrow, who had graduated from Howard University with skills gained through the female-centered campaign to desegregate public accommodations, moved to Cleveland to work simultaneously as a journalist and the chairperson of a newly formed CORE chapter. While in Cleveland, Morrow led the dramatic campaign to desegregate Euclid Beach Park, honing her skills in nonviolent direct action. As part of her work for the Cleveland *Call and Post* Morrow visited and interviewed Wallace Nelson, an African American born and raised in Little Rock, Arkansas, who had been active in the Christian student movement during the 1930s at Ohio Wesleyan. When the military assigned Nelson to a Civilian Public Service camp during World War II, he declared that he was a conscientious objector. Like other pacifists, Nelson walked away from the camp rather than cooperate with the war effort in any way. He served two years in prison for this act of conscience, the last three and a half months on a hunger strike to protest the appalling conditions.[12]

Nelson and Morrow met again in Cleveland after his release, married, and formed a household that became the center of activism in Cincinnati.

When the Nelsons arrived in Cincinnati they joined a community that had been galvanized by the struggles of 1940s radical pacifism. Nelson had just completed the 1947 Journey of Reconciliation, a precursor of the Freedom Rides that would help break the back of segregation in the early 1960s. The event was organized jointly by CORE and the Fellowship of Reconciliation (FOR) and tested the 1946 Supreme Court ruling *Morgan v. Virginia*, which ruled interstate travel could not be segregated. The action linked the pacifist and civil rights movements in a highly visible and dramatic fashion.[13] Of the sixteen volunteers who participated in the Journey, four were from Cincinnati, marking it a center of radical nonviolent activism.[14] The Journey also brought together two men who would help transform race relations in Cincinnati. Like Nelson, Ernest Bromley, a white native of New England, had become involved in the Christian student movement during the 1930s when he trained for the ministry at Duke University and Union Theological Seminary. Disillusioned with the church and increasingly committed to pacifism during World War II, Bromley moved to New York City to work for FOR.[15] From there he stepped onto the bus and met Wallace Nelson, who was to become a lifelong friend.

Like Wallace Nelson, Bromley had also found a life partner whose commitment to social justice equaled his own. Marion Coddington left her home and family in the early 1940s to move to New York City and work for FOR's director, A. J. Muste, a prominent pacifist and labor organizer who deeply influenced Martin Luther King.[16] One historian describes FOR's national office in the early 1940s as the "nerve center of American Gandhism."[17] In 1943 Coddington met Bromley in the FOR offices and the two were wed by Muste, who was also a minister. In 1948 Muste along with the Bromleys, David Dellinger, Dwight MacDonald, Bayard Rustin, and other activists founded Peacemakers, a radical pacifist organization dedicated to nonviolent direct action and war resistance. But the Peacemakers did not want to be simply a membership organization; instead they formed small communities, usually interracial, to organize on a local level and model egalitarian living.[18] When the Nelsons arrived in Cincinnati they learned that Ernest and Marion Bromley lived only fifty miles north of Cincinnati in Wilmington, Ohio. The two were doing odd jobs while working to integrate the local schools. The Bromleys and Nelsons soon took their deep belief in pacifism and interracialism to the level of everyday life by creating a radical domesticity in cold war suburbia. In 1950 they bought a modest home together in Gano, Ohio, just outside Cincinnati. They lived communally, raised the Bromleys' two children, engaged in wage work to bring in funds for the household, and refused to pay taxes as part of their continued commitment to pacifism. As they became more active in nearby Cincinnati, the two couples met Maurice McCrackin, a local white Presbyterian minister. Together they joined forces to create the Citizen's Committee for Human Rights (CCHR), an affiliate of CORE, and spearheaded a campaign to desegregate the largest public accommodation in the city, Coney Island amusement park.[19]

Cincinnati had a burgeoning black population in the wake of World War II. Between 1940 and 1970 it more than doubled as the proportion of African Americans grew from 12 to 28 percent.[20] Initially, most African Americans lived in the West End, the central neighborhood of black settlement since the turn of the century. But urban renewal, public housing, and highway construction began to displace African Americans in large numbers by the 1950s. Most moved into the Walnut Hills-Avondale section of the city, which had been a relatively integrated neighborhood of poor whites and middle-class black professionals.[21] Virginia Coffey, who opened a settlement house in Avondale, remembered, "in Avondale it was neighborhoods that had been largely Jewish but Black people were migrating . . . so you had the in-coming group and you had the group that was there and you had to try to build good relationships between the two and avoid as much friction as possible."[22] This familiar pattern of ethnic and racial succession was the backdrop for a growing civil rights community and a black population ripe for activism. As they struggled to obtain housing, decent jobs, and integrated schools, black Cincinnatians also sought to open public accommodations. Coney Island became the preeminent symbol of this struggle as the largest and most recalcitrant public accommodation in the city.

The CCHR, the CORE affiliate, was at the vanguard of civil rights militancy in Cincinnati, and its members were eager to force open the gates of Coney Island. Another civil rights organization that would play a central role in the Coney Island campaign, along a similar ideological trajectory as the MFRC, was the Cincinnati Urban League (CUL). Founded the same year as the CCHR, the Urban League spent much of its time in the late 1940s and early 1950s working to open up job opportunities for black Cincinnatians.[23] But instead of picketing and boycotting, the CUL met privately with employers to negotiate new jobs for black migrants. This two-pronged approach to fighting racial discrimination—the moral suasion used by the MFRC and CUL backed by more militant direct action techniques of the CCHR—

would prove to be highly effective in challenging segregation in the Queen City. Equally important was the bond between the Nelsons, Bromleys, and McCrackin. While on the national level there was tension between the white-dominated FOR, made up largely of peace activists, and the more radical CORE, this interracial group effectively combined religious-inspired pacifism with radical nonviolent direct action.[24] They moved between a number of organizations—the CCHR and CORE, the Peacemakers, and the FOR—with little conflict. Central to this coalition was McCrackin, the young minister A. J. Muste once described as coming "very close to being a saint."[25]

McCrackin moved to Cincinnati from Chicago, where he had served as a pastor at the Waldensian Presbyterian Church, and worked with both the FOR and CORE. Wanting to work more actively on racial issues, he accepted a position as co-pastor at St. Barnabas Church in Cincinnati's West End in 1945. St. Barnabas was a newly federated Presbyterian-Episcopal church in a largely African American neighborhood. Before McCrackin's arrival whites dominated this congregation in a community that was increasingly black. Reed Hartman, chairman of the Presbyterian Church Extension Board, warned McCrackin to proceed toward integration cautiously. "Remember that we are a northern city," said Hartman, drawing from a well-worn characterization, "but we have a southern exposure."[26] McCrackin, however, had no intention of taking a go-slow approach to integration. Only two months after his arrival he opened the Findlay Street Neighborhood House and began to invite neighboring black residents into his church. Soon McCrackin successfully integrated church-sponsored social activities, which necessitated careful negotiations for outings. McCrackin often bought tickets to theaters and skating rinks ahead of time to ensure his integrated groups would be allowed in. This strategy was not always successful—one roller rink refused entrance to children from Findlay Street and later closed rather than integrate.[27] These early experiences with recalcitrant public accommodations sharpened McCrackin's commitment to civil rights and his determination to challenge Coney Island's segregation.

In 1948 McCrackin met Wallace and Juanita Nelson, and the small group of Peacemakers began to develop the CCHR, drawing from two existing Cincinnati CORE affiliates to create a more vibrant and militant chapter.[28] Their first project was the successful desegregation of two local music schools.[29] The CCHR also used nonviolent direct action to test segregation in downtown restaurants and theaters, sending integrated teams to visit public accommodations and picketing those that refused service to blacks.[30] At this point the MFRC attempted to intervene in the increasingly heated confrontations between CCHR members and local white businessmen. They contacted the mayor and police department and offered to mediate between the different groups, echoing the work being carried out in other interracial commissions throughout the country that emphasized education and moral persuasion rather than the militancy of CORE.[31] But the effectiveness of the CCHR lay in direct action. That direct action led business owners, who feared ongoing boycotts and picketing, to agree to desegregate Cincinnati's downtown theaters and restaurants in 1950. This campaign provided a template for desegregating Coney Island and offered evidence that integration did not lead inevitably to economic decline as Cincinnati's downtown continued to flourish. An editorial calling for integration at Coney Island in 1955 noted, "history is its own best judge and observer. All races and creeds have attended the theaters and shows in Cincinnati, almost without incident. The same will apply to Coney Island." Another editorial arguing against the assumption that "if Negroes were admitted to the beautiful amusement center the white customers would quit coming" stated, "integration of downtown theaters and Bingo did not lead to decline in customers."[32] Although downtown integration proceeded relatively smoothly, not all efforts to bring African American and white Cincinnatians together were as welcomed. The color line in the city's swimming pools proved more difficult to cross.

By the late 1940s most of Cincinnati's public swimming pools were still segregated. In the West End pool near McCrackin's St. Barnabas Church, African American children were let in only after three o'clock when the white children had left. Fearful of the "contamination" of black youths, the pool manager routinely threw large amounts of chemicals in the water before allowing blacks in. One of the parents noticed the "flaking skin and bloodshot eyes" of his children and turned to McCrackin for help. The minister quickly instigated a letter-writing campaign that opened the pool to blacks for two days a week, Tuesdays and Thursdays. Following more complaints from African American parents, the pool was also opened on Saturdays to blacks but soon closed down rather than fully integrate.[33] Cincinnati's Public Recreation Commission had operated the city's public swimming pools on a segregated basis for a generation, generally reserving only two days a week for African American children. Although the commission closed the West End pool, under pressure from the growing number of civil rights organizations they agreed to open four pools on an integrated basis in 1950 and the remaining six the following summer.

Integration of the public pools was anything but smooth. The Jewish Community Relations Council reported on "intransigent elements throwing rocks, nails and glass into newly unsegregated pools and further trying to discourage interracial swimming by seeking to influence parents to prevent their children swimming with Negro youngsters."[34] When one white mother complained to the recreation director about a desegregated pool, asking, "You wouldn't want to swim with Negroes, would you?" he replied by stripping down to his swimming trunks and diving in among the African American children.[35] This act, and others like it, convinced some that integrated swimming was not the threat to public health and safety feared by some white parents. But for many whites desegregated pools reflected wider changes in race relations. Swimming had long been a compulsory course in Cincinnati's high schools—but on a segregated basis. Thus for many parents the integration of swimming pools raised the larger specter of integrated public schools. Seeking to reassure them, the Cincinnati Board of Education, working with the MFRC, announced in 1950 that swimming would now be integrated but also voluntary. The result was predictable: many white students withdrew from swimming, in some schools up to 90 percent. This tension eased within a few years, although swimming remained fairly unpopular in the city's schools.[36] It may have also been comforting that the segregated Sunlite Pool at Coney Island was only a short trip away for white Cincinnatians seeking to avoid racial conflict and "contamination" on a hot summer day.

The CCHR's decision to target Coney Island was precipitated by the actions of Marian Spencer, an African American mother of two small boys who challenged the park's policies. Spencer called the NAACP to complain and they asked Theodore M. Berry, a black lawyer who also served on the city council, to begin gathering evidence for a possible lawsuit. Spencer, however, was eager for more immediate results and notified the CCHR that Coney Island was routinely discriminating against African American children.[37] Spencer's choice is telling; by the early 1950s the radical activists in CORE had moved to the forefront of the civil rights movement.[38] Spencer's timing was also excellent—CCHR activists had successfully completed their campaign to integrate Cincinnati's music colleges and were looking for a new project. However, McCrackin, the Nelsons, and the Bromleys were surprised by the controversy the choice of Coney Island created. Ernest Bromley commented many years later, "Some people told us you would never be able to do anything there. You ought to be working on something else, like employment. To us it was the other way because Coney was such a sacred cow. The little kids saw all the advertisements on TV and heard all of the stuff on the radio and all of these enticements to come to Coney Island—and they couldn't go. It seemed like a terrible thing."[39] Even Spencer's husband, Donald, did not support the idea of carrying out a campaign against Coney Island. As a public schoolteacher, he was concerned about losing his job. The NAACP and the CUL were also hesitant about signing on to the campaign. Bromley's motivation to take on the project—the fact that Coney Island was a "sacred cow"—was, for more moderate civil rights organizations, a reason to leave it alone.

The CCHR activists followed well-honed CORE tactics in planning their campaign. They first sought to meet privately with Schott and his manager, Ralph Wachs, in January 1952 to discuss the policy of racial segregation; they sent him four letters and received no response. When McCrackin simply walked into Wachs's office to air their grievances, Wachs ignored him. After hitting this wall, the CCHR mobilized a public hearing by distributing forty thousand leaflets outlining the discriminatory practices of Coney Island. On April 23 representatives of the NAACP, the Jewish Community Relations Council, the CCHR, and other organizations testified in front of over one hundred community members. Dozens of African Americans who had been denied access to the park came to the hearing as well, demonstrating the ongoing resistance to segregation and depth of feeling in the community.[40] This meeting helped mobilize activists for the struggle ahead but received no publicity in the local media, which had long ignored Coney Island's policy of segregation.[41]

The campaign had now reached its second stage of public protest and direct action as opening day approached. The Nelsons, McCrackin, and the Bromleys mobilized teams of picketers and volunteers for "stand-ins," a technique CORE had used at the White City Roller Rink, Palisades Park, and Bimini Baths.[42] Activists waited peacefully in line, and when they were denied entry they blocked other customers by simply refusing to move. At Coney Island, however, this technique was pushed to its furthest limits as the activists practiced total noncooperation with authorities. Their first opportunity came on opening day when twenty-five black and white CCHR members drove to the large auto gate about ten miles from downtown Cincinnati. Some activists attempted to enter by foot and others by car, but all were denied entry, told by park officials that it was a "sponsor day" and they needed permission to enter. Coney Island was known for its "special days," sponsored by various clubs and organizations, including Coca-Cola Day, Burger Chef Day, Farmers Day, German Day, Shrine Day, and Masons Day. However, special days never prevented white customers from entering the park.[43] Rather, they became a convenient justification for park managers who placed the blame for racial exclusion on private sponsors.

After being denied entry, the activists calmly said, "Well, we'll just wait here then," turned off their motors, locked their doors, and threw the keys under the seat. Pedestrians had more direct physical confrontations with park officials as they attempted to block gates. Coney Island's private police force, known as the Solar Hill Rangers, often roughed them up when clearing the way for white customers. The city police, Hamilton County deputy sheriffs, and Anderson Township police joined the Solar Hill Rangers to remove civil rights protestors. Supplementing the officials were a group of local vigilantes who watched events unfolding from a bar across the street and became the unofficial protectors of the park, notifying police when activists arrived and harassing protestors with racial epithets. This type of collusion between park guards, local police, and hostile bystanders to keep blacks at bay was commonplace at amusement parks. CORE activists had confronted a similar conspiracy at Euclid Beach in Cleveland.

On opening day police arrested Marion Bromley and Wallace Nelson, the first arrests of many that summer.[44] One week later the Solar Hill Rangers, who had been instructed by Coney Island to keep out "undesirables," stopped Marion Spencer and Lois Wright's cars. As the harassment of demonstrators escalated, Ernest Bromley and Maurice McCrackin decided to directly confront several members of the Solar Hill Rangers about the morality of their actions. The two visited members of the private police force in their homes and attempted to open up a dialogue with them. They were met by anger and in one case were threatened with a police club.[45] Police targeted Wallace Nelson during the third week of demonstrations when he was arrested in his car for "illegal parking" and "resisting an officer."[46] But it was the June 22 demonstrations that led to the most dramatic events of the summer.

On that day twelve protesters arrived to find the park guards unprepared to stop them. As a result, Marion Bromley made it up to the auto ticket window and was in the process of paying the fare when park officials noticed her black passengers. She quickly threw her keys into the back seat, rolled up her window, and locked her car. Park guards then began the laborious process of pushing her car away from the entrance while rerouting traffic to an emergency gate. McCrackin quickly drove to this second gate while other activists moved toward the pedestrian entrance. With both auto gates and the pedestrian entrance blocked, traffic was tied up and white customers were growing restless. At this point park police dragged McCrackin out of his car and drove it to the side. The Nelsons were patiently standing in front of the ticket window when the police dragged them away to join Marion Bromley, who had been forcefully shoved into a police car.[47] McCrackin reported that "hoodlum elements" among the park patrons cheered when they observed the rough handling of Bromley and the Nelsons.[48]

When they were arrested, Marion Bromley and the Nelsons made a crucial decision to practice a form of radical nonviolence: total noncooperation. They went limp and had to be dragged to the police car, and when they were placed in jail they promptly went on a hunger strike that lasted until their release nine days later. Describing the decision to refuse cooperation, Juanita Nelson said, "The police had no legal or moral right to act as they did. We could not prevent legal authority from throwing us out of line, but we feel now as we did then that we were forcefully taken from the gates of Coney Island . . . that we could not cooperate with such action. At this point we feel strongly that such cooperation as eating in jail or accepting bail is tantamount to accepting the rightness of being arrested, and the rightness of the discriminatory policies upheld by Coney Island and the police."[49] Marion Bromley and the Nelsons had taken nonviolence to its furthest end and helped define a form of direct action that would inspire and anger many. During the nine-day hunger strike Ernest Bromley could be seen daily picketing the jail accompanied by his young children, Danny and Caroline. The image of this father caring for his children and supporting his wife was a direct inversion of normative gender roles in the early 1950s and an assertion of racial militancy that most do not associate with 1952. Marion Bromley and the Nelsons endured severe heat and dehydration in prison, but they emerged resolved to continue the fight.

There were four more demonstrations at the park in late June and July; these were also marred by violent confrontations. Ernest Bromley remembered local toughs smashing his car window on July 20. "The deputy sheriff was standing right there. I knew him," recalled Bromley, "As soon as they smashed the window, I said to him, 'Well, did you see that?' He said, 'No, I didn't see a thing.' It was a terrible crash. He ordered the wrecker to come over there when I wouldn't move. I fixed it so they couldn't open the door to haul us out. They would do that. They would haul you out of the car and drive your car away off the road. This time he towed the car with all of us in it."[50] Jeering white teenagers surrounded the wrecker as it left the park. A police captain approached the car and warned the occupants, "If you go back, there will be trouble. You will be hurt." It was clear who would do the hurting.[51] By the end of the season protesters found it increasingly difficult to even reach the gate. Police and guards now recognized them and their vehicles and would pull them over before they could block the entrance.[52]

Nor was the violence limited to the park itself. When Ernest Bromley decided to directly target the Coney Island headquarters in downtown Cincinnati in mid-July by picketing and distributing leaflets in front of the office, a middle-aged man approached him and said, "You put down that sign and get away from here or I'll come back with someone who will make you wish you had." Undeterred, Bromley continued his work. The man returned accompanied by an intoxicated friend who threatened him. The next day a different young man, cheered on by bystanders and also seemingly drunk, attacked Bromley, striking him hard on the face until he fell on the sidewalk. The following week, yet another attacker beat Bromley while he protested. McCrackin later reported that Bromley "asked the fellow why he had struck him, to which he replied, 'Because I don't think a nigger is as good as a white man.'" Police officers, who had earlier told him to stop leafleting, watched calmly as Bromley was beaten and allowed his attacker to walk away.[53] As the summer wore on police increasingly depended on local toughs to intimidate the nonviolent demonstrators rather than inviting unwanted publicity by arresting CCHR members.

Amid this violence the activists were also working the political front, urging the African American city council member and NAACP lawyer Theodore Berry to pass a resolution calling for an investigation of Coney Island's segregation policy. The city convened the investigating committee on the same day authorities released the fasting Marion Bromley and the Nelsons from prison. By the end of July McCrackin had drafted a report on the extent of the violence at Coney Island; however, the city council refused to let him read it into the record or to allow the subcommittee access to it. Instead the subcommittee met with Coney Island officials who assured them of their "sincere desire" to "find the proper solution" to racial problems at the park. The subcommittee made no recommendations to the council, arguing that the park was outside city limits and accepting the park's argument that their policy of racial discrimination was "within the law."[54] McCrackin replied, "Does perversion of justice and terrorism indicate a sincere desire to find a proper solution? It shows rather a planned program of intimidation and brutality so that the solution may be indefinitely delayed."[55] Given that the park would not be fully desegregated for another ten years, this statement was prescient. Violence was successfully undermining the movement for desegregation.

Frustrated by the subcommittee's inaction, Berry introduced legislation that would close the park for thirty to ninety days every time it violated Ohio's civil rights law. During the bill's discussion McCrackin was finally able to present his report to the city council; he was joined by Marian Spencer, the mother who raised her voice against her children's exclusion.[56] Detailing the collusion between Coney Island and the city council, McCrackin concluded in his report, "at Coney Island large financial interests, law enforcement agencies and the hoodlum element in our society are working hand in hand in direct violation of the Civil Rights Law of the State of Ohio and in the disgraceful and outrageous treatment of citizens seeking to secure these rights."[57] Predictably Berry's legislation failed, but by this time the wider civil rights community was standing firmly behind the CCHR. The willingness of the radical nonviolent activists to put their bodies on the line sparked solidarity and made the NAACP and CUL appear moderate, which improved their bargaining power with city officials. This dynamic became familiar during the early 1960s sit-ins in the Deep South but had its roots in the early 1950s racial struggles over public accommodations.

The next obvious step was legal action, but the CCHR's radicals resented the need to turn to the NAACP and mistrusted the courts. In his October statement to the council McCrackin complained that the call to "fight it through the courts" was inadequate. "It is not that simple, as anyone who has tried to win civil rights cases in Hamilton County knows. . . . Civil rights cases have been lost one after the other when the defendant has had comparatively little money. What then of winning a civil rights case with the money that will be poured in to its defeat if the defendant is Coney Island? Approximately 15% of our citizens are not allowed to use these facilities and are exposed to the treatment which I have just outlined; we need no court case to prove these facts."[58] McCrackin was certainly correct, but turning to the courts was a tactical decision that made sense in the social and political climate of the early 1950s. The CCHR may have gained supporters among civil rights activists and black community members, but there was virtually no publicity given to their protests and little wider community support from white Cincinnatians. A turn to the courts would force Schott to address his continual violation of the Ohio civil rights law and perhaps give the issue broader attention.

During the off-season of 1952–53 CCHR activists did their best to publicize the previous summer's conflicts. They distributed leaflets in fifty downtown stores with a picture of an African American minister being turned away at the park gates. They called on local media to stop accepting advertisements from Coney Island and urged the many churches and organizations that sponsored special days at the park to cancel any future plans until desegregation was accomplished.[59] In a letter sent to potential sponsors, CCHR highlighted an incident at the park's dance hall during a fund-raiser the Richter Jewelry Company was holding for the American Cancer Society. An African American woman, presumably an employee, arrived with a ticket and was brutally harassed by park guards. "One of the observers of this incident," reported the CCHR, "commented that it certainly resembled a Nazi scene."[60] The letters drew from the Double V rhetoric of a decade earlier and emphasized the vulnerability of an ordinary citizen, not a militant activist. These tactics sparked increased support among community members. At this stage in the struggle both the Urban League and the NAACP began to step up their involvement in the campaign. They were ambivalent about CCHR's nonviolent direct action but supported their goals. CCHR activists, meanwhile, were worn down from a season of picketing, beatings, and arrests and eager for backing from their more moderate allies.

Forcing Open the Gates

The opening day of Coney Island's 1953 season also marked the opening of a second summer of protests. Eight ministers, six white and two black, led the day's demonstrations. Park management was prepared this time and began to stop demonstrators well before they reached ticket booths, making the waiting line tactic significantly less effective.[61] Turning to legal tactics, three activists, all African American women, filed a class-action suit against the park, which was later thrown out by a local judge, a ruling reaffirmed by the Court of Appeals.[62] A second attempt at a class-action ruling was sparked by the actions of Ethel Fletcher, a black social worker and mother who attempted to enter the park on July 2 and 4. Like Marian Spencer, Fletcher was willing to directly challenge segregation at Coney Island, drawing from her roles as an activist and as a mother furious at the misleading advertising to which her young children were subjected. When she approached the gates on those two summer days, park managers informed her that their corporate sponsors had specifically requested that CCHR and NAACP members not be admitted (Fletcher was an NAACP member but had not been active in the CCHR protests). Thus, park management argued, the issue was not related to race. NAACP lawyers were eager to undermine Coney Island's claim that on sponsor days the park was a private accommodation not subject to the law and quickly filed suit on Fletcher's behalf.[63]

The Court of Common Pleas in Hamilton County did not hand down a decision on the Fletcher case until the following summer. Coney Island's lawyers argued that on the two days in question Coney Island was not "a place of public accommodation" but operated under "outing contracts" with the Second-Third Ward Civil and Social Club and the Knights of Pythias of Dayton, Kentucky. It was these organizations, they claimed, that had requested park management refuse admission to members of the NAACP and CCHR. The fact that these two sponsors were from nearby Kentucky highlighted the "southern exposure" of Cincinnati and supported Schott's contention that geography limited Coney Island's ability to integrate. Schott often employed the rhetoric of regionalism to justify his segregation policies. According to the defense, the NAACP and CCHR's "previous unlawful disorderly subversive conduct" had rendered them "undesirable persons at said picnics." This directive included white members as well as black, thus undermining the application of Ohio's civil rights law.[64]

In his decision Judge Weber rejected this argument, arguing that African Americans had not been asked about their political affiliation when they were routinely denied entrance to the park. He also argued that the park was still a public accommodation, despite the existence of contracts, pointing out that Coney Island continued "the usual advertising media for the purpose of increasing attendance" and thus the "invitation was made to the general public."[65] Weber agreed that the park had the right to exclude "troublemakers" from its grounds but demonstrated "that the plaintiff never made any trouble either inside or outside of the park."[66] Based on these findings, Weber gave a limited victory to the activists. He rejected the idea that a remedy of a fine or brief imprisonment for the defendant was adequate, pointing out that Fletcher would continue to be denied admission to the park. On this basis he granted a permanent injunction ensuring that Fletcher would never be denied admission to Coney Island. But this was not a class action; it applied to Fletcher and no one else.[67]

Fletcher was reluctant to use this injunction after it was publicized in local newspapers. She began to receive threatening phone calls during the night and anonymous letters warning that she and her family would be attacked if they attempted to come to Coney.[68] Civil rights leaders and black Cincinnatians were also deeply frustrated by the limited scope of the ruling. A group of ministers urged Coney to change its policy so "it will be unnecessary for numerous brown-skinned citizens to go through the procedure of applying to the courts for admittance to the park."[69] Others argued that the decision should inspire African Americans to attempt to cross the color line. "Mrs. Fletcher's victory against Coney Island was not just for her alone," argued an editorial in the African American paper the *Independent*. "Her victory is one which every Negro can enjoy and should—just by going to Coney Island."[70] But even this small victory was lost when the appeals court overturned Judge Weber's decision.

Angered by Weber's strong words condemning their segregation policy, Coney Island immediately filed in the Ohio Court of Appeals. In June 1955 the court argued that Fletcher was limited to the remedies provided under the civil rights statute. By a five-to-two decision the Ohio Supreme Court agreed with this second decision in April 1956. They emphasized that "privately owned and operated places of amusement and entertainment are open to all only through legislative enactments," discouraging any judicial activism on the part of the lower courts.[71] Coney Island did not have to abide by Judge Weber's injunction, which gave credence to McCrackin's contention that Ohio courts were no friend to civil rights. The NAACP's legal remedy brought some publicity to Coney Island's segregation policy, but without continued direct action this pressure was not enough to open Coney to all Cincinnatians. And the existence of a civil rights statute had done nothing to protect the rights of African Americans who wanted access to public accommodations.

The Fletcher case did convince park owner Edward Schott to reconsider the problem of segregation. He knew that the negative publicity and boycotts urged by the CCHR could have some impact on his bottom line. But Schott loathed the Nelsons, Bromleys, McCrackin, and everyone associated with CCHR. Rather than deal with them directly, he contacted the MFRC, which connected him with Joseph Hall of the CUL.[72] When Hall first spoke to Schott shortly after the NAACP filed suit in the Ethel Fletcher case, Schott's primary concern was the economic impact desegregation would have on the park. Schott felt "there would be mass movement of non-whites to the park as a result of which the swimming pool and ballroom would present serious problems." Indeed, these two facilities would become the central focus of the struggle for a desegregated park.[73] When Hall and Schott met again in the fall of 1953 Hall came armed with a study examining how extensive amusement park segregation was nationwide. This study was an effort to demonstrate to Schott, and other white owners of segregated public accommodations, that desegregation did not lead inexorably to economic decline.

The responses to Hall's request for information on amusement park segregation from local Urban League branches around the country reflected the uneven nature of racial segregation. In a single city, Portland, Oregon, one amusement park segregated only its roller rink, the second segregated its swimming pool and ballroom, and the third was entirely segregated.[74] Those that had fully desegregated provided the most useful ammunition for Hall. William Ashby, the executive director of a branch of the New Jersey Urban League, discussed the struggle to desegregate Palisades Park and Olympic Park as direct parallels to the Cincinnati experience. He reassured Hall, "It is my sincere belief that if this park is opened to non-whites, the management within thirty days will begin to wonder why they have been cheating themselves out of so much money for so long a time."[75] Parks in Providence (Rhode Island), Denver, Minneapolis, Springfield (Massachusetts), and Fort Wayne (Indiana) were open to all and economically viable.[76] These were the models of racial tolerance that Hall triumphantly presented to Schott.

But most branches of the Urban League that Hall contacted in northern cities informed him that they had reached the compromise that Schott would strive for: an integrated park with segregated swimming pools and dance halls. Pittsburgh's Kennywood Park was a primary example of this approach. When large integrated groups, such as a public high school, came to the park, Kennywood managers closed down the swimming pool and dance halls to avoid controversy.[77] In Cleveland, Euclid Beach Park continued to segregate its dance floor and roller-skating rink despite Juanita Morrow's efforts there.[78] In Grand Rapids, Michigan, Ramona Gardens barred African Americans from its roller rink.[79] At the "more exclusive" parks in Omaha that provided swimming and dancing, "Negro citizens are . . . excluded."[80] In Akron, Ohio, park managers at Summit Beach segregated their swimming pools and skating rinks.[81] Segregated spaces within desegregated parks, managers and owners believed, maintained racial order and improved the bottom line.

There were many northern parks, however, that were entirely segregated, including one in nearby Marion, Ohio. The Marion Urban League director wrote to Hall: "This fear expressed by the management of Coney Island is the initial and almost unscalable obstacle advanced by most managements when approached on the subject of integration."[82] Predictably, southern parks and those in border cities were uniformly segregated, with most allowing African Americans to attend a few designated days per year. Hall discovered that was the case in Atlanta, Louisville, Baltimore, and St. Louis.[83] Thus Cincinnati's own policy of racial segregation was well within the mainstream. Despite the mixed report on amusement park segregation nationwide, Hall concluded from these examples that integrated parks had not suffered undue economic decline. But Schott dismissed the study, arguing that Coney Island was a "unique operation" and he could "not compare our situation with any other one in the country."[84] Hall then tried another tactic common among racial liberals. He offered assurances that the first groups to integrate Coney Island would be "middle class, high school and college youngsters, well disciplined in human relations" who would not seek to dance or swim with whites. Hall also suggested that there be no public announcement of the new policy and guaranteed that the Urban League and NAACP would handpick the first African American customers.[85] These assurances bore fruit, but only after the city threatened to rescind Coney Island's license.

Civil rights leaders first raised the issue of Coney Island's license in the spring of 1954, alerting the city manager that the park was in clear violation of the Ohio civil rights statute and should be denied a license. Schott assured the city that the park would not "violate any State laws or city ordinances," and the city granted the license in part because the final decision in the Fletcher case was still pending.[86] Another summer of protests set the stage for a more formidable showdown over licensing the following year. On August 18, 1955, park officials denied entry to an interracial group of fifty children and adults organized by the CCHR.[87] Schott remained intransigent, arguing that the license "does not involve the admission gate—nor does it involve the pool—neither of them is in Cincinnati and in our opinion that city is not involved in what we do at the gate or at the pool."[88] This open resistance incensed a group of liberal religious leaders who issued a statement to the press: "At a time when our country has been making great progress in eliminating racial discrimination under the leadership of President Eisenhower, and the historic decision of the United States Supreme Court in the school segregation cases has strengthened our moral leadership throughout the democratic world, Cincinnati cannot afford to permit Coney Island to remain a monument to bigotry."[89] This time city leaders concurred and forced Schott to reconsider his position, extracting an agreement that he would cease practicing discrimination at Coney Island.

Behind the scenes Schott's compliance with the city's demands was more limited than it first appeared. He sent a member of his board of directors, Charles Sawyer, to meet with Hall and negotiate the park's opening. Sawyer made it clear that they were unwilling to open the ballroom or swimming pool to African Americans, arguing that "a large number of Kentuckians use Coney" and these facilities might be reopened as private clubs. Hall initially stood up to this threat, but because he hoped to achieve at least some desegregation at Coney, he eventually backed down. Hall then met with Schott and agreed to help open the park by handpicking individuals who would test the new policy, promising that there would be limited publicity within the African American community. Schott suggested that desegregation be a "step-by step" procedure that would keep the pool and dance floor lily-white.[90] To ensure that he would not be openly violating the law, he leased the swimming pool and dance hall to private operators after agreeing to let in African American customers. Entrance into Sunlite Pool would require a membership card, at least for those who could be visibly identified as black. And Moonlite Gardens held "private" dances each evening for its white patrons.[91] Advertisements for the park printed in the spring of 1955 advised potential customers that "admission to the Park [was] subject to requirements of the exclusive outing sponsor."[92] Again Schott was claiming it was the sponsors, not the park management, that practiced discrimination. In fact, when private companies that used the park for picnics, including General Electric, inquired as to whether it was feasible to bring in interracial groups of employees, they were told that it was "inexpedient" until some unspecified future date.[93]

When Coney Island opened its 1955 season on April 30, African American leaders feared that the violence of the previous summers would begin again. The first blacks to enter the park were Marian Spencer and her two young sons, the family most responsible for the partial victory of desegregation.[94] Their experience was a peaceful one as reported by Ray Paul, a black journalist who attended opening day with his three children and a nephew. There were no incidents that day, he reported, noting that "park personnel treated their first Negro guests with every courtesy and attention."[95] The opening had been carefully orchestrated in negotiations between management and the local NAACP and Urban League. With the exception of Ray Paul's column there was virtually no publicity about the new desegregation policy. Indeed, the *Peacemaker* stated, "one reason why more Negroes didn't visit the Park is that they didn't know of the policy change."[96] Those who did visit may have been the handpicked individuals promised by the local NAACP, who arrived "singly or in pairs" rather than in organized groups.[97] Schott had also insisted that McCrackin, the Nelsons, and the Bromleys not enter the park—an illegal demand that was nonetheless respected by the activists.

By discouraging black attendance at the park and selecting "respectable" customers, the moderate CUL and the NAACP hoped to demonstrate to Schott and white Cincinnatians that desegregation was a painless process.

This was in sharp contrast to CORE's leafleting of Harlem after opening the swimming pool at Palisades Park. There the activists put racial justice and open access over a perceived need to appease Palisades' owners. In Cincinnati careful negotiation, more emblematic of racial liberalism, won out over the Peacemakers' calls for immediacy. After opening day Joseph Hall met with Schott and Wachs biweekly to ensure that all was going well. In fact, desegregation was not going quite as smoothly as Paul's optimistic column that first day suggested. Park management reported a "few complaints" by white customers and the removal of a sign that read "Niggers don't go to Coney." Park guards also forcefully removed three black teenagers who were asking about possible employment at the park. Nevertheless, the small number of black patrons reassured Schott and his management that desegregation was not lethal to the park's success. Because these patrons did not attempt to enter the dance hall or swimming pool, the limited nature of that desegregation was also masked for a short time.[98]

The unmasking came in July 1955; not everyone at the Cincinnati NAACP was willing to bow to Schott's demands. George E. Johnson, who worked for the city's NAACP branch, chose July 4 as an appropriate day to challenge the park's policy on swimming. Johnson approached the pool with a group of white friends. The attendant manning the gate reportedly said, "I'd rather you not go in there because we have people here from everywhere and I am concerned about your personal safety."[99] By "everywhere" the attendant was referring to Kentucky. A park police officer approached Johnson and quickly pulled him out of the line. It was another four years before African Americans challenged segregation at Moonlite Gardens or the Sunlite Pool, and black attendance at the park was miniscule throughout the rest of the 1950s. It was only in 1961 that a revitalized CORE succeeded in fully integrating the park. In the case of Coney Island the distance between nominal desegregation and actual integration was wide. The willingness of radical nonviolent activists to face the brutality of park patrons and police dramatically demonstrated that African Americans would not stand for complete exclusion. But through the club method, Schott ensured they would not obtain complete inclusion.

For Cincinnati's civil rights activists, 1955 proved to be a turning point. While Coney Island reluctantly began the process of desegregation, the local chapter of CORE became embroiled in a national debate about the organization's future. Wallace Nelson made a bid for the leadership of national CORE, which he believed had become "overconcerned with 'respectability.'" Speaking from the vantage point of his experience at the front gates of Coney Island, Nelson pointed out that "no direct action can be respectable in these times."[100] Nelson's belief in direct action was solidified while leading interracial workshops in Washington, D.C., at the behest of the FOR and CORE during the first summers of the Coney Island demonstrations. In 1951 and 1952 Nelson had led a remarkable project to desegregate Rosedale playground, located in a mixed neighborhood in the nation's capital but open only to whites. The first summer the project worked to secure neighborhood support by forming the all-black Rosedale Citizens Committee. These community members, mostly women and children, picketed the playground accompanied by interracial groups of CORE activists. Local whites attacked them viciously, and there were several incidents of beatings.

On a hot June evening in 1952, the second summer of protests, a thirteen-year-old black boy climbed Rosedale's fence during the night, wanting to cool off in the restricted pool. Denied the swimming lessons given his white neighbors, the boy drowned in the unattended pool, and his death galvanized the local black community to engage in a full-frontal assault on the playground. Wallace Nelson brought his interracial workshoppers into the fray, using tactics that he had honed at Coney Island. Ten members of the interracial workshop, five white and five black, blocked the entrance to the playground. When police approached to arrest them, they immediately fell to the ground and were carried into a wagon and to the patrol house. There they refused to give their names to police or post bond at the jail. After they were imprisoned, the group went on a hunger strike. Nelson later reported that while in custody an officer kicked him to the floor, ground a lighted cigarette into his skin, and twisted his arm with a metal clamp that left permanent scars on his wrist.[101] At that point in the summer young blacks began to climb over the playground fence daily, violating the mandated segregation policy. When whites armed with baseball bats met them one afternoon, Walter Lucas, a forty-year-old black man, tried to break up the fight but was badly beaten. He ran to his nearby house to retrieve a gun and fired it into the air to disperse the crowd. A white man hurled a brick at Lucas's head, striking him unconscious. That night when the gates of playground were shut, a group of black children and teenagers jumped the fence and played in the park. Under intense pressure, the District Recreation Board finally declared it a desegregated facility, and it reopened that October to African American and white children.[102] At least the play equipment did—the pool remained white-only until the following summer.[103]

The struggle for access to Rosedale playground was brutal, but it ultimately was successful. And for Nelson it legitimized the tactics of nonviolent direct action, even when civil rights leaders deemed such action unrespectable. By the mid-1950s Nelson's commitment to radical pacifism and total noncooperation angered more conservative factions of CORE, who feared he would alienate white liberals and black moderates caught up in the cold war. Not a communist himself, Nelson fervently believed in "free expression for everyone, including those who preach a totalitarian creed."[104] Similarly, Marion Bromley complained to the national CORE office in 1953, "I take pretty strong exception to the 'non-Communist oath' on the flyer you sent."[105] The debate over anti-communism and radical tactics came to a head in 1954 when moderate CORE activists, primarily those in New York, signaled their movement away from CORE's earlier commitment to nonviolence and civil disobedience by eliminating Nelson's position as a paid field worker. Juanita Nelson, who had been elected to the position of secretary, resigned in disgust during the 1954 convention after a decade of commitment to CORE. In light of this turmoil, Cincinnati's local chapter folded in 1956 and there were, for a time, no further challenges to the discriminatory practices of Cincinnati's public accommodations.

Wallace Nelson's concerns about the limits of respectability were well founded. The private negotiations between the Urban League, NAACP, and Schott were respectful and calm compared to the scenes of brutality at Coney Island's gates in the early 1950s. But the results were disappointing. Marion Spencer and Ethel Fletcher had hoped for more for their families. They wanted to protect their children and give them the joy of an amusement park on a summer day. That goal was achieved in Washington's Rosedale playground after a protracted struggle. But Coney Island remained a white space with only token signs of desegregation. As a coveted site of recreation set apart from the city, in contrast to Rosedale's location in an urban neighborhood experiencing racial transition, white consumers and police effectively used violence in flagrant violation of the state's civil rights law to ensure Coney Island remained segregated. It would take the rediscovery of the nonviolence and civil disobedience practiced by the Bromleys, Nelsons, and McCrackin by a group of young activists at the beginning of the next decade to complete the task of integration.

Northern Struggles in the Early 1950s

Although the owners of recreational facilities in border cities like Cincinnati legitimized their racist practices by pointing to their proximity to the

South, in reality segregated leisure continued to be the practice throughout the North as well. A reinvigorated NAACP gave African Americans across the North more ammunition to pressure city officials to open recreational facilities to them and their children in the years surrounding the 1954 *Brown v. Board of Education* decision. During hot city summers, pools were often the focus of black demands for access to spaces of public leisure. Pennsylvania's two largest cities, Philadelphia and Pittsburgh, saw major campaigns to open urban waters in the early 1950s as activists pressured local officials to abide by Pennsylvania's 1939 open accommodations law. Unlike amusement parks, in these spaces white consumers of leisure could not rely on private guards but depended on local police and white toughs to enforce illegal discrimination. As the historian Karl E. Johnson argues, "Black youths seeking access to public recreational and athletic facilities were often the victims of threats, physical attack, subterfuge, and expulsion by whites in many sections of Philadelphia in the postwar era. . . . Police officers even acted as part of the local 'security force' that sought to maintain racial separation and to prevent African Americans from entering white areas."[106] By the early 1950s the American Civil Liberties Union (ACLU) and the Philadelphia NAACP had received dozens of complaints from blacks who had been turned away from public facilities, harassed, and beaten. But it was an unconventional religious figure, Father Divine, who took action at a segregated swimming pool in 1952.

Father Divine (born George Baker, Jr.) founded the International Peace Mission movement in the early 1930s and became a major figure in Harlem's political and cultural scene during the Great Depression. In the early 1940s he moved to Philadelphia and continued to preach and organize, although on a smaller scale. Like the Peacemakers in Cincinnati, Father Divine created an interracial community committed to the integration of public accommodations.[107] In the late 1940s he attempted to purchase the segregated Crystal Pool at the Woodside Amusement Park in order to open it to all races. In 1952, after a black Korean War veteran was turned away from northeast Philadelphia's lavish Boulevard pools, Father Divine responded by using his interracial congregation to test pool policies, following the CORE model. Using photographs and testimonies, Father Divine's followers documented their exclusion from Boulevard pools—the park's owners had claimed that the group was not a member of the Boulevard Swimming and Tennis Club.[108] The Peace Mission activists turned their evidence over to the city's Commission of Human Relations (CHR), which had compiled an extensive record of pool discrimination in Philadelphia. A group of blacks, who had been part of

Figure 7. Activists in Pittsburgh protesting segregation at Highland Park swimming pool. Their signs read, "We want democracy at Highland Park Pool, Mayor Lawrence, what do you want?" and "We fought together, why can't we swim together?" This language reflects the continued use of Double V rhetoric in the years following World War II. Charles "Teenie" Harris, American/1908-98, c. 1951, Carnegie Museum of Art, Pittsburgh. Heinz Family Fund.

a string of demonstrations, filed a successful class-action suit against Boulevard pools.[109] In the case of Philadelphia's pools, an eclectic mix of civil rights groups, religious organizations, and ordinary citizens forced the city and private operators to abide by the law.

A similar struggle in Pittsburgh pitted determined African Americans against white teenagers who repeatedly attacked blacks who attempted to swim in city pools. In 1951 this conflict came to a head at Highland Park pool, a large facility that blacks had struggled to enter since its opening in 1931. For twenty years small groups of blacks had attempted to swim only to be faced with mobs of white teenagers who attacked them. When police arrived they would arrest the black swimmers for inciting a riot.[110] This pattern persisted even into the war years and the heyday of racial liberalism in the late 1940s.

In 1948, for example, a progressive interracial group attempted to swim at Highland, only to be driven out by a white crowd estimated at a thousand.[111] In the summer of 1951 a white gang of teenagers threatened Alexander J. Allen, the executive secretary of the Pittsburgh Urban League, when he attempted to enter Highland Park pool. Lifeguards and police again refused to intervene, telling Allen he had the right to use the pool but that they could not guarantee his safety. The NAACP then issued this statement: "If the soft speaking of those seeking to assure Negroes the freedom to use without fear the facilities of Highland Park or any other municipal pool was not effective, the big stick of legal action would be used."[112] In response to this threat, Pittsburgh officials stepped up efforts to police the pool and reassured civil rights groups they would be protected, but most African Americans deeply feared meeting white gangs' fists and avoided Highland Park.

When the pool reopened in the summer of 1952 the Pittsburgh CORE chapter began a series of swim-ins despite threats "that we would be followed home and our homes bombed, that our leader would be hung on the telephone pole nearest the pool, that a group of determined men would be hidden in strategic spots around the pool with rifles to pick us off."[113] Such threats deeply frightened CORE members, but they managed to carry out the swim-ins with little conflict. The project was so successful that when a riot broke out in Pittsburgh's Paulson pool that same summer, white swimmers yelled, "Go on over to Highland Park; that is your pool!"[114] This perception was heightened because the city had closed Kline pool, a small, dilapidated facility that had long been known as the "colored pool."[115] Here the distinction between integration and desegregation was evident. Highland Park was desegregated successfully in 1952, but many whites considered it a black space as a result. Thus, true integration was forestalled. But for most African Americans having free access and safety at Highland Park, rather than swimming with whites, was the goal.

The violence that had pervaded Highland Park shifted to another Pittsburgh pool on Paulson Avenue, which African Americans targeted as the next recreational battleground. In the summer of 1952, when blacks finally began to enter Highland Park with relative safety, white gangs threw rocks and screamed epithets at African Americans attempting to swim at Paulson pool.[116] After a week of continual violence officials closed the pool for several days in order, they claimed, to clean out the rocks. Community groups pressured the city to provide protection for black swimmers, and the NAACP began to work on assigning a black lifeguard to Paulson pool. Despite the presence of police the harassment continued. Whites splashed and taunted a young African American couple while police looked on, and two young girls found their clothes strewn across the floor of the dressing room.[117] Racially integrated swimming would continue to be elusive in Pittsburgh despite the best efforts of the NAACP, community groups, nonviolent activists, and ordinary consumers. Death threats, rocks, and epithets warned black swimmers away from white spaces of leisure. It was only when whites perceived those spaces as black, as in Highland Park, that African Americans could swim in relative safety.

Lawsuits against northern municipalities that segregated their pools proliferated in the early 1950s. By 1952 Springfield, Illinois, had agreed to desegregate both its Memorial Pool and Lake Springfield beaches after the NAACP threatened lawsuits.[118] The NAACP filed a suit against the town of Centralia, Illinois, whose large pool in Fairfield Park had been segregated since its opening.[119] These legal measures, and those in Pennsylvania, originated from the actions of ordinary African Americans who were increasingly frustrated by the lack of access their families had to recreation. One 1955 letter from Springfield, Missouri, to the NAACP office read, "I am writing you concerning swimming in public parks in Springfield Mo. The children are playing in the parks, but my sons were refused in the swimming pools. I wrote the local paper and asked them to publish it in the paper, but they did not. . . . The children also go to the white schools here. I would like for you to write me and let me know what to do about it."[120] This letter, written after the *Brown v. Board of Education* decision ruled that "separate but equal" was unconstitutional, expressed anger that in towns where children could go to school together and even play in parks, integrated swimming was prohibited. The lack of mainstream press coverage of recreational discrimination in Springfield was typical; the demonstrators in Cincinnati had also been unable to pressure the white newspapers to cover their protests against Coney Island. Indeed, few northern papers covered nonviolent protests or NAACP lawsuits. Stories on the topic of segregated swimming generally appeared in white papers only when there was a riot. But African American papers did cover the court cases and violence that resulted from determined attempts to swim in urban pools.

Because amusement parks, like Coney Island, rarely allowed integrated swimming in their pools, even when other facilities were desegregated, they became a central target of activists and consumers. Local NAACP offices received many complaints from civic groups whose black members were barred from amusement park swimming facilities in the early 1950s. Hershey

Park, in Pennsylvania, turned away black members of a Baltimore YMCA who had traveled there for the day. In a small amusement park in Chalfonte, Pennsylvania, the swimming pool had the ubiquitous "for members only" sign and turned away black children from a church school.[121] In Colorado, a group of African Americans sued the owners of Lakeside Amusement Park for denying them entry.[122] Most often the NAACP counseled those seeking their advice to negotiate directly with facilities rather than pursuing legal action. But in select cases NAACP lawyers jumped at the opportunity to challenge segregation in the courts.

Such an opportunity appeared with a series of swimming pool cases just prior to the 1954 *Brown v. Board of Education* decision. These cases were instrumental in chipping away at the logic inherent in *Plessy v. Ferguson* that segregation was necessary to prevent interracial violence in public spaces. Those who wanted to keep amusement parks and pools white exploited fears of violence, and often government officials and courts reinforced the link between violence and integration. "The rhetoric of violence has been an important part of the rationale of racial segregation in the United States," argued a leading law journal in 1951; "it has often swayed courts as well as legislation."[123] Swaying courts in the opposite direction by arguing that segregated recreation was both unconstitutional and created, rather than forestalled, racial tension would take a massive legal effort.

The proliferation of legal challenges to pool segregation in the early 1950s reflected a grassroots effort to push for integrated recreation; this was analogous to the pressure placed on segregated schools to integrate. Indeed school segregation and recreational segregation had some similarities: both impacted children, both raised the ire of concerned black parents, and both reflected the growing spatial segregation in American cities. The legal histories of school integration and recreational integration were deeply intertwined. For example, in Kansas City, when three African Americans sued the city to gain entrance into the Swope Park swimming pool in 1952, city officials claimed the existence of a separate "Negro pool" made the segregation policy constitutional. Both the U.S. Federal District Court and the U.S. Court of Appeals disagreed, ruling that the city could not deny blacks equal access to Swope Park. In response Kansas City officials closed the pool, a relatively new and lavish facility, for two long hot summers while they waited for a ruling from the Supreme Court. When the Supreme Court term opened in the fall of 1953 they refused to review the case, upholding the ban on swimming segregation imposed by the lower courts.[124] African Americans recognized the significance of the case for the fate of *Brown v. Board of Education*. "The recent Supreme Court ruling allowing Negroes use of the heretofore segregated Swope Park Municipal swimming and wading pool at Kansas City, Mo.," reported the *Chicago Defender*, "may brighten prospects in regard to discrimination in public schools. . . . With the Supreme Court ruling against the 'separate but equal' clause in regard to recreation, it also established the possibilities that 'separate but equal' claims in education will be ditched, eliminating segregation in public schools."[125] The Swope Park swimming pool finally reopened as a desegregated facility in the summer of 1954, the same year the *Brown* decision was handed down by the Supreme Court.[126]

The case that broke the link between integration and violence in the law, if not in daily life, originated in Baltimore—like Cincinnati, another border city with a deep history of racial segregation. *Dawson v. Mayor and City Council of Baltimore* linked three swimming cases from the early 1950s. In 1950 city officials denied Robert Dawson, an African American man, use of a public beach at Fort Smallwood Park. Although the local court ordered the city to cease discrimination, it responded by setting aside separate days for black swimmers and developing a segregated beach for blacks, completed in 1952. The NAACP filed a new motion for judgment on the case ten days after *Brown v. Board of Education* was decided; however, Baltimore's Judge Roszel Thomsen denied the motion, persuaded that violence would ensue if segregated recreation were outlawed and that swimming was "more sensitive than schools." It was the white public's sensitivity to interracial swimming that the city's lawyer, Edwin Harlan, pointed to when advocating continued segregation of Baltimore's pools and beaches. "I think one of the greatest objectives is to keep order and prevent riots," he argued. "It is better for public safety in any activity involving physical contact that the races be separated."[127] Judge Thomsen agreed, and he upheld Baltimore's policy of segregated swimming at public pools and beaches despite the recent *Brown* decision. The "sensitivity" of swimming outweighed the separate but equal doctrine's demise.

At this point the NAACP bundled the *Dawson* case with another beach swimming case, *Lonesome v. Maxwell*. In the summer of 1952 guards turned away Milton Lonesome and several friends, all African American, from the white-only South Beach at Sandy Point State Park and directed them toward the black-only East Beach. Lonesome filed a complaint arguing that the two beaches were unequal, but the lower court dismissed the case. The third and final swimming incident resulted in *Isaacs v. Baltimore*, in which the NAACP challenged Baltimore's segregated swimming pools after three young African

American boys drowned in surrounding natural water.[128] In 1954 the NAACP brought the *Dawson*, *Lonesome*, and *Isaacs* cases to the U.S. Court of Appeals.[129] Early in 1955 the U.S. Fourth Circuit Court of Appeals reversed the lower court decision in the *Dawson* case, affirmed Milton Lonesome's right to use any beach he pleased, and desegregated the city's seven outdoor pools. The court did not agree with Judge Thomsen that the prevention of violence justified segregation, arguing instead that "segregation cannot be justified as a means to preserve the public peace merely because the tangible facilities furnished to one race are equal to those furnished to the other."[130] With the *Brown v. Board of Education* decision the state could no longer argue that supplying "equal" bathing facilities was sufficient. When the Supreme Court refused to review an appeal, the decision stood as a new precedent to be wielded by the NAACP in their struggle for interracial recreation.[131] Even the notoriously racist Board of Recreation in Washington, D.C., saw the writing on the wall. Rather than waiting for the final decision in the *Dawson* case, on the evening of May 17, 1954, the board released a signed statement declaring that all public recreational facilities in the District were available to African Americans. It was the evening the Supreme Court announced the *Brown v. Board of Education* decision, and the statement had been prepared in advance.[132]

The NAACP had a powerful tool to fight segregation cases after the *Brown* decision and the Baltimore swimming cases. For example, in 1955 the Kansas Supreme Court ordered the city of Parsons to open its municipal swimming pool to blacks. A local paper reported, "The decision came as no surprise here. It had been foreshadowed by action of the U.S. Supreme Court in holding segregation in public schools to be unconstitutional."[133] Attempts to open private facilities also drew on the *Brown* decision for moral and legal weight. The Castle Hill Beach Club in the Bronx had kept blacks out of its facilities since its opening in 1928, claiming it was a private club exempt from state civil rights laws and that racial mixing would lead to violence. The general manager admitted, "our only reason for not wanting to admit Negroes is that we are scared to death to admit them for fear of the untoward results which might follow their admission."[134] Anita Brown, an African American woman, filed a complaint with New York's State Commission Against Discrimination (SCAD) in 1953 after being denied a locker at the bathhouse. After extensive hearings SCAD issued an order forcing Castle Hill to stop its discriminatory practices. Charles S. Zimmerman, a labor leader in New York, hailed the order and said it "clearly parallels the historic Supreme Court decision against segregation in education."[135] The New York Supreme Court and the New York

Court of Appeals, which found that the "beach club" was, in fact, a public accommodation, upheld this ruling.[136] Like the *Dawson* case, the Castle Hill case provided a useful precedent with which to attack segregated recreation. After 1957, when the final appeal was exhausted, civil rights lawyers challenging the private club subterfuge often cited it.

Despite these legal victories, the Cincinnati Coney Island case demonstrates that not every challenge to recreational segregation in the mid-1950s succeeded. But there were more legal victories after the *Brown* and *Dawson* decisions, and these victories in turn inspired more activism. In a fund-raising letter the leaders of CORE stated, "The Supreme Court's momentous decision outlawing racial segregation in the public schools challenges us to renewed efforts to attack discrimination in all places of public accommodation."[137] Ordinary citizens, as well as activists, increasingly demanded access to recreational spaces after 1954. In Marion, Indiana, for example, the only public swimming pool at Matter Park had been segregated for decades when seven African American men attempted to swim in the wake of the *Brown* decision. They were turned away by police officers and deputized civilians who carried guns on their hips. After a confrontation at city hall, the park board offered to open the pool to blacks three days per week, an offer the local NAACP rejected. According to the local paper, "All members of the City Council at Tuesday's meeting agreed there is no question of the legal right of all citizens to swim at the pool, but they expressed fear that an integrated policy would create racial disturbances and violence."[138] Although the courts had declared segregation could no longer be justified as a means of preventing violence, fears of potential violence remained a powerful tool wielded by city officials and owners of recreational facilities. But, in the end, a NAACP lawsuit opened Matter Park to blacks.[139] In Marion the combination of a group of black men's courage in facing down an armed posse and an active NAACP chapter willing to come to their defense gave African Americans access to the local swimming pool. The changing legal landscape emboldened lawyers, activists, and ordinary African Americans to demand admission into all spaces of leisure.

Massive Resistance in the South

The swimming pool cases in the years surrounding the *Brown* decision did not end recreational segregation. It would take the 1964 Civil Rights Act to put the full weight of the federal government behind the concept that equal access to public accommodations was a fundamental right. Even then, many facilities would fight to keep blacks away from white spaces of leisure by closing or privatizing pools and parks. But it is striking that resistance to recreational segregation in the 1950s was not limited to the northern or border states. In his history of Atlanta, Kevin Kruse points out that desegregation of public spaces was the "focal point of local civil rights activities of the mid-1950s."[140] That was true in Cincinnati, but it was also true in southern cities like Atlanta where the *Brown* decision gave new hope to activists and consumers.

The summer of 1954 was a busy one for communities trying to negotiate segregated swimming in this new legal era. While whites in Marion eventually returned to the Matter Park swimming pool, in other communities with only one pool whites boycotted integrated swimming. Determined to test their new rights in the wake of *Brown*, African Americans in Ironton, West Virginia, flocked to the one municipal swimming pool in town. Previously black residents had been allowed to swim on Mondays only, despite the fact the pool was built with Works Progress Administration (WPA) funds and subject to federal nondiscrimination laws. When blacks began to swim in the pool every day during the summer of 1954, whites abandoned the pool altogether.[141] Such boycotts reflected whites' shifting strategies of segregation when black community members demanded full and equal access to public facilities.

In the South, the massive resistance to school integration that followed *Brown v. Board of Education* carried over to massive resistance to recreational integration. As historian Tony Badger argues, "What whites reacted so violently against was the notion of African Americans dictating the timetable of racial change, and what they perceived as black aggressive intrusion into white-controlled space."[142] Despite this violent reaction, southern African Americans eagerly wielded the new legal precedent to demand access to recreation. Before the *Brown* decision the NAACP and CORE had been reluctant to support direct action campaigns against segregated public accommodations in states without civil rights laws. After 1954 this pattern began to shift as local activists and consumers found more national support when they ventured across the color line. Increased challenges to segregation also forced southern whites to shore up their legal and extralegal defenses. Black willingness to challenge segregated recreation in the wake of *Brown*, for example, led to a startling discovery in San Antonio, Texas. For decades African Americans swam in only two of the city's twelve pools; but there was no law requiring segregation in the city's recreation facilities. In June 1954 a group of

African Americans swam in one of the "white" pools before guards quickly ousted them. That night a cross burned at the entrance to the pool, and the next morning the city council met in emergency session to pass a new segregation law and authorized police to guard the pools that had been temporarily closed for "cleaning and repairs."[143] Two years later, under continual pressure from its black citizens, the city repealed the ordinance.[144]

San Antonio was not unusual in having no laws on the books mandating segregation. The historian Darryl Paulson points out, "In most communities of the South, segregation in recreation facilities was maintained by local ordinance or by prevailing custom."[145] This was not the simplistic de jure versus de facto regional landscape of the national imagination. In the wake of *Brown v. Board of Education* and increased use of recreational facilities by blacks, southern cities and states passed laws explicitly segregating recreational facilities. When blacks in Florida realized that Delray Beach had no law mandating segregation, they flocked to the town's pool and beach. In response, citing an "invasion" of blacks that could incite riots, the town issued an emergency segregation ordinance.[146] Sarasota, Florida, passed an ordinance declaring that police would clear beaches if "members of different races" intermingled in order to prevent "riots, affrays, batteries and civil disorders."[147] This innovative law again pointed to violence prevention as a motivation for segregation but sheltered the city temporarily from litigation. On the state level, Louisiana passed an act in 1956 mandating that all facilities "for swimming, dancing, golfing, skating or other recreational activities ... shall be operated separately for members of the white and colored race in order to promote and protect public health, morals, and the peace and good order in this State."[148] These laws were subject to legal challenges and in 1964 would be declared unconstitutional, but their passage reflected a determined effort on the part of southern whites to forestall recreational integration. This form of massive resistance was sometimes more concerted in the area of recreation than in schools. According to Michael Klarman, Florida, for example, "never fully embraced massive resistance" and was the first state in the Deep South to desegregate a grade school.[149] But Florida towns like Delray Beach and Sarasota swiftly resisted interracial swimming.

Massive resistance to recreational integration was starkly evident in yet another Florida beach community in the mid-1950s. In 1955 a group of seven blacks attempted to purchase tickets to the Spa pool and beach in downtown St. Petersburg. The following day, ninety local whites formed a citizens' council to resist integration of city pools and beaches. This incident was the centerpiece of a successful class-action suit against the city. Although the city argued that they could not run the facilities at a profit if they were integrated, they failed to convince the courts that this was justification enough for violating the Fourteenth Amendment. On April Fool's Day in 1957 the Supreme Court upheld the lower courts' decisions. In a pattern that increasingly marked the southern strategy in recreation cases, St. Petersburg closed the Spa pool and beach the following summer when blacks attempted to exercise their rights. The city manager cited "the rise of possible derisive friction between the races" as the motivation for his decision and noted, correctly, that "While the federal courts have ordered that if the city operates the beach and pool they cannot be segregated there is nothing in the court order stating the city must operate them."[150] Closing these facilities was the simplest solution, but it was one that alienated business leaders and white taxpayers who used the facilities. By the summer of 1959 these interests prevailed over the city manager and citizens' councils, and St. Petersburg's beaches were reopened for business. In the 1960s pressure from business leaders was the Achilles' heel of massive resistance, and St. Petersburg's drama would play out in cities across the South.[151]

The *Brown* decision also enabled activists and consumers to pursue cases involving desegregation of golf courses throughout the South, most of which originated in the late 1940s and early 1950s. The earliest successful southern case was in Houston, where five African Americans filed a lawsuit to gain access to municipal golf courses in 1950. The mayor was reluctant to build a separate course for blacks and so agreed to integrate the existing links.[152] A key Supreme Court ruling on integrating Atlanta's municipal golf courses in 1955 affirmed that "separate but equal" could no longer justify segregated golf courses. This court fight began in 1951, when a group of four middle-class African American professionals attempted to play on the city's Bobby Jones golf course. After the ruling Atlanta's mayor kept the courses open but shut down the locker rooms and shower facilities and reassured whites that the city's pools and playgrounds would remain segregated.[153] In Nashville, the federal district court ordered the city in 1952 to allow blacks to use the Shelby Park Golf Course two days a week in response to complaints by local blacks But in 1956 the U.S District Court ordered the course fully desegregated in the wake of the Atlanta decision and the Baltimore pool cases.[154] These cases brought a flurry of new suits to the federal district courts, which desegregated public courses in Pensacola, Florida, in 1956; Portsmouth, Virginia, in 1956; Fort Lauderdale in 1957; Charlotte, North Carolina, in 1957; Miami in 1957; and

Greensboro, North Carolina, in 1957.[155] This success was mitigated by the fact that golf courses were not as controversial as amusement parks and swimming pools. Groups of golfers could place significant space between themselves, and the rulings applied only to public courses, not private clubs where elite whites could easily retreat. Nevertheless, the proliferation of successful court cases reflected ongoing resistance to segregated recreation in the South even prior to 1954. And the success of lawsuits would help pave the way for further struggles in the early 1960s.

Although lawsuits provide a convenient way to track the struggle against recreational segregation, there were many acts of daily resistance that are more elusive. Each lawsuit was preceded by an act of determination as African Americans crossed racial lines in parks, on golf courses, and at pools. Others chose not to participate in a segregated industry by frequenting black-owned facilities rather than visiting amusement parks and swimming pools on designated days. By eschewing limited entrance into segregated facilities, blacks boycotted both public and private facilities and denied a profit to the proprietors. In Houston, for example, whites-only Playland Park opened in 1941 in a city where there were no public swimming pools or public playgrounds for African Americans.[156] The Texas city had no pretense of a separate-but-equal recreational policy. Rather, blacks were completely excluded. At Playland Park there was one exception to the apartheid policy. Like many American amusement parks, Playland opened its gates to African Americans one day per year. In this case it was Juneteenth—commemorating when Texas slaves reportedly heard from Union troops of their emancipation on June 19, 1865. Many black families flocked to Playland on Juneteenth. State representative Al Edwards reminisced, "I think the owners of that place paid all their bills on that day. It was so crowded, you couldn't fit a feather through."[157] Pouring money into the coffers of a segregated park became too much for many by the mid-1950s, and a series of boycotts resulted. In 1956, for example, an African American father called his children to him and, much to their distress, told them that year they would attend a church picnic on Juneteenth instead of the annual outing to Playland. Other families joined in this informal boycott by the mid-1950s. These were ordinary black fathers and mothers who took their children to church picnics at Emancipation Park or on family outings to the segregated beach rather than give their dollars to Playland.[158]

The legal victories of the NAACP and the moral victories of CORE emboldened Houston's black families. But the ability to enforce the law was highly dependent on local governments and the nature of race relations in particular communities. Even before 1954, many of the states where there had been recreation riots and lawsuits had civil rights statutes on the books that prohibited racial discrimination in public accommodations. And even when municipal pools and amusement parks were desegregated African Americans encountered hostile whites or, more often, found themselves swimming or playing only with other blacks. In the South, citizens' councils and white leaders leading massive resistance to integration attempted to forestall recreational segregation through privatization, white boycotts, or closing facilities. The radical interracialism of CORE and other groups that challenged recreational segregation in northern and border states also met with limited success. Cincinnati's Peacemakers opened the gates to Coney Island, but only to a small number of African Americans, and even they could not venture onto the Moonlite Gardens dance floor or jump in the Sunlite Pool. Cincinnati was a "northern city with a southern exposure," emblematic not of regional differences but of the national landscape.

* * *

The legal cases surrounding *Brown v. Board of Education* directly challenged the logic in *Plessy v. Ferguson* that the threat of violence justified segregation. Yet even in many of the rulings overturning recreational segregation, judges and lawyers revealed their fears that racial contact on beaches, on golf courses, in swimming pools, and at amusement parks would inevitably lead to violence. When the federal district court ruled that Pensacola had to desegregate its municipal golf course in 1956, it gave the city time to "prepare" in order to "preserve the peace and tranquility of the community."[159] Despite the lingering fears of violence, 1954 was a watershed year—the state would no longer be able to justify segregation as violence prevention in a court of law. But this fact would not lessen the frequency of recreation riots or end white resistance to recreational desegregation. Increasingly local governments or owners of amusement parks and swimming pools would privatize to evade civil rights laws. And physical attacks on activists and consumers who attempted to enter white recreational spaces would continue into the late 1950s and 1960s. But the white public often dismissed these attacks as the result of juvenile delinquency and crime, not resistance to segregation. The white press and city officials viewed black teenagers who ventured into "white" pools and parks as thugs and troublemakers. A 1956 recreation riot in Buffalo, New York, illustrates how resistance to recreational segregation went well beyond the organized civil rights movement. As in Cincinnati, in Buffalo the threat of violence dictated the pace of change. Disorder and order defined accessibility, not the law.

CHAPTER 4

Violence in the City of Good Neighbors: Delinquency and Consumer Rights in the Postwar City

AFTER *Brown* the amount of formal political activity in northern states to open public accommodations declined. Racial liberals' efforts to educate the public made blatant support for the segregation of public accommodations less acceptable, and NAACP lawsuits pressured civil rights states to abide by their laws. Despite these successes, racial conflict in spaces of leisure persisted and by the late 1960s had increased dramatically. Chicago's southeast side, for example, was ground zero for recreation riots instigated by white teenagers. A series of vicious attacks in the mid-1950s in Tuley and Calumet parks pitted local African American families against whites fearing incursions into their neighborhoods. In the summer of 1957 at the Tuley Park pool hundreds of white teenagers attacked blacks attempting to swim. Nearby Calumet Park saw a major riot when a mob of thousands challenged an African American mothers' club that had reserved park facilities for a picnic. In the end police had to rescue the women and children, escorting them through the howling mob. By the early 1960s the battles at Chicago's parks, beaches, and pools were part of a consolidated movement against integration spearheaded by white teenagers.[1] One could read this increase in racial violence, as did many white southerners, as the direct result of integration: the warnings of *Plessy* come to fruition. But beginning in the 1950s reformers and the media often cast these conflicts as a symptom of a new epidemic in juvenile delinquency, unrelated to race.

For urban African Americans, however, it was clear continued recreation riots resulted from the lasting consequences of segregation. Legal victories and successful civil rights struggles may have opened the gates of some amusement parks in the North and West, but those spaces remained highly contested. Just as housing segregation and employment discrimination were not erased by civil rights legislation, recreational segregation did not end with public accommodations laws. Instead, the fight over recreational segregation raged on. But increasingly the fight was between young consumers eager to mark their territories in quickly changing urban environments. By the mid-1950s American cities were undergoing major transformations as African American migration and white flight to suburbs rapidly changed neighborhoods' racial composition. Conflict over urban space—in schools, housing, recreation, and transportation—was the result. As the historian Todd Michney argues, "racialized violence" was "a tactic in the territorialization of urban space."[2] In this environment many middle-class white consumers fled urban recreation altogether, seeking safety in private suburban neighborhoods and recreational facilities far outside the urban milieu. Emblematic of this trend, by the late 1950s the decline of the urban amusement park in an era of integration led directly to a new recreational industry: the theme park. Disneyland, which opened in 1955, was the first and most successful American theme park. Its success was premised on its dissociation from cities, in stark contrast to the traditional urban amusement parks like Buffalo's Crystal Beach.

The City of Good Neighbors

From Cincinnati's Coney Island traveling east we find another Queen City, another steamboat, another park, and another border. Buffalo had gained a reputation as the "City of Good Neighbors" by the mid-twentieth century. Unlike other industrial cities such as Chicago or Detroit, there had been no major race riots and the city prided itself on its ethnic and religious diversity. This tranquility was shattered on Memorial Day 1956 when a race riot at Crystal Beach amusement park mesmerized the nation. In the summer months Crystal Beach, a park across Lake Erie in Ontario, had long been a gathering place for Buffalonians seeking a respite from the city. They traveled across the lake on the *Canadiana*, a large steamer that began operating in 1910.[3] On the forty-five-minute trip customers danced to big bands, ate, drank, and socialized. Although the park was never formally segregated, substantial numbers of African Americans did not visit the park before the

1950s, when black southern migration to the city dramatically increased. On that fateful opening day of 1956 thousands of white and black Buffalonians packed onto the *Canadiana*. By the end of the evening all of Buffalo was talking about the riot that had broken out at Crystal Beach and continued on the boat ride back. By the next day the entire country was discussing the riot's implications in newspapers, government offices, and civil rights organizations.

Like many American cities, Buffalo in 1956 was in the throes of rapid demographic change. In the aftermath of World War II thousands of southern black migrants boarded northern-bound buses and trains to the Queen City, nearly doubling Buffalo's black population in a single decade.[4] They settled in the congested Eastside neighborhood in the Ellicott District that had housed African Americans since the nineteenth century. Overcrowded housing and urban renewal soon forced them north into the Cold Spring District and further east into the Fruit Belt. Their German, Polish, and Italian neighbors became part of a mass exodus of whites as the 1950s saw the largest drop in Buffalo's overall population. Nearly fifty thousand white city dwellers moved to nearby suburbs, leaving behind declining city services, dilapidated schools, and neighborhoods shattered by poorly planned urban renewal.

Buffalo was not unique. Increased residential segregation divided other American cities in both the North and the South as local municipalities developed racially exclusive public housing and urban renewal projects. Indeed, a recent focus on segregated housing has helped historians nationalize the history of racial conflict. As historian Stephen Meyer suggests, "Southern practices did differ from the rest of the country, but white supremacy and racial discrimination are national phenomena."[5] The fight against racial discrimination was also a national phenomenon as increased residential segregation coincided with a wholesale attack on segregation in public accommodations and education by civil rights activists. Northern cities were the site of many of these struggles to obtain full access to the bounty of postwar consumerism. Simultaneously, it seemed, American cities were coming together and apart, formally desegregating public accommodations yet segregating their ever-growing African American neighborhoods. These two trends collided in spaces of leisure.

The mid-1950s also marked the height of a perceived nationwide epidemic of juvenile delinquency. A series of congressional hearings on the issue between 1954 and 1956 kept it in the national spotlight, and social scientists and journalists produced reports, books, and articles on delinquency at a startling pace. But the discourse surrounding juvenile delinquency was a malleable one and different explanations for its persistence proliferated. Many reformers, for example, defined delinquency as a problem of lower-class values and mass media infiltrating middle-class homes.[6] When describing urban delinquency, however, they tended to focus on how the social environment of the city corrupted youth. "The sad and dangerous truth," argued the journalist Harrison Salisbury, "is that the slums are only reservoirs and, perhaps, tradition setters for antisocial adolescent conduct at all social levels. Poverty increases the pressures which drive young people into blind revolt against the world. But it is not the cause of the revolt. Delinquency is a symptom, not a disease, and the disease knows no geographical and no social boundaries."[7] Because the social and geographic boundaries of 1950s America were in dramatic flux, the disease of delinquency appeared to many to be spreading. By the early 1960s the spatial distance between African Americans in the inner city and white suburbanites was well defined. Former white juvenile delinquents by then were part of a broader "youth culture" and their black counterparts too often described simply as urban criminals.

Invoking juvenile delinquency as the cause of violence at amusement parks, swimming pools, and roller rinks deflected attention away from deteriorating race relations in cities like Buffalo. In their report following the 1956 Crystal Beach riot, for example, Buffalo's Board of Community Relations identified delinquency as the chief cause of the riot, adding "ours is not a local problem, but one of national scope." Their recommendations included stricter parental control, police presence in public spaces, and "faithful and regular family attendance at religious services."[8] Yet such pronouncements masked deeper racial conflict in American cities. Young African Americans' anger and frustration with limited access to recreation reflected their exclusion from postwar prosperity. Black teenagers could not live in the same neighborhoods, shop in the same stores, eat at the same restaurants, or swim at the same beaches as their white counterparts. When African Americans did obtain access to these resources they often faced violent reprisals from white youth who zealously defended their territory, whether it was a city block or a bowling alley. At Crystal Beach white and black teenagers gave vent to their anger and anxiety and unintentionally created a national furor.

The Riot

It was hot, blessedly hot for a city known for long, frigid winters. Young Buffalonians had anticipated this day for months. They carefully prepared their pleated pants, ducktail haircuts, and saddle shoes for the park's opening day. As one Buffalonian described it, "Crystal Beach Amusement Park *was* summer," a site beloved by generations of western New Yorkers.[9] Traditionally Memorial Day at Crystal Beach brought together teenagers from throughout the city. They wore brightly colored club jackets on the opening day of the summer season, marking neighborhood, race, ethnicity, and class as distinctly as any census map or ethnography. In a city in upheaval these youth broadcasted their allegiances to create a temporary stability and to defend their turf.

On Memorial Day 1956 there was palpable tension in the air. Rumors flew that two rival African American gangs, one from the Ellicott District and another from Cold Springs, planned a showdown at the park—a showdown that never materialized. Some young men carried switchblades, knives, and the summertime weapon of choice—firecrackers. Most were prepared to use their fists if challenged. Nevertheless, Crystal Beach patrons experienced anticipation rather than trepidation that morning. Buffalonians boarded buses in the Fruit Belt, South Buffalo, Ellicott, and Parkside and headed to Shelton Square. Most walked from there to the nearby boat dock at the foot of Commercial Street, while others hopped on the streetcar to lower Main Street.[10] Gripping their coupons from the *Buffalo Evening News*, they bought their round-trip tickets for the *Canadiana*, 99 cents for adults, 35 cents for children. The ship was Buffalo's pride—huge and sparkling white, it was appointed inside with mahogany banisters, chandeliers, comfortable deck seating, and the largest ballroom of any Great Lakes steamer. "Noble and gleaming in the morning sunshine," remembered George Kunz, "the Canadiana seemed to me to represent the ultimate in luxury and pleasure."[11] It bore no resemblance to a humble commuter ferry but encased glamour and the joys of summer as travelers danced to swing music in the boat's large ballroom. By 1956 the *Canadiana*'s swing bands were gradually giving way to jump bands and early rock 'n' roll to the delight of Buffalo teenagers, but the *Canadiana* had lost none of its magic.[12]

After a forty-five-minute ride, the outlines of the amusement park emerged on the Canadian side. Rising above it all was the Comet roller coaster, the much-feared and loved high point of the park for a generation. The park itself was in the midst of a transition, broadening its appeal to the growing numbers of young families visiting in the midst of the baby boom. Buffalonians made up around 80 percent of the park's visitors, with the rest coming from Toronto and southern Ontario.[13] There was a Kiddieland available for the very young, and there were plans to refit the large ballroom at the center of the park as a roller rink. In the evening Ralph Marterie and his Down Beat Orchestra were slated to perform in the ballroom.

Racial tension flared only minutes after the boat docked. Three white servicemen taunted a group of African American teenagers with racial epithets. One young black man responded by pushing a white soldier into Lake Erie. Although the soldier's buddies quickly fished him out, news of this incident spread rapidly through the park.[14] By mid-afternoon park authorities closed the Old Mill ride around because "teen-agers were holding back boats midway in the ride by pressing their hands against the walls."[15] Around six o'clock a group of young African American teenagers heard that white boys were harassing a black girl at the picnic grounds. They rushed to defend her but found a group of belligerent white men in their early twenties, not the teenagers they expected. The teens quickly found older African American friends to join them and the brawling began in earnest.[16] Young men pulled knives from underneath jackets and fashioned makeshift weapons from broken bottles.

As the fighting escalated there were injuries that needed medical attention. One of the injured was a young African American boy whom the police brought to the park's first aid station. He was screaming—loudly. According to one account, "His screaming could be heard out on the lake, it was so loud and immediately it aroused the white people."[17] He was carried through the gathering crowds on a stretcher and loaded on an ambulance whose shrill siren "intensified the excitement." According to an investigation by the Board of Community Relations, the boy's friend "jumped to the erroneous conclusion that racial issues were involved and sought to avenge his friend's injury."[18] The boy's cries for help also alarmed black customers who gathered around the first aid station in the Picnic Grove just west of the park.

When the young boy first screamed, only four provincial officers were on hand, although twenty-five additional police later joined them. They arrested five African Americans, four in their late teens and early twenties and one fifteen-year-old. Canadian police also took four white men of Italian descent in their late teens and early twenties into custody. An NAACP investigation revealed that these arrests were arbitrary. After observing a "series of spontaneous fights," the park police "decided to file charges against the next bunch that started fighting."[19] Each had a knife or switchblade at the time of arrest, and one had a blackjack. When news of the arrests spread throughout the crowd, hundreds of African Americans marched to the guardhouse in protest. Around the same time other witnesses spied a group of white youths moving down the midway into the center of the park where they attacked an African American man walking with his wife and child.[20] This World War II veteran ended up with a badly bruised face "swollen almost twice its normal size" and a gashed lip. He later told reporters he had witnessed fifty to one hundred fights but had no idea why he was attacked.[21]

This stage of the riot, Canadian police concurred, was racially motivated. Officers blamed white men, rather than black teenagers, for escalating the violence, describing them as "absolutely intent to injure and maim any colored person in sight. . . . I can conceive of no more violent effort on anyone's part to create a disturbance or perhaps a riot."[22] It was, testified one, "racial discrimination by hooligans."[23] Indeed, a Canadian court later dismissed charges against the black defendants for "creating a disturbance" because of lack of evidence. But the day was not over. Soon the violence would escalate aboard the *Canadiana*.

The hot day had become sultry and threatening, and black clouds loomed over the lake. The managers of the *Canadiana* knew about the rioting and became increasingly concerned about the return trips that would ferry young Buffalonians home. The boat was running behind schedule, and the large crowd of teenagers began to grow restless. Black and white teenage girls taunted one another, while boys pushed and jostled.[24] Before allowing the youths to board the 9:15 P.M. boat, the crew carefully searched young men and confiscated knives and other weapons. But the etiquette of the era made physically searching teenage girls unthinkable, allowing them to squirrel away the young men's contraband. [25] Most of these young women were African American, as were the majority of the passengers on the *Canadiana*, about 80 percent of the estimated 1,200. George Hall, Sr., the owner of Crystal Beach, had noted the "increased number of colored persons" on that Memorial Day.[26] And one of the Italian men arrested at the park noted that blacks "went out there in numbers that day."[27] White patrons at Crystal Beach and on the *Canadiana* confronted the physical manifestation of black migration.

When the teenagers boarded the boat they segregated themselves by race and age. Ordinarily older riders gravitated to the top deck to get some sun during the day while teenagers went to the first and second decks to listen to the jukebox and play pinball.[28] With impending darkness and threatening weather this rule was reversed. Several dozen of the rowdiest young blacks took over the top deck and began running back and forth, hollering and throwing firecrackers. It was a "swarming beehive" of anger, enthusiasm, noise, and mayhem.[29] Others moved to the inside of the second deck where three rival black gangs from the Ellicott and Cold Spring districts, the Aces, the Frontiers, and the Lowes, began the fighting that many had expected to see earlier in the day.[30] Teenagers seeking shelter huddled in the dining room, avoiding the surrounding chaos, their ranks growing as the passage continued. Soon the *Canadiana*'s crewmen were roping off the lower decks of the ship for the "older passengers and their families."[31]

The violence began with young African American men fighting one another, but it was the young women who escalated the interracial violence on the boat. About ten African American girls began taunting young white counterparts, pulling their hair, ripping their clothing, and making them run in fear.[32] One white girl reported to the *Buffalo Evening News*, "They kept laughing at our shorts and began hitting us, they threw some of us on the floor. They were running up and down the decks. The Negro boys joined in and fights broke out all over."[33] Some, from East High, reportedly wore black and white corduroy jackets, others "khaki colored carhop coats."[34] They weren't known to be troublemakers; they had no disciplinary record at their schools and had not been in trouble previously.[35] But this night they were angry about the rioting in the park and took out their anger on their white counterparts. The white girls who were attacked later identified a whole spectrum of black girl gangs from their distinctive clothing. The Conservative Lovers, the Sweethearts, and the El Dorados wore Bermuda shorts and brightly colored yellow or purple jackets with their club name emblazoned on the back.[36] These jackets were worn with pride, a symbol of neighborhood, school, and race. But on May 30 they became a liability. Witnesses remembered not faces but clothing and skin color, and the media and investigators singled out young African American women wearing their club colors.

Buffalo's social workers and school administrators viewed club and gang jackets as symbols of juvenile delinquency. Indeed, school officials had launched a "dress right" campaign just the year before to encourage high school students to conform to middle-class standards of attire. Administrators called this campaign the "Buffalo Plan" and it was copied throughout the country.[37] The vivid descriptions of colorful clothing in the newspaper alarmed middle-class parents of urban youth who saw the "black" styles on their own children. Young African American women, however, hotly contested the characterization of their clubs as "gangs." The El Dorados, for example, were a social club affiliated with the Buffalo Urban League, a moderate civil rights organization. After the publicity they received they complained to the league that they "were not engaged in any disorder and had no part in it."[38] Furthermore, they explained to the league that no reporters had spoken directly to them about the events. But on this day whites made no fine distinctions between high school social clubs and dangerous youth gangs.

Riders' apprehension was heightened by the weather and noise as they crossed Lake Erie. Lightning split the sky, thunder boomed, and halfway back to Buffalo the skies opened to torrential rain. One young woman later interviewed by the FBI worried "that the boat was going to sink" from the rain and heavy wind.[39] Those outside on the top deck quickly sought shelter. In the crowded conditions below, African American girls pushed one another into white girls, beginning brawls that inevitably drew in male friends and brothers as protectors. Unlike the incidents at the park, there were few weapons aboard the boat, and injuries were thus fairly minor. But unlike the park, the boat was a closed space and most passengers, black and white, felt trapped and frightened. Those trying to escape huddled on the first floor deck, listening to the noise of the storm and fighting above them.

Figure 8. Police and an anxious crowd await the docking of the *Canadiana* on May 30, 1956, on its return from the Crystal Beach amusement park. *Buffalo Courier-Express*, May 31, 1956. Courtesy Buffalo State College Archives, Buffalo Courier-Express Collection and Buffalo and Erie County Historical Society.

The trip seemed interminable, but finally the *Canadiana* docked in Buffalo. The boat was met by twenty police officers who had been forewarned by a call from the ship's captain. During the trip the *Canadiana*'s first mate managed to detain three young African American men whom police promptly arrested. But their main task was to escort a group of thirty terrified young white girls to the No. 1 Precinct and place them under protection until their parents picked them up.[40] Five people were treated for minor injuries. One, Vincent Paladino, had been arrested at the park earlier in the day and had the most serious injuries; two other young men sustained more minor cuts and bruises. And two young white girls, ages fifteen and sixteen, were treated for bruises sustained after being tripped by rioters on the boat.

In interviews of whites by journalists and investigators in the riot's aftermath, what comes across is fear: of the storm that raged, of being outnumbered by a large group of young African Americans, and of gang violence they had read about in the paper and had been warned about by parents and teachers. When interviewed by the FBI, one young white girl admitted she had "suffered no injuries, other than being extremely frightened."[41] For white Americans such fear was injury enough. When surrounded by African Americans at the park while being placed in an ambulance, the badly injured Paladino thought he would be killed.[42] Whites riding the *Canadiana* on that stormy night felt surrounded by an angry and disgruntled mob that had invaded their city and now threatened even their ability to experience leisure.

Throughout the day there were repeated incidents and rumors of incidents involving young women who needed protection. The rumor that an African American girl was being abused by a group of white men at the picnic grounds brought black defenders to her side. White boys on the boat sought to protect their female friends from the abuses of African American girls. And when the boat docked the white girls were quickly swept into the waiting arms of parents and police. But young women on the *Canadiana*, black and white, were active participants in the events of Memorial Day and not merely the recipients of male protection. As the *Buffalo Courier-Express* reported, they were "gleefully aware that they were immune from search by male police officers."[43] Protected from police searches, they used their gender to bring weapons onboard and joined the melee. The visibility of African American girl gangs and clubs, with their distinctive jackets, led to their identification as the main instigators of the riots; however, the evidence that they were primarily responsible is limited. One FBI interviewee stated, "I saw a number of girls' gangs among the people there, but I did not see any of them taking part in the fights."[44] An image of white and black girls actively participating in the upheaval was unacceptable to the media and community leaders. For many whites, viewing young black women as violent assailants and young white women as passive victims more easily fit into prevailing stereotypes of gender and race. In descriptions of the riot, young African American women's racial identity prevailed over their gender identity. The media portrayed young white women, in contrast, as hysterical, weeping, and injured. Images of African American criminal behavior and violence crossed gender lines in 1950s Buffalo, but images of white victimhood were distinctly female.

The fear and near hysteria of the white passengers were captured by two young reporters, Margaret Wynn and Dick Hirsch from the *Buffalo Courier-Express*, whose stories were widely quoted nationwide. They, like many others, had spent most of the trip huddled below deck to escape the violence above. This made them eyewitnesses to the events but also severely narrowed their view of the riot. William Evans, the executive secretary of the Buffalo Urban League, blamed the "grossly exaggerated" account by Wynn and Hirsch for stirring up "a great deal of racial resentment."[45] For example, they reported that "nearly forty white youngsters, several beaten or cut, cowered below decks in the ship's dining room for most of the trip" despite the fact that only a handful of passengers required medical treatment. Wynn and Hirsch also focused on the aggression of African American girls throughout their report, blaming the violence on "gangs of Negro girls who walked the deck, attacking and molesting young white girls." Whites, in their eyes, were merely victims of "roving groups of Negroes" who "calmly attacked the outnumbered whites. Girls were beaten mercilessly and youths who attempted to defend them were slugged and kicked without feeling." In contrast to their descriptions of marauding black girls, Wynn and Hirsch consistently portrayed young white girls as the primary victims. They interviewed one white girl who "sobbed uncontrollably" and said, "'I don't even want to talk about it. Please go away. They'll get me when I get off the boat. I know they will. They'll cut me.'"[46] These descriptions of young white girls attacked by a black mob attracted nationwide attention.

The two-inch headlines broadcasting the riot that appeared the next morning in Buffalo's white newspapers emphasized the dangers faced by young white girls. By the following day most major urban papers carried at least some account of the events, and many had follow-up articles and editorials commenting on Buffalo's recreation riot.[47] This coverage contrasts sharply with the lack of media attention paid to violent white attacks on black protestors at Cincinnati's Coney Island or Cleveland's Euclid Beach. African American papers had a decidedly different take on the riot from white newspapers. In Buffalo the *Criterion* downplayed the racial aspect of the riot and avoided the incendiary language of the *Buffalo Courier-Express*. Drawing on information from a local minister, the paper argued that the riot began because "two Negro youth gangs that had fought once earlier in May decided to have a showdown battle on Memorial Day at the Beach and the whites were inadvertently drawn into the conflict."[48] The paper did not report on racial violence but instead chalked up the events to juvenile delinquency. The *Chicago Defender* placed the riot squarely in the context of youth culture with the headline, "Teens Rock and Riot on Cruise." "Large groups of teen-agers," it reported, "added to the confusion by running from one side of the boat to the other causing the 200 foot, three-deck vessel to rock."[49] This rather lighthearted description downplayed the severity of the riot and omitted any description of "gangs of Negro girls." But the terror of the *Canadiana*'s white passengers that night had struck a nerve—in Buffalo and throughout the country.

For many Buffalonians the riot marked the end of a period when they could revel in the moniker of the City of Good Neighbors. "Race relations in Buffalo has one of the best records of any place in the world," claimed the editors of the *Criterion*, "and what a few hoodlums have done should not be set down as a pattern to judge this relationship."[50] Generally, African American leaders and white liberals in the city were eager to blame juvenile delinquency for the riot and not view the event as a harbinger of worsening race relations. Compared to the image of black gang members that would emerge by the 1960s, a juvenile delinquent was a relatively benign figure. It was also a character that in the popular imagination was a troubled white teenager, depicted in 1955 by James Dean in the film *Rebel Without a Cause*. By claiming that racial strife was the result of juvenile delinquency, civil rights leaders made white teenagers equally responsible for the violence and tapped into a national discourse on the causes of social unrest that was unrelated to race. In contrast, the mainstream white press heightened fears of racial conflict and African American behavior in its coverage of the riot by focusing on black youth. Increasingly, African American teenagers embodied the dangers of urban life.

In his examination of riots at Brighton Beach, England, the sociologist Michael Brake describes the phenomenon of "deviancy amplification." Such amplification happens when the mass media describe rioting teenagers as "deviant folk devils" who are subsequently "identified and segregated" by authorities.[51] Gang members became the "folk devils" in 1950s urban America, and African American youths were the primary targets of attempts to "identify and segregate" delinquents. After the Crystal Beach riot, for example, officers searched teenagers before they boarded the *Canadiana* and managers increased the police presence at the park. The "deviants" identified in Buffalo's white newspapers were black youth, and by amplifying their culpability and threat, they marked the African American community as culpable and threatening. White city leaders sought to contain this threat through housing policies and school redistricting. Amusement park owners, however, were losing the goodwill of white consumers whose sense of safety and security was undermined by rioting and delinquency.

A Park Transformed

The Crystal Beach riot marked an irreversible transition point for Buffalo's premier amusement park. Unlike other parks, there was no one moment, an opening day after years of protracted struggle, when African Americans could walk freely through the park grounds. Instead, the recreation riot demonstrated to Buffalo's white community that not only the city but also its amusements had been transformed by migration. Commenting on the riot, a local psychologist suggested, "the situation flared because Negro teenagers found themselves in the unusual position of being in the majority and gave vent to long smoldering resentments and hostilities."[52] For some whites the *Canadiana* had become a symbol of a changing Buffalo, with white passengers trapped and outnumbered by angry African Americans. For blacks, however, the riot suggested that true integration would not be easily achieved in this northern city. For both groups Crystal Beach had become a stage on which they could enact their right to occupy public space and enjoy the fruits of postwar leisure.

For whites, urban amusement parks like Crystal Beach had been a retreat into homogeneity and safety carefully constructed by park owners who regulated the dress and demeanor of park visitors and kept racial and ethnic groups separate.[53] For recently arrived African American migrants, entrance into the park represented their arrival north, their reward for years of planning and saving. This park was not formally segregated and they could finally exercise their consumer rights. Longtime black Buffalonians had used the park alongside their white neighbors for a generation. For them racial conflict in the park was a giant step backward, a sign that black migration was changing their city and increasing racism. William Robinson, who participated in the riot, was told by his sixth-grade teacher that the incident "set back the Negro race fifty years."[54] Other longtime black residents shared this view and lamented the toll that increased delinquency was taking on the city's race relations. A set of norms had clearly been violated at Crystal Beach and Buffalonians, black and white, mourned the result.

Amusement park managers placed limits on the transgressive potential of their facilities so they could be marketed more effectively to white consumers. At Crystal Beach, park managers carefully monitored urban customers' behavior and prohibited alcohol consumption and gambling.[55] Within limits they also celebrated the diversity of park customers. In 1955, for example, the mayor of the town of Crystal Beach, Claude Brewster, bragged, "We have every nationality here." The journalist who interviewed Brewster went on to comment that the "populace may represent every race and creed, but to the casual visitor everyone looks alike—dusky Indians. Pale faces are most conspicuous at this summer playground and street clothes taboo."[56] This description highlights the liminal nature of the amusement park—visitors could safely transgress norms, dress in beach clothing, speak in loud tones, and mix freely with others—but only if the containment strategies employed by the park worked effectively, if people followed the basic rules and regulations and interacted peacefully. In this way the park maintained and marketed itself as an "imaginary landscape" separate from the city while dependent upon it.

Crystal Beach's location across an international border also reinforced its liminal position. Canadians like to contrast themselves with their southern neighbors as a haven of racial tolerance. This is particularly true in southern Ontario, where thousands of escaped slaves braved the waters of the Niagara River and Lake Erie to cross to freedom. The "North Star Myth"—that racial discrimination, violence, and segregation were uniquely American—has defined Canadian identity since the nineteenth century.[57] Indeed, there was no *Plessy v. Ferguson* in Canada. But free access to recreational facilities and other public accommodations was also not protected under Canadian law, and Afro-Canadians experienced their own Jim Crow in the North. Beaches along Lake Erie were one of the public spaces that blacks negotiated with care.[58] Crystal Beach, which was known for its white sand, was restricted to whites by custom until the mid-1960s. One black Buffalo resident remembered, "we wanted to go swimming but we just assumed that you couldn't go swimming"; his friend explained, "it was usually all white."[59] In the 1940s an attendant at the bathing beach would warn African Americans disembarking from the *Canadiana* that "niggers aren't allowed" on the beach.[60] Indeed, park managers used racial segregation to market the bathing beach. A 1934 advertisement for the beach declared that "safeguards" had recently been installed, including "a fenced enclosure guarded and patrolled" and "no admittance to undesirables."[61] Such statements reassured white visitors that they would not be subjected to the mixing of black and white bodies on Crystal Beach.

Park operators erected less explicit barriers to reduce the possibility of racial and ethnic conflict at Crystal Beach. Park attendance was carefully structured to conform to neighborhood divisions by designating days when specific Buffalo neighborhoods could attend the park, offering them discounts on the *Canadiana* and park fees. Thomas Rizzo remembered, "Booths were set up in the main intersection of the neighborhood so that you could pre-purchase your boat and amusement tickets, at a discount . . . and when your special day finally arrived, you felt you were going on an all day outing with your neighbors."[62] Vincent Paladino recalled going to Crystal Beach with those in his neighborhood.[63] With the exception of the beach, in the early decades of the park there was less need for explicit racial segregation, as Buffalo's African American community was relatively small. Before the mid-1950s one certainly could not imagine a boat ride on the *Canadiana* where the majority of customers were black.

Buffalo's demographic shifts transformed Crystal Beach and other spaces of leisure in the city. Increasingly white consumers viewed urban leisure as dangerous because of the presence of large numbers of blacks. At the same time, white urban dwellers moved out to surrounding suburbs and turned inward toward their television sets and away from older forms of leisure.[64] Responding to these changes, investors advised that new amusement parks and "kiddielands" should be located "along major highways," in "large shopping centers," and close to "large, middle-class housing developments."[65] Thus the spatial configuration of consumers was key to the economic decline of urban parks. Their traditional clientele was physically removed from the city and low-income people of color began to make up a larger percentage of their consumer base. In addition, these new customers depended on public transportation to carry them to the parks. The most effective way to maintain racial order in the minds of many park operators, therefore, was to cut off public transportation. In the case of Crystal Beach, ridership on the *Canadiana* declined dramatically after the riot, and by the end of the 1956 season the park was accessible only by car across the Peace Bridge. "That was the end of an era of going to Crystal Beach like that," remembered one black Buffalonian, "because, they ran the boat the rest of summer . . . but it was never the same."[66]

The riot wrought other changes at Crystal Beach as park management attempted to prevent future violence. The nearby village of Crystal Beach banned the sale of fireworks and policed its streets after complaints that "children here since last Wednesday have been playing riot. They are using lollypop sticks for switchblade knives."[67] The Buffalo police also agreed to begin regular patrols on the *Canadiana*, with special details on July 4 and other days with heavy patronage. In addition, no unaccompanied teenagers were allowed on the *Canadiana* throughout its last summer of operation.[68] Like other amusement parks, Crystal Beach was trying to attract families, not young adults who could potentially disrupt uneasy race relations in an era of integration.

The integration of commercial leisure was complicated by the changing racial geography of postwar cities. The spaces of leisure African Americans laid claim to were increasingly neglected and rundown as middle-class whites moved to the suburbs. As civil rights activists and black consumers desegregated urban amusement parks and the white consuming public saw them as racialized space they lost value, in much the same way property values were devalued in integrated neighborhoods. David Nasaw argues, "Even where there were no confrontations or only minimal and sporadic disruptions, some white patrons stayed away from the parks because they were now desegregated."[69] The white youth gangs who fought with young blacks at amusement parks such as Crystal Beach were reacting to this transformation, as they defended their spaces of leisure just as they defended neighborhood lines in cities. Attempts to cut off access to the parks by cutting off public transportation such as the *Canadiana* reinforced the sense that the park had to be defended from the increasing concentration of people of color. Working-class whites who could not afford to travel to the new theme parks were particularly angered by the changes in their local amusement park. The liminal space of the amusement park and bathing beach, a space of safety and play, had become part of the city and the city's problems. When the *Canadiana* stopped running after the riot in 1956, Crystal Beach was no longer the imaginary landscape of summer childhoods.

A City in Flux

The decision to dock the *Canadiana* remapped leisure in the city. Urban teenagers and young families had depended on the *Canadiana* for access to the park during the long summer months. Now those without access to cars would find themselves trapped in a city with few recreational facilities. At the same time, the center of the African American community in the Ellicott District was soon to become dramatically altered through an urban renewal project. This renewal project, and an ongoing public housing crisis, accelerated the exodus to the suburbs. Buffalo, a city known for its interethnic and interracial neighborhoods, was increasingly a city divided.

In the summer of 1956 Buffalo's Ellicott and Cold Springs neighborhoods, where the majority of the black teenagers who had been on the *Canadiana* lived, were in the throes of a dramatic transformation. Public housing and urban renewal displaced thousands of black families just as African American migrants began to pour into the city. Meanwhile white families were leaving Buffalo's Eastside to settle in the suburban communities springing up around the city's boundaries. As a result between 1950 and 1960 the number of black residents increased by 93.5 percent, but the total population of the city fell.[70] "The exodus to the suburbs is creating a city of non-whites concentrated in substandard housing areas, and a suburban population of so-called white groups," argued the Buffalo Urban League in its annual report for 1956. "The result of this heavy concentration means serious overcrowding with all of its by-products of crime, delinquency and other social disorders."[71] Because perceptions of African American crime and juvenile delinquency accelerated white suburbanization, black leaders became increasingly concerned about media coverage of black crime. Public perceptions of the city's Eastside as a rapidly declining neighborhood also created public support for a major urban renewal project that would prove devastating for the black community. The Crystal Beach riot happened at the crux of this crisis.

By the time of the Crystal Beach riot the Buffalo Housing Authority had already marked Buffalo's black neighborhoods for demolition. In 1949 the National Housing Act created a federally funded urban renewal program to raze dilapidated neighborhoods and sell the land to private developers. After years of planning, an all-white redevelopment board appointed by Buffalo's Common Council submitted a massive plan to the federal government in 1956, the same year as the riot. When the Federal Housing Administration (FHA) approved this plan the following year the city demolished thirty-six blocks in the Ellicott District and provided no further public housing for displaced families, 80 percent of whom were African American. They joined earlier migrants and moved to the north of Ellicott, while most of the remaining white ethnics moved to the Westside or to nearby suburbs. Also displaced by the redevelopment were over 250 small businesses that had formed the economic backbone of the black community.[72] In a 1958 article on the Ellicott redevelopment project in the *Wall Street Journal*, William Sims, the head of the Buffalo NAACP, stated, "Before long most of the city will be Negro, the suburbs white. That's segregation all over again."[73]

The neighborhoods surrounding the Ellicott District, where displaced black families and recent migrants settled, experienced increased racial conflict. A planning official working on the urban renewal projects noted in the wake of the displacement, "It was remarkable how fast the tensions started arising."[74] African American teenagers felt the brunt of this tension more forcefully than most Buffalonians. The media and local officials labeled them as troublemakers responsible for a spiraling juvenile delinquency problem. But these teens were facing the redistricting of their schools and often the removal of their families. In the face of these disruptions urban leisure took on a deeper significance for African American migrants. Their presence at Crystal Beach and on the *Canadiana* signaled their arrival in the North and expressed their rights as consumers in a flourishing city. But forcefully integrating nominally desegregated public accommodations such as Crystal Beach was a form of direct action that was met with resistance, even in the City of Good Neighbors.

African American leaders watched the results of urban renewal and white flight with apprehension. Any negative publicity about the African American community, they knew from experience, made the struggle against segregation more difficult. "The frequency with which Negroes are involved in crime," lamented the director of the Buffalo Urban League in 1955, "produces a public reaction which seems to be increasingly, potentially dangerous for the whole community."[75] A year later the "crime" of the Crystal Beach riot made front-page news. For black Buffalonians it was the worst possible timing. In 1957 the Buffalo Urban League protested, "the city is rapidly becoming more non-white, and the suburbs exclusively white." The result was "street fighting, disorder in public places, rowdyism and teenage clashes in school and street," which "definitely increased racial tension in our city."[76] The head of Buffalo's Youth Bureau in the 1950s, Richard V. Carnival, pointed to the same trend: "recently there's been a high incidence of gang fights pitting whites against colored—particularly in changing neighborhoods."[77] Whites

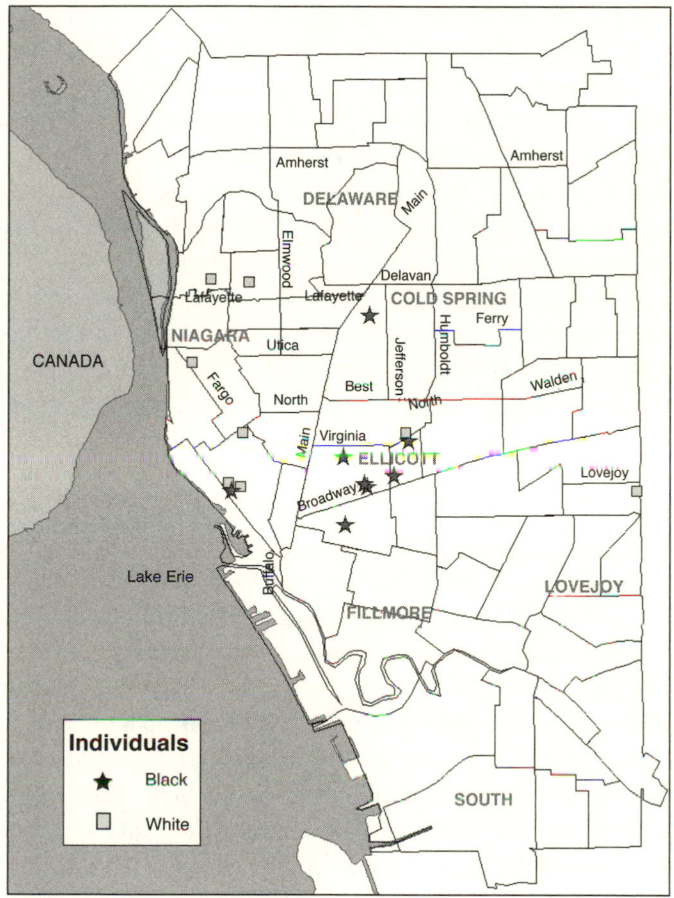

Figure 9. Map of Buffalo showing residences of individuals injured or arrested in the Crystal Beach riot in May 1956. Created by the author and Jin-Kyu Jung.

routinely justified their movement out of newly integrated neighborhoods by noting the increase in crime and delinquency. But it was, in fact, this rapid movement in the 1950s that heightened tensions across racial lines.

Mapping the residences of young Buffalonians involved in the Crystal Beach riot illustrates this dynamic. The African Americans arrested at the park and on the *Canadiana* lived in the Ellicott District, largely in the blocks surrounding the Willert Park Project. The whites arrested, who were primarily of Italian descent, lived in the Westside near Lasalle Park. However, a number of them lived in other Buffalo neighborhoods, including Robert Heberlein, who lived only one block from Maxwell McCullogh, an African American, on the Eastside. Heberlein was part of the dwindling German American community that had once dominated this neighborhood and was now leaving it in droves. Two young girls injured on the *Canadiana* were among the first generation of suburbanites in Buffalo living in Cheektowaga. These locations are suggestive—clearly African American families had significantly fewer choices about where to live than did their white counterparts. African American teens arrested during the riot lived on the Eastside, a fact noted in the newspapers, marking that neighborhood as potentially dangerous. White ethnic teens were disseminated more widely, reflecting the increased spatial mobility of their families throughout Buffalo and into nearby suburbs.

Yet many of these white urban youths lived and played with African American teenagers. "We still had white people in the neighborhood," remembered William Robinson. "Everybody knew some white people. You might have white friends or contemporaries in this thing or kids they went to school with."[78] In fact young Buffalonians were on the front lines of race relations in part because the schools they attended reflected their changing neighborhoods. The large student populations were unstable and eager to assert their territoriality in a changing city. Marking one's ethnic, class, racial, and neighborhood affiliations in these large public high schools was a daily pastime for postwar youth in Buffalo and other American cities. It was also a behavior that social workers, community leaders, and the media fixated on and gave a label: juvenile delinquency. These activities, and the publicity they engendered, were deeply rooted in the spatial reorganization of the city. With public housing, urban renewal, black migration, and ethnic succession came an enormous amount of social anxiety. Focusing on youth and their outward expressions of territoriality gave the public a more manageable set of problems to solve than discriminatory housing practices and deepening segregation. Control youth and restore Crystal Beach's reputation as a refuge and perhaps the City of Good Neighbors could be preserved.

Juvenile Delinquency in the Queen City

Buffalo's rapidly changing ethnic and racial demographics created a dilemma for city leaders who sought to stabilize social life in the city. As white ethnics moved into outlying neighborhoods or nearby suburbs and black families increasingly dominated the Ellicott, Masten, and Fruit Belt districts on the Eastside, Buffalo's large high schools experienced rapid demographic changes.[79] Some white working-class youth were able to move beyond the spatial limitations of neighborhood by taking advantage of the city's elaborate system of vocational schools.[80] The skilled trades, however, were reserved for the white working class; vocational schools barred African Americans, who were restricted to the increasingly segregated neighborhood high schools. African Americans also had little access to the city's private high schools, which were becoming increasingly popular among the city's white middle class. In 1954, concerned about the increased African American population, Buffalo's Board of Education redistricted the school system, announcing that all students living east of Main Street, the city's racial dividing line, would attend East High. This ensured that few blacks would attend the majority-white Hutchinson Central School and that East High would be increasingly African American as the remaining white population moved out of the Eastside.[81]

Despite the best efforts of the school board, Buffalo's large public high schools reflected the ethnic succession of the surrounding neighborhoods, bringing together white and black Buffalonians. Sandra Walker, whose high-school experience was shaped by redistricting, remembers that in high school young Buffalonians were often "with other ethnic groups for the first time."[82] William Graebner points out that racial conflict in urban high schools was more common among girls, who did not attend the segregated vocational schools. "By the mid-1950s," he argues, "physical encounters in which girls of one race were struck and knocked down by girls of another were a part of life in the neighborhood."[83] The violence of girls on the *Canadiana*, then, was an extension of daily violence experienced in Buffalo's schools. However, amusement parks offered even more opportunities for such conflicts as teenagers frequented them unchaperoned. Parks like Crystal Beach were also a stable geographic space that lay outside rapidly changing neighborhoods. For youth gangs, parks provided neutral territory where they could display physical prowess and racial allegiances. Thus, in amusement parks teenagers were free from their immediate neighborhoods and from their parents and teachers. They were free as well from the expectation of workplaces and schools, free to play and to fight.

When the Crystal Beach riot hit the front page of Buffalo's newspapers, a debate over whether it was a "race riot" or an instance of "juvenile delinquency" immediately ensued. Buffalo's Board of Community Relations insisted that delinquency had sparked the riot, simply characterizing it as an "outburst of teen-age hoodlumism with racial overtones."[84] Such pronouncements attempted to minimize the event and deflect attention away from deteriorating race relations in the city. The mayor of Buffalo and the Buffalo Urban League also took this stance. "We don't believe the affair was planned and therefore cannot be considered as such, a race riot," reassured one editorial in the *Criterion*.[85]

But for others urban juvenile delinquency was at its heart a problem of race. Richard Carnival stated immediately after the riot that "anyone who denies that there are tensions in certain areas of this city is either blind or dishonest."[86] Similarly, Victor Einach, Buffalo field representative for the State Commission Against Discrimination (SCAD), which the governor authorized to investigate the riot, attributed the violence to "a chip on the shoulder attitude among some Negroes and a reluctance to face racial issues on the part of some whites."[87] SCAD's characterization of the riot as primarily racial went against the local civil rights community's attempt to focus the public's attention on juvenile delinquency. Einach further angered the Buffalo Urban League when he referred to the "terrifying Memorial Day race riot at Crystal Beach" in a 1957 article in the *Buffalo Courier-Express*. Exasperated, William Evans wrote a letter to SCAD's chairman arguing that Einach had placed "the responsibility" for the riot "on Negroes" and was stirring up racial resentment in Buffalo.[88]

Evans was right to suggest that young black Buffalonians carried the weight of blame for declining race relations. City officials targeted juvenile delinquency among blacks as the city's central problem in the second half of the 1950s. Although in reality the number of youths arrested declined in the early 1950s from a high in the years immediately following World War II, Buffalo's Common Council created the Youth Board in 1955 to measure and police juvenile delinquency.[89] The board's reports, which were widely covered in the press, reinforced the public's perception that the African American Eastside generated the most crime in the city and that juvenile delinquency was rapidly destroying the social fabric of Buffalo.[90] The Youth Board connected delinquency directly to Buffalo's changing spatial organization by arguing that the city was "expanding" and "a characteristic feature of such expansion is the movement to the suburbs of some of the more stable elements of the population and the concentration within the city proper of less stable elements."[91] Social workers carefully charted those "less stable elements," noting that African Americans' arrest rate was significantly higher than that of whites. The board presented these statistics without any analysis of police brutality or the racial makeup of Buffalo's police force that patrolled black neighborhoods.[92]

In addition to analyzing the racial breakdown of juvenile delinquency, the Buffalo Youth Board also carefully examined gender dynamics in youth crime. Although generally not involved in violent crime, girls who lived in the "least favorable areas" of the city made up a larger percentage of female delinquents than boys in those neighborhoods. The Youth Board argued, "girls living in the most favorable socio-economic areas are expected to be much better behaved than boys, whereas in the case of girls in the least favorable areas, there is relatively less training and supervision in this direction." Given Buffalo's clear racial geography, the Youth Board was commenting on the prevalence of African American girls among the delinquent. Indeed they concluded, "there is a higher proportion of female offenders among Negroes than among whites."[93] The reporting in white newspapers that focused on young black women as instigators of the riot on the *Canadiana* reinforced the findings of the Youth Board that female delinquency was racial. Despite whites' prominent role in Buffalo's youth culture, police and parents viewed white girls primarily as victims. In contrast, officials viewed even the African American girls in the Urban League's El Dorado social club as gang members and delinquents.[94]

African American leaders responded to this negative publicity with calls for improved recreational facilities in Buffalo's Eastside.[95] With few options available to them, African American teenagers took advantage of church-based programs and commercial recreation to fill their leisure time. It was the latter that parents, teachers, and social workers targeted as potentially dangerous. Dance halls, roller rinks, and other spaces of leisure where young black and white Buffalonians met provided opportunities to heal racial rifts but could also be terrains of conflict. For many older white Buffalonians the prospect of young African Americans mixing socially with their sons and daughters also raised fears of interracial relationships. By 1956 those fears were particularly high as the Zanzibar Lounge, a rock 'n' roll club, had opened in the heart of the Ellicott District the year before. White and black teenagers flocked to the club to see Fats Domino, Bill Haley, Little Richard, and other emerging stars perform. Soon after the club's opening, a white disc jockey known as "Hound Dog" Lorenz broadcast these acts live on WKBW and sponsored auditorium shows similar to those produced by Alan Freed in New York City. As William Graebner argues, "Hound Dog represented the possibility of an interracial community based on a shared black youth subculture."[96] In the midst of a growing civil rights movement and rising rates of juvenile delinquency, community elites deemed that interracial subculture subversive. To them the Crystal Beach riot suggested that integration was not merely subversive but potentially destructive.

The policing of the interracial youth culture in the 1950s is aptly demonstrated by an incident that occurred in the spring of 1959. Clayton Johnson, an Afro-Canadian boy, had traveled from Toronto to Buffalo with forty-five classmates to take part in a local television program called *Dance Party*. During the show he danced with his white friend, another fifteen-year-old Toronto girl. Immediately telephone calls poured into the station demanding he be stopped. The master of ceremonies, Pat Fagan, forced the boy to leave and reportedly said, "when Buffalo teenagers appear on the program Negroes dance with Negroes and whites dance with whites."[97] Furious, Johnson left the station and walked for a mile in the rain to "cool off" after the experience.[98] He wasn't the only one left angry and frustrated. James Hemphill, the director of the Buffalo NAACP, wrote to the mayor, "If this is the practice of the City of Buffalo, then the Negro people in Buffalo are no better off than those Negroes who live in the deep South."[99] An editorial in the *Buffalo Criterion* also used the rhetoric of regionalism to lament that Fagan had "moved Buffalo to Atlanta, Georgia."[100] In this northern city interracial dancing might happen at one of the Hound Dog's auditorium shows or in the Zanzibar Lounge, but it could not be broadcast on live television. Two African American women pointed out the irony of the protest against public, as opposed to private, interracial mixing in a letter to the *Buffalo Criterion*: "It is far more desirable to have interracial couples dancing publicly in a wholesome chaperoned situation than to see numbers of white teen-age girls seeking out Negro men in the Negro neighborhoods; and conversely, to see white men obtrusively forcing their attentions on Negro girls at the various night spots as well as on the streets."[101] But for some white Buffalonians the very public nature of *Dance Party* made interracial mixing untenable, further diminishing Buffalo's reputation as the City of Good Neighbors.

The link between racial integration in commercial recreation and increased juvenile delinquency attracted the attention of the NAACP and other civil rights organizations. One of the chief issues targeted by civil rights leaders was the media's identification of delinquents' race, a widespread practice in Buffalo's newspapers and other media outlets. In 1955 the Buffalo Urban League argued, "The frequency with which Negroes are involved in crime . . . probably engenders more race prejudice than anything else in the metropolitan area. The press identifies only Negroes. Recently, the term 'white' has come into use which is less identifying, and singles out no one race or nationality."[102] In this case the Urban League recognized that the media viewed the city in black and white. No longer were Italian Americans, Polish Americans, or German Americans committing crimes; there were only two categories now. In a city where the African American population was rapidly increasing and whites left for the suburbs, ethnic conflict was supplanted by racial conflict in the media.

In 1958 the NAACP met to discuss "the effect upon our public relations of the widespread attempt to identify Negroes with criminality, particularly in view of the current wave of juvenile misbehavior."[103] The NAACP had to walk a fine line—to recognize publicly that juvenile delinquency was a problem in African American communities yet demonstrate that it was neither a uniquely black problem nor one caused by integration. In a letter to an NAACP member concerned about rising rates of juvenile delinquency, John Morsell, an officer in the national office, addressed this balance. "We are not so sure," he wrote, "that a specific action by us in connection with juvenile delinquency among Negroes would not do more harm than good. In the first place, we feel that the causes of crime are not racial." Yet Morsell also saw the need for local communities to address the issue. "In this way," he concluded, "we will be able to contribute whatever we can to solving the common problem without, at the same time, giving the opposition added grounds for saying that crime is a Negro problem."[104] In 1959 the Buffalo branch of the NAACP held a special panel discussion titled "What Approach Should Be Used to Curb Juvenile Crime?" in response to the national office's call for greater attention to the issue. Despite such public events the NAACP's attempts to dissociate juvenile delinquency from racial integration in the late 1950s proved futile. Opponents of the civil rights movement found ammunition to beat back integration any time the media publicized juvenile delinquency among African Americans. The Crystal Beach riot was no exception.

Civil Rights and Recreation

In a 1958 press release on juvenile delinquency the NAACP noted that "every incident involving Negroes and whites is cited by our enemies as an argument against non-segregated employment and non-segregated recreation."[105] After the Crystal Beach riot some of those "enemies," southern white journalists, arrived in the Queen City. "Press reports of 'race riots' in Buffalo gained national circulation," lamented the Buffalo Urban League. In the midst of the

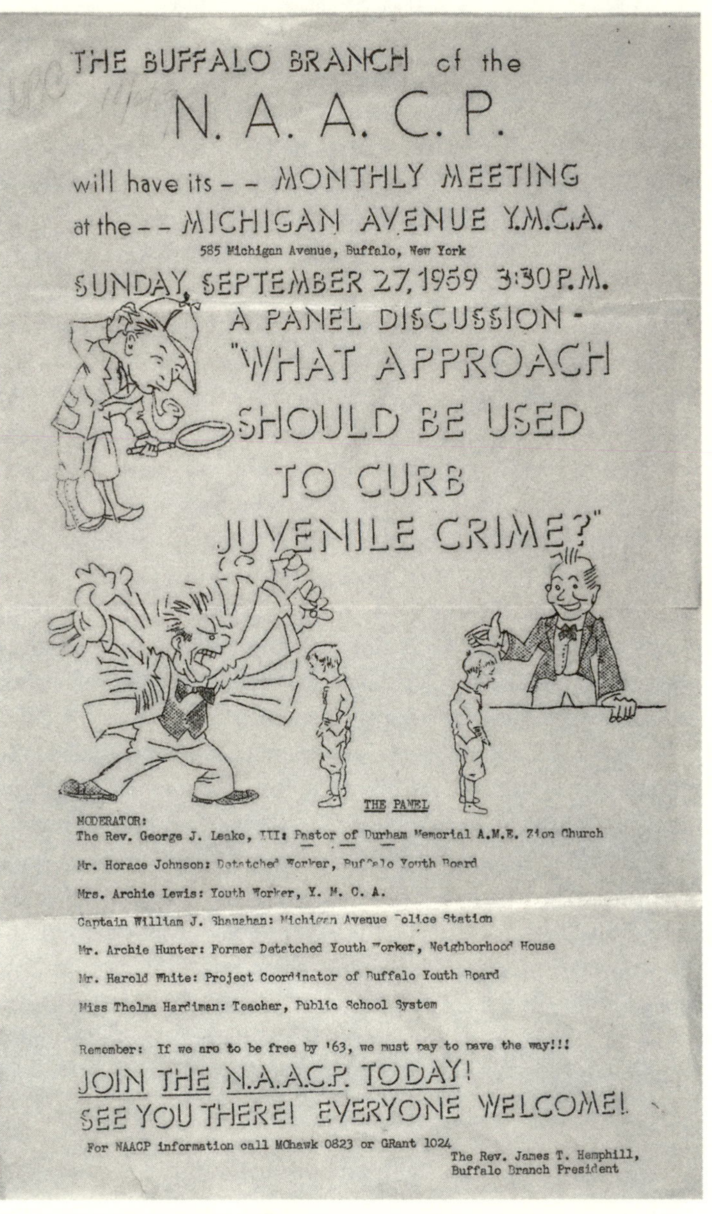

Figure 10. This 1959 flyer from the Buffalo chapter of the NAACP reflected the growing concern among national and local NAACP officials that juvenile delinquency undermined the struggle for civil rights. "What Approach Should Be Used to Curb Juvenile Crime?" Courtesy Library of Congress, Manuscript Division, Folder, "Buffalo, New York, 1958–60," Box 94, Series III, NAACP Papers.

Montgomery bus boycott and only two years after *Brown vs. Board of Education*, "newspaper reporters from the deep South came to Buffalo and wrote their own stories to prove that integration in education could not succeed."[106] African Americans in Buffalo were saddened that the publicity surrounding the Crystal Beach riot became ammunition in the southern struggle to maintain Jim Crow. Urban League officials' denial that it was a race riot was, in part, an attempt to offset the national press's focus on integration. Massive white resistance to civil rights had arrived uninvited at Buffalo's doorstep. At the same Urban League meeting where the Crystal Beach riot was discussed, William Evans reported that the national office had alerted him to the existence of "citizens' councils" in southern cities and suggested that they keep a watchful eye out for northern manifestations of these segregationist organizations. The national office was particularly concerned that white racists in Buffalo might take advantage of the Crystal Beach riot to foster racial hatred.[107]

The coverage of the Crystal Beach riot in the southern white press generally followed the lead of Buffalo's white newspapers. Headlines such as "Holiday Outing Turns into Voyage of Terror," "Negro Knifers Turn Outings to 'Nightmare,'" and "Flashing Knives, Sobs Mark Race Riot on Pleasure Boat" appeared in city papers across the South, often on the front page.[108] Some editors took the opportunity to use the riot to directly attack the civil rights movement. The *Memphis Commercial Appeal*, for example, ran an editorial stating: "When the Supreme Court began substituting sociological decisions for law, we suggested that if trouble resulted it would start more quickly elsewhere than in the South." The editors were clearly pleased to have been proven right. "The Buffalo area clashes should make all of us in the South more determined than ever to let orderly processes prevail."[109] But in fact orderly processes were not prevailing in the South during the summer of 1956. The Montgomery bus boycott was in its sixth month at the time of the riot, and in early April members of the local citizens' council attacked Nat King Cole while he was performing onstage in Birmingham, Alabama. The historian Brian Ward notes that white Alabamans in the beginning of 1956 "felt that the entire edifice of Jim Crow was under immediate and direct assault from both within and without the state."[110] Increasingly southern papers linked the perceived crisis of juvenile delinquency to the threat of integration by attacking rock 'n' roll and other manifestations of black culture. In the spring of 1956, then, Buffalo's Crystal Beach riot was another manifestation of racial integration's dangers.

White southerners' fascination with the Crystal Beach riot demonstrates the inextricable link between southern and northern segregation. In 1956 the *Nashville Tennessean* ran an editorial lamenting the "national tragedy" represented by the riot. "Pointing fingers at Buffalo now will neither obscure nor solve racial problems elsewhere," argued the editors. "Only if other cities look upon the unfortunate experience there as a warning to redouble their efforts to set their own houses in order will its meaning be captured." The "tragedy" of race no longer belonged to the South alone but was one "on which no city or section has a monopoly." Echoing this sentiment and frustrated by attempts to downplay the severity of the incident, the *Jackson Daily News* published an editorial titled, "They Can't See a Riot Unless It Is in Dixie."[111] In the 1950s southern newspaper editors often complained, as the historian Joseph Crespino points out, that "their northern counterparts sent teams of reporters to cover racial strife in the South while ignoring or minimizing racial disturbances in their own cities."[112] The southern mainstream press clearly felt vindicated by the Crystal Beach riot. Racial mixing in recreational spaces had led to violence, an inevitability in the eyes of many southern whites and a future they were struggling to forestall through massive resistance.

The widespread publicity given to the Crystal Beach riot reflected a national interest in the link between juvenile delinquency and civil rights. The media response to these events was clearly out of proportion to the scale of the confrontations. In contrast, when protestors at Cincinnati's Coney Island were brutally beaten and jailed in 1952 there was virtually no coverage in the local white newspapers.[113] Yet the violence at Crystal Beach, which was comparatively minor, was covered in the national media and perceived as a crisis by local political leaders. Clearly not all violence was created equal and the vulnerability of white consumers, particularly young white women, engendered a more powerful reaction from the white press than attacks on activists challenging the racial status quo.

The Birth of the Theme Park

By the 1950s consumerism was a central component of white Buffalonians' racial identity. Buying a house in a newly built suburb, driving to a shopping mall, or going to an amusement park were all privileges enjoyed by middle-class whites.[114] Integrating these spaces undermined their value in the eyes of postwar white consumers, including those who remained in the city. Buffalo was typical in not allowing African American bowlers to participate in league play sponsored by the American Bowling Congress, nor were there swimming pools in Buffalo's Eastside where young African Americans could cool off in summer.[115] When African American teenagers boarded the *Canadiana* to join their white neighbors at Crystal Beach they exercised their consumer rights and challenged the sanctity of segregated leisure. The actions of Buffalo's teenagers mirrored other attempts by civil rights activists and consumers to cross the color line in commercial recreation after World War II. These struggles sensitized the public, black and white, to integration at amusement parks, swimming pools, and other sites of postwar leisure. But as the process of desegregation accelerated, the parks experienced a physical and economic deterioration.

The decline of the urban amusement park in the late 1950s led to the rise of a new space of consumption and leisure: the theme park. The first theme park, created by Walt Disney, was a conscious attempt to provide American families an alternative to older parks such as Crystal Beach. The park opened on July 17, 1955, in Anaheim, California, which was populated primarily by orange groves but an easy drive from Los Angeles on the newly constructed Santa Ana Freeway. Those who analyze Disneyland—and there are many—tend to focus on its contrast to the older urban amusement parks, particularly New York's Coney Island. For example, the historian Eric Avila argues, "Extolling the virtues of consumerism, patriarchy, patriotism, and small-town Midwestern whiteness, Disneyland issued a set of cultural motifs that emphasized a retreat from the public culture of New Deal liberalism and instead asserted a privatized, suburban alternative to that culture."[116] Yet there was a significant amount of continuity in Walt Disney's image of a new "theme" park. Indeed, theming (carrying a motif through a park's exhibits) dates back to nineteenth-century world's fairs. At New York's Coney Island, Dreamland and Luna Park were both "themed" environments and Disney drew directly from these precedents. Early parks, including Coney Island, also featured lavish entrances and clear demarcations between the outside world and an interior fantasyland.[117] In addition, the desire for order, cleanliness, and safety had also been a major goal and marketing tool for urban amusement parks. Walt Disney visited Cincinnati's Coney Island, noted for its cleanliness, and consulted with its management before opening Disneyland.[118] And Disney's use of a private security force echoed the policing of visitors in amusement parks across the country.

The terms "privatized" and "suburban" are also commonly used to describe Disneyland, in contrast to the urban and more open culture of traditional parks. Historians have pointed to the advent of television and mass suburbanization in the mid-1950s as primary reasons urban parks began to decline. Americans, in this formulation, left urban amusements behind for the pleasures of private suburban homes and the television set. As Judith Adams argues, "Suddenly, the traditional lures of the local amusement park paled in contrast to the delights emanating from the small screen."[119] Indeed, park owners had become concerned about competition from television by the early 1950s.[120] But they quickly began to make use of the medium rather than viewing it as a threat. Riverview Park in Chicago began to televise advertisements in 1951, and Palisades Park brought in television personalities and staged television "giveaways" in the early 1950s. In 1952 New Jersey's Olympic Park introduced a television theater with seven large sets available for continual viewing.[121] Walt Disney took advantage of television more than any other park owner. His broadcast of the television show *Disneyland*, which premiered in 1954, financed the opening of the new park, and visitors arriving at Disneyland were already familiar with its characters through television and movies.[122] Disney constructed on a large scale what other park owners were attempting to do on a smaller scale: use the new medium to draw visitors to the park. In 1952 *Billboard* magazine reported, "Edward L. Schott, of Coney Island, Cincinnati, said TV is here to stay but that park men need not be fearful of it as a competitor because the medium cannot give the sense of participation that parks can provide for customers."[123] Schott's analysis was correct. Americans craved crowds—as long as they were orderly and unthreatening.

In the 1950s suburban Americans did not simply retreat into their private living rooms to watch television and live atomized, cocooned lives. Indeed, recent work on suburbanization suggests that suburbs were more complicated and more communal than critics have portrayed them.[124] Suburban, middle-class Americans sought out the experience of anonymity and pleasure within huge crowds. Disney provided this in a hypersanitized and controlled environment. As Michael Sorkin suggests, "Disney invokes an urbanism without producing a city."[125] Disney's Main Street, the first theme area park visitors encountered on entering, was an idealized image of an American downtown—without crime, dirt, or disorder—but it was not an image that promoted suburban shopping malls or office parks as an ideal. Disneyland was—and still is—a walking city and a model for New Urbanists seeking to promote livable spaces for postwar Americans.

But if Disneyland was not the antithesis of urbanity or a promotion for privatization, what made it truly distinct from the urban amusement park? Geographically it was cut off from the city, not accessible by public transportation. In stark contrast to the overcrowded and chaotic conditions on the *Canadiana*, visitors to Disney arrived primarily by private car, parking in the one-hundred-acre lot.[126] This blocked off access to the urban working class and teenagers unable to drive. Visitors to Disneyland also paid an entrance fee at the gate. This was an easy means of establishing class segregation and discouraged the arrival of unattended teens or working-class families who wandered the grounds.[127] Once within the park visitors were also carefully controlled. There were no sprawling picnic grounds where families could bring food from home or teenagers could congregate. Instead crowds were carefully ushered from one attraction to the next.[128] Park guards wore blazers, carried no weapons, and blended into the crowd, but they were always vigilant for signs of disorder, politely escorting troublemakers out of the park. Disney hired men who worked as schoolteachers and coaches and had experience working with teenagers—the primary cause of potential trouble.[129] These well-mannered, educated guards did not resemble the hired thugs at Euclid Beach or Cincinnati's Coney Island. The difference was a matter of degree; Walt Disney took the old mandate of amusement park managers to create safe, clean environments and made it into a science. Remarkably he did so without explicitly excluding any racial groups.

There is some debate over whether Disneyland was a segregated park at the time of its opening in 1955. Eric Avila asserts that the only blacks in the park were those performing in its exhibits, such as the Aunt Jemima House on the banks of Rivers of America. He views Disneyland as the quintessential white space in postwar America: "Placing his theme park in a suburban location, removed from the inner-city concentration of racialized poverty, Disney used racial representations to underscore the sense of whiteness that took shape along the suburban periphery of the metropolis."[130] While acknowledging the racist depictions of African Americans in Disneyland exhibits, the historian Susan Sessions Rugh argues that "Disneyland was a product of its times in conveying a racialized America in its stereotypes of African Americans, but it was in the forefront of opening its gates to anyone who wanted to be amused by its imaginary world."[131] The reality was that Walt Disney needed no explicit racial segregation to create a relatively homogenized middle-class white consumer base. He had learned the lessons of recreational segregation extraordinarily well and created an environment that was almost immune to racial conflict. Disneyland could afford to be color-blind because of careful planning. The gate fee, park guards, and crowd control were all part of that planning, but these were elements present in other amusement parks that did see racial conflict or had explicit segregation rules. More significant was Disneyland's isolation from the city, its lack of accessibility, and the absence of facilities that had most provoked racial conflict throughout the twentieth century.

Disneyland was notable in 1955 not only for the novelty of themes within the park and the exhibits innovated by Disney and his company. It was notable for the absence of hot spots of racial conflict—swimming pools, dance halls, and roller rinks. There were no rock 'n' roll dance parties in 1950s Disneyland. Disney chose the park's location, inland from the beautiful Pacific coast, because he recognized the dangers of racial mixing at bathing beaches.[132] Within the park there were no spaces where men and women could dance or swim together, eliminating concerns about interracial sexuality that sparked internal park segregation throughout the North. Privatizing particular facilities within the park, creating fictitious private clubs, or hiring a phalanx of lawyers to stave off civil rights lawsuits were simply not necessary. The Disney example demonstrates the extent to which segregation was never simply about the law. Walt Disney's greatest accomplishment may have been creating a regulated, controlled, and clean space without conflict. "The theme park presents its happy regulated vision of pleasure—all those artfully hoodwinking forms—as a substitute for the democratic public realm," argues Michael Sorkin, "and it does so appealingly by stripping troubled urbanity of its sting, of the presence of the poor, of crime, of dirt, of work."[133] For some white consumers, African American teenagers embodied the poverty, crime, and dirt of cities and their presence in parks devalued urban leisure. Disney's theme parks, in contrast, provided the cleanliness and safety that traditional parks increasingly lacked. It was fitting, then, that Disneyland successfully completed its first year at the time of the Crystal Beach riot.

* * *

Disneyland and Crystal Beach were both liminal fantasylands. Crystal Beach was across a deep river and in another country, far away from the workaday life of midcentury Buffalo. Disneyland was a trip down a freeway into a world seen only on television sets and movie screens. Despite these similarities it was Disneyland that was more successful at transporting its visitors outside the mundane. Because it was new and expensive, could not be reached by public transportation, and carefully controlled its visitors' experience, Disneyland had no recreation riots. And Disneyland drew its customers from throughout the nation, even the world, in contrast to Crystal Beach's dependence on nearby Buffalo. Therefore, Disney's customers did not bring a specific city's neighborhood conflicts into the park. In contrast, Crystal Beach and the *Canadiana* were staging areas for Buffalo's racial clashes. The 1956 riot occurred just as racial and ethnic succession were reaching their height in the city. At the center of these transformations were young teenagers, black and white, who carefully negotiated the city's large public high schools and rapidly changing neighborhoods. When large numbers of African American teenagers flocked to Crystal Beach in 1956, white consumers felt deeply threatened. The violence that broke out seemed to confirm white fears that the city had become increasingly unstable and vulnerable to outbreaks of black juvenile delinquency. Those fears were reflected in the national interest in the Crystal Beach riot. White southerners viewed it as justification for continued resistance to integration and evidence that racial problems were not uniquely southern. White northerners were mesmerized by the images of young white girls beaten and terrorized.

African American consumers of leisure had long been on the forefront of the struggle for open public accommodations. Every NAACP lawsuit began with a complaint from an African American mother who was angry about her child's exclusion or from a minister frustrated that his church outing met closed gates. But when the gates opened to blacks the struggle did not end. Many African Americans, particularly teenagers, confronted enormous anger and violence when they used recreational spaces, and they often fought back. The recreation riots in Chicago's parks and Buffalo's Crystal Beach during the mid-1950s reflect this reality. The violence devalued the facilities, which whites increasingly viewed as dangerous and emblematic of urban life, in contrast to the relative safety of suburbia. As the civil rights movement accelerated with the student movement, the confrontations between adolescents in public spaces were put in a new, more politicized, context. Demands for access to public accommodations galvanized young African Americans and sympathetic whites in the early 1960s. Many of these struggles are deeply familiar to us, such as the student-led sit-ins at lunch counters in southern cities. But the powerful student movement reached North and West and was the culmination of decades of nonviolent organizing. As in those earlier struggles pioneered by CORE activists, this movement sparked brutal reprisals by whites angered by the loss of "their" recreation. That violence gave the movement greater moral authority, but it also marked the limitations of political activism.

CHAPTER 5

Building a National Movement: Students Confront Recreational Segregation

SOON after Disneyland opened, a real estate developer from Texas, Angus G. Wynne, Jr., visited the park. Impressed by its popularity, Wynne decided to create his own theme park between Dallas and Fort Worth. Wynne's theme centered on the history of Texas. He flew six flags over his park representing the six flags in Texas history—those of Spain, France, Mexico, the Confederacy, the Republic of Texas, and the United States. Wynne divided the park into different themes corresponding to each flag, including a Confederacy section featuring a Confederate recruiting station and reenactment of romantic "old South" scenes. Confederate reenactors even demonstrated an execution of a captured Union spy at the park in its opening year.[1] Wynne's use of theming at his new park reinforced its racial exclusivity. African Americans were unwelcome at Six Flags, although there was no official policy of segregation as there was in Playland in Houston. Armed Confederate soldiers underscored this reality. Like Disneyland, Six Flags was accessible only by automobile, and Wynne promoted the park as a clean and safe alternative to older amusements in urban areas. In its unproblematic promotion of a Confederate past, Six Flags looked back to a southern history marked by racial apartheid; but in its location and amenities Six Flags was on the cutting edge of new suburbia.[2]

Wynne was not the only entrepreneur to be influenced by Disneyland. Rock 'n' roll pioneer Chuck Berry purchased land thirty miles outside St. Louis in 1957 to create Berry Park, which he opened in 1960. "I'd imagined it to be a place where people both black and white could mix together harmoniously," remembered Berry in his autobiography. "I was thinking of a place like Six Flags, but maybe only 'One Flag' in my case, to accommodate families for fun and entertainment." Berry wanted to create his "own mini Disneyland" outside the city limits with sprawling, well-groomed grounds. But this Disneyland would invite black consumers and promote interracial mixing.[3] Berry Park sported a large guitar-shaped swimming pool, nightclub and dance floor, and an assortment of rides.[4] These modern amusement parks drew from Disney's innovative theming and his placing of parks outside cities. But they offered dichotomous models of racial democracy within recreational spaces in the South. Through its celebration of a Confederate past, Wynne's Six Flags signaled to white consumers the safety and pleasure of a new generation of amusement parks. Berry Park, in contrast, invited all races to enjoy the fruits of a new rock 'n' roll subculture, a youthful racial democracy inscribed in the landscape of the park. These competing visions of the theme park presaged a new decade of racial conflict over recreational space in the South and nationwide.

While Six Flags, Disneyland, and Berry Park distanced themselves from urban problems, older amusement parks throughout the country confronted growing racial strife in the early 1960s. Most parks in southern and border states were at least partially segregated, and they increasingly faced direct challenges from a growing militant youth movement. Outside the South, where historians have generally considered integrated public accommodations a settled issue by the early 1960s, struggles over access to recreational facilities continued and in some cities became more violent.[5] The rhetoric of regionalism, with African Americans shaming cities like Los Angeles or Chicago by comparing them to Alabama, demonstrates that there was significant continuity across state lines. White thugs brutalized blacks in both Birmingham and Chicago when they threatened white-only pools and parks. Nationally student activists deployed the nonviolent direct action techniques pioneered by CORE in the 1940s to resist this brutality. Although racial liberalism continued to play a role in the African American freedom struggle, particularly within interracial commissions on the local level, it had largely become supplanted by more militant demands for immediate access to public accommodations rather than gradual negotiations. Joining the student activists were ordinary black citizens who occupied beaches, parks, and pools without deploying the well-honed techniques of nonviolence. In both cases direct action inspired brutal white attacks on demonstrators and citizens. White proprietors of recreational facilities also responded to direct action and legal challenges by privatizing and closing their pools and parks. These actions denied urban dwellers access to basic recreational facilities and would have long-ranging effects on American cities and towns. Combined with violence and white boycotts of desegregated facilities, massive white resistance to recreational integration shaped the path of the civil rights movement and the extent to which African Americans could exercise their legally enshrined freedoms.

The South Rises

In 1956 a group of African Americans in Greensboro, North Carolina, sued the city for refusing them access to the Lindley Park Swimming Pool. To ensure the white citizens of Greensboro would not have to tolerate integrated swimming, the city promptly sold the pool.[6] Four years later, on February 1, 1960, four young black college students from North Carolina Agricultural and Technical University entered a Woolworth store in Greensboro. After buying some school supplies they sat down at the white-only counter and ordered coffee, much to the consternation of the employees, who refused to serve them and closed the store early. Within a week the four were joined by hundreds of students in Greensboro protesting segregation at local lunch counters and restaurants and subjecting themselves to increasingly brutal beatings. Within a month a mass sit-in movement dominated headlines and galvanized activists throughout the country. Two months later students and their allies gathered at Shaw University and formed the Student Nonviolent Coordinating Committee (SNCC). The media attention and wide scale of the sit-ins was new in 1960, but the tactic and the goal were nearly twenty years old. CORE activists working in Chicago in 1942 initiated nonviolent sit-ins as a method of forcing integration of public accommodations, and even in the South such demonstrations at recreational facilities accelerated after 1954. The historian Aldon Morris notes that sixteen southern cities experienced sit-ins between 1957 and 1960.[7] The student movement was built on a firm foundation of nonviolent activism that was national in scope.

The privatization of Greensboro's Lindley Park Swimming Pool, which was upheld by the courts, marked the limits of state power to enforce integration. The U.S. Court of Appeals ruling on the Greensboro case noted, "a municipality may not exclude, on account of race, members of the public from the use of any of its facilities."[8] But the pool was no longer controlled by the city, and local activists hit a legal brick wall in their attempt to access basic recreational services. Selling municipal facilities in order to privatize them raised cash for local governments while ensuring that racial apartheid remained intact. Many southern municipalities employed this profitable strategy in the late 1950s when faced with growing activism within their black communities and new legal precedents in the courts.

In some cases city officials were divided on how to respond when challenged by black consumers and activists to desegregate recreational facilities. During the late 1950s Florida was a hotbed of civil rights activism focused on the state's beaches, pools, and parks. In Miami, local blacks and CORE activists pressured the city manager to desegregate the city's pools after two African American women attempted to swim at the city-owned Manor Park swimming pool in the fall of 1959. Within twenty-four hours the city commission adopted a resolution banning blacks at the city's pools, basing their decision on a state law mandating the segregation of "sanitary and washroom" facilities. The pools could be integrated but the washrooms could not, and blacks could not swim without potential damage to public health.[9] Fearful of the rising scale of protest, Florida's legislature authorized the sheriff of any county to close temporarily "any public beach, pool or other public recreation facility within his jurisdiction when disorderly conditions exist or threaten to take place."[10] This order was implemented throughout the state as nonviolent activists and ordinary black citizens directly confronted the taboo of integrated swimming in the Sunshine State.[11]

Despite the new legislation, African Americans throughout Florida continue to challenge segregation of parks, pools, and beaches. In Tampa, local blacks staged a series of attempts in 1959 to enter Lowry Park, which boasted a small zoo and Fairyland—a maze of paths surrounded by concrete statues of fairy-tale characters. After being repeatedly escorted out of the park by police, African Americans began to negotiate with the city, which offered a typical compromise of access to the park either one day per month or one weekend per month. Local blacks rejected the offer and the newly elected mayor insisted that the "traditional practice" of recreational segregation be maintained. He also appointed a biracial committee to begin negotiations for gradual integration. But Tampa had no statute mandating segregation in its public parks and no legal basis to keep African American children out of Fairyland. Instead, the city based its enforced apartheid on the threat of violence, and the courts agreed to uphold segregation when African Americans filed suit. The U.S. District Court ruled, "The plaintiffs' constitutional right to use and enjoy the parks, playgrounds and recreational facilities on an equal basis with the White citizens in the community does not encompass a right to cause a disturbance, thereby infringing upon the rights of others to peacefully enjoy and use said parks, playgrounds and recreational facilities."[12] As long as city officials claimed to be working toward integration, the constitutional rights of Tampa's African American children stopped at the rainbow bridge leading to Fairyland.

Such challenges to recreational segregation prior to 1960 were not limited to Florida. Court records reveal numerous attempts to open up parks and other facilities throughout the South before the student movement dominated the nation's headlines. At Sylvan Beach Park near Houston, four African American men drove up to the gate for a day of fishing and swimming in late May 1958. The attendant told them to return on June 19 when white patrons would be banned from the park.[13] In Montgomery, Alabama, two years after the successful resolution of the bus boycott that launched Martin Luther King, Jr., into the national spotlight, the city attempted to draw the color line at the pools and parks. The boycott and Supreme Court ruling had ended segregation on the city's buses, but recreational segregation was still rampant. Eight local African Americans, emboldened by the success of the bus boycott, filed a lawsuit in federal district court to fully integrate the city's public parks. In response the Board of Commissioners closed twelve of the parks because "this attempt poses grave problems involving the welfare and public safety of all the citizens of the City of Montgomery."[14] Many southern towns and cities would utilize this extreme response in the face of court rulings and federal legislation mandating desegregation.

Challenges to southern recreational segregation did not always fully embrace nonviolence. In the late 1950s Robert Williams, a black veteran and activist, reinvigorated the local chapter of the NAACP in Monroe, North Carolina. When a young African American boy drowned in a nearby lake in 1957, Williams's chapter took up the cause of desegregated swimming. An inevitable and deadly result of racial exclusion was the drowning of young blacks swimming in natural waters to cool off from the summer's heat.[15] Monroe's local pool had been built with federal New Deal funds, and the activists pointed out to the town's Board of Recreation that the Supreme Court rulings following *Brown* prohibited segregated swimming in facilities supported by public money. When the city failed to offer any concessions Williams led a group of eight African American youths to the pool where they engaged in a CORE-style stand-in. The local Klan responded with death threats, and armed whites drove through the black community to intimidate the activists. Monroe's white liberals quickly distanced themselves from Williams, appalled that he chose to tackle the most taboo form of integration and fearful of the growing white backlash in town. On an October night, after a huge Ku Klux Klan rally, a group of Klan members fired at the homes of NAACP members. Williams and his friends fired back, forcefully defending themselves and driving the Klan away. For the next four summers Williams continued to lead demonstrations at the pool, confronting increasingly angry white crowds and occasional gunfire. By the summer of 1961 the confrontations had escalated to full-scale battles and the city decided to drain and close the pool to end the pickets.[16] Williams's courageous decision to challenge swimming segregation in 1957 and to face violence with armed self-defense suggests a broader willingness of southern blacks to directly confront segregated recreation before the mass student movement gained public support.

After the Greensboro sit-ins and the formation of SNCC, wade-ins, stand-ins, and sit-ins at southern recreational facilities became a weekly occurrence. As in the case of Monroe, where the Klan rallied around the defense of segregated swimming, protests at beaches and pools sparked some of the most violent confrontations of the civil rights era. Local blacks had long coveted beautiful Biloxi Beach on the Mississippi Gulf Coast. In the late 1950s NAACP activist and local physician Gilbert Mason spearheaded a drive to integrate the beach, calling his campaign Operation Surf. In late April 1960 over one hundred African Americans, many of them children, attempted a wade-in of the beach despite the smoldering remains of a Klan cross that had burned the previous night. They were met by a white mob wielding blackjacks, pipes, and clubs who viciously beat them. The riot spread into the nearby town and lasted well into the night.[17] Operation Surf was a grassroots endeavor, with no national civil rights organizations' involvement. But the riot sparked an investigation by Medgar Evers, Mississippi's NAACP director. His report on Biloxi led the national NAACP to issue a call to arms to local branches throughout the country to use public beaches. Roy Wilkins, the national secretary of the NAACP, wrote to local activists, "This mob action not only violated the basic human rights of the Negroes, who were molesting no one, but also their constitutional rights."[18] Those rights had been spelled out in the Baltimore swimming cases that determined public beaches could not be segregated. It was time to put these rulings to the test on southern beaches.

Of all the civil rights organizations, CORE had the most experience holding interracial beach "parties." In 1960 they brought the parties to southern coastlines, including Miami, where they occupied several city beaches. In addition, they held a party at Virginia Beach, the segregated black Dade County beach with a large "For Colored Only" sign at the entrance. After some confusion black beachgoers welcomed the white newcomers. One white CORE staffer reported, "Color consciousness was washed away with the waves."[19] Nearby Fort Lauderdale experienced its own wave of beach parties and wade-ins the following summer. This time the local NAACP organized the protests, spurred by lack of easy access to the county's only black beach, Dania Beach. On July 4, Independence Day, the activists occupied Fort Lauderdale's popular white beaches, the backdrop of the 1960 spring-break movie *Where the Boys Are*. The wade-ins continued throughout July, in ever-escalating numbers, with no major incidents. By August local police began arresting demonstrators for "disturbing the peace" as organizers shuttled carloads of interracial beachgoers to the mile-long stretch of white sand. Remarkably, the only lawsuit in this case was filed by the city, which attempted to enjoin the NAACP from further wade-ins. They also named a white supremacist organization in the suit in an attempt to appear evenhanded. The lawsuit failed, and African American college students slowly began to join their white counterparts on Fort Lauderdale's beaches.[20]

By the early 1960s, southern communities like Fort Lauderdale had to choose to desegregate their swimming facilities, close them down, or privatize them. Because beaches could not be easily closed or privatized, activists often achieved desegregation, although only after protracted battles. Swimming pools, however, continued to serve as central battlegrounds in the legal and physical war over coveted recreation. As Baltimore's Judge Thomsen had intoned in 1954, swimming was "more sensitive than schools" and therefore the threat of violence could undermine the growing efforts of activists to use their now well-established constitutional rights. In a case that combined swimming and schools, when Houston instigated a modest school integration plan in 1960, the school board voted to eliminate swimming pools in any new schools and canceled interscholastic swimming events.[21] But urban public pools posed a more difficult challenge for city officials. In Charlotte, North Carolina, for example, the chairman of the Charlotte Park and Recreation Commission admitted in 1960 that "all people have a right under law to use all public facilitates including swimming pools." But he went on to point out that "of all public facilities, swimming pools put the tolerance of the white people to the test." His conclusion was predictable: "Public order is more important than rights of Negroes to use public facilities and any admission of Negroes must be within the bounds of the willingness of white people to observe order or the ability of police to enforce it." In practice black swimmers would not be admitted to pools if the managers felt "disorder will result."[22]

Swimming pools were often the "special case," even in relatively liberal cities, where officials advocated an extraordinarily slow process of mediated desegregation. The trade publication *Amusement Business* noted in 1961, "Amusement and recreation facilities are nearing complete integration in the South's three most progressive cities, Atlanta, Nashville and Dallas, after a summer of increased desegregation activity by Negro and white groups. The only facilities not integrated even on paper in the three cities are swimming pools."[23] Dallas desegregated parks, golf courses, and other recreational facilities in 1961 but explicitly left public pools out of their agreement with civil rights leaders.[24] While Atlanta had led the way in desegregating southern golf courses in the early 1950s, swimming pools proved to be a more intractable issue. By 1962 all municipally owned parks in the city were desegregated, but the pools remained white-only. When the city finally desegregated pools the following summer, under court order, most whites abandoned them altogether, retreating to private facilities. [25] In Nashville, when a 1961 wade-in followed by a lawsuit forced the city to desegregate their pools in 1963, officials promptly closed them. After angry protests by local whites eager to swim in the hot southern summer, the city proposed reopening the pools with a plan to have whites and blacks use them on alternating days. This would require, in the logic of bodily pollution that often accompanied fights over integrated swimming, changing the water in the pools each evening.[26] This plan was eventually rejected and the pools remained closed.

Many cities followed Nashville's model by closing pools altogether in the face of legal rulings demanding desegregation, even before the 1964 Civil Rights Act. In Lynchburg, Virginia, African Americans approached city officials asking that the city's pools be desegregated. The city denied their request and announced that all pools would close if any African Americans attempted to swim in the white pools. Defying this threat on Independence Day 1961, blacks jumped into a white pool and the city promptly closed down all pools. Lynchburg's city officials saw the writing on the wall; they could not legally maintain a segregated facility. Indeed, the federal district court demanded the city end the policy of pool segregation in response to a class-action suit, but they could not force Lynchburg to reopen the pools.[27] The summer of 1961 also marked a recreational uprising in Memphis, Tennessee, with similar results. The city had outlined a gradual recreational desegregation plan, over a ten-year period, citing the "maintenance of law and order" and "avoidance of confusion and turmoil" as justification for the slow pace of change.[28] Black residents asked the U.S. District Court to order immediate desegregation of recreational facilities, but to no avail. Two years later, however, the Supreme Court reversed this decision, arguing that there was "no indication that there had been any violence or meaningful disturbances when other recreational facilities had been desegregated." The constitutional rights of Memphis blacks, argued the court, "may not be denied simply because of hostility to their assertion or exercise."[29] But there was an easier way to deny the constitutional rights of African Americans: close the pools. Recreational massive resistance on the part of city officials easily subverted the court ruling.[30]

In the wake of the Biloxi Beach riot, African Americans in Jackson, Mississippi, faced a similar brick wall in their attempts to desegregate pools. But in contrast to Memphis, city officials had the federal district court on their side and did not have to resort to closing the pools at the first sign of danger. The district judge ruled in 1962 that any segregation in Jackson was purely "voluntary" and "members of each race have customarily used the recreational facilities located in close proximity to their homes."[31] "Voluntary segregation does not violate the Constitution of the United States," concluded the court, "which does not prohibit a municipality from permitting, authorizing or encouraging voluntary segregation."[32] Here was the argument for de facto segregation spelled out in the Deep South. There was nothing unconstitutional about voluntary segregation.

Despite the court's ruling favoring continued segregation, Jackson's city leaders closed the pools in the summer of 1963 to prevent integration efforts, which led overheated whites to check into local motels to use their segregated pools and to form neighborhood organizations to raise money for private pools.[33] The city defended its refusal to reopen the pools with a familiar call for law and order: "The personal safety of the citizens of the City and maintenance of law and order would be endangered by the operation of public swimming pools on an integrated basis."[34] Closures and privatization became the dominant strategy for whites resisting desegregation throughout the country. This strategy was effective because, unlike the right to go to school or to vote, there was no constitutional right to a public pool.

Jumping into white pools and wading into the ocean on segregated beaches were popular pastimes for young, mobilized African Americans by the summer of 1963. As in the case of Biloxi's blacks, it also served as an entry point for many young activists into the civil rights movement. The "Great Pool

Jump" at Tift Park in Albany, Georgia, suggests how challenging recreational segregation became a gateway protest for larger acts of disobedience and dissent. One of the jumpers, Randy Battle, remembered, "that was my beginning. I mean my real beginning. That's when I made my commitment."[35] Battle was one of three young African Americans who carried out the pool jump. SNCC organizers had been working with Albany youth since 1961, recruiting students from local high schools and Albany State College to join the movement. When activists learned the city had sold its pool to the publisher of the *Albany Herald* to prevent integration, they decided to carry out a swim-in. But when they approached the pool's gate they saw a group of police who had been tipped off about the event. Battle and two companions decided to jump the fence and leap into the pool in defiance of the officers. The reception they received was predictable but dramatic. Battle remembered, "When we hit that water in that pool, when they looked over there and saw 'them niggers' in that pool, goddam it them white folks and kids went straight up in the air. They didn't climb out, they went straight up in the air, and flew over to the sides—I mean that's what it seemed like to me. I bet you in half a minute there wasn't nobody in the pool but the three of us. And they started screaming and hollering, 'Niggas! Niggas!' Them white folks hit the air like dolphins, you know, right up in the air they flew. And do you know this, they drained that pool and spent three days scrubbing it down!"[36] The hysteria of Albany's white swimmers and the obvious subterfuge of privatizing the pool galvanized the black community. Albany became a central staging area for SNCC and Martin Luther King's Southern Christian Leadership Conference (SCLC). But Tift Park remained closed to blacks.

One of the most dramatic confrontations over segregated swimming directly involved King and SCLC. In the months prior to the passage of the 1964 Civil Rights Act, SCLC carried out a major desegregation campaign in St. Augustine, Florida, the oldest city in the United States and a tourist mecca. This very public campaign drew a corresponding resistance from white militants throughout northeast Florida and the Deep South, many of whom were Klan members. The two most dramatic moments of the campaign centered on swimming. On June 18 a group of interracial demonstrators jumped into the swimming pool at Monsoon Motor Lodge, a segregated facility that King and others had targeted. As soon as they entered the water the lodge owner ran to fetch a container of what he claimed was acid and poured it into the pool. The facility was quickly surrounded by approximately one hundred whites screaming, "Arrest them! Get the dogs!"[37] Local police jumped into

Figure 11. White militants attack civil rights demonstrators attempting to integrate a St. Augustine beach on June 25, 1964. © Bettmann/CORBIS.

the pool and arrested the swimmers. One week later activists took on the local segregated beach in a carefully orchestrated wade-in. Approximately eighty nonviolent demonstrators marched onto the beach where a large group of whites blocked their access to the ocean. They taunted, "Come on in, niggers! You've got the right to swim!"[38] Rev. Fred Shuttlesworth, King's advisor who joined the protest, later reported that "he feared more for his life and those with him on that occasion than at any other time during the civil rights movement."[39] White militants badly beat the few who made it into the water that day. The publicity given to the St. Augustine campaign helped facilitate growing support and the eventual passage of the civil rights bill. But SCLC pulled out of the city before a desegregation agreement was achieved, embittering some local activists who had borne the brunt of white violence.

In other cities demonstrations and lawsuits wore down city officials, who reluctantly complied with the law. In Miami, the city commission's defiant stand against desegregation was finally challenged in 1960 when a federal judge ruled that the city's public pools must be opened to blacks.[40] In 1963 the federal district court granted an injunction requiring the city of New Orleans to desegregate all its recreational facilities.[41] That same year African Americans in Little Rock, Arkansas, had similar success in federal courts when a judge issued an injunction desegregating recreational facilities.[42] But as Kevin Kruse has argued, "In the end, court-ordered desegregation of public spaces brought about not actual racial integration, but instead a new division in which the public world was increasingly abandoned to blacks and a new private one was created for whites."[43] The resistance to southern swimming pool integration was fierce in the years before the Civil Rights Act. In the end, the abandonment and closure of many public pools was the result. Not all recreational facilities, however, could be so easily replaced or privatized. Public parks, long a terrain of interracial battles in the North, were also subject to occupation by activists and desegregation orders from courts. Against all logic, some white city leaders attempted to end access even to the grass and trees designed to make urban living tolerable.

Parks, in theory, "belonged" to the residents in surrounding neighborhoods. As the racial composition of urban neighborhoods changed in the early 1960s and as civil rights activists pressured city leaders to desegregate all public spaces, blacks encroached upon white families' playing fields and picnic spots. Cities and white residents countered this threat with a variety of legal and extralegal tools. In Danville, Virginia, for example, the city council passed an ordinance in 1960 simply restricting any recreational facilities to "the neighborhood wherein they are located." Occupation of parks by "persons from other neighborhoods" represented a "breach of the peace."[44] But neighborhoods were vulnerable to racial incursions, and playgrounds and parks could not be fully "protected" from African Americans with ordinances such as Danville's. This was clearest in Birmingham, Alabama, where a protracted battle to keep blacks out of all municipal parks galvanized civil rights activists and white supremacists.

In 1910 Birmingham passed a law segregating city-owned parks, part of a larger racial zoning plan that sought to contain the black community.[45] That containment was stymied by the growth of the African American community after World War II and a newly invigorated civil rights movement. City leaders, dominated by the notorious police commissioner Eugene "Bull" Connor, openly condoned violence against black community leaders in response. Despite a bombing campaign and constant threats of violence, local activists filed a lawsuit in 1959 seeking the desegregation of all city-owned parks, golf courses, and swimming pools. The city promptly cut the park budget by 80 percent and closed the facilities targeted in the suit. Explaining the decision, Birmingham's mayor declared to white citizens, "I don't think any of you want a nigger mayor or a nigger police chief . . . but I tell you that's what'll happen if we play dead on this park integration."[46] The park closures spurred Birmingham's business leaders to stand up to city officials, putting a new city commission in place in 1963 that repealed the segregation ordinances.[47] But that decision did not end the racial violence. In September 1963 four young African American girls died in the bombing of the 16th Street Baptist Church. Those four girls would never roam the parks and playgrounds finally opened to them.

Segregated parks were a feature of not only the urban South; state and even federal parks openly barred African Americans in rural areas. Although black demands for public recreational space focused on cities and towns, in the early 1960s blacks began to file lawsuits demanding access to beaches and rural parks throughout the South. South Carolina, for example, shut down its state parks in 1961 to avoid integration after a group of African Americans attempted to enter Myrtle Beach State Park and Sesquicentennial State Park. South Carolina's twenty-seven parks remained closed until passage of the 1964 Civil Rights Act.[48] In Georgia, seven African Americans filed a lawsuit asking for desegregation of Jekyll Island State Park in 1963.[49] Even national parks segregated blacks, despite federal nondiscrimination policies. Shenandoah National Park in Virginia designated a separate campground for African Americans. Virginia park managers also segregated facilities such as lunch counters and bathrooms, and few blacks ventured into the park until the 1970s.[50] In postwar America working- and middle-class families sought out camping as an inexpensive and family-oriented vacation. But campgrounds, like urban parks and pools, were largely white spaces that African Americans had limited access to. Rural resorts on midwestern lakes, for example, were routinely segregated. "In the early 1960s," notes the historian Susan Sessions Rugh, "it was still almost impossible to find a cabin or cottage in the Midwest that was not segregated by race."[51] This reality necessitated the publication of travel guides written explicitly for black vacationers who had to navigate segregated facilities nationwide. The best-known guide, *Green Book*, was published between 1936 and 1966. Another resource, *Travelguide*, was published in 1946 and had as its motto, "Vacation and Recreation without Humiliation."[52] One strategy to avoid humiliation was to frequent black-owned resorts, like Idlewild in Michigan.[53] But exclusion from state and national parks, which were supported by public taxes, incensed postwar African Americans determined to carry out the same family-friendly vacations as their white counterparts.

As they had with parks, whites only reluctantly relinquished their segregated public golf courses. The primary method of resisting golf course desegregation was privatization, which proved to be an effective and profitable way to evade civil rights activists and federal district courts. Golf course cases during the early 1950s set clear legal precedents for activists and consumers to draw from, but many cities proved intractable to change. In Jacksonville, Florida, for example, a class action to desegregate the city's two golf courses had immediate success in the district court in 1959. Frank Hampton, a black police officer and NAACP activist known for his challenges to the city's segregationist mayor and local white supremacists, filed the suit. Just before the date set for desegregation, however, the city commission closed the courses, arguing that the presence of blacks would frighten away white golfers and decrease revenues to such an extent that they could not be maintained. Once the golf courses were closed, the city announced they were for sale at a bargain price. Activists initially failed to convince the courts to prevent the sale or force the new owners to not discriminate. But in 1961 the federal Court of Appeals overturned these rulings, stating, "If the City could not operate the courses on a non-segregated basis without losses too great to bear, it is not to be supposed that a private owner could profitably operate without discrimination, or that such an operator, who had made his purchase with little more than a token payment, could or would operate at a loss."[54] Despite this victory, few African American golfers ventured onto the unfriendly greens in Jacksonville.

Similarly, in 1958 a group of blacks, studiously ignoring the "Whites Only" sign, ventured onto the Charleston, South Carolina, municipal golf course. After being turned away they filed suit in federal district court, but it was three years before the sign came down.[55] Black golfers in Mobile, Alabama, also succeeded in opening up the municipal golf course there, but the court denied their demand for five thousand dollars for damages as compensation for years of traveling long distances to other courses.[56] Such cases were not restricted to the South. A group of African Americans filed a formal complaint with the Colorado Anti-Discrimination Commission in 1962 to gain entrance into Park Hill Golf Club in Denver.[57] City officials ordinarily cited economic concerns as the reason for privatizing public courses, as they did in Jacksonville. After the *Dawson* ruling in Atlanta the question of racial segregation in public courses was settled law. And although federal district courts were at times reluctant to enforce the law, they had little choice. Nevertheless, the responsibility for desegregation was placed on black activists and consumers who ignored "Whites Only" signs, raised money for lawsuits, and demanded entrance into white facilities. These were not the student activists of SNCC; they were more likely to be older and often affiliated with the NAACP. But the steady stream of golf course cases demonstrated blacks' determination to gain access to all forms of public recreation, including the most genteel.

Despite the changing legal landscape, white officials continued to use the threat of violence as a justification for segregating southern recreational facilities. The "disturbance" caused by activists trumped the constitutional rights promised in the Fourteenth Amendment. This was the logic of a district court in Greenville, South Carolina. A skating rink run by the city in Cleveland Park became the target of student activists in the spring of 1961. While acknowledging that the African American students had a constitutional right to use the rink, the court claimed they were there "in an effort to stir up strife and trouble and not truly seeking recreation." As a result the court ruled, "The plaintiffs' constitutional rights to use and enjoy the skating rinks on an equal basis with White citizens in the community does not encompass a right to cause a disturbance, thereby infringing upon the rights of others to peacefully enjoy and use the said skating rinks."[58] To ensure that "peace and tranquility" would reign when segregation faltered, the city simply closed the rinks. The closure of pools, parks, and skating rinks forestalled desegregation. SNCC activists and their counterparts could not sit-in or swim-in closed facilities. But these closures also marked incremental progress in southern cities. The need for extreme measures to maintain segregation demonstrated the impact activists and consumers were having. Frustrated by the lack of revenue and bad publicity, and under pressure from white business leaders, officials reopened some facilities. And these years of protests forced the federal government to pass the 1964 Civil Rights Act, as politicians finally recognized that piecemeal court decisions were not ending Jim Crow but only protracting the struggle. That legislation would soon open a new front on the racial wars in public and private recreation.

"This Is Not Alabama": Riots and Resistance Outside the South

You didn't have to be a member of SNCC to be beaten for desegregating a public park, and you didn't have to live in the South. On Memorial Day 1961, a merry-go-round in the center of Los Angeles's Griffith Park was the site of a recreation riot. The Los Angeles police chief, William Parker, blamed "the publicity coming out of the South in connection to the Freedom Rides" for the growing assertiveness of African American youth at Griffith Park.[59] By the early 1960s blacks routinely challenged white domination at Griffith Park, even on the coveted merry-go-round, long reserved for white families. On Memorial Day dozens of Los Angeles police carefully watched picnicking African Americans and had designated a special patrol for the merry-go-round. In the late afternoon the carousel operator accused a black teenager of failing to pay for his ticket. He denied the charge and refused to dismount, prompting officers to drag him off his horse and beat him mercilessly. African American teenagers quickly gathered, tearing him away from the arresting officers. The police began to beat the newly minted protestors indiscriminately, and black youths responded with bottles, rocks, and explosions of rage. They repeatedly shouted, "This is not Alabama!" Police then blocked all park entrances and demanded that it be vacated. Griffith Park was, at least temporarily, closed for business.[60] Birmingham and Los Angeles had something in common: both cities closed their public parks in the face of black defiance.

By shouting "This is not Alabama!" the crowd at Griffith Park was invoking the 1961 Freedom Rides, when whites brutally beat CORE activists, including Palisades Park veteran James Peck. Police chief William Parker invoked the same link when he blamed the Freedom Rides for provoking the riot. Both black youth and the police used the rhetoric of regionalism to tie segregation and racial conflict to the South and to signal that it was unwelcome in Los Angeles. For African Americans it was an effective rallying call to demand their full inclusion in public spaces. For white police officers it was a call for racial peace amid growing black anger. The cry "This is not Alabama!" and the startling images published in the local papers drew national and international attention. *U.S. News & World Report* ran an image from the riot with the caption, "Aftermath of the Freedom Rides?"[61] But this riot differed both from the southern protests and from earlier northern recreation riots. The 1919 Chicago riot and the 1956 Crystal Beach riot pitted young whites against African American urban dwellers seeking to use public accommodations. Griffith Park's recreation riot followed a pattern that would become more common in the urban uprisings of the 1960s. It was a riot where black residents battled the police as African Americans increasingly occupied formerly white public spaces. But the Griffith Park riot also reflected the continued fear of juvenile delinquency, which had also been evident at Crystal Beach. Editorializing that it was "not a race riot," the *Los Angeles Times* claimed it was "started by a boy full of beer and youthful belligerence."[62] As the decade continued, the white public increasingly viewed large crowds of African Americans, particularly teenagers, not as delinquents but as potentially dangerous criminals. The "rioters," as evidenced by their invocation of Alabama, saw themselves as political actors.

Recreation riots also exploded in the early 1960s in Chicago, whose beaches and parks had been battlegrounds since the 1919 riot. During the mid-1950s Tuley and Calumet parks had been the staging areas of a series of violent incidents; in the summer of 1960 Bessemer Park joined the ranks of embattled public spaces. Although African Americans had used the pool there in previous years, by the late 1950s local whites had driven them away. An all-black baseball team challenged this orthodoxy by occupying the pool one warm July night, and the next day other African Americans followed their lead. Soon a hand-painted sign appeared at the boys' entrance to the pool with the words "Niggers Keep Out," and a huge crowd of two to three thousand whites surrounded the pool wielding bats and rocks. Local police escorted black swimmers through the crowds to safety, although one young boy was struck by a rock.[63] It is striking that during the same summer SNCC was gaining publicity desegregating southern public accommodations, black Chicagoans were engaged in a parallel struggle at Bessemer Park. The rhetoric of southern exceptionalism, that only the South excluded blacks from public accommodations, did not match the reality of northern segregation and violence.

Chicago blacks' spontaneous challenge to recreational segregation at Bessemer Park was soon followed by an organized effort to use Rainbow Beach on the south shore of Lake Michigan. Rainbow Beach had long been known as a "white" beach, despite the growing community of African Americans who lived near the beach and in close proximity to the nearby steel mills. In late August 1960 a group of whites chased thirty blacks from the beach, injuring two with rocks, and the mob reportedly grew to three thousand before the police dispersed them. In response to this escalating violence, an interracial group of students working with the NAACP and CORE began a series of wade-ins in early September.[64] Thanks in part to a large police presence, their efforts at integration at first appeared successful. But white swimmers were infuriated. One nineteen-year-old predicted, "They won't always have this kind of protection." He added, "This is the only beach left for whites so why do they have to come out here."[65] The battle was on, and only the advent of cooler weather stalled it for a time.

The summer of 1961 saw a rising war between the wade-in activists, who were often joined by local blacks unaffiliated with civil rights organizations, and large white crowds that numbered in the thousands. In June, a group of whites watched uneasily while African Americans gathered for another wade-in. The mob held their fire until they saw three young African American girls accompanied by their mother in the water. At that point the rocks flew, badly injuring two and providing an eerie echo of the 1919 riot.[66] By early July there were weekly confrontations between wade-in activists and whites furious at the growing police protection of the integrationists. Activists called themselves the "Freedom Waders" and often brought guitars to accompany their rendition of freedom songs. They suffered physical blows from rocks, and continual racial epithets. One "blonde rioter" was arrested for disorderly conduct when she kicked sand in the faces of demonstrators, declaring, "They were taking my beach away!"[67] Adolph J. Slaughter, a black journalist, described the caravan of freedom waders to Rainbow Beach as a Freedom Ride "I don't believe Freedom Riders, anywhere, are fearless," he wrote. "I was scared and I'm sure I had plenty of company."[68] In early August, Freedom Waders arriving on a Sunday morning were met with a painted sign on the concrete retaining wall: "Go Home, Niggers." Further violence was only forestalled by the constant presence of police officers. [69] The following summer CORE negotiated an agreement with the police department to maintain a force of forty "plainclothes" (in this case, with bathing suits) officers to circulate and keep the peace.[70] Unlike the previous lakefront and swimming pool riots, Chicago police officers, after receiving significant pressure from city leaders and civil rights groups, protected African Americans from ever-growing crowds of disgruntled whites—not to enforce civil rights laws but to prevent riots.

The Rainbow Beach wade-ins were not initially organized civil rights demonstrations but attempts by young blacks to use recreational spaces nominally open to the public. As experienced organizers from CORE and the NAACP joined in, the demonstrations resembled similar conflicts in Mississippi and Florida, where African Americans claimed their right to recreational access on the Atlantic coast. Like those struggles it was violence that defined the limits of desegregation and the allocation of public space. The escalation of recreation riots in the early 1960s marked what the historian Andrew Diamond, writing about Chicago, labels a "broad-based white movement against integration."[71] It is significant that whites gathered at Rainbow Beach from around the city; they were not defending a specific ethnic enclave. Whites' resistance to racial integration centered on beaches, pools, and amusement parks where large crowds from around the city congregated. As Arnold

Hirsch has noted about Chicago, after World War II, "the worst violence occurred when the use of public parks and beaches was contested."[72] Because civil rights statutes covered these spaces and they were used by children and families, whose exclusion from basic rights was particularly galling, they attracted large numbers of black activists and citizens who demanded equal access to recreation.

The 1961 Memorial Day riot in Los Angeles and the Rainbow Beach conflicts kicked off a dramatic summer of activism at recreational facilities throughout the urban North. In contrast to the mobs at Rainbow Beach, some actions were more lighthearted. Nathan Boyd, an African American man, strapped himself inside a large rubber-coated ball and rode over the Horseshoe Falls in Niagara that summer. "I did it to integrate the Falls," he proclaimed. "I'm a Negro and Proud of It."[73] Boyd's daredevil act reflected a resurgence of hope and radicalism that reverberated through civil rights organizations and black citizens. They had fully embraced the immediatism championed by radical nonviolent activists in the 1940s, in contrast to racial liberals' calls to change the "hearts and minds" of white Americans. This willingness to face down white violence was fed by the courageous acts of southern activists and a greater focus in the media on nonviolent resistance. CORE, in particular, benefited from this resurgence and gained further credibility during the 1961 Freedom Rides. Northern chapters of CORE came to life, filled with newly energized members eager to be part of the freedom movement.[74] In addition to supporting southern struggles, northern CORE chapters completed the desegregation efforts at recreational facilities begun in the 1940s. There was unfinished business in amusement parks, roller rinks, and swimming pools, and these spaces became the center of organized activism in the North.

Desegregation and the Student Movement

One major piece of unfinished business was Cincinnati's Coney Island. A newly formed chapter of CORE worked closely with the local NAACP to fully desegregate the park, whose ballroom and lavish swimming pool remained all-white. They began at Moonlite Gardens in April 1961, sending an African American couple to the dance hall. This was not the first challenge to segregated dancing at the park. When rock 'n' roll concerts began to force out the more sedate ballroom dancing in the late 1950s, African American teenagers demanded to join in the fun. An African American mother, Margaret Riley, inquired whether her teenage son and his friends could attend a rock 'n' roll concert in 1959, but park officials told her not to bother. Even with no black teens present, park owner Edward Schott told the Cincinnati Urban League that "for the past two summers when rock and roll artists and name bands had appealed to the teen-age crowds," he was "not entirely satisfied with the patrons' reactions in that there has been some disorder." As Riley's inquiry suggested, interracial performances opened a Pandora's box, and Schott was "quite disturbed at the possibility of Negro youngsters being interested" in the new music.[75] Racial mixing, juvenile delinquency, and rock 'n' roll were a potent mix in the late 1950s. If he needed more justification to persist in segregating the dance floor, Schott found it in the new youth culture. But young Cincinnatians found increased inspiration to dance together at Coney Island.

After they were turned away from Moonlite Gardens, activists mobilized a series of large protests designed to humiliate Schott and force full desegregation. These protests ranged from small acts, such as pressuring the University of Cincinnati's junior class to cancel their prom at Moonlite Gardens, to dramatic confrontations with park guards.[76] For a week in late May pickets stood outside the gates with signs reading, "We believe in integration" and "Why can't we go swimming?" Meanwhile a white team entered the pool grounds, so they could testify that it was not reserved for a private group. They were followed by a black team who, when asked to leave, refused to move from the ticket lines and blocked the entrance. Behind the black activists were a second group of whites acting as a buffer from attacks by police and white customers. Park police quickly arrested the activists, charging them with disorderly conduct and trespassing. After several days of picketing and arrests the activists announced that as many as fifteen hundred protestors would converge on Coney Island, alarming city officials and park managers. Schott backed down, calling a conference with CORE, the NAACP, and the Cincinnati Urban League. He agreed to open all the facilities to African Americans on May 31 and drop all charges against those police had arrested.[77]

As was the case in 1955, when Schott opened Coney Island's grounds to African Americans, more conservative black and white leaders were deeply concerned that desegregation would inevitably lead to violence at the worst and juvenile delinquency at the least. Schott said to the press after his announcement, "I wish to say that any person whose motives are only to use the facilities we provide and who is prepared to conduct himself properly will be admitted to any part of the park."[78] Proper conduct would ensure successful racial progress. Al Roman, a columnist for the black newspaper *Cincinnati Herald*, focused on the need for restraint. "It is hoped that the patrons at

Coney Island will not try to cause any incidents; there are hoodlums, white and Negro, who would get a bang out of causing trouble," preached Roman. "It will be a struggle for minority members to keep their heads but it will be worth the effort. . . . Play the role of ladies and gentlemen and in the long run you are the real winners, in every respect."[79] Here the language of racial liberalism—persuading whites to pursue equality through respectable black behavior—combined with fears of juvenile delinquency. In the same vein, another editorial in the same paper was simply titled, "Don't Abuse Privilege."[80] The first summer of desegregation suggests that any violations of etiquette were committed by park management. "Small numbers" of African Americans reportedly used the pool without incident. But two young black children from a nearby Catholic school were "called out of line" while waiting to enter the pool. Apparently the manager did not believe they could be from the Catholic school. When the Cincinnati Urban League discussed pool attendance with the pool manager, he reported that blacks were indeed steadily entering the pool grounds. One party, he said, "drove up in a big Cadillac."[81]

Fearful of further incidents, both the NAACP and the Urban League continued to monitor attendance and ensure that "care is being taken that well disciplined people go to the park." Despite such care African Americans still experienced discrimination. On July 4, 1961, guards turned blacks away from the ballroom and told them it was open only Monday through Thursday. A pool attendant also refused entrance to a black family that summer.[82] Indeed, few African Americans attempted to enter the Moonlite dance hall or Sunlite Pool because of the possibility of being hassled by park guards or hostile whites. And outside Coney Island's gates recreational segregation in the city persisted. Cincinnati's bowling alleys, roller-skating rinks, and many dance halls continued to turn blacks away in the early 1960s.[83] But the relative success of the Coney Island campaign galvanized community leaders to change the status quo citywide. Marshall Bragdon, the director of the Mayor's Friendly Relations Committee, responded to the campaign by stating, "At no time in our history have ordinary citizens had a richer opportunity to show the power and the grace of our inherited freedoms and responsibilities."[84] Similarly the director of the local NAACP chapter, William Bowen, proclaimed, "The direct action program has created a poor community image with those who oppose us, but has created a sense of belonging unity and strength in the Negro and liberal white community."[85] It had been a decade since the Nelsons and Bromleys began their nonviolent campaign at Coney Island, but by the early 1960s the beatings and humiliations that they and their companions suffered opened the park to the African American children of Cincinnati and sparked a wider movement for racial equality.

Just south of Cincinnati in Kentucky, Louisville was a city that had long been known for its relative racial peace and its strict segregation of public accommodations before the civil rights era. The "Louisville way" centered on recreational facilities as the city agreed to open separate parks and pools for African Americans while denying them entry into "white" facilities.[86] This carefully planned "separate but equal" policy continued until, under pressure from civil rights activists, the city passed a public accommodations ordinance in 1963 forcing downtown businesses to open their doors to black customers on an equal basis.[87] One such business was Fontaine Ferry Park. The park opened in 1905, and like Euclid Beach in Cleveland and Coney Island in Cincinnati, many of its customers arrived by steamboat along the Ohio River.[88] But those customers were all white until 1964. Andrew Wade IV, a young African American man in the 1950s, was deeply scarred by this exclusion. He told his friend, white activist Anne Braden, of a time when he and his family were barred from the park.

> He and his parents and his sister were riding in their car. . . . They passed Louisville's one big amusement park, Fontaine Ferry. An amusement park is a tempting fascination to a child—the Ferris wheel turning, the music from the merry-go-round, the laughter of those within. Andrew and his sister asked to stop and go in. "No, not today. Maybe sometime. Not today," Andrew says his father replied. This happened several times, whenever they rode that way. . . . The park took on even more fascination because it was out of reach. Finally one day, evidently realizing he could no longer make excuses, Andrew's father told him the truth. "Son, I can't take you in there. . . . That park is for white people."[89]

The anger and rejection Wade felt reflected the experience of a generation of African American children and their parents. While Louisville's downtown stores had finally allowed blacks to shop freely, the amusement park remained closed to all black families.

It is not surprising that students were at the forefront of addressing recreational segregation in Louisville in 1961. Members of the NAACP Youth Council and the local CORE chapter, many of whom were high school students, targeted Fontaine Ferry during the height of the student movement.

In June 1961 a group of twenty-eight activists, mostly teenagers, attempted to buy admission tickets to the park. When the attendant turned them away they blocked all park entrances and police quickly arrested them. Meanwhile, white teens in passing cars and from within the park jeered at the demonstrators, who defiantly sang the song "Freedom" in reply.[90] The clash at Fontaine Ferry reflected an impasse between the city's leaders and an increasingly militant black community. Louisville's mayor had formed an Emergency Committee on Integration in an attempt to negotiate gradual and voluntary integration of public accommodations. But a month prior to the Fontaine Ferry demonstration the mayor disbanded the committee and refused to consider a local ordinance prohibiting discrimination in public accommodations.[91] Integration had stalled at the city's bowling alleys, skating rinks, and its sole amusement park. Despite the mass arrests, activists continued to picket Fontaine Ferry throughout the summer, facing down the inevitable crowd of white teens with freedom songs. One evening in late June after six hours of picketing, the African American demonstrators, ranging from twelve to seventeen years old, faced a crowd of five hundred whites who jeered them mercilessly. The whites had signs to counter the demonstrators: "Tickets Back to Africa" and "People Want Water in Hell, Too." Large Confederate flags hung from circulating cars, and whites responded to the black demonstrators' chants of "Everybody wants freedom, everybody wants freedom" with "Go home, niggers, go to Africa." Ignoring the handful of police, whites began to throw rocks and eggs at the picketers, who finally dispersed in the face of the escalating violence.[92]

For a time, the well-honed use of violence and intimidation to "protect" white recreational space worked to maintain segregation in Louisville. A local judge issued a temporary restraining order prohibiting further demonstrations at the park at the behest of Fontaine Ferry's management, claiming their "right to admit or exclude in or from said amusement park whomsoever they choose."[93] Dozens of young activists were on probation and both CORE and the NAACP decided to step back from the stand-ins. They had lost the first round. After protracted negotiations, Fontaine Ferry's owners finally agreed to desegregate the park in the wake of a new local antidiscrimination ordinance, knowing they would lose a new court challenge, but they were determined to maintain segregation at the swimming pool. The owners turned to the most convenient and widely used means of recreational segregation by creating a private club at the pool, exempt from civil rights laws. But as was the case at the Sunlite Pool in Cincinnati's Coney Island, this ruse was confronted by a powerful coalition of activists and local citizens.

At the forefront of the new round of demonstrations was William F. Dady, a young white aide to Martin Luther King, Jr. He led a series of sit-ins at the park and repeatedly challenged the right of the pool operators to deny blacks entry. Dady easily got a membership card to the pool, which theoretically allowed him to bring in guests for a nominal fee. Instead the interracial group was carried out bodily. Dady described these efforts as "citizens' enforcement" of the new antidiscrimination ordinance.[94] Part of this enforcement was a direct challenge to establishments that owners privatized to evade the ordinance. In the midst of continual demonstrations at the park the mayor held hearings before the city's Human Relations Commission. The commission ruled that the pool was indeed a public facility whose membership policy existed solely to resist integration. Responding to the club ruse, the local black newspaper, the *Louisville Defender*, noted in an editorial, "Many will recall that a similar tactic was employed at the Coney Island Amusement Park in Cincinnati."[95] Their hope was that the victory of Cincinnati's CORE would be repeated just south of that city. Despite the ruling, the pool operators continued to insist they were private. City leaders attacked Dady and other activists as outside agitators, and the park owner obtained a restraining order against the "rabble rousers."[96] In violation of the restraining order, Dady continued to lead demonstrations at the park gates.[97] Finally, in 1965, the city forced the fictitious "swim club" to allow African Americans entrance.

It took four years of demonstrations, lawsuits, and sacrifice to fully desegregate Fontaine Ferry Park. This was a significantly longer struggle than black activists' attempts to open up smaller downtown businesses in Louisville. Clearly Fontaine Ferry was a space more powerfully protected by white consumers and more powerfully desired by blacks such as Andrew Wade. A similar protracted and dramatic struggle unfolded just outside Washington, D.C., at Glen Echo Park in Montgomery County, Maryland. Washington had been a center of black student activism since the 1940s when Pauli Murray and Juanita Morrow challenged the city's racial segregation in public accommodations. That legacy of activism was reignited at Howard University with the student movement of 1960. There Stokely Carmichael, Cleveland Sellers, and a divinity student from Philadelphia, Lawrence Henry, joined other black students to form the Nonviolent Action Group (NAG). The students choose the segregated Glen Echo Park, an easy bus ride from the city, as a primary target. They began their protest on June 30, entering the park with picket signs determined to carry out an act of nonviolence. They decided to make their stand at the merry-go-round. There, when a security guard asked Law-

Figure 12. Lawrence Henry confronting a security guard at Glen Echo Park. Reprinted with permission of the District of Columbia Public Library, Star Collection. © Washington Post.

rence Henry, who sat astride a wooden gray rabbit, "What race do you belong to?" he replied, "I belong to the human race" and was promptly arrested. Daily picketing and direct action continued for the next five weeks. Activists, now joined by local white liberals and union members, endured taunting and jeers from counterpickets belonging to the American Nazi Party. By the end of the summer police had arrested over forty activists, but the park refused to consider desegregation as an option.[98]

The NAACP decided to use the students' arrest to challenge the unconstitutional recreational segregation and the use of park guards who were deputized as Montgomery County police to enforce segregation. In an editorial on the controversy, the *Washington Post* noted: "Like restrictive real estate covenants, segregation at an amusement park may be a permissible form of private prejudice; but the power of the state cannot properly be employed to enforce it."[99] The comparison was apt—the law was clear that neither restrictive covenants nor recreational segregation was constitutional. Nevertheless, the lived reality of African Americans was that both restrictive covenants and segregated parks were a fact of daily life, and if the state would not enforce these acts of private discrimination then violence would ensure their persistence. Two days after the Senate passed the 1964 Civil Rights Act, the Supreme Court resolved the Glen Echo case. The justices reversed the conviction of five protestors arrested at Glen Echo by park police, arguing that because the state deputized the private police force they were in violation of the equal protection clause of the Fourteenth Amendment.[100] It was too late for the Glen Echo case to have a meaningful impact on the many sit-in arrests of the early 1960s. But the students and their allies had already achieved their goal. When the park reopened in 1961 it did so on a "non-segregated basis." African American customers, however, found a newly built gate "for more effective control of persons entering and leaving the park" and a newly instituted admission charge.[101] The African Americans who did go to Glen Echo that summer generally came on the weekends in organized groups, and very few ventured into the swimming pool.[102] Their caution was well founded as five years after desegregation Glen Echo was the site of a recreation riot.

The Glen Echo demonstrations reverberated in another Maryland amusement park, Gwynn Oak just outside Baltimore.[103] Like Glen Echo, Fontaine Ferry, and Cincinnati's Coney Island, Gwynn Oak Park barred African Americans entirely. The annual All Nations Day, when Washington, D.C. embassy staffs were invited to the park along with those dressed in "ethnic attire," particularly angered the city's black community. This celebration of multiculturalism excluded embassy staff from African nations, and all African Americans. Baltimore's CORE chapter began to picket this event in 1955. For three years an interracial group of activists peacefully circled in front of the park gates holding signs decrying an All Nations Day that excluded blacks. In 1958 they added the "waiting-line technique" to their arsenal, effectively blocking the gate for a short time. James Peck, who had led the fight at Palisades Park during the previous decade, led CORE's fight in Baltimore.[104] The following year the police and white patrons were waiting for CORE when they again attempted radical nonviolence. An interracial group had managed to get into the park grounds, but an angry crowd of whites quickly surrounded them. When police arrived to arrest them the activists dropped to the ground, refusing to move. Police had to carry two of the men and forcibly dragged the remaining three. Meanwhile the crowd "spit and kicked" and shouted, "Lynch them!" at the demonstrators, whom police promptly charged with disorderly conduct and disturbing the peace.[105] This escalation of violence galvanized Baltimore's African American and liberal white communities. By 1962 CORE also convinced embassies not to participate in the annual All Nations Day, and Baltimore's archbishop forbid all parochial schools in his diocese from using Gwynn Oak for outings.[106] In 1963 the National Commission on Religion and Race, an interracial group, joined CORE to storm the gates at Gwynn Oak Park.

The result of that coalition was a massive demonstration on Independence Day 1963 that brought national attention to the subject of recreational segregation. Approximately eight hundred activists, students, community members, and clergy descended on Gwynn Oak Park. Among them were Michael Schwerner, a white student who was murdered the following summer in Mississippi, Eugene Carson Blake, executive head of the United Presbyterian Church, and Todd Gitlin, future historian and member of Students for a Democratic Society (SDS). As the activists began to block the front gate, police quickly arrested them, putting them into yellow school buses. While the demonstrators sang the "Star Spangled Banner," white onlookers screamed from the park, "Dump 'em in the bay!" and "Send 'em to the zoo!" In all, police arrested a startling 283 demonstrators, including 26 clergymen.[107] Three days later activists organized a second large demonstration, capitalizing on the media attention and continued presence of national religious leaders. But this time local whites were more prepared. A large group of whites, estimated at 1,500, stood ready at the entrance to the park cheering on the police and yelling racial epithets. Many were members of the far-right organization Fighting American Nationalists, which sought to thwart integration efforts in Baltimore. Counterpickets held signs stating "Integration Stinks" and "The United States for Whites—Africa for Blacks."

Seeking to avoid the counterpickets and actually enter the park, some young demonstrators waded across Gwynn's Falls, a stream that bordered Gwynn Oak, and snuck in through a back gate. A group of whites spotted the activists, and a well-thrown brick hit young Allison Turaj in the head. She was bloodied and received ten stitches but survived the attack. Inside the park whites spotted two African American women going into a restroom. They followed the women inside and beat them mercilessly. It was soon discovered the women were park employees. As service workers they were allowed into white space, but on that day whites perceived them as invaders. By day's end police had arrested ninety-nine demonstrators.[108] Gwynn Oak

Figure 13. Protestors practicing nonviolent passive resistance at Gwynn Oak Park, July 4, 1963. © Bettmann/CORBIS.

Park, however, was now a national symbol of intolerance. At this point Baltimore's Human Relations Commission, which had been organized after the earlier CORE demonstrations at Gwynn Oak, began negotiations with the park's intractable owners. The commission forced Gwynn Oak to desegregate and drop all charges against the demonstrators. Upon hearing the news, the Fighting American Nationalists began a series of pickets of their own, urging whites to boycott the park and holding signs such as "White Man Fight" and "White! Boycott Gwynn Oak." When privatization or closure was not an option, the white boycott was a common tactic among segregationists. And such pickets discouraged black patrons fearful of encountering violence and hostility at newly desegregated parks.

When asked why he agreed to desegregate Gwynn Oak, the park owner stated, "It's just too hard to fight when the Archbishop and the leaders of the Protestant faiths and the Jewish faith, and, let's face it, the President and the Governor and other governmental leaders tell you what should be, plus the union leaders, to say nothing of a little nudging here and there from the Congress of Racial Equality and the National Association for the Advancement of Colored People."[109] In short, when the entire establishment and a determined group of protestors are against you, it might be time to back down. On August 28, 1963, hundreds of thousands of marchers descended on Washington, D.C., to hear Martin Luther King, Jr., and other civil rights leaders demand their rights. On that same warm day, Sharon Langley, an eleven-month-old black girl cradled by her father, was the first child to ride the merry-go-round at Gwynn Oak Park. It was the first day of desegregation.[110]

When King gave his "I have a dream" speech on the mall that August he said, "This sweltering summer of the Negro's legitimate discontent will not pass until there is an invigorating autumn of freedom and equality. Nineteen sixty-three is not an end, but a beginning." For many urban amusement parks across the country, the summer of 1963 would be a new beginning of racial inclusion. In Omaha, Nebraska, the beautifully landscaped Peony Park, known for its lavish swimming pool and dance hall, had excluded African Americans since its opening early in the century. Throughout the late 1950s local blacks called for community boycotts of the dance floor and swimming pool but had little support from the city's white population.[111] By 1963, just as demonstrations in Gwynn Oak Park and Cincinnati's Coney Island were picking up, the NAACP's Youth Council in Omaha decided to take action at Peony Park. In July a carload of black youths attempted to enter the park to no avail. They returned repeatedly, only to be turned away. The park's owner decided to close Peony Park altogether, fearing "it was going to start a disturbance."[112] The park was flooded with phone calls threatening a white boycott if the pool was integrated. Several days later, on July 18, Peony Park reopened as a private club. The club ruse was ordinarily used by smaller facilities, such as rinks and pools, but the logic was the same. By privatizing the owner hoped to evade the law. On July 22 members of the Youth Council arrived at the gates and politely requested to fill out membership applications. They were told they needed sponsors and that the applications would have to be reviewed by a membership committee. Meanwhile a young black air force officer from a nearby base sued Peony Park after being denied entry. Capitulating to pressure from activists, black consumers, and liberal city leaders, Peony Park's owners reopened the park to the general public on July 26, 1963.[113]

Civil rights activists launched two additional attacks on segregated amusement parks in the summer of 1963. In St. Louis, Chain of Rocks Amusement Park had segregated swimming since its opening in 1927. The local NAACP chapter began picketing the park in early July. The activists' success was celebrated when a thirteen-year-old African American boy leaped into the pool in early August.[114] CORE joined with the local NAACP's Youth Council to take up amusement park segregation at Fairyland Park in Kansas City, Missouri, in the summer of 1963 as well. Unlike Chain of Rocks, which allowed blacks into the grounds, Fairyland was opened to blacks only once a year. In August 1963 police arrested an interracial group of sixteen CORE members picketing the park. A few protestors managed to hop on some rides, but white customers pelted them with stones and screamed racial epithets at them.[115] The actions of the young protestors, who spent the night in jail after their arrest, galvanized the city's progressive forces. A new group, People for Public Accommodations, called for a popular vote to open Fairyland and other accommodations to all city residents. Their primary target was recreational facilities, the worst offenders in the city. By a narrow margin the referendum passed in April 1964. Fairyland's owner, Marion Brancato, lamented, "There's no way out," and agreed to open the park. But Brancato also leased the Fairyland pool as a private club. The night the referendum's approval was announced, several Kansas City drive-ins and theaters opened to African Americans.[116] The escalation of protests at amusement parks was beginning to pay off in wholesale change.

Amusement parks were attractive targets for nonviolent direct action as their size and popularity highlighted African Americans' exclusion from the best urban recreation had to offer. But these campaigns were only the most visible of myriad smaller actions by ordinary black men and women. In the late 1950s and early 1960s African Americans continually pressured northern municipalities to open their pools to all and comply with state civil rights laws. In Menands, New York, near Albany, Barbara Anne Sharpe, a young black woman, attempted to enter the Mid-City Swimming Pool but was turned away. Sharpe filed a complaint with the New York State Commission Against Discrimination (SCAD), but the pool's owner simply ignored the order to apologize to Sharpe and stop discriminating. In the end the New York Supreme Court intervened by imposing a fine and threatening the owner with a jail sentence.[117] In California, a group of black high school students protested their exclusion from the swim team, which practiced in a private swimming pool that excluded African Americans. The state's attorney general ruled in 1959 that this policy was in violation of *Brown v. Board of Education* and that black students must be given an equal opportunity to swim.[118] In a small Pennsylvania amusement park, Maple Grove in Lancaster County, William and Blanch Lackey, an African American couple, attempted to swim in the park's pool in the summer of 1960. The pool guard told them they needed to be members of a club, and they promptly filed suit to challenge the policy. After a protracted court fight, all of Maple Grove's facilities, from the merry-go-round to the swimming pool, were opened to the Lackeys and other African American families.[119] These cases are representative of ongoing attempts by ordinary black consumers and citizens to realize the promise of civil rights in recreation. They did not wait for the arrival of CORE or SNCC activists but took matters into their own hands.

In communities with vibrant civil rights organizations, activists challenged even private clubs to end their discriminatory policies. In Ann Arbor, Michigan, twenty young members of CORE traveled to the Newport Beach Club on Lake Portage, where they staged a wade-in during the summer of 1960. Although they initially gained entrance into the club, when they returned a week later the club owner decided to close the beach to all for the remainder of the summer. A court order and fine convinced him to reopen the following year.[120] Young activists also worked with the Detroit Brotherhood Youth Council to challenge the segregated Crystal Beach Pool in Oak Park, a white suburb of the city, in the summer of 1961. The NAACP was reluctant to become involved in the case, as the pool was a private club and thus exempt from the state's civil rights laws. But as the mother of one of the protestors noted in a letter to Thurgood Marshall, "These youngsters went on their own. The results seem to prove that even the owner doubted that his claim to being a private club would stand up in the courts."[121] She was right. In response to ongoing pickets and direct action, the pool owner closed for the season and then sold the pool altogether rather than face further protests.[122]

Youngsters "went on their own" in Cairo, Illinois, as well. There the local Rotary Club had operated the only available swimming pool for the public since the 1940s in an open effort to maintain segregation. Jan Peterson Roddy, a black resident of Cairo, remembered riding in his family car past the restricted pool, "mesmerized by the pristine, blue water." In the hot southern Illinois summers Roddy and his friends swam in drainage ditches swollen

Figure 14. Local African Americans attempt to enter the segregated swimming pool in Cairo, Illinois, 1962. Danny Lyon, Magnum Photos.

with rain. "The water, an opaque brown, contained twigs, trash, and, from time to time, snakes," Roddy recalled.[123] Frustrated by the lack of change, in 1962 young African Americans in Cairo, many of whom were high school students, began a series of sit-ins at the pool and a segregated roller-skating rink.[124] After they were arrested for their actions, seventeen of the young activists carried out a hunger strike while in jail and the nonviolent campaign began to attract national notice, including from SNCC, which sent organizers from the national office in Atlanta to help the young activists.[125] As in many cases, it was Cairo's young black citizens who instigated the movement, with professional organizers coming into the community only after demonstrations had begun.

By late summer local white teenagers began to strike back at the demonstrators, hospitalizing a young white Chicago social worker and a pregnant African American woman and injuring a dozen more. The "white mob" was armed with "baseball bats, chains, black jacks and lead pipes," and local police offered no protection to the activists. Meanwhile an African American demonstrator, Willie B. Taylor, who had earlier attempted to integrate the

Figure 15. Demonstrators hold hands and sing freedom songs outside a segregated swimming pool in Cairo, Illinois, 1962. Danny Lyon, Magnum Photos.

swimming pool, drowned while swimming in the Ohio River.[126] City leaders remained defiant as civil rights activists repeatedly pointed out that segregation of public accommodations violated the state's civil rights law. "You may know the state law, but you don't know Cairo law" was their refrain.[127] The city closed the swimming pool for the entire 1963 swimming season and reopened it only after being ordered to do so by the courts in 1964. After two weeks of integrated swimming the city closed the pool for good, filling it with concrete, and thereafter the children of Cairo had only drainage ditches and the perilous Mississippi and Ohio rivers to swim in.[128]

Some of the worst violence in Cairo occurred outside the city's segregated Roller Bowl, where whites beat thirty-eight blacks with chains, sending several to the hospital. Roller-skating rinks were coveted facilities for northern teenagers and prominent targets for interracial activists. A 1961 skate-in at the Arcadia Roller Rink in Detroit by the Detroit Brotherhood Youth Council forced desegregation there. White skaters tripped and threatened the forty black and white teenagers who integrated the rink, but the owner relented under pressure from the courts to desegregate his facility.[129] In Bay City, Michigan, a skate-in at the Skateland rink by local African Americans succeeded in desegregating the rink in 1961 after the owner had declared it a "private club."[130] In the college town of Bloomington, Indiana, the manager of the Rollerama raceway denied entrance to an interracial group of Indiana University students but was forced to reconsider by the Indiana Civil Rights Commission.[131] The Rollercade Skating Rink in Toledo, Ohio, faced a similar challenge. When whites attempted to skate on a Monday night, the night "reserved" for blacks, management told them they had to be members of the Flying Falcons club, and when blacks attempted to skate on a Friday night they were told they needed to join the Rollercade Club. After a hearing the Ohio Civil Rights Commission declared the club system was a means to segregate the rink and ordered the rink's management to end discrimination.[132]

In all these cases groups of young blacks and whites forced skating rinks to reconsider their policies with the threat of court action. But nominally desegregated rinks were often dangerous spaces even after these efforts succeeded. In Chester, Pennsylvania, for example, the local NAACP's Youth Council challenged segregation at the Great Leopard Skating Rink but was denied entry. They soon enlisted the help of SNCC activists from nearby Swarthmore College. Together the college students and local activists repeatedly tested the rink, which reluctantly admitted them. One freshman remembered these outings as "frightening," as they encountered racial epithets, threats, and tripping from local whites.[133] Swarthmore's SNCC activists also joined with activists on the Eastern Shore of Maryland in the deeply segregated city of Cambridge. There they worked with Gloria Richardson, a black graduate of Howard University who had been drawn into the movement through the activism of her teenage daughter. Richardson founded the Cambridge Nonviolent Action Committee (CNAC) to take on all forms of segregation through direct action. Many activists from Washington, D.C.'s NAG, who had desegregated Glen Echo Park, spent time in Cambridge's jails with Richardson, SNCC students, and local protestors. By 1963, after a year of sit-ins targeting the local skating rink and movie theater, Maryland's governor called in the National Guard to forestall more violence between local whites and demonstrators. The guardsmen stationed themselves along the aptly named Race Street that divided white and black neighborhoods and remained for two years in a city essentially under martial law. Meanwhile, in a public referendum, whites repealed a public accommodations measure designed to end segregation.[134]

The growing militancy of Cambridge's white community drew Alabama governor and Democratic presidential candidate George Wallace to the city to speak out against the civil rights bill in 1964. He delivered his address at the Rescue and Fire Company's arena, a recreation center and swimming pool available only to white members that was routinely targeted by civil rights demonstrators. The day of Wallace's appearance, May 11, civil rights activists held a mass meeting and then marched to the arena. The National Guardsmen attacked the marchers, spraying Stokely Carmichael with a chemical that rendered him unconscious. His friend Cleveland Sellers rushed him to the hospital. The following day a two-year-old child was found dead; most believed the experimental gas used by the soldiers caused her death. Maryland's presidential primary, held a few days later, gave Wallace nearly half the Democratic vote.[135] In the end, Congress passed the Civil Rights Act of 1964 that summer, which gave the CNAC demonstrators the legal power to desegregate the arena and swimming pool that had been the site of repeated battles.[136] But the casualties on Race Street continued to mount, as Cambridge's activists battled local whites for full access to public space throughout the 1960s. Radical nonviolence proved effective at opening amusement parks, roller rinks, and swimming pools throughout the country. But whites who resisted recreational segregation employed every tool at their disposal to defy desegregation. They provoked recreation riots by physically and verbally attacking demonstrators and boycotting desegregated facilities. Owners and city officials closed some facilities, only to reopen them as private clubs. And proprietors raised gate fees or cut off public transportation in an effort to deny access to local blacks.

* * *

The student movement in the early 1960s in many cases did finish the job of desegregation. Coney Island, Glen Echo, Gwynn Park, and many other facilities opened under pressure from young activists and local black citizens. But desegregation and integration were not the same. In the years following court orders and reluctant agreements, amusement parks and rinks remained dangerous spaces for African Americans. Generally they entered the grounds of desegregated recreation in large groups and on weekends, being careful to regulate their behavior. Especially in the enclosed space of a roller rink or swimming pool, racial taunts and physical blows were a constant threat. And many facilities, particularly in the South, closed down rather than comply with the law. This massive resistance to recreational segregation was effective. It could not be fought in the courts, although the NAACP did try to force some municipalities to reopen closed facilities. There was little recourse for black consumers when facilities simply disappeared, as in the case of Cairo's swimming pool. Despite these limitations, the wide array of activism discussed in this chapter, national in scope, suggests that African Americans carried out a movement to claim public space that has gone largely unrecognized. This movement was made up of not only familiar names such as Stokely Carmichael in Cambridge or Martin Luther King, Jr., in Birmingham but also teenagers at the Memorial Day riot in Los Angeles's Griffith Park, the baseball team in Chicago's Bessemer Park pool, and the many mothers holding children by the hand who entered amusement parks and playgrounds. Drawn in by the student movement, increasing numbers of liberal and progressive white activists joined African Americans in this struggle. Together they began to dismantle the recreational apartheid that had marked American cities for a century.

Urban whites who were invested in Jim Crow responded to this mass movement with a variety of tactics: some white city officials schemed to subvert the law and prevent integration, members of the Nazi Party carried out counterpickets at Glen Echo, huge crowds of teenagers and young men patrolled Chicago's parks and beaches, and white customers threw bricks at Fontaine Ferry in Louisville. Their anger over the growing success of the movement is palpable in these incidents. With the passage of the Civil Rights Act in 1964 that anger would grow but also shift. Increasingly some whites viewed the urban recreational spaces to which African Americans had finally gained access as unsafe and unclean. Massive resistance to desegregation continued, particularly in the South, but integrated facilities were also simply abandoned by many white consumers. And the urban rebellions that marked the 1960s closed many of the remaining parks and pools for good.

CHAPTER 6

"Riotland": Race and the Decline of Urban Amusements

IN the wake of a recreation riot at Glen Echo Park, Dick West, a columnist for the *Chicago Defender*, suggested a "new type of amusement park, a place called 'Riotland,'" be built to accommodate rebellious teenagers. "It would feature such attractions as a 'Tunnel of Hate' where the young patrons could give vent to their hostilities. Instead of tickets, they would buy facsimiles of draft cards, which would be burned upon admittance. This would entitle them to throw a brick through a store window, participate in overturning an automobile and toss soft drink bottles at policemen." West's proposed slogan was "Come to riotland for your next rumble. Good, clean, wholesome violence for the entire family.'"[1] For West and many other Americans, teenagers were no longer overly boisterous delinquents whose comic books needed to be confiscated.[2] Instead they posed a larger threat to social stability and to law and order. In West's column youthful opponents of the Vietnam War were as culpable for this new culture of violence as rioting young blacks. But for many white Americans, the breakdown of law and order was deeply racialized. The urban uprisings of the mid-1960s shifted the national conversation about recreational access from one of racial justice to one of racial culpability. It was rioting black teenagers—or the threat of them—who posed a danger at amusement parks and swimming pools. They had turned the nation's Playlands into Riotlands.

In the 1960s the visibility of suspected black violence and criminality in spaces of leisure erased the decades of white violence that preceded it in the national imagination. Indeed, the National Commission on the Causes and

Prevention of Violence accused Americans of "historical amnesia" that had expunged memories of white vigilantism and other forms of violence before the riots.[3] By the late 1950s, argues Michael W. Flamm, "the changing face of America's cities, coupled with the emergence of the civil rights movement, led to a greater focus on the racial composition of youth crime."[4] By 1964, when the first major race riots broke out in Harlem and Rochester, Republican presidential candidate Barry Goldwater had made "law and order" part of the national political culture. "Security from domestic violence, no less than from foreign aggression," argued Goldwater during his acceptance speech at the Republican convention, "is the most elementary and fundamental purpose of any government."[5] In 1965 the Democratic president, Lyndon Johnson, declared a "war on crime" and promised to ensure every American's personal safety. And by 1968 the issue of law and order launched Richard Nixon into the White House as the majority of Americans listed "crime and lawlessness" as the most important domestic problem.[6] This rhetoric justified the mass incarceration of African Americans that has profoundly marked American society after 1970.[7] Crime rates did rise in the second half of the 1960s; however, for many white Americans larceny and theft were conflated with civil rights and antiwar activities. Activists and criminals alike, they argued, choose which laws to abide by.

The conflation of civil rights activism and criminality during the 1960s undermined efforts to desegregate and make use of recreational facilities. After passage of the Civil Rights Act in 1964 there were fewer nonviolent activists staging protests to demand recreational access. Instead, racial conflicts in amusement parks and other facilities were more often sparked by large groups of African American teenagers who, in their occupation of these public spaces, intimidated white consumers and clashed with police. These recreation riots reinforced the notion that the very presence of blacks created disorder and devalued spaces of leisure they favored. Even recreational spaces that saw no violence or disorder were vulnerable, as rumors of muggings and vandalism kept customers away and justified closings. As a result many Americans blamed urban decline, represented by drained swimming pools and closed amusement parks, on black criminality.[8] This declension narrative was premised on a mythical golden age of urban recreation that erased memories of white racial violence and exclusion. The disparagement of urban leisure and nostalgia for an imagined past were not the result envisioned by student activists and their allies in the early 1960s who carried out mass demonstrations at parks and pools. However, these activists' courage elicited enough sympathy and moral outrage among Americans to facilitate passage of the 1964 Civil Rights Act. But that legislation proved not to be the easy solution to either the legal or the social problem of recreational segregation.

The 1964 Civil Rights Act

When President John F. Kennedy first introduced the Civil Rights Act to Congress in 1963 he said, "No action is more contrary to the spirit of our democracy and Constitution—or more rightfully resented by a Negro citizen who seeks only equal treatment—than the barring of that citizen from restaurants, hotels, theaters, recreational areas and other public accommodations and facilities." Kennedy recognized that segregation in public accommodations was central to the freedom movement. And the civil rights movement's "master narrative" marks the 1964 Civil Rights Act as the successful culmination of the nonviolent struggle to integrate public accommodations. Simply put, the 1964 Civil Rights Act was to public accommodations what *Brown v. Board of Education* was to education. Although decades of legal challenges and grassroots struggles had forced individual states to abide by existing civil rights laws, Title II of the act ended de jure segregation nationally. But like the *Brown* decision, the Civil Rights Act encountered resistance, violence, and uneven implementation throughout the country. The end of de jure segregation in public accommodations was nearly as elusive as its end in education and housing. When civil rights activists eventually achieved success in the courts, they shifted the battlefield over access to recreation in two ways.[9] The legislation helped create the historical amnesia around white racial violence and racial apartheid. Increasingly, whites viewed integrated urban recreational facilities as dangerous and crime-ridden spaces. Large-scale recreation riots seemingly legitimated these fears, and in response many whites retreated into private or suburban spaces of leisure. In addition, the Civil Rights Act added more fuel to the "conservative counterrevolution" against federal government interference.[10] The federal government was forcing whites to directly confront central taboos such as interracial swimming and denying them their "right" to control entrance into private businesses or public parks.

Although Title II of the Civil Rights Act outlawed racial discrimination in public accommodations, the wording of the act was unclear. Did "any motion picture house, theater, concert hall, sports arena, stadium or other place of exhibition or entertainment" include amusement parks?[11] What were the parameters of the "private club" exemption in the act? A slew of court cases in the years following 1964 clarified this language, but actual desegregation was often slow and incremental. The most important court challenge that tested the constitutionality of Title II came with the *Heart of Atlanta Motel Inc. v. United States* case. The Supreme Court's decision in December 1964 upheld the Civil Rights Act based on the commerce clause of the Constitution. The motel, like many in the South, refused to shelter black customers. The Supreme Court argued that this discrimination violated interstate trade, and therefore the Court upheld Title II of the Civil Rights Act.[12] But not all facilities were so clearly defined under the purview of the act, and soon challenges to segregation cluttered court dockets. Behind these cases were consumers and activists determined to make the rhetoric of ending Jim Crow match the reality of their lives. A mother and her two children in Baton Rouge, Louisiana, exemplify their courage.

Baton Rouge's Fun Fair Park lured customers in the early 1960s with its "Everybody Come" slogan. In reality the park was segregated. Nevertheless, Patricia Miller took her two children, Daniel, age twelve, and Denise, age nine, to the park to ice skate. The attendant initially gave her light-skinned daughter, Denise, a pair of skates. Denise realized they were too tight and returned for a new pair. The manager, realizing the family was black, grabbed the skates and told Miller and her children they would not be served. Denise began to cry as the white customers laughed at their predicament. Miller whisked her children away and filed a lawsuit against the park arguing that their segregation policy violated the 1964 Civil Rights Act. The lower court ruled against Miller, arguing that Fun Fair Park was not a "place of entertainment" and therefore was not covered by the act.[13] Indeed, they argued that an amusement park "which offers no exhibitions for the entertainment of spectators" was not protected under the Civil Rights Act.[14] In 1968 the Court of Appeals reversed the earlier decision, arguing that amusement parks did provide entertainment: "It is obvious to us that many of the people who assemble at the park come there to be entertained by watching others, particularly their own children, participate in the activities available. In fact Mrs. Miller's presence at the park was to see her children perform on ice."[15] It took a full four years after the passage of the Civil Rights Act for the courts to affirm that it applied to amusement parks.

Judges and lawyers debated the question of what the Civil Rights Act covered throughout the 1960s. Bowling alleys, for example, were not explicitly named in the legislation and were not a place of "entertainment." But restaurants were explicitly covered, and if an alley served food it would have to abide by the law. This was the issue in a 1967 case at Fazzio's Bridge Bowl in New Orleans, an all-white bowling alley in the Algiers neighborhood. Fazzio's argued that because they served more beer than food, they did not have to abide by the law. The "beer is not food" argument did not hold up in court; the bowling alley was a public accommodation covered by the act.[16]

By far the most successful tactic available to recreational facilities seeking to remain segregated after 1964 was to use the private club exemption to the Civil Rights Act. Most of the litigation connected to the act sought to determine whether a facility was a club or a public accommodation. Courts focused on whether the facility advertised to the general public and made a profit—both of which would mark it as a public accommodation. But the primary factor was membership. Private clubs could not simply exclude all blacks and admit all whites; they had to demonstrate membership criteria other than race.[17] For example, in 1966 the New Jersey Supreme Court declared the Clover Hill swimming club a public accommodation because it advertised to the public. When it denied the membership application of a local black doctor and his family, it violated state and federal law. "Clearly not every establishment using the 'club' label can be considered 'distinctly private,'" ruled the court. "Self-serving declarations by the owner of an accommodation are not determinative of its character."[18] But the "self-serving" declarations dramatically increased throughout the country as a direct result of the private club exemption, and they were often successful.

Many municipalities transformed their recreational parks, which often included a swimming pool or beach area, into private clubs. Little Rock, Arkansas, boasted two recreational parks, Lake Nixon and Spring Lake, which successfully kept African Americans out of their "clubs."[19] The city of Edwards, Mississippi, sold its recreational park, including a large swimming pool, so that it could operate as a private club and exclude African Americans.[20] A Fairfax County, Virginia, recreational park, Little Hunting Creek Park, successfully maintained it was a private club and the court refused the African American plaintiff the damages he requested for "psychological harm" to him and his family.[21] Remarkably, an entire amusement park, Lakeland Park near Memphis, Tennessee, transformed itself into a private club after the passage of the Civil Rights Act. The park had opened in 1961 as a segregated facility that the courts recognized as a public accommodation. In 1964 it became the Lakeland Fun and Recreation Club where white families could buy an annual membership for five dollars.[22] Added to these examples are many more pools, parks, and rinks that were not challenged by African Americans and therefore do not appear in court records. In St. Louis alone, where the Fairgrounds recreation riot had shocked the city in 1949, three golf courses and five pools became private clubs upon passage of the Civil Rights Act.[23]

Lakeland Park was not the only large amusement park to use the club exemption in the wake of the Civil Rights Act. Doe Doe Park in the small city of Lawton, Oklahoma, near the army base of Fort Sill also attempted to evade the legislation by calling itself a private club rather than a public accommodation. But this case sparked a freedom march for recreational access in the summer of 1966, the same summer James Meredith was gunned down during his March Against Fear to publicize the voting registration drive in Mississippi. Martin Luther King, Jr., Stokely Carmichael, and hundreds of activists completed Meredith's march in the hot summer days of June. During those same weeks in Oklahoma there was another march that confronted white violence and hatred—one to desegregate the "private" Doe Doe Recreation Park. A group of about one hundred marchers, most members of the NAACP youth chapter, walked the one hundred miles from Oklahoma City to Lawton. While on the road they encountered hostile groups of whites who yelled epithets, spat at them, and threw bricks and stones their way. Upon arrival in Lawton three days later, the marchers embarked on a series of sit-ins in an effort to open the park. African Americans in Lawton joined the marchers, swelling the activist ranks to two hundred. The demonstrations culminated on July 4 when mass arrests of protestors signaled the city's open support of the park's segregation policy. Under pressure from demonstrators the city council agreed to pass a public accommodations bill, but it specifically excluded swimming pools and amusement parks. The federal district court found the Civil Rights Act did not cover Doe Doe Recreation Park after the NAACP filed suit because it was not a public accommodation. In 1968 the park's owner did agree to desegregate the park, largely because of pressure from the nearby military base, but African Americans found Doe Doe a hostile place to play until it closed in 1985.[24]

Commercial businesses that transformed themselves into private clubs could sometimes skirt the Civil Rights Act, but the ultimate solution, particularly in the case of swimming pools, was closing down recreational facilities entirely. This form of massive resistance predated the Civil Rights Act, particularly in states with strong civil rights laws. Cairo, Illinois, for example, closed down its public pool in the face of student protests in 1963. Many southern states waited until federal legislation sounded the death knell for Jim Crow. In the fall of 1964 citizens of Statesville, North Carolina, voted by a three-to-one majority to close their two pools rather than desegregate them.[25] Little Rock, Arkansas, closed its two segregated pools, one black and one white, rather than integrate. The park superintendent in Huntsville, Alabama, followed the same model for the "best interests of the city" after local blacks attempted to desegregate the town pool. Park Bluff, Arkansas, closed its municipal pool at Oakland Park after demonstrations there. Memphis, the home of the private Lakeland Park, also closed its pools after passage of the Civil Rights Act.[26] In Griffin, Georgia, city officials closed two swimming pools and two recreation centers to "prevent any possible disorder" in the city.[27] And by 1966 Baton Rouge had still failed to reopen its closed swimming pools.[28] The historian Timothy Tyson has noted that the city leaders in his hometown of Oxford, North Carolina, closed both the baseball diamond and city pool in response to the Civil Rights Act. Local businessmen then bought the pool, which had been built by the Works Progress Administration, and ran it as a private club.[29]

While many whites became club members or built their own backyard pools, there were some immediate legal successes that led to desegregation, even in the Deep South. In New Orleans, Pontchartrain Amusement Park had been segregated since its opening in 1939. African Americans instead frequented Lincoln Beach, which had been constructed explicitly to offset black complaints of exclusion.[30] After the passage of the Civil Rights Act the park's owners complied with the law, agreeing to open the gates to New Orleans's black community. This seeming success was mitigated by other factors. The city immediately closed Lincoln Beach, cutting off access to a black leisure space important to the community. And Pontchartrain Park closed its swimming pool, installed a fence around the park, and began a one-price ticket policy to keep out customers who were not there to spend money. Changes in park policies such as these often followed racial unrest in newly desegregated parks. In New Orleans they were preemptive; the park was openly trying to limit black attendance to appease white customers. Despite these changes white attendance plummeted at Pontchartrain.[31]

In nearby Baton Rouge the Civil Rights Act undercut the long-held argument that the potential for violence justified segregation. More than a decade earlier, in 1953, African Americans had filed a class-action suit against the city demanding access to segregated recreational facilities, including swimming pools and skating rinks. That initial suit failed but was reheard in 1964 when the district judge proclaimed, "It is no defense under the present state of the law to show that desegregation of these facilities might result in interracial disturbances, violence, riots, and community confusion and turmoil."[32] The force of law was also effective in exposing the most obvious club ruses, as in Ohio where the Holiday Sands recreation park had refused admission to a group of African Americans challenging its segregation policies. The recreation park routinely admitted whites who were not members of the "club," and the Ohio Civil Rights Commission concluded that Holiday Sands was a public accommodation that must follow the Ohio civil rights law, now backed by a federal law.[33] The explicit inclusion of restaurants, lunch counters, and motels in Title II of the act also helped undercut private golf courses' attempts to exclude black players. In Greensboro, North Carolina, the Sedgefield Club had to open its course to any guests of the attached Sedgefield Inn, and in Richmond, Virginia, Laurel Links could not exclude black players who had legal access to their lunch counter.[34]

As these cases suggest, the Civil Rights Act had an uneven impact on public accommodations. Restaurants and motels were clearly within its purview, but many recreational facilities could either become private clubs to avoid the law or claim that Title II did not cover them. In some cases cities passed local ordinances in the wake of the Civil Rights Act to make it more inclusive. In the fall of 1964, after bruising demonstrations at Gwynn Oak Park, Baltimore passed a broad ordinance prohibiting discrimination in public accommodations, including swimming pools, amusement parks, and roller-skating rinks.[35] And in Oklahoma City the city council passed a public accommodations ordinance that provided for "entry and services of all races at swim pools, skating rinks, bowling lanes, fun parks and theaters frequented by the general public."[36] By a razor-thin margin, Kansas City, Missouri, also passed an antidiscrimination ordinance in 1964. "There's no way out," lamented Marion Brancato, the owner of the city's Fairyland Park. "The city can take your license away after three convictions, and you can't operate without one." To compensate for his predicted losses, Brancato leased Fairyland's pool as a private club and applied for a zoning change to help him sell the park if "there's too much trouble."[37] Brancato's reaction to the Kansas City ordinance echoed the reaction of many white owners of recreational facilities. They predicted economic losses and increased "trouble" from racial conflict. By creating private clubs, neglecting their facilities, or simply closing them down, owners' predictions became self-fulfilling prophecies.

Civil rights organizations joined ordinary citizens in pressuring recreational facilities to be more inclusive in the wake of the Civil Rights Act. Activists organized one of the most ambitious plans to apply CORE's direct action tactics to a recreational space during the 1964 New York World's Fair. The Urban League of New York had protested for several years that the fair's planners, including Robert Moses, were hiring few African Americans for technical or construction jobs. They picketed the construction site and brought in African delegates from the United Nations to see firsthand that their own country's pavilions were built with white labor.[38] When the Brooklyn chapter of CORE discovered that the Louisiana exhibit would feature a minstrel show they began to organize a "stall-in." The plan was to have two thousand cars "stall" on the highways leading into the fair site. James Farmer and Bayard Rustin, veteran CORE activists, arrived in New York City to join the protests on opening day. Along with hundreds of activists, Farmer and Rustin drowned out President's Johnson's welcoming speech with shoots of "Freedom now!" Police arrested them outside the New York Pavilion, which they had managed to barricade from fairgoers. James Farmer declared that his goal in leading the fair protests was to publicize "the melancholy contrast between the idealized, fantasy world of the Fair and the real world of brutality, prejudice, and violence in which the American Negro is forced to live."[39] The world of the fair was similar to the world of the amusement park—a celebration of consumerism, leisure, and technological progress. Farmer's distinction between this fantasy world and the reality of racial violence reflected two decades of protests against recreational segregation.

Despite the success of the opening day demonstrations, the CORE stall-in proved a disappointment. Farmer opposed the plan, which was badly organized and not well coordinated. The city let protestors know their cars would be towed away and impounded, discouraging many from joining in. In the end police quickly towed the few cars that "ran out of gas" on the highways. Police also swarmed city subways to thwart a parallel plan to pull emergency-stop cords on subway cars, preventing passengers from arriving at the fair. Farmer suspended the Brooklyn chapter of CORE for the debacle, which received an enormous amount of negative media attention.[40] Despite the failed "stall-in," Rustin, Farmer, and their fellow activists succeeded in publicizing the discriminatory hiring practices of the fair's organizers and exhibitors. Their use of picketing and sit-ins at the fair was reminiscent of dozens of similar campaigns at amusement parks and swimming pools across the country. But their primary goal was to highlight economic discrimination.

Linking economic and social goals was always integral to the civil rights movement, even in its "classical" phase. As Ella Baker wrote in 1960, soon after the founding of SNCC, "current sit-ins and other demonstrations are concerned with something much bigger than a hamburger or even a giant-sized Coke."[41] The students were looking for not only consumer rights but also human rights, including the right to a decent job and freedom from violence. After the passage of the 1964 Civil Rights Act, however, this link between public accommodations and broader rights seemed broken in the eyes of some civil rights leaders. Most notably, Bayard Rustin, in his seminal 1965 article "From Protest to Politics," asked, "What is the value of winning access to public accommodations for those who lack money to use them?" Rustin argued that "desegregating public accommodations . . . affected institutions which are relatively peripheral both to the American socio-economic order and to the fundamental conditions of life of the Negro people."[42] His essay called for a turn toward a coalition politics that would transform social and economic conditions for all working-class Americans. But as Nikhil Pal Singh argues, "By fantasizing that the U.S. political economy could simply be lifted out of its racial matrix, Rustin underestimated the cultural and economic investment in white supremacy."[43] Segregated public accommodations were not an ephemeral barrier to civil rights, easily defeated by the nonviolent movement. Instead, they were the most visible manifestation of a broader racialization of public space in America. And many African Americans, even after the victory of 1964, found access to the most coveted accommodations blocked.

Urban Rebellions in America's Parks

Noting the rise of mid-1960s racial rebellions, Thomas Sugrue has argued, "The passage of the Civil Rights Act was a beginning not an end."[44] African American anger during racial uprisings was in part directed at the continued lack of jobs and police brutality in American cities. But the continued reluctance to open public accommodations to blacks, despite the new law, was also an intolerable situation. It is not surprising, then, that the 1960s saw a continuation of recreation riots and activist and consumer demands to fully open spaces of leisure. But these recreation riots were less often attacks by whites defending spaces of leisure, like the 1919 Chicago Race Riot or attacks on protesters at Cincinnati's Coney Island. More frequently frustrated African Americans, many of them teenagers, fought back against excessive policing and exclusion from recreational facilities now nominally opened to them. White Americans often viewed this violence as part of a crisis of law and order rather than a crisis of racial justice.

Playlands across the country transformed into "riotlands" in the summer of 1965. One New Jersey amusement park, Olympic Park, brought fears of urban violence into a suburban enclave. Olympic Park was located in Irvington, near Newark. By 1965 Newark had a rapidly growing black population that was increasingly politicized around the issues of housing and police brutality. Despite New Jersey's civil rights laws, Olympic Park remained segregated until the mid-1950s and Newark's black community felt unwelcome even when they gained access to the park.[45] By 1965, however, young blacks began to take buses to the park to enjoy daylong excursions. On opening day of 1965 a large group of Newark teenagers, numbering perhaps one thousand, arrived at the park. They expected to pay only ten cents per ride, a tradition on opening day that the park owner had eliminated that year. By the evening many had run out of money as a result. Fearing trouble, park officials tried to close early. Guards ushered the angry teenagers from the park, but there were no buses to take them back to Newark because of the early closing time. The crowds then descended on downtown Irvington, shattering some shop windows and "frightening" pedestrians. Other than a handful of minor injuries, some vandalized park exhibits, and the smashed shop windows, the teens did not cause major damage. Indeed, Irvington's police captain stated, "It was not a riot. There was no looting, no breaking into stores. And it certainly had no racial aspects. It was vandalism."[46] This claim echoed the official response to the Crystal Beach riot in Buffalo a decade earlier—this was juvenile delinquency, not racial conflict. But white customers fearful of the influx of Newark's teenagers did not perceive the riot as merely "vandalism." Many viewed Olympic Park as a space of danger and violence, dominated by black youth and now shunned by white families.[47]

Irvington's town council was also concerned about the attraction Olympic Park held for Newark's young black residents. Two weeks after the riot the council met to discuss denying the park's license renewal. One member of the council argued that "property and life in the area around the park were in danger," and many whites agreed with this assessment.[48] After the park's owner threatened to file a lawsuit, the council reversed this decision.[49] But this reprieve did not save the park from closure. By the end of the season the owners had sold Olympic Park to land developers, and Newark youth no longer had access to any major amusement parks. Fittingly, what is left of Olympic Park today is a magnificent Liberty carousel, a huge ride with beautifully carved wooden horses. This carousel was first erected in Detroit's Belle Isle Park, site of the 1943 race riot, and was then bought by Olympic Park. When the park closed in 1965 Walt Disney bought the historic carousel and erected it as the centerpiece of Fantasyland's medieval courtyard at Walt Disney World. It is now known as Cinderella's carousel, and all the horses have been painted white.[50] The Olympic Park recreation riot demonstrated to white community members and the park owners that desegregated recreation threatened law and order in their suburban community. In their perception the park thrived when the owners barred blacks entirely, although this unwritten policy was a clear breach of state law. Once blacks entered the park in large numbers disorder followed, threatening not only the park but also the surrounding neighborhood. This narrative was reinforced in parks across the country in the mid-1960s.

In Glen Echo amusement park outside Washington, D.C., another classic carousel was the site of a successful desegregation effort by civil rights activists in 1960. Six years later, on the Monday following Easter, large numbers of African American teenagers boarded buses in Washington and headed to Glen Echo. It was a school holiday, and black teenagers took advantage of the opportunity to enjoy the park. Alarmed by the crowds and fearing vandalism, park operators shut down their rides early, around 6:00 P.M. The youths had purchased ride tickets that they could not use and were frustrated and angry. At this point the bus company decided to suspend service back to the city because they could not be guaranteed police protection. Several hundred teenagers had to walk many miles to their urban homes. During this walk they threw bottles and stones, frightening nearby residents and smashing some windows on cars and houses. Nevertheless, a citizens' report later noted, "No instances were reported where violence was directed at the person of any fellow walker, policeman, passing motorist or homeowner."[51] The local white press reported the incident as a riot, quoting a Montgomery County police officer describing the black teenagers as "a bunch of savages." That same officer was quick to point out that there were "no racial overtones" in the rioting, an opinion not shared by the local civil rights community, angered that park officials expelled young blacks and forced them to walk home.[52]

Civil rights leaders in Washington suggested that the riot was an unfortunate incident of "youthful restlessness," in the words of the director of the Washington Urban League. But some whites were incensed by what they perceived as alibis for criminal behavior. Arthur Krock, a Washington-based reporter, wrote in his *New York Times* column that the riot could be blamed on "the preachment of Dr. Martin Luther King that individuals have a right to select the laws they will obey on their judgment of which is or is not just and nondiscriminatory." He also lamented the protection of "criminals at the expense of social order" and especially "the special condonation of such infractions by Negroes, on the ground of the injustices and discriminations they have suffered."[53] The complete exclusion of blacks from Glen Echo prior to 1960 and the abject fear their large numbers sparked in 1966 were not part of Krock's evaluation of the riot. Instead, he viewed the events as part of the crisis in law and order that had turned Glen Echo into a "riotland."

Glen Echo reopened a week after the riot, but the city and the park quickly made changes to prevent future incidents. These changes paralleled the response to the Crystal Beach riot a decade before. Like Crystal Beach, transportation to the park was limited to private cars when D.C. Transit ended its bus service from Washington. In addition, Glen Echo began to charge admission at the gate rather than allowing patrons to roam the park and pay for individual rides.[54] In doing so they transformed the amusement park from a public space that could be entered at will to a private space of consumerism and surveillance. But even these efforts failed to stem the park's decreasing popularity. The final season for Glen Echo was 1968. In the spring of 1969, just prior to what would have been opening day, the owner's attorney announced, "It was determined that the public no longer has an interest in what the park has to offer. . . . The closing indicated itself through the turnstiles."[55] Glen Echo's proximity to Washington, D.C., like Olympic Park's proximity to Newark, marked it as a black space after desegregation. Silent turnstiles were the result.

Traditional urban amusement parks in cities across the country saw increased numbers of recreation riots by the mid-1960s. New York's Coney Island, the quintessential trolley park, exploded a few weeks after Glen Echo's riot in 1966 when four thousand teenagers, most of whom were black and Latino, engaged in a daylong battle with police.[56] Coney Island had been experiencing a steady decline in the decade before the riot. By 1964 the *New York Times* described it as a "good place for people who hate crowds." Coney Island's white concessionaires' main explanation for the decline was the "influx of negroes" that "discouraged some white persons from visiting the area." They also cited increasingly unsafe subways and "teen-age hoodlums," whom they viewed as part of the declining law and order evidenced by African Americans' increased presence in the city's public spaces.[57] As one police officer who patrolled Coney Island stated, "I think people are afraid of subways, afraid of Coney Island. Just afraid to be here."[58] By the end of the dismal 1964 season, Steeplechase Park, the very first of Coney Island's parks to open in 1897, turned off its bright lights for the final time. Steeplechase had become notorious among local blacks for its whites-only policy at its large resort pool. That final summer the park closed the pool rather than invite blacks to swim.[59] Marie Tilyou, the granddaughter of Steeplechase's original builder, George Tilyou, called Steeplechase a "gorgeous rosebud in a garbage can."[60] In this case the rose was white and surrounded by an increasingly dark city.

Tilyou's vivid image aptly reflected the white public's growing distaste for the country's first amusement park. Postwar Coney Island had become the reverse image of its turn-of-the-century heyday, a dystopia that reflected urban problems rather than a utopia that set itself apart from the city. In the 1950s Robert Moses had overseen the construction of public housing projects and private high-rises, including the Luna Park Houses, near the remaining amusements. As late as 1950 Coney Island's black population was less than 2 percent, but by the mid-1960s Coney Island's population was majority black and Puerto Rican as a result of urban renewal and public housing. Public fears of racial violence were realized in the 1966 melee when thousands of teenagers ran through the park, reportedly shouting "anti-white and anti-police" slogans. Like the Griffith Park riot in Los Angeles, police and teenagers battled at Coney Island. The teens threw bottles at police and smashed some of the prizes at the game booths.[61] Fearing further disturbances, the police department transferred many African American and Puerto Rican officers to Coney Island and increased their patrols fourfold.[62]

Much of the conflict around Coney Island was concentrated at the subway stop on Stillwell Avenue, where police patrolled heavily. In July 1966 police arrested six young African Americans for making speeches "to incite acts of violence in contempt of lawful authority."[63] Often police patrolling the park grounds would herd groups of young people back to the subway station, insisting they leave the area. On hot days when the trains were already crowded, the result was often rowdy groups of teens "terrorizing" passengers and vandalizing subway cars. On Easter Sunday in 1968, for example, thousands of young African Americans crowded onto trains, pulling emergency cords, frightening passengers, and smashing windows. The youths claimed that police herded blacks onto the trains, where they waited for two hours before the trains began to move.[64] Angry white residents called the *New York Amsterdam News* in outrage. One stated, "We're arming ourselves and going to kill all the Negroes out here."[65] The Transit Authority responded to this latest incident by installing iron gates at the entrance of the Stillwell Avenue subway station, designed to safely enclose park visitors in case of future violence. The gates would also cordon off "unruly" young blacks and Puerto Ricans when police herded them into the station.[66] Unlike most trolley parks on the very outskirts of cities, Coney Island never had the option of sealing itself off from its urban population. The park itself was surrounding by a mixed African American and Puerto Rican community, which was increasingly impoverished by the late 1960s. And it was a short subway ride from other black and brown neighborhoods. The presence of the iron gate was a symbolic and chilling attempt to stem the flow.

Some white ethnics living near the Stillwell subway station blamed the unrest on black power activists, whom they believed had "infiltrated" the community's antipoverty agencies in the late 1960s.[67] Similarly, in Idora Park outside Youngstown, Ohio, a 1967 riot was blamed on black militants raising black power fists on the park grounds. Idora Park had been losing customers to Cedar Point in Sandusky, Ohio, which was located far from any major city and had few black customers.[68] In 1967 Idora's owners tried to appease customers concerned about juvenile delinquency and crime by instituting a pay-one-price policy on holidays. This policy drew criticism from park customers, and a few days after the park opened police arrested two African American men for inciting a riot. The men had reportedly been shouting "Black power!" in an impromptu protest that drew a crowd of teenagers. Following the arrests and the publicity that surrounded them, Idora Park began to lose more customers. The park's manager instituted a daily general admission charge in order to get "rid of the loafers, of the gangs of hoodlums who made the place uncomfortable for a family trade."[69] Youngstown's families, black and white, suffered from the shutdown of the steel mills in the 1960s and 1970s, and with rapidly declining attendance and dilapidated facilities the park closed in 1984.

Across the country, at Playland Park in San Francisco, a group of African American teenagers rampaged through the grounds in 1967, reportedly breaking windows and stealing from ticket booths. Riot-equipped police quickly cleared away the group of black teens.[70] Black youth occupying public accommodations at Idora and Playland were at times actively protesting what they viewed as discriminatory entrance policies or police harassment. At times they were engaging in criminal behavior or simply enjoying time with friends. Regardless, the police and larger white public often viewed their presence as a threat to safety and increasingly the parks they "invaded" became racialized spaces deemed unsafe for whites. It was these recreation riots that were most remembered by the white public and blamed for the parks' decline. Lost to memory were the white racial violence and discriminatory policies that preceded them.

Oklahoma City's Springlake Park and Louisville's Fontaine Ferry Park illustrate how park owners, city officials, and the white media blamed black teenagers for the decline of urban recreation. Springlake was fully segregated before the 1964 Civil Rights Act. After the legislation's passage blacks began to enter the park grounds tentatively, but the management kept the pool segregated by creating the Aquatic Club to subvert the law. Finally, in 1967, the park management transformed the pool into an aquarium in an effort to avoid conflict.[71] But racial tensions at Springlake Park remained high, in part because of demographic changes in the city. When the park was opened in the early twentieth century it was located in a white neighborhood. By the 1960s, however, it became a "white island in a black sea" as African Americans began to move north into the surrounding neighborhood.[72] On opening day, Easter Sunday, in 1971, a false rumor spread through the park that a white teenager had pushed an African American off the Big Dipper roller coaster. A dramatic fight broke out between blacks and whites inside the park. Park guards managed to throw most of the teenagers out of the park, but the teens confronted police in the surrounding parking area. Soon police fought with African American teenagers, who were joined by youth from nearby housing projects. In the end police arrested thirty blacks and no whites. Following the riot, park managers tried to bar all men between the ages of thirteen and twenty-six from entering the park.[73] This ploy was short-lived, and white attendance at the park plummeted.

Fontaine Ferry Park was also located in a transitional neighborhood and saw similar violence after the 1964 desegregation campaigns. During the next five years the desegregated park began a slow and steady slide toward disrepair. This was, in part, a reflection of the changing racial geography of the city. Fontaine Ferry was in the West End of Louisville, on the river just north of Shawnee Park, a largely African American neighborhood by the 1960s. The park itself, however, had a nearly entirely white staff and was still attended largely by white patrons. The contrast was stark. In 1968 a major race riot in the West End followed a rumor that the city had prevented Stokely Carmichael, leader of SNCC, from landing in the city. Carmichael had planned to join an ongoing protest against a police officer who was reinstated despite his beating an unarmed African American teenager. After several days of rioting, the National Guard patrolled the West End, over forty people were treated for injuries, and several hundred were arrested. Two black teenagers, one fourteen and a second nineteen, were shot and killed in the violence.[74] Thus racial tensions in the West End were high by the time Fontaine Ferry Park opened for business in 1969.

On opening day in 1969 nearly eight thousand people flooded into the park. Many were young black teenagers, some of whom had been involved in the uprising the year before. By midafternoon a group of youths began to smash equipment and rob cashiers at rides and stands. Park management closed the gates two hours early, and the next day the owner announced Fontaine Ferry was closed for good.[75] Fontaine Ferry had been fully desegregated for only four years before closing. The park opened briefly again in 1972, aptly named Ghost Town on the River, but closed again in 1975.[76]

Traditional amusement parks had become "riotlands" by the late 1960s and many of them ghost towns by the early 1970s. Vandalism and juvenile delinquency marked them as dangerous spaces that no longer offered safety and escape to white families. Park owners, meanwhile, invested less in upkeep and innovation after desegregation efforts and were tempted by lucrative offers from developers who sought to buy up valuable land. Marie Tilyou, for example, sold Steeplechase to the developer Fred Trump, Donald Trump's father, for redevelopment into high-rise apartment buildings.[77] The Guenther family, who owned Olympic Park in New Jersey, sold their valuable property to urban developers after closing it down.[78] These park owners profited from their decision to abandon urban recreation, but they did not point to this reality as their primary motivation. Instead the white public perceived the closure of major urban amusement parks as a direct result of the violence and vandalism propagated by black urban teenagers.

When young African Americans fought with police and vandalized park facilities, the white mobs yelling racial epithets of the late 1950s and early 1960s fell out of the public's memory. Instead, the nation's attention was turned to the cause of widespread racial uprisings during the long hot summers of the 1960s. When the commission chaired by Illinois governor Otto Kerner published its *Report of the National Commission on Civil Disorders* in 1967, the most memorable finding was that "Our Nation is moving toward two societies, one black, one white—separate and unequal."[79] After decades of integration efforts by ordinary black consumers and trained civil rights activists, this reality was devastating. And as in earlier generations, it was violence rather than racial justice that was at the center of the debate over the state of race relations in America. The Kerner Commission investigated seventy-five "disorders" that had erupted in the previous two years. Number four on the list of grievances African Americans pinpointed as having begun the riots was "poor recreation facilities and programs."[80] The Cincinnati riot in 1967, for example, began on a ninety-degree summer day when only two swimming pools were available to black children and teenagers. And the Atlanta neighborhood where a riot began that same summer lacked a swimming pool and accessible park.[81]

When Martin Luther King, Jr., arrived in Chicago in the summer of 1966, he experienced firsthand how the lack of pools and parks could lead to violent uprisings between police and young blacks sweltering in the summer heat. Chicago's vibrant open housing movement attracted King, and he was eager to draw attention to northern segregation after the passage of the 1964 civil rights and 1965 voting rights bills. In 1966 King moved into a West Side apartment and began to hold a series of marches and rallies in conjunction with local activists. To King's disappointment, his Chicago Freedom Movement encountered resistance from some Chicago blacks, particularly young African Americans who had suffered repeated beatings at the hands of whites and police officers when crossing the color line. It was these young people who had been at the front lines at Bessemer Park and Rainbow Beach. By 1966 they increasingly turned away from the nonviolent protests that provoked unrelenting violence from the city's white population.[82]

King confronted that violence on July 12 when a riot exploded outside his apartment building. A group of young black children had opened a fire hydrant on a particularly hot summer day. Although illegal, their actions were understandable given that African Americans had full access to only one of the four pools within walking distance of the neighborhood. Indeed, playing in the spray of an open fire hydrant was part of growing up for Chicago children. Nevertheless, on this day two police officers closed the hydrants, and a protesting crowd gathered, angry at the harassment. After the police arrested seven black teenagers, rumors began to spread that the arrestees had been beaten and that police were turning off hydrants in black neighborhoods across the city. These rumors sparked riots in the neighborhood, despite the efforts of King and his staff to act as peacemakers. After the National Guard ended the riot there was two million dollars' worth of damage, over five hundred people had been arrested, and three people were dead, shot by police.[83]

Mayor Daley met with King after police quelled the riot and addressed the recreational inequality that had sparked the melee. He agreed to add sprayer attachments to the fire hydrants, enforce equal access to parks and pools, and construct more swimming pools and playgrounds in black neighborhoods. He was significantly more reluctant to address the police brutality that had prolonged the violence.[84] The liberal columnist Mike Royko wrote of the agreement, "City Hall embarked on a crusade to make Chicago's blacks the wettest in the country. Portable swimming pools were being trucked in. Sprinklers were attached to hundreds of hydrants, and water was gushing everywhere. The city's department of planning mobilized to launch a long-range program of black wetness. . . . One cynical civil rights worker said, 'I think they're hoping we'll all grow gills and swim away.'"[85] This stopgap measure did not address the recreational segregation that had defined the city since the first Great Migration. The portable pools were small and nothing like the resort pools enjoyed by a generation of urban whites. King was infuriated by this partial response. In an open letter to supporters he noted, "How ironic it is that in Chicago, four days of rioting were precipitated by the shutting of water hydrants; the authorities then found $10,000 for portable pools but meanwhile the State was spending $100,000 per day for the National Guard."[86]

After signing the agreement to provide more recreational facilities to the black community, the Chicago Freedom Movement sought to hold the mayor to his promise by combining their open housing campaign with an open recreation campaign. Activists "tested" realtors to see if they would be steered to segregated neighborhoods and picketed realtors who had offered listings to whites only. They also held large integrated picnics in white parks, using all the accommodations available, including swimming pools. This exposed the shallow nature of Daley's response to recreational segregation. In late July, for example, two hundred interracial picnickers in the volatile Gage Park had their automobiles damaged and had to dodge rocks when they were forced to retreat from the park. When activists targeted Riis Park they found the pool closed; park officials claimed there was glass on the bottom.[87] In the weeks that followed, marches through white neighborhoods became increasingly violent. Whites screaming, among other things, "Burn them like Jews!" surrounded open housing marchers in the Gage Park neighborhood.[88]

The violence and hatred that met King in Chicago have long been part of the civil rights narrative—illustrating the limits of nonviolence in the northern context. But a closer examination of the Chicago movement reveals the centrality of struggles over recreational space, which was integral to a viable open housing movement. Chicago's working-class white communities rose up because their entire neighborhoods had been "invaded"—not just their homes but parks, playgrounds, and pools. Mayor Daley's promise of swimming pools backfired because of this connection between recreational space and open housing. As Royko points out when explaining white anger, "He had given the rioting blacks swimming pools, now the police were beating home-owning whites."[89] The civil rights marches in Chicago's white neighborhoods confronted increasingly hostile crowds of whites as the summer dragged on. In the end King signed another agreement with Daley that ended the marches and professed a commitment to open housing, but it had no legal standing. The following year Daley won the mayoral race in a landslide and promised in his inauguration speech that "law and order will prevail."[90] The infamous Democratic Convention in 1968 would reveal Daley's definition of law and order. In the meantime, cities and towns across the country were staging grounds for new recreation riots.

As Thomas Sugrue and Andre Goodman have argued, not all of the 1960s uprisings took place in large cities. Suburban communities and towns also saw a surprising amount of racial unrest. One such town was Plainfield, New Jersey, about twenty miles outside Newark and home to a growing black population by 1967. High rates of unemployment, police brutality, residential segregation, and educational inequality beset the town. One gauge of this inequality was the almost complete lack of recreational facilities in African Americans' West End neighborhood. There were no swimming pools or ball fields in the black community, even though African Americans paid relatively high taxes to subsidize these facilities in white neighborhoods. In response to complaints, the town agreed to bus African Americans to nearby Rahway to visit that town's pool for a small fee. In 1966 young African Americans furious at their continued exclusion from the town's facilities threw "firebombs and stones" at cars in the center of town.[91]

The following summer, days after the large Newark uprising and following several cases of police brutality in Plainfield, young blacks from the West End began to fill the streets. They met in public parks and on street corners, had numerous clashes with the police, looted stores, overturned cars, and burned down white-owned stores. After several days of violence one police officer was beaten to death after having shot a black man; in all, police wounded dozens of black residents and arrested over one hundred.[92] The Kerner Commission, which investigated the riot in its immediate aftermath, found that the young blacks who had engaged in the violence were northern born, relatively well educated, and politically astute. Black participants viewed the uprising as a form of political protest, and it did create some real change. Notably, the town built a pool in the West End in 1968 and placed two more pools in the community during the early 1970s.[93]

The uprisings in Plainfield and Chicago were not solely about recreation. In both cases police brutality played a particularly large role in the motives for and outcomes of the riots. But clearly young African Americans were deeply angered by their continued exclusion from swimming pools and parks in post–Civil Rights Act America. And even in this era blacks fought openly with white defenders of recreational spaces who screamed insults and threw projectiles at them in Chicago and elsewhere. White citizens, city officials, and police officers too often viewed blacks' presence in urban and suburban public spaces, particularly parks, as inherently threatening. Young blacks believed this was a basic right too often denied to them. The violent rebellions that ensued when police and National Guardsmen "cleared" young blacks from parks and streets were a clash of these two worldviews.

One clash between armed authorities and African Americans over access to recreation proved particularly deadly. In Orangeburg, South Carolina, there was only one bowling alley, All Star Bowling Lanes, run by Harry Floyd, who refused to allow African Americans through his doors. The Civil Rights Act covered bowling alleys only if they served food, in which case segregated snack bars were prohibited. The confusion over this aspect of the law led to a proliferation of challenges to segregated bowling in both the North and South throughout the late 1960s.[94] After 1964, African American college students enrolled in two historically black colleges in Orangeburg, South Carolina State and Claflin College, began to protest the segregated alley. A year earlier students had staged mass protests against segregated lunch counters in the downtown of the conservative, rural town. Police turned fire hoses on the students and arrested dozens, but the desegregation campaign was ultimately successful. Floyd was a holdout who insisted on maintaining the color line. One State College student, John Stroman, was particularly determined to open the alley. Stroman, a league bowler, was weary of driving forty miles to Columbia, South Carolina, in order to bowl. In early February 1968 Stroman led a group of black students to the alley. They entered through the back door, avoiding the "Privately Owned" sign Floyd had recently erected in place of his "For Whites Only" sign. Forty students managed to enter the alley before Floyd called the police and closed the business for the evening. The following day the students returned to face locked doors and a large group of police officers carrying batons. The students retreated.[95]

At this point Stroman decided he needed support from a visiting black radical, Cleveland Sellers. Sellers was a veteran of the efforts to integrate Glen Echo Park and the brutal desegregation campaign in Cambridge, Maryland. By 1968 he had renounced nonviolence as a primary tactic and, like others in SNCC, was an advocate of black power. When Stroman sought his support Sellers dismissed him, stating that the bowling alley should not be a priority for the movement. "Integration," Sellers wrote in his autobiography about the request, "was an irrelevant issue."[96] But the black students in Orangeburg disagreed. For them segregated recreation continued to be a priority, not because they were clamoring for integration but because they viewed access to public accommodations as a right. Students also were calling for full enforcement of the hard-fought Civil Rights Act and they rallied to Stroman's side.

On the night of February 8 students again protested outside the alley; this time police directly confronted them and arrested fifteen for disorderly conduct. The remaining students rushed back to campus where they gathered hundreds together and led them to the alley. Fire trucks awaited them, reminiscent of the fire hoses in 1963, and police held weapons at the ready. Police viciously beat the protestors, and as the students retreated back to campus some activists threw rocks at store windows and vandalized cars. Back on campus the wounded sought help at the infirmary, while others drew up a list of grievances that began with, "Close down the All Star Bowling Lanes immediately and request the management to change his policy of racial discrimination before reopening."[97] In the wake of the police riot Sellers rethought his previous position and became a more visible leader in the emerging movement. He believed this was now an issue of police brutality rather than an integrationist cause. In the meantime city officials, fearful of racial violence, called in the National Guard.

In the two days that followed students grew increasingly angry about the lack of response to their demands. The male students, who made up the majority of the protestors, were particularly incensed that the police had beaten several female students. Describing the events, the journalists Jack Nelson and Jack Bass argued, "Basically, it was a question of honor—of asserting their manhood in the presence of the all-white police power that had clubbed black girls."[98] By this time local police and the National Guard had stationed themselves around the perimeter of the South Carolina State campus. On the evening of February 10 students decided to build a large bonfire on the

Figure 16. Police officers at South Carolina State College in Orangeburg guard two badly injured students after officers shot dead three students protesting police brutality and segregation at the All Star Bowling Lanes. This event became known as the Orangeburg massacre. © Bettmann/CORBIS.

edge of campus. They gathered around it singing, "We Shall Overcome" and "We Shall Not Be Moved." Some students also shouted epithets at the nearby officers and threw the occasional projectile their way. As the police began to approach the students moved away, heading back to their dormitories. One officer was hit with a wooden stick and fell to the ground, hard. Other officers assumed he was shot and opened fire. They fired directly on the crowd of fleeing students for ten seconds, hitting dozens. When the shots finally died down three students, Delano Middletown, Henry Smith, and Samuel Hammond, lay dead on the ground. Twenty-seven others lay wounded, among them Cleveland Sellers, who had been shot in the arm.[99] After Sellers was treated at the local segregated hospital, police arrested him, charging him with "inciting to riot." This arrest allowed the governor, Robert McNair, to claim that "black power advocates" were to blame for the riot and (falsely) that snipers had been taking pot shots at the police prior to the shooting. Students singing "We Shall Overcome" and attempting to flee the violence did not fit the prevailing white image of black resistance in 1968.[100]

Meanwhile the All Star Bowling Lanes remained segregated and open for business. By this point the Justice Department was under considerable pressure to respond to the shootings. Martin Luther King, Jr., just six weeks before his assassination, sent a letter to Attorney General Ramsey Clark demanding an investigation of both the segregated alley and the shootings: "We demand that you act now to bring justice to the perpetrators of the largest armed assault undertaken under color of law in recent Southern history."[101] On February 11, the day after the massacre, the Justice Department sued to desegregate Floyd's bowling alley. Floyd responded, "I believe every man has a right to operate his place as he sees fit."[102] He then closed his snack bar in an effort to circumvent the law. Despite this move, the federal district judge ordered Floyd's alley closed pending the outcome of the suit.[103] Finally bowing to the inevitable, Floyd reopened the alley to all residents of Orangeburg. John Stroman and his friend James Davis were among the first bowlers when it reopened.[104] The only individual who served any prison time as a result of the massacre was Cleveland Sellers. An all-white jury found the nine white police officers tried for the shootings not guilty.

The standard narrative of the civil rights movement after 1965 seldom places struggles over public accommodations center stage. Even contemporary civil rights and black power leaders felt that police brutality, housing issues, and employment were at the core in this "new phase" of the movement. Cleveland Sellers, for example, was uninterested in students' protests until the conflict became an issue of police brutality. In part this reflected the perception that the struggle had moved north, where many civil rights leaders believed nonviolence and opening public accommodations were not relevant. Writing in 1967, Martin Luther King argued, "The increases in segregated schools and the expanded slums are developments confined largely to the North. Substantial progress has been achieved in the South. The struggles of the past decade were not national in scope; they were Southern; they were specifically designed to change life in the South, and the principal role of the North was supportive."[105] This North-South binary, however, erased the role of nonviolence in 1940s Chicago where pacifists founded CORE and attacked segregated recreation. And as the events in Orangeburg demonstrated, the job of opening public accommodations in the South was not completed.

The Glen Echo riot, Plainfield riot, Chicago's fire hydrant riot, and the ongoing efforts to enforce the Civil Rights Act suggest that King and Sellers did not fully grasp the importance of public accommodations and the occupation of leisure spaces for urban blacks. Full and equal access to recreational facilities continued to be a priority for many ordinary African Americans in both the North and the South. This demand was not divorced from other priorities—police brutality was the result when black students in Orangeburg challenged bowling segregation, and the struggle to occupy Chicago's parks was directly linked to the open housing movement. Indeed, the 1960s uprisings were an occupation of public space in the most profound sense. As Thomas Sugrue suggests, "The urban riots were, above all, about turf and control."[106] Rioters occupied city streets and claimed them as their own. The Rochester, New York, race riot in 1964, for example, began as a black street party that local police broke up. African Americans who were part of the urban rebellions also engaged in what the historian Alison Isenberg identifies as "consumer revolts" when they targeted white businesses, including commercial recreation, that had exploited or excluded them in the past.[107] Finally, blacks were rebelling against ongoing white violence and antagonism, from the white residents holding up swastikas in the streets of Chicago to the brutal beatings by white police officers. Their occupation of public space was a defiant and often destructive one. In its aftermath was despair but also the glimmerings of hope. As Isenberg suggests, "The riots and civil rights demonstrations highlighted in their respective ways that urban commerce was a critical place where the different people of America came together. If business sites and commercial transactions could spark such conflict, then urban commercial sites were also places where race relations might be repaired."[108] But the recreational spaces where this repair took place were rarely in the urban centers that were the staging grounds for racial rebellion.

From Trolley Park to Theme Park

By the late 1960s the amusement park was a potential "riotland" in a country newly obsessed with law and order. Whites conflated the rising crime rate with the urban riots and increased protests against the Vietnam War. This was not the juvenile delinquency that plagued the 1950s but a more threatening scourge. As one contemporary observer remarked, "In 1967 the violent crime rate was twice that of 1963, a figure backlighted by the glare of burning cities."[109] The race riots fueled the crisis in law and order and hastened the decline of newly desegregated spaces. Because amusement parks had linked cleanliness and order to racial exclusion for decades, the influx of African American consumers raised white concerns that they were no longer safe. Recreation riots at amusement parks since World War II reinforced this notion. Park owners were also increasingly tempted by offers to sell their land to private developers. Therefore, they neglected upkeep in their parks and failed to adequately police teenagers who roamed the grounds. Owners effectively hid this profit motive behind the veil of race. Closing parks in the face of desegregation also paralleled the massive resistance against recreational integration in the South. The result was the demise of nearly all of the traditional trolley parks and the continued rise of the theme park.

Although some have suggested that rising crime and disorder in amusement parks after desegregation led to their downfall, there is little evidence that such behavior was rampant. Parks were beset by recreation riots because of white resistance to sharing these spaces with their black neighbors, but they were not beset by black crime. Even the recreation riots at Glen Echo and Olympic Park were sparked by mistreatment of black teenagers by park officials. Perhaps the best example of how the rumor, rather than the reality, of black crime could become the leading explanation for a park's closing comes from Riverview Park in Chicago. Because of white violence, the park was a dangerous space for Chicago blacks until the early 1960s. Before then, blacks who ventured into the park, according to the local historian Scott Newman, "were often viciously attacked by white thugs for their refusal to submit to white authority."[110] Blacks, however, were present in the park as one of the exhibits—the notorious African Dip, where white customers threw balls at a target to dunk a black man seated on a wooden bench inside a cage suspended above a pool of water. The exhibited "Africans" became masters of inciting white rage by taunting young white men by complimenting their girlfriends and wives. In the late 1950s the NAACP succeeded in closing down the African Dip, but the racial animosity remained.[111]

By 1967 Riverview Park was showing the typical signs of an aging urban amusement park and was increasingly considered a "dangerous" space by white customers fearful of muggings and petty crimes by larger crowds of black customers.[112] One white commentator mourned the days when "Two plainclothesmen were all that was needed to maintain law and order with no difficulty. . . . There would be an occasional pick-pocket arrest, and young girls and children were protected from molesters."[113] Those "simple" times, when young girls were protected, were also times of racial homogeneity. Now that more African Americans ventured into Riverview, city officials, particularly Mayor Daley, became concerned about possible rioting. When the 1967 fire hydrant riot broke out, for example, the mayor ordered Riverview closed for several days.[114] But despite such fears the reality was that there were no major riots at Riverview Park and no evidence of a dramatic increase in criminal behavior. Instead the park became associated with the surrounding urban environment. Closing the park was a preventive rather than reactive measure. Riverview's owner reported "that a contributing reason for the sale of the park was the rising problems of violence and disorder. Although police 'have done a commendable job' in preventing any major disturbance, the problem was on the increase."[115] Preventing potential violence had long been the justification for recreational segregation. As in the South, closing parks and other facilities was a simple way to solve the problem of integration and the problem of violence.

African Americans writing to the *Chicago Defender* did not see Riverview as a dangerous space. In fact, the park was less dangerous for blacks in the late 1960s than it had been in the late 1950s when white customers routinely harassed them. One young black woman wrote, "This has been a place where all children have set their minds on going every summer. It was one of the few places in the city where the entire family could go and have fun." Another lamented upon hearing the park would close down, "It just seems to be part of a horrid thing which is happening in Chicago. There are so many vacant lots where places, not all of them run-down, have been demolished. Then nothing is erected in the vacant areas. Riverview was a children's paradise. Now that will be taken too."[116] A children's paradise and a place for families would be replaced with an industrial park. For urban blacks without the ability to travel to faraway suburban parks, this was a tremendous loss. It was the same loss felt by Newark's African American community when Olympic Park closed down, by Washington, D.C.'s young blacks when Glen Echo closed, and by the West End youth in Louisville when Fontaine Ferry shut its gates.

Across the country the urban amusement parks that blacks had fought so hard to gain access to closed or rapidly fell into disrepair. Springlake Park in Oklahoma City, for example, never recovered from the Easter riot in 1971. The park's owners attempted to assuage the white public's fears that the park was unsafe, promising "protection, security and supervision" and "clean, safe, wholesome fun." But the combination of the black neighborhood surrounding the park and the well-publicized riot undermined this effort. After 1968 traditional urban parks closed in rapid succession. Cincinnati's Coney Island closed the same year as the Springlake riot, replaced by a new theme park, Paramount's Kings Island. This park opened in 1972, north of Cincinnati in Mason, and was inaccessible by public transportation.[117] As one of the activists who helped open Coney Island in 1961 noted, "Just as soon as we won it, they closed it down and moved it to Kings Island. We said, 'We're here,' but it's gone. And it's not only what it costs to get in. Look at how far away it is. It became a transportation challenge, you can come—but it's a long walk."[118] The new Kings Island incorporated a Coney Island section, Old Coney Island, to indulge the nostalgia of park visitors, many of whom now lived in Cincinnati's suburbs.[119] But city dwellers with no cars were out of luck. Reinforcing the image of the theme park as a safe space for white American families, Kings Island was featured in two prominent situation comedies in the early 1970s—*The Partridge Family* (1972) and *The Brady Bunch* (1973). Some urban parks found competition with suburban parks and theme parks insurmountable. Cleveland's Euclid Beach Park, for example, had to compete with Cedar Point in Sandusky and Geauga Lake Park in Aurora for customers. But Euclid Beach's decision to close in 1969 was also the result of continued racial conflict, long after CORE's 1946 campaign to desegregate its swimming pool and dance hall. Chroniclers of Euclid Beach's history blame its open-gate policy for attracting "a number of gangs and undesirables [that] scared off the patrons with money to spend."[120] Many others citied "racial tensions" and "racial incidents" as reasons for the park's demise.[121]

These descriptions of Euclid Beach's closing place blame squarely on Cleveland's African Americans who frequented the park. They were the "undesirables" who created "racial tension." Absent from such descriptions are potentially divisive events such as the Italian Power Day held in Euclid Beach the season it closed.[122] Also absent is the justifiable anger black patrons felt about their ongoing exclusion. "Rather than open some facilities to blacks," remembered an African American newspaper editor, "they shut them down one by one in the years prior to the park's actual closing."[123] One native Clevelander, criticizing the popular and nostalgic histories of the park, noted, "The authors treat the park's financial failure in 1969 as an unfathomable mystery. It's no secret in this town that it was due, in large measure, to racial bigotry."[124] There was, no doubt, an increase in vandalism at Euclid Beach Park in the years before its closure. But the park's owners also deliberately abandoned its facilities. Describing the park in the 1960s, one author states, "The vacant, darkened spaces on the countenance of Euclid Beach Park were like teeth absent from an aging face."[125] The owners shuttered exhibits, closed rides, and generally neglected the grounds as their middle-class white customers sought out Cedar Point, which was now accessible from the interstate highway.

Letting amusement parks "go to seed" was a common tactic among owners who blamed black consumers for declining revenues. Pacific Ocean Park in

Los Angeles, for example, had become dilapidated by 1967 but many blamed the presence of "undesirables" for shutting the park down.[126] Similarly, Riverside Park in Indianapolis had been opened to African Americans only since the early 1960s after repeated protests. Indeed, it was one of the few parks north of the Mason-Dixon Line that openly displayed "Whites Only" signs at the gates. After desegregation the park lost much of its white customer base, and the owners allowed the premises to deteriorate, closing the park in 1970.[127] Most of the parks discussed in this book closed during the same period. Houston's Playland Park, where African Americans carried out boycotts in the 1950s, closed in 1968. Palisades Park, another site of the World War II–era struggles to open public accommodations, closed in 1971. Gwynn Oak Park in Baltimore, where some of the most dramatic civil rights demonstrations took place in the early 1960s, closed in 1972.[128] The Chain of Rocks Amusement Park in St. Louis, which opened its pool in 1963 after intense picketing by young activists, closed in 1977. Kansas City's Fairyland Park, which saw similar protests in the early 1960s, also closed in 1977. And this is not an exhaustive list of the traditional parks that did not survive the desegregation struggles and mass suburbanization of the late 1960s and 1970s.

A handful of urban parks survived the late 1960s and 1970s for a decade or more. Idora Park, which had closed its swimming pool rather than integrate it, shut its doors in 1984.[129] Crystal Beach, across the lake from Buffalo, remained open until 1989 despite the lack of ferry service. Bob-Lo Island, where Sarah Elizabeth Ray challenged her exclusion from the park in 1945, remained open until 1991. Peony Park in Omaha, which admitted blacks only after concerted protests in 1963, closed its gates in 1994. An even smaller number of traditional trolley parks remain open today. Some, like Kennywood Park near Pittsburgh, were far enough from the city center that they avoided the "taint" of urban crowds. Judith Adams, writing about Kennywood, argues, "Lack of access by public transportation was a blessing for the park, enabling it to avoid the destruction, danger, and vandalism generated by urban gangs in other parks."[130] Adams exaggerates the presence of gangs, but certainly the perception that other parks had become ganglands impacted their ability to stay open. David Nasaw also views lack of access by public transportation as key to Kennywood's survival, as well as Cedar Point in Ohio and Coneaut Lake Park in western Pennsylvania.[131] These suburban parks have transformed themselves into theme parks, with massive roller coasters and large water parks supplemented by the major traditional exhibits. A few surviving urban parks, such as Seabreeze in Rochester, actively

Figure 17. Historic plaque at Seabreeze in Rochester, New York. Photograph by the author.

market themselves as spaces of nostalgia. Most rides sport a historical plaque with photographs of revelers from a bygone era.

One could argue that the decline of urban amusement parks was part of a general privatization of American leisure, a turning inward to television sets and backyard playgrounds and pools. Indeed, many commentators on the decline of parks point to television as a primary culprit. But the problem with such a hypothesis is that theme parks boomed in the late 1960s and 1970s. Between 1960 and 1979 Disneyland's attendance went from 5.9 million per year to 10.8 million. And the number of amusement parks overall increased from 400 in 1954 to 786 by 1967.[132] Texas's Six Flags dramatically increased its franchise in the 1970s. Walt Disney World's Magic Kingdom took over suburban Orlando in 1971, Great Adventure opened in New Jersey in 1974, and Busch Gardens opened in Tampa in 1975. Amusement parks had become *more* popular, not less. Americans had become particularly enthralled with roller coasters and thrill rides in the 1970s, exhibits that sprawling theme parks had the space and the money to launch. There was no retreat into the private world of the suburban home, but rather a retreat from urban leisure spaces many perceived as dangerous.

* * *

After desegregation, the owners of traditional parks cut off public transportation, instituted pay-one-price plans, and tried to reassure their white customers that their parks were safe. However, knowing the land the parks occupied was valuable, they also let the facilities decline and sold them to the highest bidder. Meanwhile, city dwellers without access to cars or the price of admission would never experience the joys of an amusement park after they closed. Therefore, the lack of equitable access to recreation continued into late twentieth-century America. But the inequality that marked public accommodations had become a spatial inequality. By the 1970s many viewed the city as a space of danger, to be avoided. Perceptions of a rapid decline in law and order meant that violence became a justification for white consumers and residents and some members of the black middle class to abandon cities and towns. Many whites blamed the racial uprisings of the 1960s for the decline of cities like Detroit and Newark. Similarly, whites blamed recreation riots instigated by blacks for the decline of amusement parks. Fearing a law and order crisis and attracted by suburban amenities and low taxes, urbanites leaving for the suburbs left behind not only homes but also pools and parks that were now shuttered.

Throughout the twentieth century owners and managers marketed their amusement parks as wholesome and safe spaces of leisure. This carefully drawn image was dependent on African Americans' exclusion. The racial makeup of park customers signaled safety and security to white consumers, while the exclusion of blacks reflected the limitations of citizenship for African Americans. Integrating these parks became a potent symbol of black advancement in the civil rights era. But racial integration also changed the parks' liminal position by bringing them into the turmoil of urban America. Whites no longer perceived them as safe havens for families, and as a result most closed by the early 1970s. This fact demonstrates the limits of the 1964 Civil Rights Act. Because racial inequality is deeply spatial, legislation cannot change the association of black-dominated spaces with disorder. The myth of a golden age in recreation reinforced this association, and by the 1990s many Americans came to express a powerful nostalgia for the urban recreation of the mid-twentieth century. Old wooden roller coasters, lavish swimming pools, and swinging dance halls have been celebrated in documentary films and other forms of public history. Rarely, however, do these public depictions of the past highlight the racial exclusion on which recreation was premised.

Conclusion

WHEN Walt Disney opened his new theme park in 1955, Anaheim was at the outskirts of suburban Los Angeles. By the 1980s, however, Disneyland was accessible by public transportation and frequented by local teenagers with discounted annual passes in hand. Customers began to complain that groups of young Latinos and blacks dominated the park grounds. And Disneyland was showing its age with peeling paint and burned-out bulbs.[1] The original Disneyland had become part of Los Angeles rather than a distinct fantasy world. But Americans seeking the Disney experience had another option. Disney World's Magic Kingdom opened in 1971 outside Orlando. This time the Disney Company bought such an extensive property that there was no risk of urban incursion. The park was open to anyone who could afford the price of admission, but Disney carefully controlled the heterogeneous crowds through planning, policing, and landscaping. As Disney executive Jeffrey Katzenberg commented, "think of Disney World as a medium-sized city with a crime rate of zero."[2] In 2000 fourteen million middle-class Americans and foreign visitors flocked to the Disney World resorts.

But not everybody was celebrating the Disney experience. Increasingly, social commentators and critics lamented the "Disneyfication" of the American landscape.[3] Malls, restaurants, casinos, and cruise ships began to sport themes to distinguish themselves from competitors. Many critics felt these "variations on a theme park" appeared commodified and sterile, reflecting a decline in public life.[4] Themed spaces, they suggested, were disconnected from local culture and lacked the authenticity of gritty, urban neighborhoods. But laments about Disney's lack of authenticity are replete with their own nostalgia. As Bryant Simon has argued in his analysis of Atlantic City, "the much-revered public experiences of going downtown or hanging out on the front stoop were just as unreal, just as exclusionary, and just as contrived as the Disneyland public experience of today."[5] There was never a "golden age" of amusements that was more democratic or more "authentic" than today's themed environments. Instead, racial exclusion defined amusement parks, roller-skating rinks, and swimming pools as safe places for white consumers. The historical amnesia that surrounds this reality is fueled by nostalgia for urban amusements generally.

Nostalgia is a form of historical memory that is deeply tied to place and identity.[6] People are nostalgic for the places where they grew up, which they often perceive as safer and more fulfilling than today's suburban neighborhoods or themed environments. The urban amusements that suburbanites pine for have generated a veritable industry of nostalgia. Arcadia Publishing, which specializes in local history, has an extensive list of books on defunct urban amusement parks catering to this nostalgia.[7] The National Amusement Park Historical Association publishes a glossy newsletter on old parks, and most defunct parks have their own fan clubs online. To take only one example, Crystal Beach Park outside Buffalo is fondly remembered in at least nine documentary films, including the aptly titled *Things That Aren't There Anymore*.[8] Titles of books that remember Crystal Beach reflect similar sentiments, such as *The Last Fine Time* and *Crystal Beach: The Good Old Days*.[9] "Many things change as time goes on; many gentle customs are replaced by harsher sights and sounds. But not childhood, not fun, not the love of parents for their children—and not Crystal Beach waffles and cinnamon suckers," remembers one local journalist.[10] Those suckers are still sold at neighborhood ice cream parlors, and older Buffalonians will talk at great length about the glories of their lost park. Implicit in these conversations is a lost city, one that may not have existed in reality but remains fixed in memory. This lost Buffalo is the City of Good Neighbors without the deepening poverty, segregation, and violence of the postwar period. But it is also part of a world that King spoke of in his letter from Birmingham Jail, a world where his six-year-old daughter Yolanda watched Funtown from beyond the gates.

Buffalonians' reminiscences of Crystal Beach are echoed across the country with similar documentaries, books, and memorabilia. Rarely do these depictions incorporate the longing African American children expressed to ride on roller coasters, skate in rinks, or dive into swimming pools. White suburbanites continue to wax nostalgic about urban amusement parks, viewing them as symbols of the melting pot and memories of halcyon days.

Recollections of African Americans growing up in the Jim Crow era, in contrast, are replete with the closed gates of leisure. Eleanor Jordan, who grew up in Louisville near Fontaine Ferry Park during the 1950s, remembers, "Whenever we passed that amusement park . . . you see the lights, the big Ferris wheel that had green lights on it. And we would always ask the same question: 'Can we go?' And my mother and father would almost simultaneously say, 'No, you can't go.' We'd kind of sit there, and then as we passed it, we'd say, 'Well, why can't we go?' And that's when there was just this deafening silence in the car. And my mother always, her eyes would always fill up with tears, and my father would just kind of look away, and we knew something was wrong."[11] Nostalgia for Fontaine Ferry runs high in Louisville, but the memories are as segregated as the park once was. One African American man recalled, "I didn't realize I was black, and black was different until I stood outside Fontaine Ferry one day. We didn't understand why we couldn't go in there. When you are a child and you see other children having fun, you can't understand why you can't do it too. It was a very sad feeling. Even after they let us go in, nobody really felt welcome."[12]

Contrast this reminiscence with that of a white resident who went to the park during the years of racial violence, 1961–69: "Over the years I did visit the park many times, along with several trips to the swimming pool and the skating rink (with its authentic calliope music). I was never old enough to go to Gypsy Village, which always seemed like such a mysterious place to me. Lastly, let's not forget about the prizes you'd win—from the straw hats, bamboo canes, and all those chalk figurines!"[13] Or this one: "It's probably hard for kids nowadays to believe that in a world of video games and high tech 'everything' and the monster amusement parks we have today that kids from my day could be so thoroughly entertained by something called 'Mirror Maze,' 'Jungle Land,' 'The Caterpillar' or 'Hilarity Hall.' . . . Growing up in Louisville though, that was reality and I couldn't think of any other way I would have wanted it."[14] Some whites do recall the decline of the park and its recreation riot in the midst of happier memories. For example, one contributor to a blog wrote, "It was a sad situation when the 60's brought such racial tensions into the area. It got so it was too dangerous to even go into the west end of Louisville, let alone Fontaine Ferry Park. When this excellent old park was tragically destroyed, I think a little bit of each of us went with it."[15]

The granddaughter of Fontaine Ferry's owners admitted that the park maintained a segregated dance hall and swimming pool up until its closing. She writes, "I wish that my grandparents had had the foresight to have changed the policies of the park in not admitting blacks. In light of the racial tensions of 1968 they should have made changes by the following season."[16] On websites and in popular documentaries and books that celebrate traditional urban amusement parks it is the late 1960s and "racial tensions" that end the golden age of the parks. The blame here is clearly laid upon urban blacks who, upon gaining entry to amusement parks, also laid waste to them. These are the same historical actors who supposedly laid waste to traditional downtowns and ethnic neighborhoods. Urban historians have largely debunked the notion that the 1960s race riots were to blame for industrial cities' economic and physical decline. But these lessons need to be applied to the decline of urban amusements. Their closure was not a harbinger of a larger declension story but a reflection of a century of segregation and exclusion. Above all the disinvestment in urban recreation is evidence of racialized space's power in twentieth-century American cities.

African Americans who remained in urban centers suffered greater losses than their suburban counterparts did when local amusements closed down. Large city parks remain, but few have working swimming pools or skating rinks in operation as they once did. By the mid-1960s the Federal Housing Administration (FHA) openly discouraged public ownership of recreational facilities. Instead, they promoted private homeowner associations in planned developments.[17] Today there are significantly fewer resources put toward urban recreational facilities, particularly swimming pools.[18] During times of fiscal austerity cities and towns often close down their pools or drastically cut hours. In Sacramento, California, for example, there were thirteen public pools in 2001. As a result of budget cuts, only three will remain open by summer 2012.[19] And there can be deadly consequences to the lack of public pools for urban children who have no access to private backyard pools or swimming lessons. Two children drowned in a natural pond at Squaw Island Park in Buffalo over one year, with no other swimming facilities readily available.[20] Such deaths in natural waters are a grim reminder of the many children who died in rivers and ponds because of their exclusion from segregated pools and beaches in the twentieth century. The defunding of these resources in contemporary America has carried those tragedies into the new century.

The nostalgia for more vibrant urban leisure crosses racial lines with the decline of recreational facilities after 1970. African Americans lament the loss of urban recreation that they had limited access to. And there is also nostalgia for the segregated past, what Michelle R. Boyd has identified as "Jim Crow nostalgia": "a yearning for and a celebration of black life during the period of legalized racial segregation."[21] In this discourse, integration marks the end of what some blacks perceived as vibrant, self-sufficient black communities in the mid-twentieth century. Boyd suggests that "Jim Crow, a period of violent, repressive, state-sanctioned racism, has come to be popularly understood as a racial utopia, a haven from the uncertainty, disappointment, and inadequacy of the contemporary period."[22] In particular, critics of integration point out that black businesses suffered from white competition after the passage of the Civil Rights Act. This was true of some small black amusement parks, such as Sea View Beach in Norfolk, Virginia, and Lincoln Beach in New Orleans. When Norfolk's whites only Ocean View Beach was forced to admit blacks after 1964, Sea View Beach lost many of its black customers.[23] Similarly, Lincoln Beach closed after the courts forced segregated Pontchartrain Beach to open to blacks.[24] Smaller black-owned parks had difficulty competing with their larger, better-appointed counterparts.

The economic and cultural costs of desegregation, as these examples suggest, should not be dismissed. But there were relatively few black-owned recreational facilities that closed as a result of integration. Compared to black-owned restaurants and stores, most recreational facilities required a significant amount of capital to run. This was particularly true of large facilities like amusement parks and resort pools. In addition, when cities entirely segregated their public facilities and built no black counterparts, African Americans had no access to public recreation. Remembering growing up in Portsmouth, Virginia, John W. Brown remarked, "Anything that was public was also white. For example, the public park, the public playground, they were white."[25] Opening public facilities did not hold the same correlating economic costs for the black community as opening commercial recreation. Rather than integration undermining black autonomy, the struggle to open public accommodations created new black spaces and new opportunities. For many black consumers, particularly the teenagers who sought to make use of recreation, the goal was the occupation of space rather than racial integration. African Americans in cities like Chicago were seeking safety and play by frequenting beaches and parks. Too often they encountered rocks, racial epithets, and a constant limitation on their freedom of movement. As James Baldwin said, rather than being "'accepted' by white people," blacks "simply don't wish to be beaten over the head by the whites every instant of our brief passage on this planet."[26] Yet African Americans' desire for an end to racial violence and intimidation is too often absent from memories of Jim Crow.

Racial tension in recreational spaces did not end with the 1964 Civil Rights Act or the many legal struggles that subsequently desegregated facilities. We still live with what Anders Walker calls the "ghost of Jim Crow."[27] Walker argues that southern moderates crafted and promoted justifications for continuing segregation while complying with the law. These justifications were often cultural as they "exaggerated the extent to which they [blacks] suffered from illegitimacy, immorality, and other social ills."[28] Sharing space with blacks, whether in a classroom or a swimming pool, continued to be objectionable to some whites. This overt racism in public accommodations did not disappear when the legal questions were finally settled. A skating rink outside Washington, D.C., still refused to allow blacks in 1978. And as recently as 2009 the owner of a private swim club in Philadelphia excluded black children attending a Philadelphia day care center, saying they would change the "complexion" of the club.[29] But the expressed motivation for racial separation by the mid-1970s rarely invoked the virulent racism of massive resistance so common earlier in the century. Instead, a color-blind discourse suggested that choices about where to live, work, and play were individual decisions separate from the legacy of racism. When amusement parks and other facilities barred entry to customers, they reportedly did so because of safety concerns or disorderly conduct, not race. For example, San Francisco's Great America Amusement Park barred a group of black and Hispanic young men in 1991 for reportedly wearing "gang attire." And Magic Mountain near Los Angeles has routinely barred young black and Hispanic customers as part of their policy of screening suspected gang members.[30]

Although urban amusements have suffered a precipitous decline in both quality and quantity, there has been remarkable progress in the extent to which whites and blacks mix in some recreational spaces. This change in social mores, although by no means complete, is a direct result of the struggle for desegregated recreation. Often it is the most expensive facilities, like Disney World, where one can view significant amounts of racial integration. African American families that have the means to travel to Orlando and pay the gate fees freely mix with their white counterparts. And the growing popularity of water parks, now ubiquitous across suburban America, suggests that swimming no longer engenders the fear of racial mixing that it once did.[31] But the boom in new water parks and theme parks created often insurmountable barriers for low-income urban residents who have no ready access to such facilities. Not all of these underserved city dwellers are black, but their economic and spatial exclusion is racial in origin. And the racial makeup of smaller recreational facilities such as roller-skating rinks and swimming pools, because they attract families from their surrounding communities, are more homogenous than large theme parks. As long as housing segregation persists, recreational segregation will persist.

An open conversation about recreational segregation in modern America has been stymied by the desire to wax nostalgic about past urban amusements. There are moments, however, when the hidden history of recreational segregation is revealed. In the summer of 2005 two real estate developers in Stonewall, Mississippi, Gilbert Carmichael and Tom Sebring, saw a piece of concrete sticking up from the ground on property they had recently purchased. Further excavation revealed a swimming pool complete with tile work and underwater lights. The town leaders had hastily buried the pool in the early 1970s rather than allow local blacks to swim alongside their white children. In 2007 Carmichael and Sebring attended the opening of the Historic Stonewall Mill Community Swimming Pool, now open to all Stonewall families. Carmichael called the pool "a symbol of reconciliation."[32] Racial reconciliation has been an ongoing project in Deep South states for the last several decades. But such ceremonies should ideally take place in Chicago or suburban New Jersey as well. Reconciliation should be a national project, just as segregation was throughout the twentieth century.

Many whites in the North and South associated disorder with the presence of African Americans. This association allowed political leaders and the courts to justify segregation as a form of law and order—whether through a "Whites Only" sign or the creation of a private club. Their fears of violence seemed validated when desegregated urban recreational facilities experienced problems of vandalism and delinquency. These incidents became part of a larger national image of cities in distress. Playlands had become Riotlands because of the presence of African Americans. Meanwhile, decades of white hostility and violence aimed at blacks who attempted to use recreational facilities have been largely forgotten. This violence took a variety of forms, from the young toughs who beat blacks attempting to swim at a city beach to the hidden violence of shutting down recreational facilities rather than desegregating them. But much of the blame for the wholesale decline of urban amusements lies in white abandonment of recreational facilities. And this abandonment, rooted in a refusal to share public space, had devastating consequences for the daily lives of urban dwellers.

Full access to public accommodations—the occupation of public space—was central to the freedom struggle because it is itself a central freedom. The

African American mothers who demanded equality for their young children understood this. So did young student activists, black and white, and the lawyers who advocated for them. Black teenagers hoping to ride a roller coaster or jump in a pool also understood recreation as an expression of freedom. It is past time twenty-first-century Americans understood the connection between freedom and fun.

Notes

Introduction

1. The term "public accommodation" is a fluid one within the law and in general practice. This study examines three broad categories of recreational accommodations. The first is the most heavily impacted by state and federal civil rights statutes: public recreational facilities owned and run by municipalities or other governmental entities. Municipal swimming pools, state parks, and picnic grounds all fall under this category. In order to avoid desegregation orders, however, such accommodations at times leased their facilities to private individuals or organizations. For example, city managers often transformed public swimming pools into private swimming clubs. These private clubs, the second category, were most impervious to legal challenges. The third, and most numerous example in this study, are commercial recreational facilities. Amusement parks, for example, are generally owned by private individuals but are considered forms of "public accommodations" because they are open to the general public.

2. There is a rapidly growing literature on the long civil rights movement. Representative works include Martha Biondi, *To Stand and Fight: The Struggle for Civil Rights in Postwar New York City* (Cambridge, Mass.: Harvard University Press, 2003); Jacquelyn Dowd Hall, "The Long Civil Rights Movement and the Political Uses of the Past," *Journal of American History* 91, 4 (March 2005): 1–28; Matthew J. Countryman, *Up South: Civil Rights and Black Power in Philadelphia* (Philadelphia: University of Pennsylvania Press, 2006); Glenda Elizabeth Gilmore, *Defying Dixie: The Radical Roots of Civil Rights, 1919–1950* (New York: W. W. Norton, 2008); Thomas Sugrue, *Sweet Land of Liberty: The Forgotten Struggle for Civil Rights in the North* (New York: Random House, 2008); Jeanne F. Theoharis and Komozi Woodward, eds., *Freedom North: Black Freedom Struggles Outside the South, 1940–1980* (New York: Palgrave Macmillan, 2003); and Robert Self, *American Babylon: Race and the Struggle for Postwar Oakland* (Princeton, N.J.: Princeton University Press, 2003). For a critique of the long civil rights movement, see Sundiata K. Cha-Jua and Clarence E. Lang, "The 'Long Movement' as Vampire: Temporal and Spatial Fallacies in Recent Black Freedom Studies," *Journal of African American History* 92, 2 (2007): 265–88.

3. See, for example, Risa L. Goluboff, *The Lost Promise of Civil Rights* (Cambridge, Mass.: Harvard University Press, 2007). In "The Long Civil Rights Movement and the Political Uses of the Past," Jacquelyn Hall states, "The economic dimensions of the movement lie at the core of my concerns" (2). Martha Biondi, in *To Stand and Fight*, focuses on the economic goals of the "Black Popular Front." Nikhil Pal Singh, in *Black Is a Country: Race and the Unfinished Struggle for Democracy* (Cambridge, Mass.: Harvard University Press, 2004), criticizes civil rights scholars for reinforcing a "formal, legalistic view of black equality" (6). In her book *Defying Dixie*, Gilmore argues that the media's focus on "school integration, access to public accommodations, and voting

rights . . . erased the complexity of a drive to eliminate the economic injustices wrought by slavery, debt peonage, and a wage labor system based on degraded black labor" (9). Finally, in *Freedom Is Not Enough: The Opening of the American Workplace* (New York: Russell Sage Foundation, 2006), Nancy MacLean states, "The quest for jobs and justice, in turn, involved a more robust vision of equality than the legal change evoked by the phrase 'civil rights'" (5–6).

4. Steven Hahn has been the most outspoken historian to critique the "integrationist framework" in African American history. See, in particular, Steven Hahn, *The Political Worlds of Slavery and Freedom* (Cambridge, Mass.: Harvard University Press, 2009). Hahn argues that historians who use the integrationist framework "have privileged and lent legitimacy to African American struggles for inclusion and assimilation, for individual rights, and for citizenship, while at the same time regarding African American interest in separatism and community development, in collective rights, and in forms of nationalism as the products of failure and defeat, as somehow lacking in integrity" (160).

5. Both Robert E. Weems, Jr., and Susannah Walker argue that black businesses were undermined by integration. See Robert E. Weems, Jr., "African American Consumers Since World War II," in *African American Urban History Since World War II*, ed. Kenneth L. Kusmer and Joe W. Trotter (Chicago: University of Chicago Press, 2009), 359–75; and Susannah Walker, "Black Dollar Power: Assessing African American Consumerism Since 1945," in *African American Urban History Since World War II*, 376–403.

6. Like many scholars I have been deeply influenced by the spatial turn in the humanities and social sciences. This work has argued, in the most general sense, that space is socially produced and can both constrain and enable human agency. Most influential to my own thinking about space have been the following: Mark Gottdeiner, *The Social Construction of Urban Space* (Austin: University of Texas Press, 1985); David Harvey, *Social Justice and the City* (Baltimore: Johns Hopkins University Press, 1973); Henri Lefebvre, *The Production of Space* (Oxford: Blackwell, 1974); Mike Davis, *City of Quartz: Excavating the Future in Las Vegas* (New York: Vintage Books, 1992); Sharon Zukin, *Landscapes of Power: From Detroit to Disneyworld* (Berkeley: University of California Press, 1991); Edward W. Soja, *Seeking Spatial Justice* (Minneapolis: University of Minnesota Press, 2010); and Don Mitchell, *The Right to the City: Social Justice and the Fight for Public Space* (New York: Guilford Press, 2003).

7. For example, in *How Racism Takes Place* (Philadelphia: Temple University Press, 2011), George Lipsitz suggests, "Attacks on Blacks seeking to enter spaces reserved for whites constituted actual rather than imagined criminal behavior. Yet because it was criminality exercised on behalf of whiteness, its perpetrators knew that ultimately they would be protected and supported by legally constituted authorities" (26).

8. There is an ongoing debate among historians about the term "riot" when describing the racial uprisings of the 1960s. Generally those who wish to highlight the political nature of the disorders call them "uprisings" or "rebellions," while those who focus on the negative outcomes call them "riots." The phrase "recreation riot" encompasses a variety of disorders in spaces of recreation, from white attacks on blacks seeking leisure to blacks protesting mistreatment. The term "riot" best encompasses this broad category of disorders. For particularly insightful discussions of this debate, see Heather Thompson, "Urban Uprisings: Riots or Rebellions?" in *The Columbia Guide to America in the 1960s*, ed. David R. Farber and Beth L. Bailey (New York: Columbia University Press, 2001), 109–17; and Amanda I. Seligman, "'But Burn-No': The Rest of the Crowd in Three Civil Disorders in 1960s Chicago," *Journal of Urban History* 37, 2 (2011): 230–55.

9. Arnold H. Hirsch, *Making the Second Ghetto: Race and Housing in Chicago, 1940–1960* (Cambridge: Cambridge University Press, 1983); Thomas J. Sugrue, *The Origins of the Urban Crisis: Race and Inequality in Postwar Detroit* (Princeton, N.J.: Princeton University Press, 1996); Stephen Grant Meyer, *As Long as They Don't Move Next Door: Segregation and Racial Conflicts in American Neighborhoods* (Lanham, Md.: Rowman and Littlefield, 2000).

10. Meyer, *As Long as They Don't Move Next Door*, 118–19; Hirsch, *Making the Second Ghetto*, 53–54. The Cicero riot was covered widely in the national media. See, for example, Charles Abrams, "The Time Bomb That Exploded in Cicero," *Commentary* 12 (November 1951): 407–14; "The Cicero Riots," *New York Times,* July 15, 1951, E8; and Helen Henley, "Indictments Hit in Cicero Riot Case," *Christian Science Monitor*, September 21, 1951, 3. Hirsch notes that the Cicero riot was "the most widely publicized racial disorder" of the 1950s, including front-page stories in Southeast Asia and the Middle East (53).

11. "Fight Palisades Backsliding," *CORE-lator*, October 1951, p. 3, microfilm, Reel 13, EIII, CORE Papers, Addendum. This incident happened despite the fact that the New Jersey courts had forced Palisades Park to desegregate as a direct result of CORE's campaign in the late 1940s. For an explicit comparison of housing and recreation, see Allen D. Grimshaw, "Negro-White Relations in the Urban North: Two Areas of High Conflict Potential," in *Racial Violence in the United States*, ed. Allen D. Grimshaw (Chicago: Aldine Publishing Company, 1969), 455–65.

12. Biondi, *To Stand and Fight*, 82–84; James Peck, "The Proof of the Pudding," *The Crisis* 56, 10 (November 1949): 292–355; Jim Peck, *Cracking the Color Line: Non-Violent Direct Action Methods of Eliminating Racial Discrimination*, 11–12, microfilm, Reel 19, EIII, CORE Papers, Addendum; "Pickets Resume Palisades Pacing," *Billboard* 59, 36 (September 13, 1947): 47.

13. For a critique of de jure versus de facto dichotomy, see Matthew D. Lassiter, "De Jure/De Facto Segregation: The Long Shadow of a National Myth," in *The Myth of Southern Exceptionalism*, ed. Matthew D. Lassiter and Joseph Crespino (New York: Oxford University Press, 2010), 99–120.

14. Randall Kennedy, "The Struggle for Racial Equality in Public Accommodations," in *Legacies of the 1964 Civil Rights Act*, ed. Bernard Grofman (Charlottesville: University Press of Virginia, 2000), 161. Kennedy goes on to say, "It was therefore a largely regional problem, unlike the national problem of racial discrimination in employment" (161).

15. For a dismantling of this myth, see Lassiter and Crespino, *The Myth of Southern Exceptionalism*. Heather Ann Thompson calls for a "synthetic analysis of black resistance" that is national in scope ("All Across the Nation: Urban Black Activism, North and South, 1965–1975," in *African American Urban History Since World War II*, 181). In his work *As Long as They Don't Move Next Door*, Meyer makes a similar plea for a national understanding of spatial segregation.

16. Jeanne Theoharis, "Hidden in Plain Sight: The Civil Rights Movement Outside the South," in *The Myth of Southern Exceptionalism*, 49–73.

17. "Beach Parties," *Chicago Defender*, July 16, 1921, 16.

18. For analyses of "performative" violence, see Allen Feldman, *Formations of Violence: The Narrative of the Body and Political Terror in Northern Ireland* (Chicago: University of Chicago Press, 1991); and Joel P. Rhodes, *The Voice of Violence: Performative Violence as Protest in the Vietnam Era* (Westport, Conn.: Praeger, 2001). In *The Ghost of Jim Crow: How Southern Moderates Used Brown v. Board of Education to Stall Civil Rights* (New York: Oxford University Press, 2009), Anders Walker argues that moderate southern governors used violence prevention as a justification for slowing the pace of racial integration.

19. Focusing on spaces rather than people has helped me avoid personality-centered social movement history. For another work employing this approach, see Anne Enke, *Finding the Movement: Sexuality, Contested Space, and Feminist Activism* (Durham, N.C.: Duke University Press, 2007).

20. Here I have been influenced by *The Right to the City: Social Justice and the Fight for Public Space* (New York: Guilford Press, 2003) by Don Mitchell, who argues that "Representation, whether of oneself or of a group, demands space" (33).

21. In *To End All Segregation: The Politics of the Passage of the Civil Rights Act of 1964* (New York: University Press of America, 1990), Robert D. Loevy argues, "The primary impact of the successful passage of the Civil Rights Act of 1964, therefore, was that virtually overnight black Americans could and did receive services in innumerable places of public accommodation that had previously

been unavailable to them" (331). Kevin Kruse, in *White Flight: Atlanta and the Making of Modern Conservatism* (Princeton, N.J.: Princeton University Press, 2005), disputes this formulation, noting that whites in Atlanta continued to struggle to keep "their" accommodations white.

22. Heather Ann Thompson, "Why Mass Incarceration Matters: Rethinking Crisis, Decline, and Transformation in Postwar American History," *Journal of American History* 97, 3 (December 2010): 706.

23. Lizabeth Cohen, *A Consumers' Republic: The Politics of Mass Consumption in Postwar America* (New York: Alfred A. Knopf, 2003), 189. For an analysis of the importance of family vacations on the civil rights movement, see Susan Sessions Rugh, *Are We There Yet? The Golden Age of American Family Vacations* (Lawrence: University Press of Kansas, 2008).

24. Rob Shields, *Places on the Margin: Alternative Geographies of Modernity* (New York: Routledge, 1991), 84. The term "liminality" comes from the work of Victor Turner, who used it to describe the period in which an individual passes from one category or status to another. Victor Turner, *Dramas, Fields, and Metaphors* (Ithaca, N.Y.: Cornell University Press, 1974). For a discussion of how amusement parks could overturn "conventional restraints," see John Kasson, *Amusing the Millions: Coney Island at the Turn of the Century* (New York: Hill & Wang, 1978), 49.

25. Zukin, *Landscapes of Power*, 259. Zukin's use of the term "imaginary landscape" is derived from poststructuralists' analysis of the "social imaginary" (Lefebvre) "to refer to a mythologized, but internalized, set of cultural meanings" (Sharon Zukin, "From Coney Island to Las Vegas in the Urban Imaginary: Discursive Practices of Growth and Decline," *Urban Affairs Review* 33, 5 [May 1998]: 628). See also Sharon Zukin, *The Culture of Cities* (New York: Blackwell, 1995).

26. Richard Moore, a Presbyterian pastor, quoted in Judith A. Bechtel and Robert M. Coughlin, *Building the Beloved Community: Maurice McCrackin's Life for Peace and Civil Rights* (Philadelphia: Temple University Press, 1991), 80. Within their gates amusement parks incorporated a variety of commercial businesses including restaurants, swimming pools, roller-skating rinks, and dance halls.

27. See Matthew D. Lassiter, *The Silent Majority: Suburban Politics in the Sunbelt South* (Princeton, N.J.: Princeton University Press, 2007); and David M. Freund, *Colored Property: State Policy and White Racial Politics in Suburban America* (Chicago: University of Chicago Press, 2007).

Chapter 1

1. Dorothy Height, *Open Wide the Freedom Gates: A Memoir* (New York: Public Affairs, 2003), 18, 114–17, 126.

2. "Race Pressure in City Called 'Rough on Kids,'" *Pittsburgh Post-Gazette*, September 10, 1963, 1. Johnson went on to report, "This is why I'm on the United Negro Protest Committee. I don't intend to stand for this kind of thing."

3. Judith A. Adams, *The American Amusement Park Industry: A History of Technology and Thrills* (Boston: Twayne Publishers, 1991), 63.

4. For a critique of the "golden age," see John Hannigan, *Fantasy City: Pleasure and Profit in the Postmodern Metropolis* (New York: Routledge, 1998), esp. 15–32; Andrew W. Kahrl, "'The Slightest Semblance of Unruliness': Steamboat Excursions, Pleasure Resorts, and the Emergence of Segregation Culture on the Potomac River," *Journal of American History* 94, 4 (March 2008): 1116; Bryant Simon, *Boardwalk of Dreams: Atlantic City and the Fate of Urban America* (New York: Oxford University Press, 2004), esp. 6–18. Similarly, in *Downtown America: A History of the Place and the People Who Made It* (Chicago: University of Chicago Press, 2004), Alison Isenberg argues that downtown was an "idealized public place" (5).

5. Adams, *The American Amusement Park Industry*, 57–59; Al Griffin, *"Step Right Up Folks!"* (Chicago: Henry Regnery Company, 1974), 1–2; William F. Mangels, *The Outdoor Amusement Industry: From Earliest Times to the Present* (New York: Vintage Press, 1952), 17–22; Jon Sterngass,

First Resorts: Pursuing Pleasure at Saratoga Springs, Newport & Coney Island (Baltimore: Johns Hopkins University Press, 2001), esp. 105–9.

6. Mark S. Foster, "In the Face of 'Jim Crow': Prosperous Blacks and Vacations, Travel and Outdoor Leisure, 1890–1945," *Journal of Negro History* 84, 2 (Spring 1999): 130–49; Charles A. Lofgren, *The Plessy Case: A Legal-Historical Interpretation* (New York: Oxford University Press, 1987), 13–17.

7. Quoted in *Plessy v. Ferguson: A Brief History with Documents* (New York: Bedford Books, 1997), 58. See also Bernard Weisberg, "Racial Violence and Civil Rights Law Enforcement," in *Racial Violence in the United States*, ed. Allen D. Grimshaw (Chicago: Aldine Publishing Company, 1969), 320–29.

8. Quoted in "Decision Awaited in Md. Pool Cases," *Afro-American*, July 3, 1954. See also Jeff Wiltse, *Contested Waters: A Social History of Swimming Pools in America* (Chapel Hill: University of North Carolina Press, 2007), 156–58; Sanford B. Hertz, "Constitutional Law: Equal Protection: Discrimination Against Negroes in State Recreation Facilities," *Michigan Law Review* 53, 4 (February 1955): 614–16. The decision to uphold segregated swimming in Baltimore was overturned in 1955 by the U.S. District Court in *Dawson v. Mayor and City Council of Baltimore* in the wake of the 1954 *Brown v. Board of Education* decision.

9. Milton R. Konvitz, "Legislation Guaranteeing Equality of Access to Places of Public Accommodation," *Annals of the American Academy of Political and Social Science* 275 (May 1951): 47–52; Valeria W. Weaver, "The Failure of Civil Rights, 1875–1883, and Its Repercussions," *Journal of Negro History* 54, 4 (October 1969): 373–74; Richard Kluger, *Simple Justice: The History of Brown v. Board of Education and Black America's Struggle for Equality* (New York: Alfred A. Knopf, 1976), 77; John R. Howard, *The Shifting Wind: The Supreme Court and Civil Rights from Reconstruction to Brown* (Albany: State University of New York Press, 1999), 124–33. Justice Harlan also wrote a dissent in the 1883 *Civil Rights Cases* in which he pointed out that the state licensed public amusements and that they should, therefore, be covered by the Fourteenth Amendment.

10. C. Vann Woodward, *The Strange Career of Jim Crow* (New York: Oxford University Press, 1955). The debate over Woodward's thesis has produced numerous significant works including Howard N. Rabinowitz, *Race Relations in the Urban South, 1865–90* (Urbana: University of Illinois Press, 1980); Charles E. Wynes, *Race Relations in Virginia, 1870–1902* (Charlottesville: University of Virginia Press, 1961); Joel Williamson, *After Slavery: The Negro in South Carolina During Reconstruction, 1861–1877* (Chapel Hill: University of North Carolina Press, 1965); Edward L. Ayers, *The Promise of the New South: Life After Reconstruction* (New York: Oxford University Press, 1992), esp. 136–46; Leon F. Litwack, *Trouble in Mind: Black Southerners in the Age of Jim Crow* (New York: Alfred A. Knopf, 1998).

11. Litwack, *Trouble in Mind*, 233.

12. Ayers, *The Promise of the New South*, 140. On heterosociability, see Kathy Peiss, *Cheap Amusements: Working Women and Leisure in Turn-of-the-Century New York* (Philadelphia: Temple University Press, 1986).

13. Grace Elizabeth Hale emphasizes the "modern" character of southern segregation, especially in sites of consumption. See *Making Whiteness: The Culture of Segregation in the South, 1890–1940* (New York: Vintage Books, 1998), esp. 121–98. David R. Goldfield notes that segregation was "an evolving institution, and accompaniment of modernization that followed the urban and economic development of the region" (*Black, White, and Southern: Race Relations and Southern Culture 1940 to the Present* [Baton Rouge: Louisiana State University Press, 1990], 11).

14. Michael J. Klarman, *From Jim Crow to Civil Rights: The Supreme Court and the Struggle for Racial Equality* (New York: Oxford University Press, 2004), 22–23; Konvitz, "Legislation Guaranteeing Equality of Access to Places of Public Accommodation," 48.

15. Weaver, "The Failure of Civil Rights," 376–77. Weaver notes that there was a "roller skating craze" in Ohio from 1882 to 1885 that led to the cases. See also Dwight W. Hoover, "Roller-Skating Toward Industrialism," in *Hard at Play: Leisure in America, 1840–1940*, ed. Kathryn Grover (Amherst: University of Massachusetts Press, 1992), 61–76. Charles S. Johnson notes in *Patterns of Negro*

Segregation (New York: Harper & Bros, 1943) that "The fact that civil rights laws in the North are continually being tested in the courts indicates both the need for such laws and the reluctance of some individuals to change their customary practices to conform with the requirements of the law" (192–93). For a discussion of the difficulty facing early civil rights cases in recreation, see Henry J. McGuinn, "Commercial Recreation," in *Negro Problems in Cities*, ed. T. J. Woofter (1928; reprint, College Park, Md.: McGrath Publishing Co., 1969), 258–61.

16. Donna M. DeBlasio, "The Immigrant and the Trolley Park in Youngstown, Ohio, 1899–1945," *Rethinking History* 5, 1 (2001): 82–83; Rick Shale and Charles J. Jacques, Jr., *Idora Park: The Last Ride of Summer* (Jefferson, Ohio: Amusement Park Journal, 1999), 15.

17. Forrester B. Washington, "Recreational Facilities for the Negro," *Annals of the American Academy of Political and Social Science* 140 (November 1928): 273. Other studies of African American recreation during the first half of the twentieth century include Ernest T. Attwell, "The Recreation Movement and Colored Americans," *Southern Workman* (February 1923): 78–85; William H. Jones, *Recreation and Amusement Among Negroes in Washington, D.C.* (Washington, D.C.: Howard University Press, 1927); McGuinn, "Commercial Recreation"; Charles H. Williams, "Recreation in the Lives of Young People," *Southern Workman* (February 1917): 95–100. For a discussion of the role of recreation in disciplining migrants during the first Great Migration, see Victoria W. Wolcott, *Remaking Respectability: African American Women in Interwar Detroit* (Chapel Hill: University of North Carolina Press, 2001), 53–64, 93–106. Concerns over the lack of respectable recreation continued into the postwar period. See Virgil A. Clift, "Recreational and Leisure-Time Problems and Needs of Negro Children and Youth," *Journal of Negro Education* 19, 3 (Summer 1950): 333–40.

18. Washington, "Recreational Facilities," 274–76. Only six out of forty private swimming pools in northern cities had "no segregation" (275). Many allowed blacks to attend on specific days. For further discussions of recreational segregation in the first half of the twentieth century, see Gunnar Myrdal, *An American Dilemma: The Negro Problem and Modern Democracy* (New York: Harper and Brothers, 1944), 982–86; St. Clair Drake and Horace R. Cayton, *Black Metropolis: A Study of Negro Life in a Northern City* (1945; reprint, Chicago: University of Chicago Press, 1993), 102–6; Johnson, *Patterns of Negro Segregation*, 26–30, 72–75, 143–46.

19. Idora Park had a yearly All-American Colored Night during the 1920s and 1930s. See *Pittsburgh Courier*, September 27, 1924, 14, August 28, 1926, 14, and July 13, 1929, 9. Camden Park was opened to African Americans one day per year. See Dave Lavender, "Camden Park Celebrates Centennial," *Herald-Dispatch*, June 15, 2003.

20. Washington, "Recreational Facilities," 277.

21. Ibid., 280–81; David Nasaw, *Going Out: The Rise and Fall of Public Amusements* (New York: Basic Books, 1993), 92; Kahrl, "'The Slightest Semblance of Unruliness,'" 1108–36. By midcentury there were also black-owned parks in New Orleans (Lincoln Beach Park), Oklahoma City (Lyons Park), and Deanwood, Maryland. See "Amusement Parks," http://www.okhistory.mus.ok.us/enc/amuseparks.htm (accessed August 1, 2008), 2; "Close La. Negro Fun Park," *Amusement Business* 76, 33 (August 22, 1964): 13. Reformers considered black amusement parks, and the steamboat excursions that took customers to parks, as less genteel than the resorts frequented by the black elite. See Foster, "In the Face of 'Jim Crow,'" 138; and Jones, *Recreation and Amusement Among Negroes*. Jones notes that Suburban Gardens in Deanwood was "not frequented to a great extent, however, by the upper classes of Negroes" (100).

22. Suzanne E. Smith, *To Serve the Living: Funeral Directors and the African American Way of Death* (Cambridge, Mass.: Harvard University Press, 2010), 92–93.

23. Frank Driggs and Chuck Haddix, *Kansas City Jazz: From Ragtime to Bebop* (New York: Oxford University Press, 2005). I'd like to thank David Peavler Trowbridge for alerting me to Lincoln Electric Park.

24. For an analysis of Jim Crow signs, see Elizabeth Abel, *Signs of the Times: The Visual Politics of Jim Crow* (Berkeley: University of California Press, 2010).

25. Johnson, *Patterns of Negro Segregation*, 193. Some northern proprietors did use "Whites Only" signs. For example, in 1919 the new owner of Riverside Park in Indianapolis, Lewis A. Coleman, instituted a segregation policy and mounted "Patronage Whites Only Solicited" signs at the park. See David J. Bodenhamer, Robert Graham Barrows, and David Gordon Vanderstel, eds., *The Encyclopedia of Indianapolis* (Bloomington: Indiana University Press, 1994), 1198; and "Private Amusement Park Flouts Indiana State Civil Rights Law," *New York Amsterdam News*, August 28, 1948, 22.

26. Amusement Park Books, *Euclid Beach Park Is Closed for the Season* (Fairview Park, Ohio: Amusement Park Books, 1977), 25–27. See also Leo O. Bush, "Euclid Beach Park . . . More Than Special," *Amusement Park Journal* 5, 2+3 (1983): 26–28, 30–33. For discussions of racial discrimination at Euclid Beach, see Dale Samuelson, *The American Amusement Park* (St. Paul, Minn.: MBI Publishing, 2001), 118–19; Nasaw, *Going Out*, 243; and Cyril Dostal, "Paradise Misplaced," *Cleveland Magazine* (September 1977): 128–29.

27. David Nasaw points out that the "monumental entrances" of early twentieth-century amusement parks accentuated their separation from the "outside world" (*Going Out*, 86). For a discussion of liminality and recreation see also Sterngass, *First Resorts*, 4.

28. John Kasson, *Amusing the Millions: Coney Island at the Turn of the Century* (New York: Hill & Wang, 1978), 49. See also Gary S. Cross and John K. Walton, *The Playful Crowd: Pleasure Places in the Twentieth Century* (New York: Columbia University Press, 2005), esp. 4–8.

29. Quoted in John F. Cuber, "Patrons of the Amusement Parks," *Sociology and Social Research* 24 (September–October 1939): 64.

30. For a discussion of regulations at parks, see Adams, *The American Amusement Park Industry*, 59; Nasaw, *Going Out*, 86–88; Hannigan, *Fantasy City*, 22–23.

31. "Coney Island: Originally Parker's Apple Orchard," *Home Office News*, 1970, clipping file, "Amusements and Amusement Parks," Cincinnati Historical Library, Cincinnati, Ohio. On the early years of Coney Island, see Charles Jacques, *Cincinnati's Coney Island: America's Finest Amusement Park* (Jefferson, Ohio: Amusement Park Journal, 2002), 6–22; Samuelson, *The American Amusement Park*, 114–15; Mangels, *The Outdoor Amusement Industry*, 19–20. Jacques points out that African Americans "were not permitted into Coney Island" during this period (12). Neither Samuelson nor Mangels mentions the segregation policy at Coney Island.

32. Quoted in DeBlasio, "The Immigrant and the Trolley Park in Youngstown," 78–79.

33. Shale and Jacques, *Idora Park*, 24.

34. Ibid., *Idora Park*, 43; "Youngstown to Welcome 'Chocolates' Mon.," *Pittsburgh Courier*, June 9, 1934, A8.

35. "Civil Rights Case Ends in Big Victory," *Atlanta Daily World*, January 15, 1935, 2. There is contradictory evidence about whether the park practiced full segregation. DeBlasio ("The Immigrant and the Trolley Park in Youngstown") and Shale and Jacques (*Idora Park*) state that the park segregated its dance pavilion only. But interviews with African Americans in Youngstown and contemporary evidence suggest that the park was entirely segregated. Most likely Idora's private police and ticket sellers discouraged blacks from entering the park gates except on the two "colored days." See also Ginny Pasha, "Idora Park," Center for Working Class Studies, http://cwcs.ysu.edu/resources/cwcs-projects/culture/idora-park (accessed May 15, 2007).

36. DeBlasio, "The Immigrant and the Trolley Park in Youngstown," 86; Peiss, *Cheap Amusements*, 118. Roy Rosenszweig, in *Eight Hours for What We Will: Workers and Leisure in an Industrial City, 1870–1920* (Cambridge: Cambridge University Press, 1983), argues that amusement parks helped foster "a multiethnic working-class culture" (182). However, sponsor days simultaneously reinforced existing ethnic identities.

37. Sherry Lee Linkon and John Russo, *Steeltown U.S.A.: Work and Memory in Youngstown* (Lawrence: University Press of Kansas, 2002), 33.

38. Chuck Wlodarczyk, *Riverview: Gone But Not Forgotten: A Photo History, 1904–67* (Chicago: Riverview Publications, 1977), 95; Pasha, "Idora Park."

39. For a discussion of welfare capitalism and leisure, see Lizabeth Cohen, *Making a New Deal: Industrial Workers in Chicago, 1919–1939* (New York: Cambridge University Press, 1990), 176–80.

40. Stephen Meyer III, *The Five Dollar Day: Labor Management and Social Control in the Ford Motor Company, 1908–21* (Albany: State University of New York Press, 1981), 99.

41. Drake and Cayton, *Black Metropolis*, 106.

42. Ibid.; Myrdal, *An American Dilemma*, 617.

43. Simon, *Boardwalk of Dreams*, 39–40. Officials also segregated Atlantic City's boardwalk during this period. For discussions of segregated swimming, see Wiltse, *Contested Waters;* and Jearold Winston Holland, *Black Recreation: A Historical Perspective* (Chicago: Burham Publishers, 2002), 148–51.

44. Quoted in Daniel Wolff, *4th of July Asbury Park: A History of the Promised Land* (New York: Bloomsbury, 2005), 35.

45. "Drawing the Color Line," *New York Times*, July 19, 1885, 1.

46. Wolff, *4th of July Asbury Park*, 38.

47. Quoted in ibid., 45.

48. Wiltse, *Contested Waters*, esp. chaps. 3 and 4. Wiltse does not examine southern swimming pools, where racial segregation at the turn of the century was more prevalent.

49. "Omaha Race Riot Breaks Out over Use of Swimming Pool," *Chicago Defender*, July 26, 1930, 13.

50. Wiltse, *Contested Waters*, 85–86; Josh Sides, *L.A. City Limits: African American Los Angeles from the Great Depression to the Present* (Berkeley: University of California Press, 2003), 21; Douglas Flamming, *Bound for Freedom: Black Los Angeles in Jim Crow America* (Berkeley: University of California Press, 2005), 216–18, 290–91; "The Race Problem at Swimming Pools," *American City* 47 (August 1932): 77; Lawrence Culver, *Frontier of Leisure: Southern California and the Shaping of Modern America* (New York: Oxford University Press, 2010), 66–74. The NAACP and local activists filed multiple lawsuits designed to integrate the pools and beaches, and in 1932 the California Supreme Court ruled that the Los Angeles Department of Playgrounds and Recreation could not segregate its pools, a ruling that the city did not fully implement until the 1940s.

51. Jones, *Recreation and Amusement Among Negroes*, 37.

52. William M. Tuttle, Jr., *Race Riot: Chicago in the Red Summer of 1919* (New York: Atheneum, 1972); Janet L. Abu-Lughod, *Race, Space, and Riots in Chicago, New York, and Los Angeles* (New York: Oxford University Press, 2007), 58–61; Chicago Commission on Race Relations, *The Negro in Chicago: A Study of Race Relations and a Race Riot* (Chicago: University of Chicago Press, 1922); James Grossman, *Land of Hope: Chicago, Black Southerners, and the Great Migration* (Chicago: University of Chicago Press, 1989), 178–80; Allan H. Spear, *Black Chicago: The Making of a Negro Ghetto* (Chicago: University of Chicago Press, 1967), vii–viii, 214–21. There are a number of versions of the events surrounding the riot; the one I reproduce here is now widely accepted.

53. Abu-Lughod points out that Charles Johnson, the primary author of *The Negro in Chicago*, and Allen Spear, author of *Black Chicago*, emphasize housing as a primary motivation for the riot. In contrast, labor historians, such as William Tuttle, Jr., and Herbert Guttman, emphasize labor competition (*Race, Space, and Riots*, 55). Abu-Lughod sides with Tuttle and Guttman, noting, "Economic competition was a fundamental 'cause' of the riot" (55). James Grossman, in *Land of Hope*, offers an interpretation of the riot that blends these two perspectives.

54. Two exceptions are Colin Fisher, "African Americans, Outdoor Recreation, and the 1919 Chicago Race Riot," in *"To Love the Wind and the Rain": African Americans and Environmental History*, ed. Dianne D. Glave and Mark Stoll (Pittsburgh: University of Pittsburgh Press, 2006), 63–76; and Robin F. Bachin, *Building the South Side: Urban Space and Civic Culture in Chicago, 1890–1919* (Chicago: University of Chicago Press, 2004), 249–50, 290–95. Fisher makes an argument similar to the one I present here, although he emphasizes that the riot was a "conflict over access to nature" (66). Bachin points out that "the riot reflected the increasingly important part leisure spaces played in structuring race relations within the city" (249–50).

55. "Race Divisions on Public Beaches," *Encyclopedia of Chicago*, http://www.encyclopedia.chicagohistory.org/pages/300066.html (accessed June 15, 2007).

56. Chicago Commission on Race Relations, *The Negro in Chicago*, 3; Grossman, *Land of Hope*, 178; Bachin, *Building the South Side*, 290–92. For descriptions of racial violence in Chicago's recreational facilities prior to 1919, see Chicago Commission on Race Relations, *The Negro in Chicago*, 288–95.

57. Grand jury foreman quoted in Chicago Commission on Race Relations, *The Negro in Chicago*, 16.

58. Chicago Commission on Race Relations, *The Negro in Chicago*, 272, 274, 277–78, quote on p. 286.

59. Ibid., 11–17, 596. In "Hoodlums, Rebels, and Vice Lords: Street Gangs, Youth Subcultures, and Race in Chicago, 1919–1968" (Ph.D. diss., University of Michigan, 2004), Andrew Diamond argues that the "harassment of African Americans had become something of a competitive sport among the athletic clubs" in the years surrounding the riot, and "nowhere was this sport engaged in more frequently and more enthusiastically than in the parks, beaches and playgrounds around the edges of the Black Belt" (39). See also Andrew J. Diamond, *Mean Streets: Chicago Youths and the Everyday Struggle for Empowerment in the Multiracial City, 1908–1969* (Berkeley: University of California Press, 2009), esp. 17–64.

The authors of *The Negro in Chicago* also viewed the athletic clubs' policing of urban recreation as a major cause of the riot and a potential target of reform. A young Richard Daley, who would become Chicago's mayor, was a member of the Hamburg Social and Athletic Club and may have participated in the riots (Mike Royko, *Boss: Richard J. Daley of Chicago* [New York: E. P. Dutton, 1971], 31).

60. "Beach Parties," *Chicago Defender*, July 16, 1921, 16.

61. "Breeding Trouble," *Chicago Defender*, July 18, 1925, A9. Policeman quoted in "Park Board Denies Part in Beach Segregation," *Chicago Defender*, July 25, 1925, 4. The *Chicago Defender* editors noted "the riots of 1919 grew out of just such similar disturbance." The couple filed a formal complaint with the park board, which claimed not to support segregation on the city's beaches. Fannie Williams, who, along with her sister and several children, was driven off the beach in 1928, filed a similar complaint. See "Bathing at Jackson Park," *Chicago Defender*, September 1, 1928, A2. In 1929 fifteen young white boys and men accosted a group of African Americans visiting the Jackson Park Beach. See "Trouble at Jackson Park Beach," *Chicago Defender*, August 10, 1929, A2. In 1931 whites beat and burned with cigarettes a young black man at Jackson Park. See "Youth Burned by Hoodlums in Jackson Park," *Chicago Defender*, July 11, 1931, 4.

62. "Trouble at Jackson Park Beach." Sources in the 1920s identify the 31st Street Beach as the primary "black" beach in Chicago.

63. "Racial Conflict at the Beaches," *Chicago Tribune*, August 5, 1929, 14.

64. Quoted in "The Tribune Speaks," *Chicago Defender*, August 10, 1929, A2.

65. Quoted in Drake and Cayton, *Black Metropolis*, 104. Black leaders called for police protection throughout the 1920s, lamenting in an editorial in the *Chicago Defender*, "We still have clashes on bathing beaches, at which time police forget their oaths and range themselves along with white law violators" ("Have They Done All These Things in Vain," *Chicago Defender*, August 29, 1925, A10).

66. Drake and Cayton, *Black Metropolis*, 105; McGuinn, "Commercial Recreation," 231.

67. James J. Gentry, "Bronzeville in Chicago," *Chicago Defender*, July 17, 1937, 1. See also A. L. Foster, executive secretary, Chicago Urban League, letter to the editor, *Chicago Defender*, August 7, 1937, 16.

68. The Chicago Urban League also campaigned against the fence and encouraged African Americans to swim on the "white" side. See "About the Beaches," *Chicago* Defender, August 7, 1937, 16. I have not been able to determine exactly when the Jackson Park fence was finally

dismantled. The *Encyclopedia of Chicago* notes that "Jackson Park Beach remained a beach used predominantly by whites through most of the twentieth century" ("Race Divisions on Public Beaches," *Encyclopedia of Chicago*, http://www.encyclopedia.chicagohistory.org/pages/300066.html [accessed June 15, 2007]).

69. Drake and Cayton, *Black Metropolis*, 105–6.

70. Roberta W. Booker, letter to the editor, *Pittsburgh Courier*, September 10, 1927, 8.

71. "Race Ignores Jim-Crow Park," *Pittsburgh Courier*, August 7, 1937, 1; "Ohioans Rebel Against Discrimination," *Atlanta Daily World*, August 7, 1937, 8.

72. "Park Scored by Cleveland School Board," *Pittsburgh Courier*, July 28, 1934, 5. In the summer of 1940 the school board faced a challenge to this resolution but voted to maintain it. See "Cleveland Fights Move to O.K. Jim-Crow Beach," *Chicago Defender*, July 13, 1940, 3; and "Cleveland School Board Refuses to Rescind Ban on Park," *Chicago Defender*, July 27, 1940, 4.

73. "Moral Victory Won in Beach Cases," *Pittsburgh Courier*, January 12, 1935, A3; and "Civil Rights Case Ends in Big Victory," *Atlanta Daily World*, January 15, 1935, 2.

74. "Youths Settle in Jim Crow Suits," *Chicago Defender*, January 16, 1943, 3.

75. "Clevelanders Demand Quiz on Brutality," *New York Amsterdam News*, August 20, 1938, 10.

76. For a representative sample of this literature, see Kenneth Jackson, *Crabgrass Frontier: The Suburbanization of the United States* (New York: Oxford University Press, 1987); Gail Radford, *Modern Housing for America: Policy Struggles in the New Deal Era* (Chicago: University of Chicago Press, 1997); David Freund, *Colored Property: State Policy and White Racial Politics in Suburban America* (Chicago: University of Chicago Press, 2010); Ira Katznelson, *When Affirmative Action Was White: An Untold History of Racial Inequality in Twentieth-Century America* (New York: W. W. Norton, 2006); Arnold Hirsch, *Making the Second Ghetto: Race and Housing in Chicago, 1940–1960* (Chicago: University of Chicago Press, 1998); Amanda Seligman, *Block by Block: Neighborhoods and Public Policy on Chicago's West Side* (Chicago: University of Chicago Press, 2005); Thomas Sugrue, *Origins of the Urban Crisis: Race and Inequality in Postwar Detroit* (Princeton, N.J.: Princeton University Press, 2006).

77. Susan Currell, *The March of Spare Time: The Problem and Promise of Leisure in the Great Depression* (Philadelphia: University of Pennsylvania Press, 2005), 7.

78. Wiltse, *Contested Waters*, 93. Wiltse notes that there were also 1,681 wading pools built as public works projects. In 1934 Robert Moses, Park Commissioner for New York City, oversaw the construction of seventy-seven playgrounds, three golf courses, thirteen swimming pools, and several tennis and handball courts, all funded through the federal government. "Park Work Relief to Speed Projects," *New York Times*, December 31, 1934, 14. For a history of New Deal public works projects, see Jason Scott Smith, *Building New Deal Liberalism: The Political Economy of Public Works, 1933–56* (New York: Cambridge University Press, 2006).

79. W. G. Lambe to NAACP, April 16, 1946, Folder 9, "Discrimination, Swimming Pools, Ironton, Ohio, 1946," Box B66, Series II, NAACP Papers, Library of Congress, Washington, D.C.

80. "A Jim Crow Pool—Whitewashed," *Pittsburgh Courier*, June 16, 1934, 1. For an extensive discussion of the Highland Park pool, see Wiltse, *Contested Waters*, 125–32. See also "The Race Problem at Swimming Pools," *American City* 47 (August 1932): 76; and Betty Beaver, "End Bias at Pool," *CORE-lator*, October 1952, p. 1, microfilm, Reel 13, EIII, CORE Papers, Addendum.

81. Quoted in Gregory Bush, "Politicized Memories in the Struggle for Miami's Virginia Key Beach," in *"To Love the Wind and the Rain,"* 172.

82. John A. Stuart, "Liberty Square, Florida's First Public Housing Project," in *The New Deal in South Florida: Design, Policy, and Community Building, 1933–40*, ed. John A. Stuart and John F. Stack, Jr. (Miami: University Press of Florida, 2008), 206.

83. Marvin Dunn, *Black Miami in the Twentieth Century* (Gainesville, Fla.: University Press of Florida, 1997), 160–61.

84. Consumerism has become a central focus of scholarship in African American history. See, for example, Adam Green, *Selling the Race: Culture, Community, and Black Chicago, 1940–1955*

(Chicago: University of Chicago Press, 2009); Michelle Mitchell, *Righteous Propagation: African Americans and the Politics of Racial Destiny After Reconstruction* (Chapel Hill: University of North Carolina Press, 2004); and Davarian Baldwin, *Chicago's New Negroes: Modernity, the Great Migration, and Black Urban Life* (Chapel Hill: University of North Carolina Press, 2007). For a discussion of blacks as "citizen consumers" in the 1930s, see Lizabeth Cohen, *A Consumers' Republic: The Politics of Mass Consumption in Postwar America* (New York: Alfred A. Knopf, 2003), 41–53.

85. Cohen, *A Consumers' Republic*, 53.

86. E. B. Henderson, "The Participation of Negro Youth in Community and Educational Programs," *Journal of Negro Education* 9, 3 (July 1940): 417–18.

87. Ibid., 421–22.

88. "Pupil Sues Skate Rink," *Los Angeles Sentinel*, July 19, 1934, 1.

89. Quoted in Jacques, *Cincinnati's Coney Island*, 58. (Mangels, *The Outdoor Amusement Industry*, 20; Jacques, *Cincinnati's Coney Island*, 49–54, 91).

90. Jacques, *Cincinnati's Coney Island*, 75.

91. Virginia Coffey, interview by Stephanie Corsbie, c. 1980, Cincinnati Women Working Collection, 1904–81, arranged by Alden N. Monroe, pp. 7–8, Cincinnati Historical Library. Coffey successfully integrated the Girl Scout camps in the 1950s. See also Cincinnati Working Women, "Stitches, Whistles, Bells and Wires: An Oral History of Cincinnati's Working Women, 1904–81," 1980, Folder 15, Box 1, Virginia Wilson Coffey Papers, Cincinnati Historical Library.

92. Quoted in Thomas R. Cole, *No Color Is My Kind: The Life of Eldrewey Stearns and the Integration of Houston* (Austin: University of Texas Press, 1997), 131. The black-owned Greenwood Park in Nashville offered African American Scouts a rare opportunity to hold a summer camp. "Historic Nashville," http://historicnashville.wordpress.com/2009/03/09/greenwood-park/ (accessed May 23, 2011).

93. David I. Macleod, *Building Character in the American Boy: The Boy Scouts, YMCA, and Their Forerunners, 1870–1920* (Madison: University of Wisconsin Press, 1983), 213–14.

94. Quoted in Nancy Marie Robertson, *Christian Sisterhood, Race Relations, and the YWCA, 1906–46* (Chicago: University of Illinois Press, 2007), 117. Robertson notes that the black YMCA supported the construction of the pool, reflecting the more conservative slant of the male organization.

95. Nina Mjagkij, *Light in the Darkness: African Americans and the YMCA, 1852–1946* (Lexington: University Press of Kentucky, 1994), 126–27. For a description of the work of segregated YMCAs, see George R. Arthur, *Life on the Negro Frontier* (New York: Association Press, 1934).

96. Martha Biondi, *To Stand and Fight: The Struggle for Civil Rights in Postwar New York City* (Cambridge, Mass.: Harvard University Press, 2003), 88. In 1950 CORE picketed the Bedford YMCA in Brooklyn, which refused to allow local blacks access to its swimming pool or gym. See *CORE-lator*, October 1950, p. 2, microfilm, Reel 13, Series 3, CORE Papers.

97. Nelson Peery, *Black Fire: The Making of an American Revolutionary* (New York: The New Press, 1994), 52–58, 69–71, quote on 56. Peery later became an organizer for the Communist Party, an activist in the civil rights movement, and an author. Histories of African Americans and communism include Glenda Elizabeth Gilmore, *Defying Dixie: The Radical Roots of Civil Rights, 1919–1950* (New York: W. W. Norton, 2008), esp. 15–156; Mark Solomon, *The Cry Was Unity: Communists and African Americans, 1917–1936* (Jackson: University Press of Mississippi, 1998); Mark Naison, *Communists in Harlem During the Depression* (Urbana: University of Illinois Press, 1983); and Robin D. G. Kelley, *Hammer and Hoe: Alabama Communists During the Great Depression* (Chapel Hill: University of North Carolina Press, 1990).

98. "Skaters Break Up Jim Crow Policy of New York Rink," *Chicago Defender*, December 24, 1938, 4.

99. Lizabeth Cohen coined the term "culture of unity" to describe the common ground that brought industrial workers together in the CIO. See Cohen, *Making a New Deal*, 333.

100. Andrew Hurley, *Diners, Bowling Alleys and Trailer Parks: Chasing the American Dream in the Postwar Consumer Culture* (New York: Basic Books, 2001), 184–90.

101. "Jim-Crowism Blacked at N.Y. Skating Rink," *Chicago Defender*, March 18, 1939, 4.

102. "Pennsy Park Ops Found Guilty of Race Ban Charge," *Billboard* 60, 52 (December 25, 1948): 54.

103. "File $1,000 Suit Against Skating Rink," *Chicago Defender*, September 30, 1939, 5. The owner of the rink, a target of civil rights activists for the next two decades, claimed it was open to "members" only.

104. Risa L. Goluboff, *The Lost Promise of Civil Rights* (Cambridge, Mass.: Harvard University Press, 2007). See also Robert Korstad and Nelson Lichtenstein, "Opportunities Found and Lost: Labor, Radicals, and the Early Civil Rights Movement," *Journal of American History* 75 (1988): 786–811.

105. Marie G. Baker to Thurgood Marshall, July 14, 1941, Folder 3, "Discrimination, Swimming Pools, Decatur, Illinois, 1941–2," Box 66, Series II, NAACP Papers.

106. Thurgood Marshall to Marie G. Baker, June 30, 1942, Folder 3, "Discrimination, Swimming Pools, Decatur, Illinois, 1941–2," Box 66, Series II, NAACP Papers; "Win Civil Rights in Beach Case," *Chicago Defender*, July 4, 1942, 8.

107. Marie G. Baker to Thurgood Marshall, July 9, 1942, Folder 3, "Discrimination, Swimming Pools, Decatur, Illinois, 1941–2," Box 66, Series II, NAACP Papers.

108. G. Gordon Brown, *Recreational Facilities and Negro-White Relations in Philadelphia* (Philadelphia: Bureau of Municipal Research of Philadelphia, 1947), 17.

109. "Riot Flares as Whites Dunk Boy in Pool," *Chicago Defender*, July 12, 1941, 4; "30 Injured in Race Riot in Philadelphia," *New York Amsterdam Star-News*, July 5, 1941, 1; "Negroes and Whites Clash at Swimming Pool," *Chicago Daily Tribune*, July 2, 1941, 10. See also Karl E. Johnson, "Police-Black Community Relations in Postwar Philadelphia: Race and Criminalization in Urban Social Spaces, 1945–1960," *Journal of African American History* 89, 2 (Spring 2004): 118–34.

110. "League Fights Jim Crow at Bathing Pool," *Chicago Defender*, July 20, 1940, 3; Charles H. Loeb, *The Future Is Yours: The History of the Future Outlook League, 1935–46* (Cleveland: Future Outlook League, 1947), 70–71. On the Future Outlook League, see Kimberley L. Phillips, *Alabama North: African-American Migrants, Community, and Working-Class Activism in Cleveland, 1915–45* (Chicago: University of Illinois Press, 1999), 3–4, 190–252.

111. Ordinance cited in "See Effort to Segregate at N.J. Beaches," *Chicago Defender*, June 18, 1938, 2.

112. "Why Should Race Wear Beach Tags?" *Chicago Defender*, July 29, 1939, 3; Kevin Mumford, *Newark: A History of Race, Rights, and Riots in America* (New York: New York University Press, 2007), 46–47.

113. Quoted in Howard Shorr, "Thorns in the Roses: Race Relations and the Brookside Plunge Controversy in Pasadena, California, 1914–1947," in *Law in the Western United States*, ed. Gordon Morris Bakken (Norman: University of Oklahoma Press, 2000), 524.

114. Quoted in Arnold Rampersad, *Jackie Robinson: A Biography* (New York: Ballantine Books, 1998), 35. Robinson was also excluded from the local YMCA and Boy Scouts in the 1930s. I am indebted to Jane Margolis for giving me the Jackie Robinson reference.

115. Rampersad, *Jackie Robinson*, 64–65.

116. Press release, "California Court Opens Swimming Pool to Negroes," November 28, 1941, Folder 2, "Discrimination, Swimming Pools, California, 1940–41," Box B66, Series II, NAACP Papers; Shorr, "Thorns in the Roses," 522–28; "Sue Coast City for Jim Crow Pool," *Chicago Defender*, July 22, 1939, 5; Culver, *Frontier of Leisure*, 70. See also Rampersad, *Jackie Robinson*, 21, 27, 35, 64–65 for memories of Brookside Plunge.

117. Mr. Reeves to Thurgood Marshall, May 7, 1941, Folder 11, "Discrimination, Galveston, Texas Pier, 1941," Box B62, Series II, NAACP Papers. The city tried to build a second pier for blacks but

could only get permission for one new pier on the Gulf. In correspondence Thurgood Marshall suggested that they find a Texas lawyer for the case.

118. Earl Brown, *Why Race Riots?* (New York: Public Affairs Committee, 1944), 2.

119. Dominic J. Capeci, Jr., *Layered Violence: The Detroit Rioters of 1943* (Jackson: University of Mississippi Press, 1991), 188.

120. Aflred McClung Lee and Norman D. Humphrey, *Race Riot* (New York: Dryden Press, 1943), 27.

121. For descriptions of the 1943 riot, see Capeci, *Layered Violence*; Richard W. Thomas, *Life for Us Is What We Make It: Building Black Community in Detroit, 1915–1945* (Bloomington: Indiana University Press, 1992), 166–72; Brown, *Why Race Riots?*; George W. Beatley, *Background Causes of the 1943 Race Riot* (Princeton, N.J.: Princeton University Press, 1954); Lee and Humphrey, *Race Riot*; and Sugrue, *The Origins of the Urban Crisis*, 29–30, 260.

122. Marilynn S. Johnson, "Gender, Race, and Rumours: Re-Examining the 1943 Race Riots," *Gender and History* 10, 2 (August 1998): 252–77.

123. Brown, *Why Race Riots*? 29–30.

124. Leaflet of the Detroit Interracial Committee, United Community Services, Central Files, Folder 17, Box 140, Wayne State University Archives of Labor and Urban Affairs, Detroit, Michigan.

125. Robert C. Weaver, "Whither Northern Race Relations Committees?" *Phylon* 5, 3 (1944): 206.

126. Ibid., 207.

127. Johnson, *Patterns of Negro Segregation*, 227.

128. Cuber, "Patrons of the Amusement Parks," 67.

Chapter 2

1. St. Clair Drake and Horace R. Cayton, *Black Metropolis: A Study of Negro Life in a Northern City* (1945; reprint, Chicago: University of Chicago Press, 1993), 753–54. In a speech on January 6, 1941, President Franklin D. Roosevelt identified the four freedoms as: freedom of speech, freedom of worship, freedom from want, and freedom from fear.

2. Robert Westbrook argues, "Strictly speaking, Americans in World War II were not instructed to fight, work, and die for their country. More often than not, they were urged to wage war as fathers, mothers, husbands, wives, lovers, sons, daughters, and consumers—not as citizens" (*Why We Fought: Forging American Obligations in World War II* [Washington, D.C.: Smithsonian Books, 2004], 8–9).

3. Statement of Albert T. Luster, "Euclid Beach Controversy," undated document, p. 3, microfilm, Reel 9, Series 3, CORE Papers; "Ohio Police Maul Negro," *Chicago Defender*, September 7, 1946, 7. Luster filed a successful lawsuit for $50,000 against the park, and one of the guards, Julius Vago, was convicted on assault and battery charges. See "Blame 'Reds' for Jim Crow Exposé," *New York Amsterdam News*, October 19, 1946, 2.

4. Gunnar Myrdal, *An American Dilemma: The Negro Problem and Modern Democracy* (New York: Harper and Brothers, 1944), xvii.

5. For discussions of the role of racial liberalism and Myrdal's work at midcentury, see Wendell E. Pritchett, *Robert Clifton Weaver and the American City: The Life and Times of an Urban Reformer* (Chicago: University of Chicago Press, 2008); David Southern, *Gunnar Myrdal and Black-White Relations: The Use and Abuse of an American Dilemma, 1944–69* (Baton Rouge: Louisiana State University Press, 1987); Walter A. Jackson, *Gunnar Myrdal and America's Conscience: Social Engineering and Racial Liberalism, 1938–1987* (Chapel Hill: University of North Carolina Press, 1990); Thomas Sugrue, *Sweet Land of Liberty: The Forgotten Struggle for Civil Rights in the North* (New York: Random House, 2008), 59–84; and Daniel Kryder, *Divided Arsenal: Race and the American State During World War II* (New York: Cambridge University Press, 2000), 5–16.

6. G. Gordon Brown, *Recreational Facilities and Negro-White Relations in Philadelphia* (Philadelphia: Bureau of Municipal Research of Philadelphia, 1947), 16.

7. Steven F. Lawson, ed., *To Secure These Rights: The Report of President Harry S. Truman's Committee on Civil Rights* (New York: Bedford Books, 2004), 183. For a discussion of Myrdal's influence on the Truman report, see Jackson, *Gunnar Myrdal and America's Conscience*, 275–55; and Sugrue, *Sweet Land of Liberty*, 99.

8. Southern, *Gunnar Myrdal and Black-White Relations*, 108.

9. Kryder, in *Divided Arsenal*, suggests that "Americans were less familiar with the aims of the war and their relationship to democratic ideals than Myrdal believed" (10).

10. Roy Wilkins, "The Negro Wants Full Equality," in *What the Negro Wants*, ed. Rayford W. Logan (Chapel Hill: University of North Carolina Press, 1944), 127.

11. Sterling A. Brown, "Count Us In," in *What the Negro Wants*, 336.

12. Charles S. Johnson, *Patterns of Negro Segregation* (New York: Harper & Bros, 1943); Lizabeth Cohen, *A Consumers' Republic: The Politics of Mass Consumption in Postwar America* (New York: Alfred A. Knopf, 2003), 88–100.

13. Howard W. Odum, *Race and Rumors of Race: Challenge to American Crisis* (Chapel Hill: University of North Carolina Press, 1943), 8. On racial violence during World War II, see Warren Schaich, "A Relationship Between Collective Racial Violence and War," *Journal of Black Studies* 5, 4 (June 1975): 374–94; and Sugrue, *Sweet Land of Liberty*, 57–58, 63–70.

14. Cohen, *Consumers' Republic*, 91; Sugrue, *Sweet Land of Liberty*, 65. On the zoot suit riots, see Mauricio A. Mazon, *The Zoot-Suit Riots: The Psychology of Symbolic Annihilation* (Austin: University of Texas Press, 1984); Edwardo Obregan Pagan, *Murder at the Sleepy Lagoon: Zoot Suits, Race, and Riot in Wartime L.A.* (Charlotte: University of North Carolina Press, 2006); and Kevin Allen Leonard, *The Battle for Los Angeles: Racial Ideology and World War II* (Albuquerque: University of New Mexico Press, 2006), 114–47.

15. "Race Tension Back of Fort Dix Riot," *Chicago Defender*, April 11, 1942, 1. Black soldiers' most common complaint on military bases was segregated seating or lack of access to movie theaters and other forms of entertainment. See Phillip McGuire, ed., *Taps for a Jim Crow Army: Letters from Black Soldiers in World War II* (Lexington: University Press of Kentucky, 1983), 18, 82–83, 173.

16. Kryder, *Divided Arsenal*, 153–58, 228–37.

17. Cohen, *Consumers' Republic*, 93; Thomas Borstelmann, *The Cold War and the Color Line* (Cambridge, Mass.: Harvard University Press, 2001), 43.

18. Pvt. Bert B. Babero to Atty. Truman K. Gibson, February 13, 1944, in *Taps for a Jim Crow Army*, 51. Babero reported in the same letter that black soldiers initially could attend only one of the five theaters on base and that theater had outside seating. After protesting, officers allowed black soldiers in the other theaters but only on a segregated basis (50). Writing from Camp Livingston in Louisiana (January 12, 1944 to James Evans), Private James Pritchett reported, "the German P.W.'s here have more rights and freedom" (23). For descriptions of racial discrimination in the military, see also Maggie M. Morehouse, *Fighting in the Jim Crow Army: Black Men and Women Remember World War II* (New York: Rowman and Littlefield, 2000).

19. Jeanette Cohen, "Across the Color Line," *New York Amsterdam News*, August 24, 1943, 7.

20. George Houser, *Erasing the Color Line* (New York: Fellowship Publications, 1945), 14.

21. On Randolph and the MOWM, see Sugrue, *Sweet Land of Liberty*, 32–33, 44–58, 73–75; and Paula F. Pfeffer, *A. Philip Randolph, Pioneer of the Civil Rights Movement* (Baton Rouge: Louisiana State University Press, 1990), 45–88. Other works on Randolph and the MOWM include Lucy G. Barber, *Marching on Washington: The Forging of an American Political Tradition* (Berkeley: University of California Press, 202), 108–40; and Jervis Anderson, *A. Philip Randolph: A Biographical Portrait* (New York: Harcourt Brace Jovanovich, 1973).

22. Pfeffer, *A. Philip Randolph*, 48. In fact, Randolph was organizing local churches, schools, and private homes to host the marchers.

23. A. Philip Randolph, "March on Washington Movement Presents Program for the Negro," in *What the Negro Wants*, 149.

24. Ibid., 150.

25. Sugrue, *Sweet Land of Liberty*, 145; John D'Emilio, *Lost Prophet: The Life and Times of Bayard Rustin* (New York: Free Press, 2003), 53; Jeffrey Podair, *Bayard Rustin: American Dreamer* (New York: Rowman and Littlefield, 2009), 18–25.

26. Art Dole, "Pattern in Black and White," undated document, c. 1941, microfilm, Reel 14, Series 3, CORE Papers; Rusty Brown, "Red-Led Group Tries to Stir Race Riot at Swimming Pool," undated clipping, microfilm, ibid.; Houser, *Erasing the Color Line*, 29–32; Sugrue, *Sweet Land of Liberty*, 156; Larry Gara and Lenna Mae Gara, *A Few Small Candles: War Resisters of World War II Tell Their Stories* (Kent, Ohio: Kent State University Press, 1999), 1, 59–60. After Juanita Morrow organized a CORE chapter in Cleveland in 1944, the nonviolent protests at Garfield Park continued until at least 1948.

27. August Meier and Elliott Rudwick, *CORE: A Study in the Civil Rights Movement* (Chicago: University of Illinois Press, 1975), 6–15; Marian Mollin, *Radical Pacifism in Modern America: Egalitarianism and Protest* (Philadelphia: University of Pennsylvania Press, 2006), 21–24; Lawrence S. Wittner, *Rebels Against War: The American Peace Movement, 1941–60* (New York: Columbia University Press, 1969), 67; Sugrue, *Sweet Land of Liberty*, 145–48.

28. For descriptions of protests at White City before 1946, see *CORE Comments*, August 1943, August 1944, and August 1945, microfilm, Reel 10, Series 3, CORE Papers. See also Houser, *Erasing the Color Line*, 34–35; George M. Houser, "A 'Nordic' Meets Mr. Jim Crow," *The Crisis* 53, 5 (May 1946): 146–47, 155; and James Tracy, *Direct Action: Radical Pacifism from the Union Eight to the Chicago Seven* (Chicago: University of Chicago Press, 1996), 28.

29. Descriptions of this protest can be found in "Arrest Jim Crow Skating Rink Head," *Chicago Bee*, January 13, 1946, 1; "Sue White City Skating Rink for Barring Negroes," *Chicago Defender*, January 19, 1946, 14; "Citizens! This Is Your Case," undated leaflet, microfilm, Reel 12, Series 3, CORE Papers; draft of press release, January 17, 1946, ibid.; and Meier and Rudwick, *CORE*, 27.

30. "We Want 'In' Too!" leaflet, microfilm, Reel 12, Series 3, CORE Papers.

31. Newspaper clipping, "Reverend Carey Leads White City Picket Line," February 9, 1946, newspaper unknown, microfilm, Reel 12, Series 3, CORE Papers; and "Join the March on White City," ibid.

32. "Anti-Negro Skating Rink Loses Suit to Halt Pickets," *Chicago Defender*, March 9, 1946, 2; "Chicago Skating Rink Offers to Drop Color Ban Policy," *Chicago Defender*, March 16, 1946, 3; "White City Rink Race Ban Dropped," *Chicago Defender*, June 1, 1946, 5.

33. "Arrest Jim Crow Skating Rink Head."

34. *The Call*, February 5, 1943. Randolph noted that in the South "non-violent disobedience and non-cooperation will take the negative form of boycotting Jim Crow cars on trains and surface lines and calling upon the parents of children to refuse to send their children to school during the week that is designated for the application of the social strategy."

35. "Youth Group Plans Lawsuit Against Jim Crow Park," *Chicago Defender*, August 3, 1946, 9. Descriptions of the Euclid Beach demonstrations can be found in John Hannigan, *Fantasy City: Pleasure and Profit in the Postmodern Metropolis* (New York: Routledge, 1998), 46–47; Euclid Beach Park Riot, *Encyclopedia of Cleveland History*, http://ech.case.edu/ech-cgi/article.pl?id=EBPR (accessed July 10, 2008); and David Nasaw, *Going Out: The Rise and Fall of Public Amusements* (New York: Basic Books, 1993), 243.

36. "Euclid Beach Controversy," undated document, pp. 1–2, 4, microfilm, Reel 9, Series 3, CORE Papers.

37. "Ask Grand Jury Probe of Police Assaults," *Atlanta Daily World*, October 25, 1946, 1. The leaders of CORE were uncomfortable with the fact Lynn Coleman, the off-duty officer, went to the park armed. See George Houser to Juanita Morrow, October 2, 1946, microfilm, Reel 9, Series 3, CORE Papers.

38. "Euclid Beach Shutters to Avoid Trouble," *Billboard* 58, 40 (October 5, 1946): 46.

39. Quoted in "Stall on Anti-Bias Ordinance," *Chicago Defender*, December 28, 1946, 2.

40. "Cleveland Council Passes Anti–Jim Crow Park Bill," *Chicago Defender*, March 1, 1947, 9; "Euclid Beach Not to Close Officials Say," *Billboard* 59, 11 (March 15, 1947): 75, 80.

41. Thaddeus K. Tekla, letter to the editor, *Cleveland News*, September 22, 1946, microfilm, Reel 9, Series 3, CORE Papers.

42. "Euclid Beach Ballroom Dark Opening Night," *Billboard* 59, 17 (May 3, 1947): 48; "Mayor Orders Club Be Granted License for Euclid Dances," *Billboard* 59, 22 (June 7, 1947): 77; "2d Private Club at Euclid Beach Given City Okay," *Billboard*, 59, 23 (June 14, 1947): 89. Although there was an investigation to determine whether the clubs were subterfuges, the mayor's support of Euclid Park's segregation policy seems to have persuaded the city to grant licenses to the new concessions.

43. Vince Guerrieri, "Youngstown's Million Dollar Playground," *The New Colonist*, http://www.newcolonist.com/youngstown.html (accessed August 10, 2009); Rick Shale and Charles J. Jacques, Jr., *Idora Park: The Last Ride of Summer* (Jefferson, Ohio: Amusement Park Journal, 1999), 79. Shale and Jacques suggest "two suits charging racial discrimination had been filed against the Idora Roller Skating Rink in early April, and the owners may have seen the pool as a potential source of trouble" (79).

44. "Kennywood," http://www.wqed.org/education/pghist/logs/kennywood.shtml (accessed July 6, 2008); Sugrue, *Sweet Land of Liberty*, 157.

45. "Democracy Group Pickets Pool on Behalf of Negroes," *Billboard* 58, 31 (August 3, 1946): 89; "50G Suit Charges Discrimination by Philly Pool Ops," *Billboard* 63, 38 (September 22, 1951): 66; "Father Divine May Buy Philly Woodside Swim Pool," *Billboard* 62, 25 (June 17, 1950): 68; "Woodside Park," http://www.rcdb.com/pd1301.htm (accessed April 8, 2009). Woodside Amusement Park, on Philadelphia's West Side, was a trolley park established in 1897 adjacent to Fairmount Park.

46. Minutes, National CORE Conference, June 16, 1948, p. 1, microfilm, Reel 9, Subgroup C: National Action Council and Conventions, 1944–67, CORE Papers.

47. James Peck, *Freedom Ride* (New York: Simon and Schuster, 1962), 31.

48. James Peck, "The Proof of the Pudding," *The Crisis* 56, 10 (November 1949): 293. The membership club, in this case the Sun and Surf Club, was the same device employed at White City in Chicago and the Crystal Pool in Philadelphia. While whites simply paid an admission fee, blacks were told they needed to join a "club" and therefore could not be admitted. *Race Relations: A Monthly Summary of Events and Trends* 5, 1–2 (October–November 1947): 32.

49. Quoted in "Judge's Decision Favors Palisades in $260,000 Suit," *Billboard* 60, 8 (February 21, 1948): 50. See also "Palisades Is Sued as a Jim Crow Pool," *Billboard* 59, 33 (August 23, 1947): 86; and "Pickets Resume Palisades Pacing," *Billboard* 59, 36 (September 13, 1947): 47. Several other court decisions also found that the Sun and Surf Club was constitutional. See "Judge Voids Convictions in Palisades Pool Case," *Billboard* 60, 11 (March 13, 1948): 53; and "Civil Suit Against Palisades Dismissed," *Billboard* 60, 45 (November 6, 1948): 66.

50. Quoted in James Peck, *Cracking the Color Line: Non-Violent Direct Action Methods of Eliminating Racial Discrimination*, p. 12, microfilm, Reel 19, EIII, CORE Papers, Addendum.

51. Peck, *Freedom Ride*, 29.

52. In *To Stand and Fight: The Struggle for Civil Rights in Postwar New York City* (Cambridge, Mass.: Harvard University Press, 2003), Martha Biondi argues that "Discrimination at Palisades undermines the notion that a clear-cut distinction between de jure segregation in the South and de facto segregation in the North characterized the pre–civil rights era" (84).

53. Biondi, *To Stand and Fight*, 82–84; Peck, "The Proof of the Pudding," 292–355; Peck, *Cracking the Color Line*, 11–12; "Pickets Resume Palisades Pacing"; Sugrue, *Sweet Land of Liberty*, 156.

54. Philip Greenwood, "How History Was Made in State of New Jersey," *Crisis* 57, 5 (May 1950): 277. The act also covered public schools and hospitals in New Jersey.

55. Of the eighteen states that passed laws guaranteeing equal access to public accommodations, only twelve allowed damage suits in addition to criminal prosecution. Milton R. Konvitz, "Legislation Guaranteeing Equality of Access to Places of Public Accommodation," *Annals of the American Academy of Political and Social Science* 275 (May 1951): 50–52.

56. Peck, *Cracking the Color Line*, 11; "Pool Observing Anti-Bias Pact," *CORE-lator*, June–July 1953, p. 2, microfilm, Reel 13, Series 3, CORE Papers.

57. Peck, *Freedom Ride*, 36.

58. "Bimini Place Story Project," http://www.bresee.org/biministories/pages/home.html (accessed August 13, 2007). See also Sugrue, *Sweet Land of Liberty*, 156. Adjacent to Bimini Baths was Palomar Ballroom, where blacks could neither perform nor watch the popular swing bands. There is speculation that Palomar Ballroom was deliberately burned down to prevent Count Basie from performing there in 1939.

59. Peck, "The Proof of the Pudding," 293–94; Minutes, National CORE Conference, June 19, 1948, microfilm, Reel 9, Subgroup C: National Action Council and Conventions, 1944–67, CORE Papers; "Discrimination Stops at Bimini," *Workshop Bulletin*, July 31, 1948, Folder, "CORE Projects: Interracial Workshops, 1947–54," Box 1, Congress of Racial Equality Papers, Swarthmore Peace Archives, Swarthmore, Pa. Using health inspections to bar blacks from pools was relatively common. In 1944, for example, a group of African American girls from the Detroit YWCA had their feet and arms inspected by a "health examiner" at the Rouge Park pool. Despite their protests the pool attendant refused to let them in. The white girls on the outing were allowed into the pool with no inspection. "Summary of Some Incident Reports," October 26, 1944, Folder 17, Box 140, United Community Services, Central Files, Archives of Labor and Urban Affairs, Wayne State University, Detroit, Michigan. An African American woman was asked for a health certificate before swimming at the Pottowottamie Park swimming pool in Chicago when she attended a company picnic of the Radiant Manufacturing Company. "News Release, Chicago Branch NAACP," undated, pp. 3–5, Papers of the NAACP, microfilm, Chicago Branch Files.

60. See, for example, Tera Hunter, *To 'Joy My Freedom: Southern Black Women's Lives and Labors After the Civil War* (Cambridge, Mass.: Harvard University Press, 1998), chap. 7; Keith Wailoo, *Dying in the City of Blues: Sickle Cell Anemia and the Politics of Race and Health* (Chapel Hill: University of North Carolina Press, 2000); and David McBride, *From TB to Aids: Epidemics Among Urban Blacks Since 1900* (Albany: State University of New York Press, 1991).

61. David M. Oshinsky, *Polio: An American Story* (New York: Oxford University Press, 2005). For examples of polio outbreaks in recreation areas in 1949, see "Ill. State Fair Belted by Polio," *Billboard* 61, 34 (August 20, 1949): 47; "Polio Scare Hurts Biz at K.C. Funspot," *Billboard* 61, 35 (August 27, 1949): 62; "Rain, Polio, Tax Bump 12% Off Gross of Cincy's Coney," *Billboard* 61, 40 (October 1, 1949): 64 ; and "Polio Epidemics in Midwest Blamed by Owners, Ops for Drop in Attendance and Biz," *Billboard* 61, 42 (October 15, 1949): 68.

62. Quoted in Peck, "The Proof of the Pudding," 294.

63. "Bimini Place Story Project."

64. Houser, *Erasing the Color Line*, 11.

65. Quoted in Pfeffer, *A. Philip Randolph*, 76. The masculinity of radical pacifism suggested in the term "virile" is analyzed in Marian Mollin, "The Limits of Egalitarianism: Radical Pacifism, Civil Rights, and the Journey of Reconciliation," *Radical History Review* 88 (2004): 112–38. Physically putting one's body on the line through nonviolent direct action also reinforced the individualism and masculine heroism of the World War II and cold war eras, even when it was women's bodies being dragged and beaten. During the war itself this manly individualism was

symbolized by the conscientious objectors who spent the war years in prison, often fighting segregation and brutality within the prison walls.

66. "Private Amusement Park Flouts Indiana State Civil Rights Law," *New York Amsterdam News*, August 28, 1948, 22. There was a civil rights law in Indiana, but when the NAACP contacted the park asking them to explain the policy, the management refused to respond.

67. "What the Branches Are Doing," *The Crisis* 53, 9 (September 1946): 280.

68. *Bob-Lo Excursion Co. v. People of the State of Michigan,* 333 U.S. 28 (1948); Michael J. Klarman, *From Jim Crow to Civil Rights: The Supreme Court and the Struggle for Racial Equality* (New York: Oxford University Press, 2004), 223–25; Sugrue, *Sweet Land of Liberty*, 158; John R. Howard, *The Shifting Wind: The Supreme Court and Civil Rights from Reconstruction to Brown* (Albany: State University of New York Press, 1999), 288–90; "Bob Lo Racial Appeal Denied," *Billboard* 59, 17 (May 3, 1947): 48; Fiona Lawless, "Sarah Elizabeth Ray and the SS Columbia: The Unknown Story of One Woman's Fight for Racial Freedom," for the National Trust for Historic Preservation, http://blogs.nationaltrust.org/preservationnation/?p=3221#more-3221 (accessed March 3, 2009). Lawless points out that Ray later went on to found Action House in Detroit, "a community center for the young and poor that helped neighbors forge positive interracial relationships for the next 25 years."

69. Minutes, National CORE Conference, June 16, 1948, microfilm, Reel 9, Subgroup C: National Action Council and Conventions, 1944–67, CORE Papers; Minutes, Executive Committee of CORE, January 22–23, 1949, microfilm, ibid.; *CORE-lator*, October 1949, microfilm, Reel 13, Series 3, CORE Papers; Andrew Hurley, *Diners, Bowling Alleys and Trailer Parks: Chasing the American Dream in the Postwar Consumer Culture* (New York: Basic Books, 2001), 188. CORE also convinced a high school bowling team in Evanston, Illinois, to open membership to blacks in 1951. See "Jimcrow High School Bowling Club Ended," *CORE-lator*, January 1951, p. 2, microfilm, Reel 13, Series 3, CORE Papers.

70. Houser, *Erasing the Color Line*, 33.

71. "End Color Bar at Skating Rink," *Chicago Defender,* August 14, 1943, 6. On the NAACP, see Patricia Sullivan, *Lift Every Voice: The NAACP and the Making of the Civil Rights Movement* (New York: The New Press, 2009).

72. "Jury Gives Nod to Sefferino in Cincy Race Case," *Billboard* 58, 39 (September 28, 1946): 82.

73. Constance B. Motley to Gloster Current, February 17, 1956, Folder, "Discrimination: Skating Rinks, 1956, 1962," Box A110, Series III, NAACP Papers, Library of Congress, Washington, D.C.

74. "Youth Group Pickets Rink in Protest Against Bias," *New York Amsterdam News*, May 18, 1946, 15.

75. In 1960 the sit-in movement that led to the formation of the Student Nonviolent Coordinating Committee (SNCC) grew primarily from NAACP Youth Councils in southern college towns. See Gilbert Jonas, *Freedom's Sword: The NAACP and the Struggle Against Racism in America, 1909–69* (New York: Routledge, 2005), 105, 173–74. For a history of the Youth Councils, see Tommy L. Bynum, "'Our Fight if for Right': The NAACP Youth Councils and College Chapters' Crusade for Civil Rights, 1936–1965" (Ph.D. diss., Georgia State University, 2007).

76. Bynum, "'Our Fight If for Right,'" 105–7.

77. "Core Skating Parties Continue," *Chi-CORE News* 4 (November and December 1946): 1, 4, microfilm, Reel 12, Series 3, CORE Papers.

78. Houser, *Erasing the Color Line*, 35–36; Houser, "A 'Nordic' Meets Mr. Jim Crow," 147. Two African American women filed a lawsuit against Skateland in 1939 after being told the rink was open to "members only" ("File $1,000 Suit Against Skating Rink," *Chicago Defender*, September 30, 1939, 5).

79. Account compiled from "Statement of Eroseanna Robinson Concerning Skateland Roller Rink," microfilm, Reel 9, Series 3, CORE Papers; "Statement of E. Robinson and M. Coffey," ibid.; "Report on Coffey and Sis Robinson meeting with Al Campana and Charles Horvath," August 1, 1952, ibid.; and "Tests 'Democracy' at Skateland; Girl Winds Up with Broken Arm," undated newspaper

clipping, ibid. Robinson joined the Peacemakers in 1954 and was jailed in 1960 for refusing to pay taxes. While imprisoned she went on a hunger strike and was force-fed by authorities. See Victoria W. Wolcott, "Eroseanna Robinson: The Long Civil Rights Movement and Interracial Pacifism in Postwar America" (paper presented at the Berkshire Conference of Women Historians, June 10, 2011).

80. George Houser to Sis Robinson, August 26, 1952, microfilm, Reel 9, Series 3, CORE Papers.

81. "Statement of Eroseanna Robinson," 2. Skateland's manager and owner blamed the violence on white southerners who were migrating to Cleveland during the war years.

82. "Report on Coffey and Sis Robinson," 2.

83. "Statement of E. Robinson and M. Coffey about visit to Play-More," July 16, 1952, p. 2, microfilm.

84. "Philly Club Plans Rollery for Negroes," *Billboard* 58, 33 (August 17, 1946): 89; "Negro Skating Clubs Set in Philly, Chester," *Billboard* 64, 46 (November 8, 1952): 64. The Sepia Skating Club used the Elmwood Roller Rink on Tuesday nights only. At other times only white members of the Elmwood Skating Club had access to the facility. "Philly Negroes Skate Tuesdays at Elmwood," *Billboard* 64, 48 (November 22, 1952): 51.

85. "Skating Rinks Agree to End Race Bias," *Pittsburgh Courier*, June 27, 1953, 7. See also press release, "NAACP Youth Break Rink Segregation," June 4, 1953, Folder 9, "Discrimination, Skating Rinks, 1953–54," Box A238, Series II, NAACP Papers. For a discussion of racial liberalism in Philadelphia, see Matthew J. Countryman, *Up South: Civil Rights and Black Power in Philadelphia* (Philadelphia: University of Pennsylvania Press, 2006), esp. 13–47.

86. *Race Relations Law Reporter* 3, 1 (February 1958): 46, 48.

87. Ibid., 45–49. The court relied on New York's 1957 Castle Hill Beach Club Case, which argued the club was established only to exclude African Americans.

88. "Bradley Fined $25 on Discrimination Charge in Br'port," *Billboard* 61, 6 (February 5, 1949): 76; "Bridgeport Mgr. Fined and Jailed in Race Action," *Billboard* 61, 20 (May 14, 1949): 83.

89. "Chase Boys from Ohio Swim Pool," *Chicago Defender*, August 9, 1941, 8. There had been racial conflict at the pool for many years.

90. Robert B. McKay, "Segregation and Public Recreation," *Virginia Law Review* 40, 6 (October 1954): 717.

91. Handwritten letter to Walter White from Richard Sims, Jr., president, Summit Branch NAACP, June 20, 1945, Folder 7, "Discrimination, Swimming Pools, New Jersey, 1945–9," Box B66, Series II, NAACP Papers.

92. Doris Berman, Paterson American Youth for Democracy, to Franklin Williams, August 2, 1946, Folder 7, "Discrimination, Swimming Pools, New Jersey, 1945–9," Box B66, Series II, NAACP Papers. On segregated swimming in New Jersey, see also Kevin Mumford, *Newark: A History of Race, Rights, and Riots in America* (New York: New York University Press, 2007), 45–49.

93. Harold A. Lett to Roby Wilkins, September 1, 1949, Folder 7, "Discrimination, Swimming Pools, New Jersey, 1945–9," Box B66, Series II, NAACP Papers.

94. Handwritten letter to NAACP from Walter Haas, chairman, Anti-Discrimination Committee, Thomas Jefferson High School, Brooklyn, January 9, 1945, Folder 8, "Discrimination, Swimming Pools, New York, 1945–47," Box B66, Series II, NAACP Papers; and Jim Robinson, "Core Gets in the Swim," *COREspondent*, January 1947, microfilm, Reel 8, Series 3, CORE Papers. CORE also targeted Manhattan hotels that often barred blacks from their indoor pools. By 1950, for example, they had successfully desegregated the Hotel Shelton's pool. See "Negro Ban Ended at Swimming Pool, Restaurant," *Core-lator*, January 1950, microfilm, Reel 13, EIII, CORE Papers, Addendum.

95. Frank Reed, president, NAACP York Branch, to Gloster Current, July 16, 1947, Folder 12, "Discrimination, Swimming Pools, Pennsylvania, 1948," Box B66, Series II, NAACP Papers.

96. Theresa M. Johnson, secretary, NAACP York Branch, to Gloster B. Current, July 8, 1948, Folder 12, "Discrimination, Swimming Pools, Pennsylvania, 1948," Box B66, Series II NAACP Papers.

97. Theresa M. Johnson, secretary, NAACP York Branch, to Gloster B. Current, July 8, 1948, Folder 12, "Discrimination, Swimming Pools, Pennsylvania, 1948," Box B66, Series II, NAACP Papers.

98. Telegram to Gloster Current from Frank Reed, May 3, 1948, Folder 12, "Discrimination, Swimming Pools, Pennsylvania, 1948," Box B66, Series II, NAACP Papers.

99. Newspaper clipping, "City Restricts Use of Pool," *Washington Reporter*, May 1, 1948, Folder 12, "Discrimination, Swimming Pools, Pennsylvania, 1948," Box B66, Series II, NAACP Papers.

100. For a summary of the case, see Marian Wynn Perry to Maurice Frink, August 20, 1948, Folder 10, "Discrimination, Swimming Pools, Warren, Ohio, Correspondence, 1947–49," Box B66, Series II, NAACP Papers; and Jeff Wiltse, *Contested Waters: A Social History of Swimming Pools in America* (Chapel Hill: University of North Carolina Press, 2007), 159–62, 165–66. Wiltse points out that the appeal's success was based on a similar case in Montgomery, West Virginia, where a municipal pool was leased to the Montgomery Park Association. The local NAACP branch successfully filed suit in federal district court, which ruled that the exclusion of black swimmers violated the Fourteenth Amendment unless a separate but equal facility was provided for blacks. The city promptly closed the pool, but the case, *Lawrence v. Hancock*, did provide a useful precedent for future cases challenging recreational segregation (162–66).

The NAACP's Legal Defense Fund, headed by Thurgood Marshall, was reluctant to support the Warren case, concerned that the evidence the Veterans Swim Club was purely a subterfuge was not strong enough. See Thurgood Marshall to W. M. Howard, Esq., February 6, 1948, Folder 10, "Discrimination, Swimming Pools, Warren, Ohio, Correspondence, 1947–49," Box B66, Series II, NAACP Papers. Marshall based his decision on the research of Marian Wynn Perry, a lawyer from the National Lawyer's Guild who joined his staff in 1945. Memorandum, Marian Wynn Perry to Messrs. Marshall, Dudley, and Williams, January 12, 1948, Folder 10, "Discrimination, Swimming Pools, Warren, Ohio, Correspondence, 1947–49," Box B66, Series II, NAACP Papers.

101. Wiltse, *Contested Waters*, 166.

102. Dorothea Kahn, "A Backward Look at Gary's Race Clash," *Christian Science Monitor*, February 19, 1946, 18.

103. Quoted in "Police Close Beach over Racial Dispute," *New York Times*, August 29, 1949, 23. See also "Another Segregation Riot Reported Far out of South," *Chicago Defender*, September 17, 1949, 7, reprinted from the *Clarion Ledger*, Jackson, Mississippi; Memorandum, Clifford E. Minton to Mayor Peter Mandich, July 14, 1953, "Progress Report on Marquette Park Beach Case," microfilm, Reel 19, Chicago Urban League Papers, University of Illinois at Chicago, Daley Library; Andrew Hurley, *Environmental Inequalities: Class, Race, and Industrial Pollution in Gary, Indiana, 1945–1980* (Chapel Hill: University of North Carolina Press, 1995), 120–22. Hurley describes a second incident in 1953 when a group of black women from the local NAACP occupied the beach. While they sunbathed white teenagers vandalized their car and waited for them to return to the parking lot. The women escaped when a police car arrived to break up the gang, and this time the city pledged to protect black beachgoers. However, this promised protection soon dissipated and in 1961 a group of whites severely beat a black man, which led to another round of protests (121–22). See also "Report on Incident at Marquette Beach Park," July 1, 1953, microfilm, Reel 19, Chicago Urban League Papers.

104. Hurley, *Environmental Inequalities*, 122.

105. George Schermer, "The Fairgrounds Park Incident," pp. 12–13, unpublished report, 1949, Folder, "Discrimination: Beaches and Swimming Pools, 1949," Box A234, Series II, NAACP Papers. CORE activist Billie Ames suggested that the mayor may have been attempting to attract African American votes in a period when the city's black population was growing rapidly. See Billie Ames to George Houser, June 21, 1949, microfilm, Reel 13, EIII, CORE Papers, Addendum. For analyses of the Fairground Park riot, see Wiltse, *Contested Waters*, 78–86, 166–80; Joseph Heathcott, "Black Archipelago: Politics and Civic Life in the Jim Crow City," *Journal of Social History* 38, 3 (Spring

2005): 726–27; and Clarence Lang, *Grassroots at the Gateway: Class Politics and Black Freedom Struggle in St. Louis, 1936–75* (Ann Arbor: University of Michigan Press, 2009), 83–86.

106. Schermer, "The Fairgrounds Park Incident"; "Opening Pools to Negroes Starts St. Louis Race Riots," *Christian Science Monitor*, June 22, 1949, 3; "St. Louis Closes Pools Following Race Disorders," *Los Angeles Times*, June 23, 1949, 16.

107. Schermer, "The Fairgrounds Park Incident," 13; "Blast St. Louis Mayor for Rescinding Pool Order to Quiet White Rioters," *Chicago Defender*, July 2, 1949, 1.

108. Quoted in Bernard Weisberg, "Racial Violence and Civil Rights Law Enforcement," in *Racial Violence in the United States*, ed. Allen D. Grimshaw (Chicago: Aldine Publishing Company, 1969), 323–24. See also Wiltse, *Contested Waters*, 174, 176–80.

109. Pauli Murray, *Song in a Weary Throat: An American Pilgrimage* (New York: Harper and Row, 1987), 200. On segregation in Washington, D.C., see Myrdal, *An American Dilemma*, 632; Constance McLaughlin Green, *The Secret City: A History of Race Relations in the Nation's Capital* (Princeton, N.J.: Princeton University Press, 1967); and National Committee on Segregation in the Nation's Capital, *Segregation in Washington: A Report of the National Committee on Segregation in the Nation's Capital* (Chicago, 1948).

110. For descriptions of the campaign, see Murray, *Song in a Weary Throat*, 200–209, 222–31; "Howard Students Picket Jim Crow Restaurant," *Chicago Defender*, April 24, 1943, 5; Mollin, *Radical Pacifism*, 24–26; Flora Bryant Brown, "NAACP Sponsored Sit-Ins by Howard University Students in Washington, DC, 1943–44," *Journal of Negro History* 85, 4 (Autumn 2000): 274–86; Cohen, *Consumers' Republic*, 98–99; Bynum, "'Our Fight if for Right,'" 63–65; and Glenda Elizabeth Gilmore, *Defying Dixie: The Radical Roots of Civil Rights, 1919–1950* (New York: W. W. Norton, 2008), 384–93. For studies of female activists during the 1940s and 1950s that focus on race, see Susan Lynn, *Progressive Women in Conservative Times: Racial Justice, Peace, and Feminism, 1945 to the 1960s* (New Brunswick, N.J.: Rutgers University Press, 1992); Ruth Feldstein, *Motherhood in Black and White: Race and Sex in American Liberalism, 1930–65* (Ithaca, N.Y.: Cornell University Press, 2000); and Melinda A. Plastas, *A Band of Noble Women: Race and the Women's Peace Movement* (Syracuse, N.Y.: Syracuse University Press, 2011). Morrow and Murray's friendship went beyond Washington, D.C. When Morrow was directing CORE in Cleveland, Murray visited and raised money for local causes (Juanita Morrow to George Houser, February 24, 1947, microfilm, Reel 9, Series 3, CORE Papers).

111. Houser, *Cracking the Color Line*, 10. Houser said the campaign was effective, but it was not until a 1951 campaign targeting the Playhouse, an art theater, that CORE successfully desegregated a Washington, D.C., theater. See also Meier and Rudwick, *CORE*, 50–51. CORE continued to hold summer interracial workshops in Washington, D.C., until 1954.

112. "Top U.S. Dramatists Back Washington Jim Crow Ban," *Billboard* 58, 47 (November 23, 1946): 1; "Equity Seeks United Front in Capital Race-Ban Drive," *Billboard* 59, 2 (January 11, 1947): 1; "Files Jim Crow Suit vs. Nat'l," *Billboard* 59, 6 (February 8, 1947): 1; "Non–Jim Crow D.C. Theater?" *Billboard* 60, 36 (September 4, 1948): 1, 42; Green, *Secret City*, 290.

113. Quoted in National Committee on Segregation in the Nation's Capital, *Segregation in Washington*, 4. For discussions of the report, see Green, *Secret City*, 286–88; and "Capital Race Bias Declared 'Worse,'" *New York Times*, December 11, 1948, 17. Works that emphasize the role of the cold war in shaping early civil rights include Borstelmann, *The Cold War and the Color Line*; Mary L. Dudziak, *Cold War Civil Rights: Race and the Image of American Democracy* (Princeton, N.J.: Princeton University Press, 2002); and Penny M. Von Eschen, *Race Against Empire: Black Americans and Anticolonialism, 1937–1957* (Ithaca, N.Y.: Cornell University Press, 1997).

114. National Committee on Segregation in the Nation's Capital, *Segregation in Washington*, 91.

115. Jackson, *Gunnar Myrdal and America's Conscience*, 275–77; Sugrue, *Sweet Land of Liberty*, 99; Southern, *Gunnar Myrdal and Black-White Relations*, 111.

116. Lawson, *To Secure These Rights*, 124, 128. The report specifically called for prohibition of discrimination and segregation in Washington, D.C.'s recreational facilities (184).

117. Green, *Secret City*, 292; "Six Negroes Booed out of Anacostia Pool," *Washington Post*, June 27, 1949, B1; "Interior and Recreation Board Compromise on Segregation," *Washington Post*, July 2, 1949, 1; "U.S. and City Fuss over Policy After Washington Swim Pool Riot," *Chicago Defender*, July 9, 1949, 1. The fact that the lifeguards worked for the Board of Recreation reflected the complexity of segregation at the pools as the board ran segregated swimming instructions at the city pools in the morning, and Government Services, Inc. operated the pools in the afternoon. After blacks integrated the McKinley and Anacostia pools the board canceled its morning swim instruction. See "Krug, D.C. Officials Confer Today on Segregation Policy," *Washington Post*, July 1, 1949, B1.

118. Green, *Secret City*, 270.

119. "Citizens Committee Against Segregation in Recreation Report of Initial Meeting," July 20, 1945, Folder, "Citizens Committee Against Segregation in Recreation—Reports," Box 78-14, NAACP—DC Branch Papers, Moorland Springarn Research Center, Washington, D.C.; "Report on Citizens Committee Against Segregation in Recreation Meeting," August 8, 1945, ibid. The committee was made up of twelve civic groups, nine labor organizations, and four churches with the NAACP taking the most prominent role. The recreation commission based their map on a 1929 "Recreation System Plan" that marked specific play areas for blacks and whites. See Green, *Secret City*, 263, 271.

120. Green, *Secret City*, 272. One veteran wrote to the Board of Recreation, "at the very moment when the peace of the world depends on emphasizing the brotherhood of man, we exalt the foundation of fascism, racial intolerance" (272).

121. "Citizens Committee Against Segregation in Recreation Report," May 20, 1948, p. 20, Folder, "Committee on Recreation Reports," Box 78-14, NAACP—DC Branch Papers. This report notes that in one week in October 1947 only ten white children used a playground in a "border" area while the thousand black students in a junior high school across the street had no facilities (19–20). For a discussion of the instability inherent in racial zoning, see Charles E. Connerly, *"The Most Segregated City in America": City Planning and Civil Rights in Birmingham, 1920–80* (Charlottesville: University of Virginia Press, 2005), esp. 71–101.

122. Statement by Alice C. Hunter, p. 5, Folder, "DC Recreation Board 1945—Statements," Box 78-15, NAACP—DC Branch Papers. Hunter was the sole African American on the recreation commission. See also Green, *Secret City*, 262–63.

123. "Six Negroes Booed out of Anacostia Pool"; Green, *Secret City*, 292. African Americans regularly used Banneker and Francis pools, and whites Takoma, East Potomac, McKinley, and Anacostia pools. While there was racial violence at the Anacostia pool in 1949, blacks swam at the McKinley pool undisturbed, although there was a drop in white attendance. See "Krug, D.C. Officials Confer Today on Segregation Policy."

124. Green, *Secret City*, 291; "Interior and Recreation Board Compromise on Segregation," *Washington Post*, July 2, 1949, 1; "Krug Asserts Non-Jim Crow Firm Policy of Interior Department," *Atlanta Daily World*, September 8, 1949, 1.

125. "SE Residents Ask Swimming Pool Opening," *Washington Post*, July 30, 1949, B1. In an editorial the *Washington Post* argued that reopening the pool without a clear settlement would "suggest to rival white and Negro groups that, since the governmental agencies in charge have been unable to settle their differences, force and hoodlumism may be the determining factors in deciding the policy to be followed. In these circumstances, it would be difficult to avoid tragic consequences" ("Anacostia Pool," *Washington Post*, August 15, 1949, 6). In stark contrast a group of twenty-five white and black mothers asked for the pool to be reopened "on a nonsegregated basis" with police presence "to quell any attempted hoodlumism" ("Twenty Five Mothers Ask Krug to Reopen Pool to All Races," *Washington Post*, August 16, 1949, 10).

126. Quoted in "Racial Violence and Civil Rights Law Enforcement," *University of Chicago Law Review* 18, 4 (Summer 1951): 774.

127. "Plea to Truman Urged in Play Area Dispute," *Washington Post*, July 10, 1949, M14.

128. John N. Daniels, Jr., letter to the editor, "Segregated Swimming," *Washington Post*, August 8, 1949, 6.

129. Chalmers M. Roberts, "Board Rejects Krug Proposal on Play Areas," *Washington Post*, July 13, 1949, 1; "Police to Enforce Jim Crow Ban at D.C. Pools," *Chicago Defender*, March 18, 1950, 1. Although Truman's stance on civil rights may have reflected his growing dependence on the black vote, African American activists had reason to believe he would be receptive to their arguments to desegregate Washington's recreational facilities. See Michael R. Gardner, *Harry Truman and Civil Rights: Moral Courage and Political Risks* (Carbondale: Southern Illinois University Press, 2003).

130. Typewritten note, June 1950, Folder 4, "Discrimination, Beaches and Swimming Pools, 1953–55," Box A234, Series II, NAACP Papers; Gloster B. Current, director of branches, to branch officers, March 20, 1950, ibid.; "Board Committee to Seek Conference with Chapman on Swimming Operation," *Washington Post*, March 31, 1950, 27.

131. "Swimming Pools," *Washington Post*, April 10, 1950, 8.

132. Mrs. B. Parent, letter to the editor, *Washington Post*, April 15, 1950, 8; Loren Sorenson, letter to the editor, *Washington Post*, April 20, 1950, 10.

133. "Attendance at Six Pools Off One Third," *Washington Post*, September 6, 1950, B1. Although some civil rights activists claimed the drop-off in attendance was due to weather, the two segregated white pools run by the District Recreation Board showed no decline in attendance.

134. Wiltse, *Contested Waters*, 184–85. In 1960 the government shut down McKinley pool.

135. Green, *Secret City*, 292; "McKinley Pool Offer Not Taken, Says Wender," *Washington Post*, August 10, 1949, B1; Peck, "The Proof of in the Pudding," 294; "CORE Plan for Pool Operation Acclaimed in Washington and St. Louis," *CORE-lator*, January 1950, microfilm, Reel 13, EIII, CORE Papers, Addendum.

136. Quoted in William M. Blair, "Segregation in Parks of St. Louis Is Denounced as Violation of Law," *New York Times*, August 2, 1949, 14.

137. Thomas J. Sugrue, "Affirmative Action from Below: Civil Rights, the Building Trades, and the Politics of Racial Equality in the Urban North, 1945–1969," *Journal of American History* 91, 1 (June 2004): 149.

138. Schermer, "The Fairgrounds Park Incident," 26.

139. Quoted in "Racial Violence and Civil Rights Law Enforcement," 772.

140. See Kevin Kruse, *White Flight: Atlanta and the Making of Modern Conservatism* (Princeton, N.J.: Princeton University Press, 2005), 119–24; and Richard B. Pierce, *Polite Protest: The Political Economy of Race in Indianapolis, 1920–1970* (Bloomington: Indiana University Press, 2005).

141. Sol Rabkin, "Racial Discrimination in Places of Public Accommodation," *Journal of Negro Education* 23, 3 (Summer 1954): 260.

142. John P. Frank, "Can the Courts Erase the Color Line," *Journal of Negro Education* 21, 3 (Summer 1952): 309. Frank worked with Thurgood Marshall on the *Brown v. Board of Education* case, defended Ernesto Miranda in front of the Supreme Court, and was a legal advisor for Anita Hill during the nomination proceeding of Clarence Thomas to the Supreme Court. See "John P. Frank, 1918–2002," *Journal of Blacks in Higher Education* 38 (Autumn 2002): 27.

143. Frank, "Can the Courts Erase the Color Line," 310. For another view of Washington, D.C., as a success story, see "Racial Violence and Civil Rights Law Enforcement," 774–75.

144. "Another Segregation Riot Reported Far out of South."

145. Lisa Levenstein, *A Movement Without Marches: African American Women and the Politics of Poverty in Postwar Philadelphia* (Chapel Hill: University of North Carolina Press, 2009), 52.

Chapter 3

1. Charles J. Jacques, Jr., *Cincinnati's Coney Island: America's Finest Amusement Park* (Jefferson, Ohio: Amusement Park Journal, 2002), 130–31; Judith A. Bechtel and Robert M. Coughlin, *Building the Beloved Community: Maurice McCrackin's Life for Peace and Civil Rights* (Philadelphia: Temple University Press, 1991), 79. Beginning in the early 1950s, numerous live radio and TV shows were broadcast from the park, which increasingly targeted its amusements to young children.

2. Quoted in Jacques, *Cincinnati's Coney Island*, 141.

3. This phrase first appears in James H. Robinson, "The Cincinnati Negro Survey and Program," *Proceedings of the National Conference on Social Work* (June 1–8, 1919): 524.

4. Jacques, *Cincinnati's Coney Island*, 23–34, 47–48. Three smaller steamboats were also lost: the *Morning Star*, *Chris Greene*, and *Tacoma*.

5. William F. Mangels, *The Outdoor Amusement Industry: From Earliest Times to the Present* (New York: Vintage Press, 1952), 20.

6. Jacques, *Cincinnati's Coney Island*, 49–54, 91.

7. Quoted in ibid., 58.

8. Harold D. Snell, NAACP, to Richard N. Bluestein, July 29, 1946, Folder 14, Box 14, Jewish Community Relations Council Papers, American Jewish Archives, Cincinnati, Ohio; "Cincinnati Branch, National Association for the Advancement of Colored People, Digest of Cases Involving Police Irregularities," ibid.

9. Kathryn Veith to George Houser, May 7, 1947, microfilm, Reel 8, Series 3, CORE Papers: Jacques, *Cincinnati's Coney Island*, 23–34.

10. Minutes, Mayor's Friendly Relations Committee, May 24, 1961, p. 2, Folder 6, Box 26, Jewish Community Relations Council Papers; Robert A. Burnham, "The Mayor's Friendly Relations Committee: Cultural Pluralism and the Struggle for Black Advancement," in *Race and the City: Work, Community, and Protest in Cincinnati, 1820–1970*, ed. Henry Louis Taylor (Urbana: University of Illinois Press, 1993), 267–68; August Meier and Elliott Rudwick, *CORE: A Study in the Civil Rights Movement* (Chicago: University of Illinois Press, 1975), 258–79.

11. "Queen's Gone, But All's Well at Coney!" *Cincinnati Enquirer*, April 9, 1948; Jacques, *Cincinnati's Coney Island*, 121–26, 129. The boat exploded at a Pittsburgh dock, killing nineteen crew members.

12. Meier and Rudwick, *CORE*, 31, 44; Bechtel and Coughlin, *Building the Beloved Community*, 70.

13. Meier and Rudwick, *CORE*, 31–39. On the Journey of Reconciliation, see James Peck, *Freedom Ride* (New York: Simon and Schuster, 1962), 10–16; Jo Ann Ooiman Robinson, *Abraham Went Out: A Biography of A. J. Muste* (Philadelphia: Temple University Press, 1981), 113–14; John D'Emilio, *Lost Prophet: The Life and Times of Bayard Rustin* (New York: Free Press, 2003), 135–40; Raymond Arsenault, "'You Don't Have to Ride Jim Crow': CORE and the 1947 Journey of Reconciliation," in *Before Brown: Civil Rights and White Backlash in the Modern South*, ed. Glenn Feldman (Tuscaloosa: University of Alabama Press, 2004); Derek Charles Catsam, *Freedom's Main Line: The Journey of Reconciliation and the Freedom Rides* (Lexington: University Press of Kentucky, 2009), 13–46; and Marian Mollin, "The Limits of Egalitarianism: Radical Pacifism, Civil Rights, and the Journey of Reconciliation," *Radical History Review* 88 (2004): 112–13.

14. These activists included one white volunteer, Worth Randle, a biologist and peace activist, and three black volunteers: Andrew Johnson, a law student and CORE member, Nathan Wright, a social worker, and Wallace Nelson. In addition, Ernest Bromley moved to Cincinnati soon after the Journey. Arsenault, "'You Don't Have to Ride Jim Crow,'" 50.

15. Bechtel and Coughlin, *Building the Beloved Community*, 73. The authors note that Bromley was heavily influenced by Edgar Scheffield Brightman, who later taught a young Martin Luther King, Jr.

16. Bechtel and Coughlin, *Building the Beloved Community*, 72–74. On Muste, see Robinson,

Abraham Went Out. On Marion Bromley, see Marion Bromley, "Feminism and Nonviolent Revolution," in *Reweaving the Web of Life: Feminism and Nonviolence*, ed. Pam McAllister (Philadelphia: New Society Publishers, 1982), 143–54.

17. Arsenault, "'You Don't Have to Ride Jim Crow,'" 34. James Peck, Bayard Rustin, and James Farmer all worked in this office during the 1940s.

18. Bechtel and Coughlin, *Building the Beloved Community*, 74; Robinson, *Abraham Went Out*, 94–95; Maurice Isserman, *If I Had a Hammer . . . The Death of the Old Left and the Birth of the New Left* (New York: Basic Books, 1987), 137; D'Emilio, *Lost Prophet*, 128–29. See also David L. Chappell, *A Stone of Hope: Prophetic Religion and the Death of Jim Crow* (Chapel Hill: University of North Carolina Press, 2004), esp. 44–66; Lawrence S. Wittner, *Rebels Against War: The American Peace Movement, 1941–60* (New York: Columbia University Press, 1969), 156–60; James Tracy, *Direct Action: Radical Pacifism from the Union Eight to the Chicago Seven* (Chicago: University of Chicago Press, 1996), 60–67. In protest of the growing militarism of postwar America, the Peacemakers also became tax refusers. This marked them as outlaws and set them apart from the more moderate FOR.

19. Burnham, "The Mayor's Friendly Relations Committee," 267–68; Meier and Rudwick, *CORE*, 44; Marian Mollin, *Radical Pacifism in Modern America: Egalitarianism and Protest* (Philadelphia: University of Pennsylvania Press, 2006), 44–72; Marion Bromley to James Peck, June 4, 1953, microfilm, Reel 8, Series 3, CORE Papers; Juanita Nelson Morrow to Catherine Raymond, March 10, 1955, ibid. The Gano Peacemakers, as they called themselves, welcomed activists from around the country, including Eroseanna Robinson. See Marion Bromley to Ernest Bromley, August 20, 1951, Folder, "Letters from Marion to Ernest Bromley, August 1951–September 1951," Box 1, Bromley Papers, Swarthmore Peace Collection, Swarthmore, Pa.

20. The black population grew from 55,593 to 125,070. Henry Louis Taylor, introduction to *Race and the City*, 14.

21. Charles F. Casey-Leininger, "Making the Second Ghetto in Cincinnati: Avondale, 1925–70," in *Race and the City*, 232–57.

22. Virginia Coffey, interview by Stephanie Corsbie, c. 1980, p. 11, Cincinnati Women Working Collection, 1904–81, arranged by Alden N. Monroe, Cincinnati Historical Library.

23. Nina Mjagkij, "Behind the Scenes: The Cincinnati Urban League, 1948–63," in *Race and the City*, 281.

24. CORE was largely dependent on the significantly better financial resources of the FOR, while Muste and other FOR activists made a distinction between the nonviolent direct action promoted by civil rights activists (including those involved in A. Philip Randolph's March on Washington Movement) and the religious pacifism of the FOR. Robinson, *Abraham Went Out*, 113–17; Meier and Rudwick, *CORE*, 19–20; Arsenault, "'You Don't Have to Ride Jim Crow,'" 43–44.

25. Quoted in Robinson, *Abraham Went Out*, 97. McCrackin joined the FOR while a theology student in Chicago in the late 1920s. After graduating from McCormick Seminary in 1930, he set sail for Persia (Iran) and spent five years there as a missionary. Upon his return he worked as a minister in Kirkwood, Illinois, near Monmouth, and then in Hessville, Indiana, a blue-collar town devastated by the Great Depression. During this time McCrackin began to attend FOR meetings in Evanston and became increasingly aware of racial discrimination, discovering that before his arrival the Ku Klux Klan had routinely held meetings in his church. After he decided to broadcast his belief in racial equality, McCrackin joined the NAACP and befriended local black leaders while speaking out against the impending war, which led to an outcry in his congregation. Seeking more freedom to develop his activism, McCrackin accepted an offer to become a pastor at the Waldensian Presbyterian Church in Chicago. But the settlement house attached to the church served an Italian community that was actively resisting racial integration. In 1967 white teenagers burned down the church and settlement house after an African American family joined the congregation. See Bechtel and Coughlin, *Building the Beloved Community*, 51–54.

26. Quoted in Bechtel and Coughlin, *Building the Beloved Community*, 59.

27. Ibid., 62–63.

28. Meier and Rudwick, *CORE*, 58; Burnham, "The Mayor's Friendly Relations Committee," 270–71; Roger C. Hansen, "Pioneers in Nonviolent Action: The Congress of Racial Equality in Cincinnati, 1946–55," *Queen City Heritage: The Journal of the Cincinnati Historical Society* 52 (Fall 1994): 24. On the early work of CCHR, see CORE Executive Committee Meeting, April 17, 1948, microfilm, Reel 9, Series 3, CORE Papers; Minutes Executive Committee, January 22 and 23, 1949, ibid. The all-black West End Civic League had carried out "Don't Buy Where You Can't Work" campaigns in the 1930s and 1940s to pressure white business owners to employ African American workers. Many of its members eagerly joined the CCHR. A predominantly white CORE chapter founded in 1946 by social worker Nathan Wright was also folded into the CCHR.

29. Bechtel and Coughlin, *Building the Beloved Community*, 74–75. On the integration of music schools, see "Cincinnati," p. 2, *CORE-lator*, January 1950, microfilm, Reel 13, Series 3, CORE Papers; "Cincinnati," pp. 1–2, *CORE-lator*, May 1951, ibid.; "First Negro in Music School," pp. 1–2, *CORE-lator*, October 1951, ibid.; and "Ask Support in Combating Racism," *The Peacemaker* (April 21, 1951): 5.

30. Burnham, "The Mayor's Friendly Relations Committee," 268; Hansen, "Pioneers in Nonviolent Action," 25–26.

31. Burnham, "The Mayor's Friendly Relations Committee," 268–69. MFRC board members argued, "Our effectiveness lay in consultation with all parties concerned" (269).

32. "Coney Island a Background for Bias," *Leader*, January 15, 1955, newspaper clipping, Folder 3, Box 9, Urban League of Greater Cincinnati Papers, Cincinnati Historical Society Library, Cincinnati, Ohio; "Did Safety Commission Err in Granting Coney Island 1954 License?" *Leader*, February 27, 1954, newspaper clipping, ibid.

33. Bechtel and Coughlin, *Building the Beloved Community*, 64.

34. Untitled document, October 1951, Folder 17, Box 14, Jewish Community Relations Council Papers.

35. Charles Posner to Joseph B. Robinson, December 28, 1951, Folder 17, Box 14, Jewish Community Relations Council Papers.

36. Robin M. Williams, Jr., and Margaret W. Ryan, *Schools in Transition: Community Experiences in Desegregation* (Chapel Hill: University of North Carolina Press, 1954), 43; Charles Posner to Joseph B. Robinson, December 28, 1951.

37. Bechtel and Coughlin, *Building the Beloved Community*, 79.

38. Arsenault, "'You Don't Have to Ride Jim Crow,'" 32–33. Arsenault argues that these activists had "seized the opportunity to take the desegregation struggle out of the courts and into the streets" and that they "transcended the cautious legal realism of the NAACP" (32).

39. Quoted in Bechtel and Coughlin, *Building the Beloved Community*, 80.

40. Rev. Maurice McCrackin, statement made at the meeting of the Cincinnati City Council, October 1, 1952, p. 5, Folder 5, Box 52, McCrackin Papers, Cincinnati Historical Society Library, Cincinnati, Ohio; Hansen, "Pioneers in Nonviolent Action," 27–28.

41. Bechtel and Coughlin, *Building the Beloved Community*, 85; Jacques, *Cincinnati's Coney Island*, 140; Rev. Maurice McCrackin, statement made to City Council, August 7, 1952, p. 9, Folder 7, Box 15, Jewish Community Relations Council Papers.

42. Jim Peck, *Cracking the Color Line: Non-Violent Direct Action Methods of Eliminating Racial Discrimination*, 1960, microfilm, Reel 9, Series 3, CORE Papers; James Peck, "The Proof of the Pudding," *The Crisis* 56, 10 (November 1949): 292–355.

43. See lists of special days and sponsors in Jacques, *Cincinnati's Coney Island*, 219–20. In one case an African American CCHR member whose mother was dying of cancer was turned away on Cancer Day (Bechtel and Coughlin, *Building the Beloved Community*, 81).

44. Bechtel and Coughlin, *Building the Beloved Community*, 81–82; McCrackin, statement made

to City Council, August 7, 1952; McCrackin, statement made at the meeting of the Cincinnati City Council, October 1, 1952, p. 5; "More 'Fireworks' at Coney Island," *CORE-lator*, October 1951, p. 1, microfilm, Reel 13, Series 3, CORE Papers. Much of this second statement is identical to the one McCrackin presented in August, but there are some minor revisions and additions.

45. McCrackin, statement made to City Council, August 7, 1952, p. 5.

46. "More 'Fireworks' at Coney Island," , p. 1. For other descriptions of the 1952 demonstrations at Coney Island, see Hansen, "Pioneers in Nonviolent Action," 28–30; Bechtel and Coughlin, *Building the Beloved Community*, 80–86; Jacques, *Cincinnati's Coney Island*, 140–42; Michael Washington, "The Stirrings of the Modern Civil Rights Movement in Cincinnati, Ohio, 1943–53," in *Groundwork: Local Black Freedom Movements in America*, ed. Jeanne Theoharis and Komozi Woodard (New York: New York University Press, 2005), 215–34; and Meier and Rudwick, *CORE*, 58–59.

47. "More 'Fireworks' at Coney Island," p. 2; "Three Peacemakers Jailed as Participants in Campaign to End Park Segregation," *The Peacemaker* (July 12, 1952): 1; McCrackin, statement made to City Council, August 7, 1952, pp. 2–3.

48. McCrackin, statement made to City Council, August 7, 1952, p. 3.

49. Quoted in Hansen, "Pioneers in Nonviolent Action," 29. For a description of their time in jail, see "Greetings from Gano," 1952, Folder, "Bromley Christmas Letters," Box 7, Bromley Papers.

50. Quoted in Bechtel and Coughlin, *Building the Beloved Community*, 82.

51. McCrackin, statement made to City Council, August 7, 1952, p. 4.

52. "More 'Fireworks' at Coney Island," p. 2.

53. McCrackin, Statement Made to City Council, August 7, 1952, p. 8; Bechtel and Coughlin, *Building the Beloved Community*, 85.

54. "Coney Island Report," *The Peacemaker* (September 27, 1952): 4; Bechtel and Coughlin, *Building the Beloved Community*, 86.

55. McCrackin, statement made at the meeting of the Cincinnati City Council, October 1, 1952, p. 4.

56. "Coney Island Action Considered by Cincinnati City Council," *The Peacemaker* (October 11, 1952): 1; Bechtel and Coughlin, *Building the Beloved Community*, 86–87.

57. McCrackin, statement made at the meeting of the Cincinnati City Council, October 1, 1952, p. 1.

58. McCrackin, statement made at the meeting of the Cincinnati City Council, October 1, 1952, p. 3.

59. "The Good Work of CORE," *CORE-lator*, January–February 1953, p. 1, microfilm, Reel 13, Series 3, CORE Papers. This was an editorial originally published in the *Pittsburgh Courier* on November 7, 1952. See also "Coney Island Drive Goes On," June–July 1953, p. 2, ibid.; and Hansen, "Pioneers in Nonviolent Action," 29–30.

60. CCHR to Fred R. Raugh, Cincinnati Gas & Electric Company, June 3, 1953, microfilm, Reel 8, Series 3, CORE Papers.

61. "Coney Island Drive Goes On," 2.

62. The women were Vivian Colbert, Lois Wright, and Marybelle Brown. NAACP press release, July 16, 1953, Folder, "Discrimination: Parks and Playgrounds 1952–55," Box A238, Series II, NAACP Papers, Library of Congress, Washington, D.C.; Bechtel and Coughlin, *Building the Beloved Community*, 87.

63. NAACP press release, July 16, 1953; "Ethel Fletcher v. Coney Island, Inc.," *Race Relations Law Reporter* 1, 2 (April 1956): 360–65. For discussions of the Fletcher case, see Bechtel and Coughlin, *Building the Beloved Community*, 87; Jacques, *Cincinnati's Coney Island*, 141; and Hansen, "Pioneers in Nonviolent Action," 30.

64. "Ethel Fletcher v. Coney Island, Inc.," Opinion, p. 2, Folder, "Discrimination: Parks and Playgrounds 1952–55," Box A238, Series II, NAACP Papers.

65. "Ethel Fletcher v. Coney Island, Inc.," Opinion, p. 5.

66. Ibid., p. 7.

67. Sol Rabkin and Theodore Leskes to CRC Offices, ADL Regional Offices, AJC Area Offices, November 1, 1954, p. 2, Folder 7, Box 15, Jewish Community Relations Council Papers.

68. "Warned Not to Enter Coney Island," newspaper unknown, July 31, 1954, Urban League clippings, Folder 3, Box 9, Urban League of Greater Cincinnati Papers.

69. Quoted in "Warned Not to Enter Coney Island."

70. "Coney Island Decision 'Involves' More than Mrs. Fletcher," editorial, *Independent*, July 31, 1954, Urban League clippings, Folder 3, Box 9, Urban League of Greater Cincinnati Papers.

71. Sol Rabkin and Theodore Leskes to CRC Offices, ADL Regional Offices, AJC Area Offices, May 24, 1956, p. 2, Folder, "Discrimination: Parks and Playgrounds, 1956–1965," Box A110, Series III, NAACP Papers.

72. "Summary of Contacts," July 18 and November 19, 1953, January 18 and 21, 1954, Folder 3, Box 9, Urban League of Greater Cincinnati Papers; Hansen, "Pioneers in Nonviolent Action," 30.

73. Ibid.

74. John S. Holley to Joseph Hall, neighborhood secretary, Urban League of Portland, December 12, 1952, Folder 5, Box 36, Urban League of Greater Cincinnati Papers.

75. William M. Ashby, executive director, Urban League of Eastern Union County, N.J., to Joseph Hall, November 24, 1952, Folder 5, Box 36, Urban League of Greater Cincinnati Papers.

76. James Williams, executive secretary, Providence Urban League, to Joseph Hall, December 2, 1952, Folder 5, Box 36, Urban League of Greater Cincinnati Papers; Sebastian Owens, executive secretary, Urban League of Denver, to Joseph Hall, November 28, 1952, ibid.; Shelton Granger, executive secretary, Minneapolis Urban League, to Joseph Hall, November 26, 1952, ibid.; telegram via Western Union, AB Mapp, Springfield, Mass., Urban League, to Joseph Hall, November 24, 1952, ibid.; Jeanette Foster, community relations secretary, Fort Wayne Urban League, to Joseph Hall, November 20, 1952, ibid. Denver had two amusement parks, Elitch's Gardens and Lakeside. The ballrooms were segregated until the early 1940s and Lakeside still segregated its swimming pool in 1952.

77. Gaines T. Bradford, director of health and welfare, Urban League of Pittsburgh, to Joseph Hall, December 15, 1952, Folder 5, Box 36, Urban League of Greater Cincinnati Papers; Alexander Allen, director, Urban League of Pittsburgh, to Joseph Hall, December 1, 1952, ibid.

78. Arnold Walker, executive secretary, Urban League of Cleveland, to Joseph Hall, December 3, 1952, Folder 5, Box 36, Urban League of Greater Cincinnati Papers.

79. Paul Phillips, executive secretary, Grand Rapids Urban League, to Joseph Hall, November 25, 1952, Folder 5, Box 36, Urban League of Greater Cincinnati Papers.

80. Whitney Young, executive secretary, Omaha Urban League, to Joseph Hall, November 24, 1952, Folder 5, Box 36, Urban League of Greater Cincinnati Papers.

81. Ray B., Akron Urban League, to Joseph Hall, November 22, 1952, Folder 5, Box 36, Urban League of Greater Cincinnati Papers.

82. Donald Hawkins, acting executive director, Marion Urban League, to Joseph Hall, December 15, 1952, Folder 5, Box 36, Urban League of Greater Cincinnati Papers.

83. Harry L. Alston, industrial secretary, Southern Field Division, National Urban League (Atlanta), to Joseph Hall, December 4, 1952, Folder 5, Box 36, Urban League of Greater Cincinnati Papers; Charles T. Steele, executive secretary, Louisville Urban League, to Joseph Hall, November 25, 1952, ibid.; Furman Templeton, executive director, the Baltimore Urban League, to Joseph Hall, November 25, 1952, ibid.; Henry von Avery, director, Urban League of St. Louis, to Joseph Hall, November 21, 1952, ibid.

84. "Summary of Contacts."

85. Ibid.; Mjagkij, "Behind the Scenes," 284.

86. "Comments on Coney," 1954, Folder 3, Box 9, Urban League of Greater Cincinnati Papers.

87. Mjagkij, "Behind the Scenes," 284; Bechtel and Coughlin, *Building the Beloved Community*, 88.

88. Clippings from Urban League files, *Cincinnati Enquirer*, January 10, 1955, "Statement Outlines Coney Views . . . Park Licensing Under Discussion" [incomplete], Box 9, Folder 3, Urban League of Greater Cincinnati Papers.

89. "A Statement to the People of Cincinnati, the Safety Director and the Management of Coney Island," January 13, 1955, Folder 7, Box 15, Jewish Community Relations Council Papers.

90. Joseph Hall, "Summary of Contacts," undated, c. 1959, Folder 3, Box 9, Urban League of Greater Cincinnati Papers; "Park License Ordered," *New York Times*, January 15, 1955, 15.

91. Al Roman, "Cincy's Coney Island Challenges Liberalism," *Cincinnati Call-Post*, January 15, 1955.

92. "Report on Summer of Integration at Cincinnati's Coney Island," *The Peacemaker* (1955): 2.

93. Mjagkij, "Behind the Scenes," 286; Joseph Hall, Summary of Contacts," undated, c. 1959.

94. Bechtel and Coughlin, *Building the Beloved Community*, 89; "Late Flash to the CORE-lator—Win Coney Island Campaign," undated, microfilm, Reel 8, Series 3, CORE Papers.

95. Ray Paul, "Coney Island Admits Negroes for the First Time," *Cincinnati Call-Post*, May 7, 1955.

96. "Report on Summer of Integration at Cincinnati's Coney Island," 2.

97. Joseph Hall, "Summary of Contacts," April 1955, and Joseph Hall, "Summary of Contacts," undated, c. 1959, Folder 3, Box 9, Urban League of Greater Cincinnati Papers.

98. Joseph Hall, "Summary of Contacts," May–June 1955, Folder 3, Box 9, Urban League of Greater Cincinnati Papers.

99. Ray Paul, "Park Policemen Used to Prevent Negro Swimming," *Cincinnati Call-Post*, July 9, 1955.

100. Quoted in Meier and Rudwick, *CORE*, 67.

101. "Fourteen Arrested in Picketing at Rosedale," *Washington Post*, July 18, 1952, 23; "D.C. Heads Get Rosedale Plea Today," *Washington Post*, July 21, 1952, 13. The interracial group of students and social workers had convened from Kansas, Oregon, Missouri, Wisconsin, Indiana, and Michigan.

102. Meier and Rudwick, *CORE*, 52–53; "2 Men Charged After Affray at Playground," *Washington Post*, September 17, 1952, 23; Summer Interracial Workshop, "Brotherhood Bulletin," July 31, 1952, Folder, "CORE Projects: Interracial Workshops, 1947–54," Box 1, CORE Papers, Swarthmore Peace Collection, Swarthmore, Pa; "Rosedale—2 Years Later!" "Brotherhood Bulletin," July 20, 1954, Folder, "CORE Newsletters, 1947–54," Box 2, CORE Papers; "Segregation End Advised at Rosedale," *Washington Post*, September 23, 1952, 17; "Segregation Ended at Play Center by 5-to-2 Ballot of Recreation Board," *Washington Post*, October 17, 1952, 27; "Board of Recreation Ends Segregation at Rosedale," *Washington Post*, October 25, 1952, 17.

103. "D.C. Recreation Board to Open Rosedale Swim Pool for All," *Washington Post*, April 15, 1953, 25.

104. Quoted in Meier and Rudwick, *CORE*, 66.

105. Marion Bromley to James Peck, August 26, 1953, Folder, "CORE Projects: Interracial Workshops, 1947–54," Box 1, CORE Papers.

106. Karl E. Johnson, "Police-Black Community Relations in Postwar Philadelphia: Race and Criminalization in Urban Social Spaces, 1945–1960," *Journal of African American History* 89, 2 (Spring 2004): 118.

107. Works on Father Divine include Kenneth E. Burnham, *God Comes to America: Father Divine and the Peace Mission Movement* (Boston: Lambeth Press, 1979); Robert Weisbrot, *Father Divine and the Struggle for Racial Equality* (Urbana: University of Illinois Press, 1983); and Jill Watts, *God, Harlem U.S.A: The Father Divine Story* (Berkeley: University of California Press, 1992).

108. Johnson, "Police-Black Community Relations," 120; "Father Divine May Buy Philly Woodside Swim Pool," *Billboard* 62, 25 (June 17, 1950): 68. The Boulevard pools were located in a large

park containing four pools and other facilities. The protest inspired one white man to send a hate letter to the national office of CORE, which stated, "I intend to lead a peaceful, non-violent counter picket line of white people this summer, if the niggers get into the Boulevard Club Swimming Pool in Niggerdelphia." The writer underlined "club" to indicate that he felt the pool was private. William H. Osmond to CORE, April 11, 1955, Folder, "Congress of Racial Equality," Box 2, CORE Papers.

109. The Court of Common Pleas initially ruled on the case in 1953. Sol Rabkin and Theodore Leskes to CRC Offices, ADS Regional Offices, AJC Area Offices, December 9, 1953 and January 24, 1955, Folder, "Discrimination, Beaches and Swimming Pools, 1953–55," Box A234, Series II, NAACP Papers; "50G Suit Charges Discrimination by Philly Pool Ops," *Billboard* 63, 38 (September 22, 1951): 66; "Leo Everett et al. v. Paul F. Harron et al.," *Race Relations Law Reporter* 1, 2 (April 1956): 366–70. The court cited *Fletcher v. Coney Island* in its decision.

110. "A Jim Crow Pool—Whitewashed," *Pittsburgh Courier*, June 16, 1934, 1; Joe W. Trotter and Jared N. Day, *Race and Renaissance: African Americans in Pittsburgh Since World War II* (Pittsburgh: University of Pittsburgh Press, 2010), 86–88; Jeff Wiltse, *Contested Waters: A Social History of Swimming Pools in America* (Chapel Hill: University of North Carolina Press, 2007), 125–32. Wiltse argues that Highland Park's policy of gender integration led to the violence. He found that municipal pools where men and women swam at different times did not experience this same level of violence.

111. Trotter and Day, *Race and Renaissance*, 86. The protesters were members of the Pittsburgh Urban League and the Progressive Party.

112. "Civic Group to End Pool Bias," *Pittsburgh Courier*, July 7, 1951, 1. See also "NAACP Calls for Proof Highland Pool Is Safe," *Pittsburgh Courier*, July 28 1951, 1; "Pool Under Test Remainder of Summer," *Pittsburgh Courier*, August 11, 1951, 1.

113. Betty Beaver, "End Bias at Pool," *CORE-lator*, October 1951, p. 1, microfilm, Reel 13, EIII, CORE Papers, Addendum; "CORE Quite Busy Using Non-Violence on Bias," *Pittsburgh Courier*, April 4, 1953, 30.

114. Quoted in "1500 Negroes Used Highland Pool in '52," *Pittsburgh Courier*, July 12, 1952, 1.

115. "Police Thwart Mobs at Pools," *Pittsburgh Courier*, June 28, 1952, 1.

116. Ibid. Whites badly beat a nine-year-old boy at the Paulson pool in 1935. See Wiltse, *Contested Waters*, 131–32.

117. "Minor Incidents at Paulson Pool to Be Stopped," *Pittsburgh Courier*, July 4, 1953, 1.

118. "Springfield Wins Beach Fight," July 1952, *Illinois State NAACP NewsLetter*, microfilm, Reel 1, NAACP Papers—Illinois State, Library of Congress; "NAACP Breaks Down Segregation at Lake Springfield, Ill., Beaches," *Chicago Defender*, July 26 1952, 3.

119. Press release, "NAACP Sues City of Centralia to End Swimming Pool Segregation," May 27, 1954, Folder, "Discrimination, Beaches and Swimming Pools, 1953–55," Box A234, Series II, NAACP Papers.

120. N. E. Adams to Gloster Current, June 14, 1955, Folder, "Discrimination, Beaches and Swimming Pools, 1953–55," Box A234, Series II, NAACP Papers.

121. Linn Creighton to Walter P. Offutt, Jr., July 1953, Folder, "Discrimination, Beaches and Swimming Pools, 1953–55," Box A234, Series II, NAACP Papers; Linwood G. Koger, Jr. to Walter White, July 30, 1953, ibid.

122. "Opal Doris Jernigan, et al. v. Lakeside Park Company et al.," *Race Relations Law Reporter* 2, 6 (December 1957): 1124–26.

123. "Racial Violence and Civil Rights Law Enforcement," *University of Chicago Law Review* 18, 4 (Summer 1951): 781.

124. Theodore Leskes and Sol Rabkin to CRC Offices, AJC Area Offices, ADS Regional Offices, September 30, 1953, and October 27, 1953, Folder 4, "Discrimination: Beaches and Swimming Pools, 1953–55," Box A234, Series II, NAACP Papers; Robert B. McKay, "Segregation and Public

Recreation," *Virginia Law Review* 40, 6 (October 1954): 717–18; press release, "Supreme Court Bans Jim Crow Swimming," October 15, 1953, Folder 4, "Discrimination: Beaches and Swimming Pools, 1953–55," Box A234, Series II, NAACP Papers.

125. "High Court Kills K.C. Pool Bias," *Chicago Defender*, October 24, 1953, 1.

126. "People, Places and Things," *Chicago Defender*, July 3, 1954, 9.

127. Quoted in "Decision Awaited in Md. Pool Cases," *Afro-American*, July 3, 1954. See also Wiltse, *Contested Waters*, 156–58; and Sanford B. Hertz, "Constitutional Law: Equal Protection: Discrimination Against Negroes in State Recreation Facilities," *Michigan Law Review* 53, 4 (February 1955): 614–16.

128. McKay, "Segregation and Public Recreation," 710–11; Wiltse, *Contested Waters*, 156.

129. NAACP Legal Defense and Educational Fund, press release, "Appeal Two Cases Challenging Maryland Segregation Policy," December 20, 1954, Folder 4, "Discrimination: Beaches and Swimming Pools, 1953–55," Box A234, Series II, NAACP Papers. A 1953 flyer urged African Americans in Baltimore to enter the water at the black East Beach in Sandy Point Park and swim to the white South Beach. "They as Americans have the right to use the public waters up to the high tide mark without molestation by anyone." Flyer, "What Are You Going to Do About It?" July 16, 1953, ibid.

130. "Dawson v. Mayor and City Council of Baltimore," *Race Relations Law Reporter* 1, 1 (February 1956): 163. See also NAACP Legal Defense and Educational Fund, press release, "Bias at Public Park Outlawed," March 18, 1955, Folder 4, "Discrimination: Beaches and Swimming Pools, 1953–55," Box A234, Series II, NAACP Papers.

131. Wiltse, *Contested Waters*, 157–58. Wiltse points out that white attendance in the Baltimore pools plummeted after desegregation. Many commercial recreational facilities, such as Gwynn Oak amusement park, remained segregated into the 1960s. For a discussion of the southern reaction to the Baltimore cases, see Darryl Paulson, "Stay Out, the Water's Fine: Desegregating Municipal Swimming Facilities in St. Petersburg, Florida," *Tampa Bay History* 4, 2 (1982): 6–19.

Mark V. Tushnet, in *Making Civil Rights Law: Thurgood Marshall and the Supreme Court, 1936–1961* (New York: Oxford University Press, 1994), argues that the Supreme Court's refusal to hear the *Dawson* case reflected their belief that *Brown v. Board of Education* invalidated all Jim Crow legislation (301). See also Richard Kluger, *Simple Justice: The History of Brown v. Board of Education and Black America's Struggle for Equality* (New York: Knopf, 1976), 750. On the same day the Supreme Court affirmed the Baltimore decision it mandated integration in Atlanta's golf courses. Two other 1954 decisions also directly challenged segregation in recreation. In *Muir v. Louisville Theatrical Park Association* the lower court had barred blacks from an amphitheater in a white park, but the Supreme Court vacated the decision and sent the case back (see "Muir v. Louisville Park Theatrical Association," *Race Relations Law Reporter* 1, 1 [February 1956]: 14–15). In *Holcombe v. Beal* the Supreme Court upheld a lower court decision desegregating Houston's golf courses.

132. Constance McLaughlin Green, *The Secret City: A History of Race Relations in the Nation's Capital* (Princeton, N.J.: Princeton University Press, 1967), 310–11; McKay, "Segregation and Public Recreation," 705–6.

133. "State Court Decrees Equal Privileges at Parsons Pool," *Parsons Sun*, July 6, 1955, clipping, Folder, "Discrimination, Beaches and Swimming Pools, 1953–55," Box A234, Series II, NAACP Papers; "Warren H. Morton v. The City Commissioners of Parsons," *Race Relations Law Reporter* 1, 1 (February 1956): 177–78. The Kansas civil rights law did not cover municipal pools; therefore, each community had to be sued separately. See McKay, "Segregation and Public Recreation," 720.

134. Quoted in Paul Hartman and Theodore Leskes to CRC Offices, ADL Regional Offices, AJC Area Offices, June 3, 1957, Folder, "Discrimination: Swimming Pools, 1956–1961," Box A111, Series III, NAACP Papers. The management made the mistake of listing Castle Hill under "Bathing Beaches—Public" in the telephone book even after creating the membership corporation. For an in-depth analysis of the case, see Brian Purnell, "Desegregating the Jim Crow North: Racial

Discrimination in the Postwar Bronx and the Fight to Integrate the Castle Hill Beach Club, 1953–73," *Afro-Americans in New York Life and History* 33, 2 (July 2009): 47–78.

135. Press release, December 30, 1954, Folder 4, "Discrimination: Beaches and Swimming Pools, 1953–55," Box A234, Series II, NAACP Papers.

136. "Castle Hill Beach Club, Inc. v. Ward B. Arbury," *Race Relations Law Reporter* 1, 1 (February 1956): 186–91; *Chicago Defender*, July 9, 1955, 1; Hartman and Leskes to CRC Offices, ADL Regional Offices, AJC Area Offices, June 3, 1957. Purnell points out that even after the final ruling the Castle Hill Beach Club had no black members. In 1961 two young African American families filed a second complaint to force the club to open its doors (Purnell, "Desegregating the Jim Crow North," 68–71). Swimming pool segregation in the Bronx using the "club method" was relatively common in the early 1950s. See M. Richards to NAACP, c. 1954, Folder 4, "Discrimination: Beaches and Swimming Pools, 1953–55," Box A234, Series II, NAACP Papers.

137. CORE to "Friend," 1954, Folder, "CORE Program Work—1950s," Box 1, CORE Papers.

138. "Marion Officials Resign in Huff in Rights Fight," *Indianapolis Recorder*, July 24, 1954, 3, clipping, Folder, "Discrimination, Beaches and Swimming Pools, 1953–55," Box A234, Series II, NAACP Papers.

139. Oral history with Jim Perkins, http://www.wikimarion.org/Jim_Perkins (accessed May 26, 2009); oral history with Roger Smith, http://www.wikimarion.org/Roger_Smith (accessed May 26, 2009); "Marion Officials Resign in Huff in Rights Fight"; "Marion Citizens Protest Swimming Pool Jim Crow," *Indianapolis Recorder*, July 10, 1954, clipping, Folder, "Discrimination, Beaches and Swimming Pools, 1953–55," Box A234, Series II, NAACP Papers. Marion was infamous in 1930 for the brutal lynching of three African American men, and in 1952 there was another attempted lynching. Two members of the city council resigned rather than support any desegregation efforts at the pool.

140. Kevin M. Kruse, *White Flight: Atlanta and the Making of Modern Conservatism* (Princeton, N.J.: Princeton University Press, 2005), 106; "Holmes v. City of Atlanta," *Race Relations Law Reporter* 1, 1 (February 1956): 146–51. The Supreme Court cited the *Dawson* case as the precedent for their decision. See also Alton Hornsby, Jr., "A City That Was Too Busy to Hate: Atlanta Businessmen and Desegregation," in *Southern Businessmen and Desegregation*, ed. Elizabeth Jacoway and David R. Colburn (Baton Rouge: Louisiana State University Press, 1982), 124. On the increased attempts to desegregate public accommodations after the *Brown* decision, see A. K. Sandoval-Strausz, *Hotel: An American History* (New Haven, Conn.: Yale University Press, 2007), 304–6. Sandoval-Strausz notes that the segregationists' response to this activism was "a wave of privatization intended to shift the struggle onto more favorable legal terrain" (305).

141. "Negroes Refuse Segregation: W. Va. Whites Quit Swim Pool," *New York Office Courier*, July 24, 1954, clipping, Folder 5, "Segregation and Integration," Box I: N83, National Urban League Papers, Library of Congress, Washington, D.C.

142. Tony Badger, "*Brown* and Backlash," in *Massive Resistance: Southern Opposition to the Second Reconstruction*, ed. Clive Webb (New York: Oxford University Press, 2005), 51. See also Numan V. Bartley, *The Rise of Massive Resistance: Race and Politics in the South During the 1950's* (Baton Rouge: Louisiana State University Press, 1969); and George Lewis, *Massive Resistance: The White Response to the Civil Rights Movement* (New York: Oxford University Press, 2006). Lewis argues for a broad definition of massive resistance: "At its central, binding core was the preservation and continued maintenance of a segregated, white-dominated society" (185).

143. "No Jim Crow Law; San Antonio Closes Pools," *Chicago Defender*, July 3, 1954, 4.

144. "Swimming Pools-Texas," *Race Relations Law Reporter* 1, 3 (June 1956): 589–90.

145. Paulson, "Stay Out, the Water's Fine," 1.

146. "Emergency Ordinance No. 236," *Race Relations Law Reporter* 1, 4 (August 1956): 733–37; "Fla. Resort Votes Race Ban at Beach," *Chicago Defender*, July 2, 1956, 1; "Delray Beach Ousts Negroes," *Chicago Defender*, June 16, 1956, 10.

147. "Ordinance No. 913," *Race Relations Law Reporter* 1, 5 (October 1956): 945–46.

148. "Segregation—Louisiana," *Race Relations Law Reporter* 1, 4 (August 1956): 731–32. The state legislature passed this ordinance after blacks had begun using the beaches in large numbers in 1954 and 1955, a practice encouraged by the NAACP. See Gloster Current to Neil Humphrey, October 24, 1955, Folder 4, "Discrimination: Beaches and Swimming Pools, 1953–55," Box A234, Series II, NAACP Papers.

149. Michael J. Klarman, *From Jim Crow to Civil Rights: The Supreme Court and the Struggle for Racial Equality* (New York: Oxford University Press, 2004), 400–401.

150. Paulson, "Stay Out, the Water's Fine." On the court battle, see "Alsup et al. v. City of St. Petersburg," *Race Relations Law Reporter* 1, 3 (June 1956): 531; "Alsup et al. v. City of St. Petersburg," *Race Relations Law Reporter* 2, 1 (February 1957): 119–21; and "Supreme Court Hits Texas Bias," *Chicago Defender*, April 2, 1957, 1.

151. Jacoway and Colburn, *Southern Businessmen and Desegregation.*

152. Howard Beeth and Cary D. Wintz, *Black Dixie: Afro-Texan History and Culture in Houston* (College Station: Texas A&M Press, 1992), 163. In 1950 the Supreme Court also ruled in *Sweatt v. Painter*, the case that opened graduate and professional schools at the University of Texas to blacks and served as an important precedent for *Brown v. Board of Education*. For the history of African Americans and golf, see George B. Kirsch, *Golf in America* (Chicago: University of Illinois Press, 2009), 146–62; Marvin P. Dawkins and Graham C. Kinloch, *African American Golfers During the Jim Crow Era* (Westport, Conn.: Praeger, 2000); and Pete McDaniel, *Uneven Lies: The Heroic Story of African Americans in Golf* (Greenwich, Conn.: The American Golfer, Inc., 2000).

153. Kruse, *White Flight*, 118–19; Kirsch, *Golf in America*, 153–54.

154. "Hayes v. Crutcher," *Race Relations Law Reporter* 1, 2 (April 1956): 346–47.

155. "Augustus v. Pensacola," *Race Relations Law Reporter* 1, 4 (August 1956): 681; "Holley, III v. City of Portsmouth," *Race Relations Law Reporter* 1, 6 (December 1956): 1089; "Holley, III v. City of Portsmouth," *Race Relations Law Reporter* 2, 3 (June 1957): 609–11; "Moorhead v. City of Fort Lauderdale," *Race Relations Law Reporter* 2, 2 (April 1957): 409–11; "Leeper et al. v. Charlotte Park and Recreation Commission," *Race Relations Law Reporter* 2, 2 (April 1957): 411–12; "Ward et al. v. City of Miami," *Race Relations Law Reporter* 2, 3 (June 1957): 603–5; "Simkins v. City of Greensboro," *Race Relations Law Reporter* 2, 3 (June 1957): 605–8; "Simkins v. City of Greensboro," *Race Relations Law Reporter* 2, 4 (August 1957): 818–21. Many of these courses had allowed blacks access one day per week, usually a Monday.

156. Beeth and Wintz, *Black Dixie*, 88; James M. SoRelle, "Race Relations in 'Heavenly Houston,' 1919–45," in *Black Dixie*, 187. See also Clifton F. Richardson, Sr., "Houston's Colored Citizens: Activities and Conditions Among the Negro Population in the 1920s," in *Black Dixie*, 133.

157. Quoted in "Freedoms Are Renewed in Recalling Deliverance," *New York Times*, June 19, 1989, A12.

158. Kenneth F. Bunting, "The Day the Fun Went out of Playland Park," *Los Angeles Times*, September 3, 1982, OC3. When the park closed in 1968, at the height of Houston's boomtown status, African Americans had gained some access to the park's grounds as a result of these informal protests. A NAACP Youth Council in Dallas forced the Texas State Fair to admit African Americans to the amusement park rides on days other than Negro Day in 1955. See Tommy L. Bynum, "'Our Fight if for Right': The NAACP Youth Councils and College Chapters' Crusade for Civil Rights, 1936–1965" (Ph.D. diss., Georgia State University, 2007), 4.

159. "Augustus v. Pensacola."

Chapter 4

1. On the Calumet and Tuley park recreation riots, see Andrew J. Diamond, *Mean Streets: Chicago Youths and the Everyday Struggle for Empowerment in the Multiracial City, 1908–1969* (Berkeley: University of California Press, 2009), 221–24; Arnold R. Hirsch, *Making the Second Ghetto:*

Race and Housing in Chicago, 1940–1960 (Cambridge: Cambridge University Press, 1983), 64–67; "Southside Racial Violence," August 1, 1957, Folder 9, Box 9, American Civil Liberties Union (ACLU), Illinois Division Papers, University of Chicago, Special Collections, Regenstein Library, Chicago, Ill.; and Chicago Commission on Human Relations, "A Preliminary Report on Racial Disturbances in Chicago for the Period July 21 to August 4, 1957," ibid.

2. Todd M. Michney, "Race, Violence, and Urban Territoriality: Cleveland's Little Italy and the 1966 Hough Uprising," *Journal of Urban History* 32, 3 (March 2006): 405.

3. For reminiscences of the *Canadiana* and Crystal Beach, see M. C. Herwood, comp., *All the Old Familiar Places: Memories of South Buffalo* (Buffalo: Herwood Enterprises, 1999), 9, 22, 30, 41, 96; "Diamond Jim's Canadiana," *Buffalo News Magazine*, August 17, 1980; Thomas M. Rizzo, "Memories of the Crystal Beach Boat and Ballroom," unpublished document, 1996, clipping file, Buffalo Historical Society, Buffalo, New York; and Erno Rossi, *Crystal Beach: The Good Old Days* (Port Colborne, Ontario: Seventy Seven Publishing, 2005). For an analysis of the Crystal Beach riot, see Victoria W. Wolcott, "Recreation and Race in the Postwar City: Buffalo's 1956 Crystal Beach Riot," *Journal of American History* 93, 1 (June 2006): 63–90.

4. Between 1950 and 1960 the number of blacks increased by 34,259, or 93.5 percent. There had been a similar increase in the 1940s, when the black population rose from 3.1 percent of the total population to 6.3 percent. See Arthur Butler, Henry Louis Taylor, Jr., and Doo-Ha Ryu, "Work and Black Neighborhood Life in Buffalo, 1930–1980," in *African Americans and the Rise of Buffalo's Post-Industrial City, 1940 to Present: Volume 2*, ed. Henry Louis Taylor, Jr. (Buffalo: Buffalo Urban League, 1990), 118, 130.

5. Stephen Grant Meyer, *As Long as They Don't Move Next Door: Segregation and Racial Conflict in American Neighborhoods* (New York: Rowman and Littlefield, 2000), 5.

6. See, for example, Richard E. Harris, *Delinquency in Our Democracy* (Los Angeles: Wetzel Publishing Company, 1954); Harrison E. Salisbury, *The Shook-Up Generation* (New York: Harper and Brothers, 1958); Sheldon and Eleanor Glueck, *Delinquents in the Making* (New York: Harper and Brothers, 1952); and Albert Cohen, *Delinquent Boys: The Culture of the Gang* (Glencoe, Ill.: Free Press, 1955).

7. Salisbury, *The Shook-Up Generation*, 16.

8. "Unit Investigating Hoodlumism Urges Thirteen Reforms," *Buffalo Evening News*, June 26, 1956, 1. The Buffalo Common Council created the Board of Community Relations in 1945 in response to wartime race riots in other cities and growing racial tensions over public housing. See Neil Kraus, *Race, Neighborhoods, and Community Power: Buffalo Politics, 1934–1997* (Albany: State University of New York Press, 2000), 76–78. For a history of juvenile delinquency, see James Gilbert, *A Cycle of Outrage: America's Reaction to the Juvenile Delinquent in the 1950s* (New York: Oxford University Press, 1986).

9. Peter Goodspeed, "Amusement Park Meant Summer for Thousands," *Toronto Star*, April 11, 1983, A11.

10. Rizzo, "Memories of the Crystal Beach Boat and Ballroom."

11. George Kunz, *Buffalo Memories: Gone But Not Forgotten* (Buffalo: Canisius College Press, 2002), 271. Other descriptions of the *Canadiana* include Marge Thielman Hastreiter, "Canadiana, Where Are You?" newspaper unknown, July 17, 1971, clipping file, Fort Erie Public Library, Fort Erie Museum Board, Fort Erie, Ontario; *Many Voices: A Collective History of Greater Fort Erie* (Fort Erie: Fort Erie Museum Board, 1996), 206–15; and Verlyn Klinkenborg, *The Last Fine Time* (New York: Alfred A. Knopf, 1991), 21.

12. Patti Meyer Lee and Gary Lee, *Don't Bother Knockin' . . . This Town's a Rockin': A History of Traditional Rhythm and Blues & Early Rock 'n' Roll in Buffalo, New York* (Buffalo: Buffalo Sounds Press, 2001), 7–8; *Many Voices*, 212.

13. Elizabeth Cuddy, "Sun and Fun at Crystal Beach," *Toronto Telegram*, November 1, 1955, Crystal Beach Binder, Fort Erie Public Library.

14. "Youths Injured in Clash on Boat," *New York Times*, May 31, 1956, 50. For the importance

of rumor in riot behavior, see Marilynn S. Johnson, "Gender, Race, and Rumours: Re-Examining the 1943 Race Riots," *Gender and History* 10, 2 (August 1998): 252–77. This precipitating incident is reminiscent of other race riots, particularly the Detroit riot of 1943, where a young black mother and her child were supposedly pushed off the Belle Isle bridge into the Detroit River.

15. "Gangs Spread Terror at Beach and on Boat; Many Hurt, Arrested," *Buffalo Evening News*, May 31, 1956, 1.

16. William Robinson and Zaid Islam, interview by William Graebner, November 9, 1985, 9–11, transcript in author's possession.

17. "Unjustly Criticized, Crystal Beach's Reeve Says of Incident," *Times-Review*, June 1, 1956, 8.

18. "Report of the Subcommittee of the Board of Community Relations," June 27, 1956, p. 1, Courier Express Collection, Butler Library, Buffalo State University, Buffalo, New York.

19. Current to Wilkins, June 1, 1956, Folder, "Racial Tension, 1956–57," Box A265, Series III, NAACP Papers, Library of Congress, Washington, D.C. For an analysis of a race riot in 1960s Cleveland between Italian Americans and African Americans, see Michney, "Race, Violence, and Urban Territoriality."

20. "FBI Probes Teen Rock, Riot Cruise," *Chicago Defender*, June 9, 1956, 1; "Five Buffalo Youths Fined for Disturbance," *Times-Review*, June 21, 1956, 16.

21. "50 to 100 Fights, Says Injured Man," *Buffalo Courier-Express*, May 31, 1956, 1.

22. "Five Buffalo Youths Fined for Disturbance." The judge fined three of the white defendants for "creating a disturbance by fighting in a public place," while he fined two of the black defendants for carrying concealed weapons.

23. "Five Buffalo Youths Fined for Disturbance"; "Unjustly Criticized," p. 1.

24. "Report of Subcommittee," 1–2.

25. William Robinson, interview by William Graebner, September 1985, 4, transcript in author's possession.

26. "George Hall, Sr. Speaks About Beach Incidents," *Times-Review*, June 14, 1956, 17; "Youths Injured in Clash on Boat."

27. Vincent Paladino, phone interview by Victoria W. Wolcott, June 7, 2011.

28. Robinson and Islam interview, pp. 4–5; Robinson interview, pp. 9–10.

29. FBI file, BU 45–82, notes, p. 6.

30. Ibid., p. 21.

31. "Gangs Spread Terror at Beach and on Boat."

32. FBI file, BU 45–82, notes, pp. 7, 13, 14–15; Robinson interview, pp. 5, 8.

33. "Gangs Spread Terror at Beach and on Boat," p. 12.

34. FBI file, BU 45–82, notes, pp. 3, 54.

35. Ibid., p. 13.

36. Ibid., pp. 7, 54. On Buffalo gangs, see William Graebner, *Coming of Age in Buffalo: Youth and Authority in the Postwar Era* (Philadelphia: Temple University Press, 1990), 52–58; and William Graebner, "Outlawing Teenage Populism: The Campaign Against Secret Societies in the American High School, 1900–1960," *Journal of American History* 74, 2 (1987): 411–35.

37. Graebner, *Coming of Age in Buffalo*, 99–103.

38. One of the El Dorados' members was the daughter of a prominent councilman, King Peterson. "Buffalo Urban League, Inc., Directors' Meeting," June 20, 1956, p. 3, microfilm, Buffalo Urban League Corporate Minutes, 1927–77, Butler Library, Buffalo State College.

39. FBI File, BU 45–82, notes, p.12.

40. Ibid., p. 6; "Holiday Outing Is Day-Long Race Riot," *Washington Daily News*, May 31, 1956, 3.

41. FBI file, BU 45–82, notes, p. 8.

42. Paladino interview.

43. Margaret Wynn and Dick Hirsch, "Terror Marks Boatride," *Buffalo Courier-Express*, May 31, 1956, 1.

44. FBI file, BU 45-82, interview, p. 16.

45. William Evans to Charles Abrams, March 25, 1957, Folder, "Buffalo, 1950–1960," Box 39, Series 5, National Urban League Papers, Library of Congress, Washington, D.C.

46. Wynn and Hirsch, "Terror Marks Boatride," 1.

47. For northern white newspapers' coverage of the riot, see "Youths Injured in Clash on Boat"; "Five Fined in Beach Riots," *New York Times*, June 15, 1956, 27; "FBI Launches Probe of Holiday Ship Riots," *New York Herald Tribune*, June 1, 1956, A14; "Knife Wielding Gangs Fight on Boat and Park," *Chicago Daily Tribune*, May 31, 1956, 7; "Excursion Boat Terrorized by Teen-Age Mob," *Los Angeles Times*, May 31, 1956, 13; "FBI Begins Inquiry in Race Riot on Ship," *San Francisco Chronicle*, June 1, 1956, 10; and "Rioting Breaks Out on Vessel Between Buffalo, Crystal Beach," *Rochester Democrat and Chronicle*, May 31, 1956, 11.

48. "Deplore Beach Conduct," *Buffalo Criterion*, June 2, 1956, 1.

49. "Teens Rock and Riot on Cruise," *Chicago Defender*, June 2, 1956, 1. Generally African American newspapers did not report widely on the riot. No stories appeared in the *Los Angeles Sentinel*, *Pittsburgh Courier*, *Amsterdam News*, *Cleveland Call and Post*, or *Louisiana Weekly*.

50. Editorial, *Buffalo Criterion*, June 2, 1956, 2.

51. Michael Brake, *Comparative Youth Culture: The Sociology of Youth Cultures and Youth Subcultures in America, Britain and Canada* (Boston: Routledge and Kegan Paul, 1985), 64. Brake writes about conflicts between mods and rockers in 1960s Brighton Beach. See also Stanley Cohen, *Folk Devils and Moral Panics: The Creation of the Mods and Rockers* (London: MacGibbon and Kee, 1972).

52. "Psychologists Blame Riot on Economic, Social Ills," *Buffalo Courier-Express*, June 3, 1956.

53. Judith A. Adams, *The American Amusement Park Industry: A History of Technology and Thrills* (Boston: Twayne Publishers, 1991), 59; John Hannigan, *Fantasy City: Pleasure and Profit in the Postmodern Metropolis* (New York: Routledge, 1998), 22–23.

54. Robinson interview, p. 15.

55. *Many Voices*, 206–13. In the 1920s Crystal Beach had "an excellent protective social service" agency on-site maintained by "the YWCA of Buffalo in co-operation with the management." L. H. Weir, *Recreation Survey of Buffalo* (Buffalo: Department of Parks and Public Buildings, City Planning Committee of the Council, Buffalo City Planning Association, 1925), 88. For a discussion of regulations at parks, see Adams, *The American Amusement Park Industry*, 59.

56. Cuddy, "Sun and Fun at Crystal Beach."

57. James W. St. G. Walker, *Racial Discrimination in Canada: The Black Experience* (Ottawa: Canadian Historical Association, 1985), 6.

58. Ibid., 16–17; Leo W. Burtley, *Canada and Its People of African Descent* (Pierrelands, P.Q.: Bilongo Publishers, 1977), 209; James W. St. G. Walker, *A History of Blacks in Canada* (Quebec City: Canadian Government Publishing Centre, 1980), 90. In the 1960s a Canadian civil rights movement challenged segregation using tactics drawn from African American organizers.

59. Robinson and Islam interview, pp. 8–9. Both Barbara Seals Nevergold and Sandra Walker, African American residents of Buffalo, remarked that they never swam on the beach or knew other African Americans who did. Barbara Seals Nevergold, personal interview by Victoria W. Wolcott, July 9, 2003, p. 4, transcript in author's possession; Sandra Walker, telephone interview by Victoria W. Wolcott, July 17, 2003, p. 2, transcript in author's possession.

60. Cathy Herbert, telephone interview by Victoria W. Wolcott, June 30, 2003, p. 1, transcript in author's possession.

61. Crystal Beach advertisement, newspaper unknown, 1934, clipping file, Fort Erie Public Library. An article in the same paper reported, "They [regulations] can now be enforced because the beautiful white sand beach at Crystal Beach has been fenced off. Admission is possible only through the turnstiles, with ticket-takers acting as inspectors. The undesirables have been shut out,

including some few unlikely humans, along with dogs, ponies, and other animals." "Praise Heard on Every Side for Beach Bathing Safeguards."

62. Rizzo, "Memories of the Crystal Beach Boat and Ballroom," 2; Hastreiter, "Canadiana, Where Are You?"

63. Paladino interview. Memorial Day was an exception to the neighborhood days model, as the entire city was encouraged to visit the park on the opening weekend.

64. David Nasaw, *Going Out: The Rise and Fall of Public Amusements* (Cambridge, Mass.: Harvard University Press, 1993), 252–55; Adams, *The American Amusement Park Industry*, 66–68, 164–65; Dale Samuelson, *The American Amusement Park* (St. Paul, Minn.: MBI Publishing, 2001), 51, 55; Al Griffin, *"Step Right Up Folks!"* (Chicago: Henry Regnery Company, 1974), 15–26; Sharon Zukin, "From Coney Island to Las Vegas in the Urban Imaginary: Discursive Practices of Growth and Decline," *Urban Affairs Review* 33, 5 (May 1998): 627–54.

65. Norris Willatt, "Amusement Parks," *Barron's*, May 25, 1959, 13.

66. Robinson interview, pp. 12–13. Similarly Barbara Nevergold, who was eleven at the time of the riot, remembered thinking after the riot: "how [are] people going to get to the beach without cars and also how are we going to get there?" She reported that after the *Canadiana* was discontinued she and her family went to Crystal Beach less frequently. Nevergold interview, p. 5. After 1956 the *Canadiana* was used for excursions between Put-In Bay, Toledo, and Bob-Lo Island, an amusement park in the Lower Detroit River, until it crashed into the Toledo Railroad Terminal Bridge on July 31, 1959. In 1963 teenagers began to use the abandoned ship for parties. "Moored Ship Scene of Teenagers Party," *Buffalo Courier-Express*, February 11, 1963.

67. "Fireworks Sale Banned at Beach," *Buffalo Courier-Express*, June 5, 1956.

68. "Cops Will Board Steamer Canadiana," *Buffalo Courier-Express*, June 20, 1956; "Special Details to Guard Resorts Against Hoodlums," *Buffalo Courier-Express*, July 4, 1956.

69. Nasaw, *Going Out*, 254.

70. Taylor, *African Americans and the Rise of Buffalo*, 118.

71. "The Thirtieth Annual Report of the Buffalo Urban League," 1956, p. 4, microfilm, Buffalo Urban League Papers, Butler Library, Buffalo State University, Buffalo, New York.

72. Kraus, *Race, Neighborhoods, and Community Power*, 95–100. See also Mark Goldman, *City on the Lake: The Challenge of Change in Buffalo, New York* (Buffalo: Prometheus Books, 1990), 13–25. For an overview of the Ellicott district before renewal, see "Economic Life Study Group," May 8–9, 1953, Vertical File, "Board of Community Relations," Buffalo Public Library.

73. Quoted in Peter B. Bart and Louis Kraar, "Rising Negro Influx Stirs New Trouble for Harried Civic Planners," *Wall Street Journal*, April 7, 1958, 1.

74. Ibid.

75. "The Twenty-Ninth Annual Report of the Buffalo Urban League," 1955, p. 7, Folder, "Buffalo, 1926–60," Box 6, Series 13, National Urban League Papers.

76. "The Thirty-First Annual Report of the Buffalo Urban League," 1957, pp. 4, 9, Folder, "Buffalo, 1926–60," Box 6, Series 13, National Urban League Papers.

77. Quoted in Bart and Kraar, "Rising Negro Influx," p. 13.

78. Robinson interview, p. 14.

79. Graebner persuasively argues that creating and maintaining a segregated school system was part of an effort by Buffalo's community leaders to erect "institutional and ideological barriers to protect white, middle-class youth from the working class and blacks." "Buffalo's social engineers" believed this separation would combat juvenile delinquency (*Coming of Age in Buffalo*, 117).

80. Generally school officials would simply reject applications from African American students. Graebner, *Coming of Age in Buffalo*, 103. See also Goldman, *City on the Lake*, 101. Goldman points out that the most celebrated vocational high school in the 1950s, Buffalo Technical, was located in a majority-black neighborhood, yet almost no African Americans were enrolled in the school.

81. Goldman, *City on the Lake*, 100–101. According to Goldman, "the purpose of the 1954 plan

was to keep blacks in their neighborhoods and whites in theirs" (101). The discriminatory practices of the Buffalo school board led the New York State Commissioner of Education to order the board to implement a desegregation plan in 1972. When this failed, federal court judge John T. Curtin ordered the city to desegregate. See Steven J. L. Taylor, *Desegregation in Boston and Buffalo: The Influence of Local Leaders* (Albany: State University of New York Press, 1998); Goldman, *City on the Lake*, 93–166; and Kraus, *Race, Neighborhoods, and Community Power*, 149–78.

82. In 1958 Sandra Walker, an African American woman, had planned to attend nearby Bennett High School. Because of redistricting she was sent to Lafayette High School instead. Her memory was that the school board was "worried about too many African Americans at Bennett." Walker interview, p. 1. Graebner calls Buffalo's large high schools "a special kind of social pressure cooker" (*Coming of Age in Buffalo*, 88). Michney notes, "In an era of social and political ferment, the comparatively intimate settings of neighborhood and public school became sites of particularly intransigent racial conflict lasting into the 1970s" ("Race, Violence, and Urban Territoriality," 405).

83. Graebner, *Coming of Age in Buffalo*, 84.

84. "Unit Investigating Hoodlumism Urges Thirteen Reforms."

85. Editorial, *Buffalo Criterion*, June 2, 1956, 2. See also "Deplore Beach Conduct."

86. "Social Agencies and Youth Groups Discuss Problem," *Buffalo Evening News*, June 1, 1956, 1.

87. Quoted in "Buffalo Presses Teen Riot Inquiry," *New York Times*, June 16, 1956, 60.

88. Evans to Abrams, March 25, 1957.

89. The 1958 report of the Buffalo Youth Board notes that there were "approximately 20% fewer arrests, annually, from 1950 thru 1957 than during the period 1946–1949." Buffalo Youth Board, *Delinquency and Youth Crime* (Buffalo: Buffalo Youth Board, 1958), 20.

90. See "Youth Crime Rate Here Higher than New York City," *Buffalo Courier-Express*, October 24, 1958; "Youth Delinquency Up Here Since Workshop Ended in '52," *Buffalo Evening News*, July 16, 1958, section 3, p. 46; Manuel Bernstein, "Juvenile Crime Rate Here Is Climbing," *Buffalo Courier-Express*, February 17, 1955, 11; and Ernie Gross, "Delinquency Data Gathered as Aid to Social Agencies," *Buffalo Evening News*, October 23, 1958.

91. Buffalo Youth Board, *Delinquency and Youth Crime*, 20.

92. Ibid., 25.

93. Ibid., 15, 27–28.

94. For discussions of adolescent female sexuality and delinquency, see Susan K. Cahn, *Sexual Reckonings: Southern Girls in a Troubling Age* (Cambridge, Mass.: Harvard University Press, 2007), esp. 241–68; and Rachel Devlin, "Female Juvenile Delinquency and the Problem of Sexual Authority in America, 1945–65," in *Delinquents and Debutantes: Twentieth-Century American Girls' Cultures*, ed. Sherrie A. Inness (New York: New York University Press, 1998), 83–108.

95. "The Thirty-First Annual Report of the Buffalo Urban League," 7–8.

96. Graebner, *Coming of Age in Buffalo*, 34. See also Lee and Lee, *Don't Bother Knockin'*, 23–24. The popular disc jockey Alan Freed is often credited with introducing African American music to young white audiences through the radio and interracial rock 'n' roll dance parties in the 1950s.

97. Quoted in James Hemphill to Frank Sedita, undated, Folder, "Buffalo, New York 1958–60," Box C94, Series III, NAACP Papers. Hemphill was the president of the Buffalo branch of the NAACP at the time of the incident. He wrote letters to both the mayor of Buffalo and the governor of New York, Nelson Rockefeller.

98. "Danced with White Girl: Metro Boy Banned on TV," *Toronto Daily Star*, May 25, 1959. Both the Canadian Association for the Advancement of Colored People and the local chapter of the NAACP requested an investigation, but there is no evidence that the national office carried one out.

99. Hemphill to Sedita, undated.

100. "It Happened Here," *Buffalo Criterion*, June 6, 1959, 2. See also "Racism in WGR Saturday Program," *Buffalo Criterion*, May 30, 1959, 1; "NAACP President Hits TV Racism," *Buffalo Cri-*

terion, June 6, 1959, 1; letter to the editor, "AME Zion Ministers Hit Race Bars of TV Program Director in Recent Case," *Buffalo Criterion*, June 13, 1959, 2. There was only one short article on the incident in the white newspapers. "Discrimination Probe Sought," *Buffalo Courier-Express*, May 26, 1959, 26.

101. Lydia W. Evans and Harriette H. Everette, letter to the editor, "Petitioners Rap WGR's Pat Fagan in Racist Episode of Saturday, May 23," *Buffalo Criterion*, June 6, 1959, 2.

102. "The Twenty-Ninth Annual Report of the Buffalo Urban League," 7. The Buffalo Urban League had received assurance from local papers that "only in exceptional cases would race and nationality be mentioned in connection with crime news" as early as 1945. Trying to ensure that the papers kept their promise was a losing battle. See William Evans, "Urban League Report to the Board of Directors," January 16, 1945, p. 7, Vertical File, "Buffalo Urban League," Buffalo Historical Society.

103. Roy Wilkins to Members of the Board of Directors, April 7, 1958, Folder, "Crime Blamed on Integration, 1956–59," Box A90, Series III, NAACP Papers.

104. John A. Morsell to Obadiah Williams, March 7, 1958, Folder, "Crime Blamed on Integration, 1956–59," Box A90, Series III, NAACP Papers.

105. Press release, 1958, Folder, "Crime: Juvenile Delinquency 1958–67," Box A91, Series III, NAACP Papers.

106. "Thirtieth Annual Report of the Buffalo Urban League," 1956, 8.

107. "Buffalo Urban League, Director's Meeting Minutes," June 20, 1956, p. 4, microfilm, Buffalo Urban League Papers.

108. "Holiday Outing Turns into Voyage of Terror," *Dallas Times Herald*, May 31, 1956, 1; "Negro Knifers Turn Outings to 'Nightmare,'" *Arkansas Gazette*, May 31, 1956, 10A; "Flashing Knives, Sobs Mark Race Riot on Pleasure Boat," *Atlanta Journal*, May 31, 1956, 8; "Savage Race Riot on Boat Being Investigated by FBI," *Memphis Commercial Appeal*, June 1, 1956, 1; "Teen-Age Riot Turns Ship into Nightmare," *Charlotte Observer*, May 31, 1956, 2; "American Negroes in Canadian Riot," *Clarion Ledger*, May 31, 1956, 1; "Negro Rioters Turn Cruise into Bedlam," *Orlando Sentinel*, May 31, 1956, 1; "Riots Turn Boat Trip into Voyage of Terror," *Arkansas Democrat*, May 31, 1956, 1; "Teenagers Fight on Cruise Ship: Negro Youths Flash Knives and Attack Outnumbered Whites," *Nashville Tennessean*, May 31, 1956, 1.

In his 1958 book *The Shook-Up Generation*, Harrison E. Salisbury suggests that it was common for the white southern press to report incidents of juvenile delinquency: "Southerners eagerly devour reports that Negro and Puerto Rican teenage mobs rule the roost in the New York schools. New York is worse than Little Rock, they say" (135).

109. "Trouble Came Elsewhere," *Memphis Commercial Appeal*, June 1, 1956, 6.

110. Brian Ward, "Racial Politics, Culture and the Cole Incident of 1956," in *Race and Class in the American South Since 1890*, ed. Melvyn Stokes and Rick Halpern (Providence, R.I.: Berg Publishers, 1994), 189.

111. "A National Tragedy," *Nashville Tennessean*, June 1, 1956, 22; "They Can't See a Riot Unless It Is in Dixie," *Jackson Daily News*, June 11, 1956, 4.

112. Joseph Crespino, "Mississippi as Metaphor: Civil Rights, the South, and the Nation in the Historical Imagination," in *The Myth of Southern Exceptionalism*, ed. Matthew D. Lassiter and Joseph Crespino (New York: Oxford University Press, 2010), 109.

113. Maurice McCrackin, statement made to City Council," August 7, 1952, p. 10, Folder 7, Box 15, Jewish Community Relations Council, American Jewish Archives, Cincinnati, Ohio.

114. Andrew Hurley, *Diners, Bowling Alleys and Trailer Parks: Chasing the American Dream in the Postwar Consumer Culture* (New York: Basic Books, 2001); Robert E. Weems, Jr., *Desegregating the Dollar: African American Consumerism in the Twentieth Century* (New York: New York University Press, 1998), esp. 31–55; Lizabeth Cohen, *A Consumers' Republic: The Politics of Mass Consumption in Postwar America* (New York: Alfred A. Knopf, 2003), 166–91.

115. William Evans, "Inventory for 1952, Buffalo Urban League," Annual Report, Folder, "Buffalo, 1926–60," Box 6, Series 13, National Urban League Papers. For a discussion of segregation in bowling alleys, see Hurley, *Diners, Bowling Alleys and Trailer Parks*, 184–90.

116. Eric Avila, *Popular Culture in the Age of White Flight: Fear and Fantasy in Suburban Los Angeles* (Berkeley: University of California Press, 2004), 107. For the contrast between Disneyland and Coney Island, see Raymond M. Weinstein, "Disneyland and Coney Island: Reflections on the Evolution of the Modern Amusement Park," *Journal of Popular Culture* 26, 1 (1992): 131–64.

Works on the Disney parks include Avila, *Popular Culture in the Age of White Flight*, 106–44; Adams, *The American Amusement Park Industry*, 87–104; John M. Findlay, *Magic Lands: Western Cityscapes and American Culture After 1940* (Berkeley: University of California Press, 1992), 52–116; Leonard Mosely, *Disney's World* (New York: Scarborough House, 1985); Steven Watts, *The Magic Kingdom: Walt Disney and the American Way of Life* (Columbia: University of Missouri Press, 1997); Margaret J. King, "Disneyland and Walt Disney World: Traditional Values in Futuristic Form," *Journal of Popular Culture* 15 (1981): 116–40; Weinstein, "Disneyland and Coney Island"; Michael Sorkin, ed., *Variations on a Theme Park: The New American City and the End of Public Space* (New York: Hill and Wang, 1992), 205–32; Gary S. Cross and John K. Walton, *The Playful Crowd: Pleasure Places in the Twentieth Century* (New York: Columbia University Press, 2005), 167–202; Richard Schickel, *The Disney Version: The Life, Times, Art and Commerce of Walt Disney* (Chicago: Ivan R. Dee, 1997); James Howard Kunstler, *The Geography of Nowhere: The Rise and Decline of America's Man-Made Landscape* (New York: Simon and Schuster, 1993), 219–28; Sharon Zukin, *Landscapes of Power: From Detroit to Disneyworld* (Berkeley: University of California Press, 1991); Sharon Zukin, *The Culture of Cities* (Oxford: Blackwell, 1995), 49–77; Susan Sessions Rugh, *Are We There Yet? The Golden Age of American Family Vacations* (Lawrence: University Press of Kansas, 2008), 92–117; and George Lipsitz, "The Making of Disneyland," in *True Stories from the American Past*, ed. William Graebner (New York: McGraw Hill, 1993), 209–25.

117. On theming, see Mark Gottdiener, *The Theming of America: American Dreams, Media Fantasies, and Themed Environments* (New York: Westview Press, 2001), esp. 116–30; and Scott A. Lukas, *Theme Park* (London: Reaktion Books, 2008), esp. 74–80. On Coney Island as a theme park, see Lynn Sally, "Luna Park's Fantasy World and Dreamland's White City: Fire Spectacles at Coney Island as Elemental Performativity," in *The Themed Space: Locating Culture, Nation, and Self*, ed. Scott A. Lukas (New York: Lexington Books, 2007), 39–56.

118. "In a Week Coney Will Only Be a Memory," *Forest Hills Journal*, September 1, 1971; Karal Ann Marling, "Imagineering the Disney Theme Parks," in *Designing Disney's Theme Parks: The Architecture of Reassurance*, ed. Karal Ann Marling (New York: Flammarion, 1997), 66. Given that Cincinnati's Coney Island was still strictly segregated when Disney visited, his admiration for the park is notable.

119. Adams, *The American Amusement Park Industry*, 164.

120. "War, Video Pose Problems in 1951," *Billboard* 62, 51 (December 23, 1950): 44; "Chi Riverview Steps up Sked of Video Time," *Billboard* 63, 25 (June 23, 1951): 50; "Palisades Uses Video to Buck Gate Threat," *Billboard* 63, 47 (November 24, 1951): 90; "TV to Originate at Palisades, Says Rosenthal," *Billboard* 64, 6 (February 9, 1952): 64.

121. Alan A. Siegel, *Smile: A Picture History of Olympic Park, 1887–1965* (Irvington, N.J.: Irvington Historical Society, 1983), 130.

122. Weinstein, "Disneyland and Coney Island," 148–49; Findlay, *Magic Lands*, 59–61.

123. "Park Men See TV as Weak Attraction," *Billboard* 64, 50 (December 13, 1952): 64.

124. Kevin Kruse and Thomas Sugrue, eds., *The New Suburban History* (Chicago: University of Chicago Press, 2006).

125. Michael Sorkin, "See You in Disneyland," in *Variations on a Theme Park*, 231. Cross and Walton argue that "Disney's dream of Main Street represents a kind of protest against both suburban sprawl and the dirt and alienation of big city centers, two lasting consequences of modern

consumer capitalism" (*The Playful Crowd*, 181). Findlay suggests that it was Disney World, not Disneyland, that was explicitly anti-urban (*Magic Lands*, 105).

126. "Disney's Kingdom," *The Economist*, December 22, 1956, 1055–56. There was also a heliport in the park so those arriving at Los Angeles International Airport could fly directly there.

127. Nasaw, *Going Out*, 255. Gate fees would soon become commonplace in older amusement parks such as Crystal Beach as well.

128. The internal architecture and crowd control at Disneyland are often commented on in works on the park. Avila, *Popular Culture in the Age of White Flight*, 106–7; Gottdiener, *The Theming of America*, 117–30; Sorkin, "See You in Disneyland," 205–32.

129. Findlay, *Magic Lands*, 82; Cross and Walton, *The Playful Crowd*, 187.

130. Avila, *Popular Culture in the Age of White Flight*, 137. In the late 1960s park guards turned hippies away from the park to prevent possible conflict. See Findlay, *Magic Lands*, 83, 113; and Cross and Walton, *The Playful Crowd*, 185.

131. Rugh, *Are We There Yet*, 115. Rugh points out that "Photographs and movies of the early years do show African Americans among the park visitors, and in the 1960s the Disney company stepped up publicity of its black visitors like baseball player Maury Wills of the Los Angeles Dodgers and Sammy Davis Jr." (115). Bryant Simon also points out there was no explicit segregation at Disneyland: "Disney's racial discourse, however, was never explicit. During its glory days, the nation's playground didn't pretend for a moment not to exclude" (*Boardwalk Dreams: Atlantic City and the Fate of Urban America* [New York: Oxford University Press, 2004], 130). In 1963 CORE protested Disneyland's hiring policy, but no blacks were hired in "people contact" positions until 1968 (Findlay, *Magic Lands*, 94).

132. Lipsitz, "The Making of Disneyland," 215.

133. Sorkin, *Variations on a Theme Park*, xv.

Chapter 5

1. http://www.youtube.com/watch?v=be9JEfT1c3c (accessed July 12, 2009).

2. Six Flags was not the first theme park to be modeled after Disney. Two other parks, Pleasure Island in Massachusetts and Freedomland in the Bronx, closed soon after opening. For the growth of theme parks in 1960, see "Education with Fun and Shivers," *Life*, August 1, 1960, 26–32. On Six Flags, see Dale Samuelson, *The American Amusement Park* (St. Paul, Minn.: MBI Publishing, 2001), 151–52; Judith A. Adams, *The American Amusement Park Industry: A History of Technology and Thrills* (Boston: Twayne Publishers, 1991), 107–8; John Hannigan, *Fantasy City: Pleasure and Profit in the Postmodern Metropolis* (New York: Routledge, 1998), 39–41; and "Confideracy Section," http://parktimes.com/sections/confideracy/ (accessed July 10, 2009). In *The Confederate Battle Flag: America's Most Embattled Emblem* (Cambridge, Mass.: Harvard University Press, 2005), John M. Coski addresses the controversy over the use of the Confederate flag at Six Flags theme park (274). Eventually the Confederate section of the park was renamed Old South and the flags made into solid colors.

3. Chuck Berry, *Chuck Berry: The Autobiography* (New York: Harmony Books, 1987), 179. I am deeply grateful to Emily Morry for alerting me to the existence of Berry Park.

4. Bruce Pegg, *Brown Eyed Handsome Man: The Life and Hard Times of Chuck Berry* (New York: Routledge, 2002), 159–60.

5. Thomas Sugrue, for example, argues that by the early 1960s "northern blacks had joined the consumer society of postwar America" by gaining access to public accommodations. However, he does acknowledge that "there were still deep pockets of resistance to integration in many smaller towns and in resort areas" (*Sweet Land of Liberty: The Forgotten Struggle for Civil Rights in the North* [New York: Random House, 2008], 256). In *Up South: Civil Rights and Black Power in Philadelphia* (Philadelphia: University of Pennsylvania Press, 2006), Matthew J. Countryman argues

that by the end of the 1950s "Segregated public accommodations substantially disappeared from Philadelphia" (46).

6. "Deloris Tonkins, et al. v. City of Greensboro, North Carolina, et al.," *Race Relations Law Reporter* 4, 4 (Winter 1959): 988–92; "Deloris Tonkins, et al. v. City of Greensboro, North Carolina, et al.," *Race Relations Law Reporter* 5, 2 (Summer 1960): 460–62.

7. Aldon D. Morris, *The Origins of the Civil Rights Movement: Black Communities Organizing for Change* (New York: The Free Press, 1984), 188–89. There was a direct link between the CORE pioneers and young SNCC activists. Bayard Rustin and other veterans of radical nonviolence trained a new generation at Highlander Folk School and in regional meetings.

8. "Deloris Tonkins, et al. v. City of Greensboro," 461.

9. "Resolution No. 31329," *Race Relations Law Reporter* 4, 4 (Winter 1959): 1066–67; Marvin Dunn, *Black Miami in the Twentieth Century* (Gainesville: University Press of Florida, 1997), 215–16; August Meier and Elliott Rudwick, *CORE: A Study in the Civil Rights Movement* (Chicago: University of Illinois Press, 1975), 90–91; James Peck, *Cracking the Color Line: Non-Violent Direct Action Methods of Eliminating Racial Discrimination*, p. 20, microfilm, Reel 19, EIII, CORE Papers, Addendum. According to Peck, the first Deep South nonviolent sit-in occurred not in Greensboro but in Miami in 1959. In April that year a group of twenty interracial CORE activists sat-in at Grant's lunch counter, an act that launched a new chapter in CORE's southern activism and after a year of constant sit-ins succeeded in desegregating thirty downtown restaurants (18–20). CORE activists also successfully desegregated Miami's Crandon Beach in 1958.

10. "House Bill No. 990 of the Florida State Legislature," *Race Relations Law Reporter* 4, 3 (Fall 1959): 772–73.

11. In Jacksonville, Florida, for example, black activists successfully filed suit to desegregate all municipally owned recreational facilities. Although the city insisted this segregation was the result of "local custom" and was necessary to preserve the peace, the district court ruled that segregation was "not a proper exercise of police power." See "Hampton v. City of Jacksonville," *Race Relations Law Reporter* 5, 4 (Winter 1960): 1145–49. As early as 1956 city officials in Daytona Beach, Florida, challenged African Americans who staged wade-ins to desegregate their oceanfront (William G. Crawford, Jr., "The Long Hard Fight for Equal Rights: A History of Broward County's Colored Beach and the Fort Lauderdale Beach 'Wade-Ins' of the Summer of 1961," *Tequesta* 67 [2007]: 27, 37).

12. "Henry Cabot Lodge Bohler, et al. v. Julian Lane, et al.," *Race Relations Law Reporter* 7, 1 (Spring 1962): 208. Tampa officials invoked the Florida state law mandating separate toilet facilities to justify segregation in public parks.

13. "Willie v. Harris County, Texas," *Race Relations Law Reporter* 5, 1 (Spring 1960): 146–51; "Willie v. Harris County, Texas," *Race Relations Law Reporter* 7, 1 (Spring 1962): 199–203; David G. McComb, *Houston: A History* (Austin: University of Texas Press, 1969, 1981), 170. The men engaged in a four-year legal struggle to desegregate the park.

14. "Board of Commissioners Resolution," December 1958, *Race Relations Law Reporter* 4, 1 (Spring 1959): 206. The U.S. District Court and the U.S. Court of Appeals ruled that the city had the right to close the parks as long as they did not violate the Fourteenth Amendment when they reopened. See "Georgia Theresa Gilmore v. City of Montgomery," *Race Relations Law Reporter* 4, 1 (Spring 1959): 977–88; and "Georgia Theresa Gilmore v. City of Montgomery," *Race Relations Law Reporter* 5, 2 (Summer 1960): 455–59.

15. For example, in the summer of 1954 a fifteen-year-old African American boy drowned in the Mississippi River after being refused admission to the public pool in Madison, Illinois. See State of Illinois Commission on Human Relations, "Sixth Biennial Report, 1953–55," March 1, 1955, Folder, "Miscellaneous," Box 37, ACLU, Illinois Division Papers, University of Chicago, Special Collections, Regenstein Library, Chicago, Ill.

16. Timothy B. Tyson, *Radio Free Dixie: Robert F. Williams and the Roots of Black Power* (Chapel Hill: University of North Carolina Press, 1999), 83–89, 201–2, 251–58.

17. See Gilbert R. Mason with James Patterson Smith, *Beaches, Blood, and Ballots: A Black Doctor's Civil Rights Struggle* (Jackson: University Press of Mississippi, 2000), 65–87; J. Michael Butler, "Biloxi Beach Riot of 1960," in *Encyclopedia of American Race Riots*, ed. Walter Rucker and James Nathaniel Upton (New York: Greenwood Press, 2006), 31–33; James Patterson Smith, "Local Leadership, the Biloxi Beach Riot, and the Origins of the Civil Rights Movement on the Mississippi Gulf Coast, 1959–1964," in *Sunbelt Revolution: The Historical Progression of the Civil Rights Struggle in the Gulf South, 1866–2000*, ed. Samuel C. Hyde, Jr. (Gainesville: University Press of Florida, 2003), 210–33; John Dittmer, *Local People: The Struggle for Civil Rights in Mississippi* (Chicago: University of Illinois Press, 1995), 86–87; and Memo, Secretary to NAACP Branch and Youth Officers, May 13, 1960, Folder, "Discrimination: Parks and Playgrounds, 1956–65," Box A110, Series III, NAACP Papers, Library of Congress, Washington, D.C.

18. Memo, Secretary to NAACP Branch and Youth Officers, May 13, 1960; "State Reports," *Student Voice* 1, 2 (August 1960): 10, reprinted in Martin Luther King, Jr. Papers Project, *The Student Voice, 1960–1965* (Wesport, Conn.: Meckler, 1990). Activists held a second wade-in at Biloxi Beach in the summer of 1963, but it was not until 1968 that the Mississippi Gulf Coast beaches were fully desegregated by the courts. See Smith, "Local Leadership, the Biloxi Beach Riot, and the Origins of the Civil Rights Movement."

19. Gordon R. Carey, "The Interracial Actions," *CORE-lator*, September 1960, microfilm, Reel 13, Series 3, CORE Papers. Virginia Beach, on Virginia Key, was the first bathing beach established for black swimmers in Miami in 1945. See Gregory Bush, "Politicized Memories in the Struggle for Miami's Virginia Key Beach," in *"To Love the Wind and the Rain": African Americans and Environmental History*, ed. Dianne D. Glave and Mark Stoll (Pittsburgh: University of Pittsburgh Press, 2006), 164–88.

20. Crawford, "The Long Hard Fight for Equal Rights," 19–51. In Savannah, Georgia, the Youth Strategy Committee, affiliated with SNCC, staged a major wade-in at Savannah's public beach the summer of 1962 ("Savannah Groups Tries Beach Entry," *Student Voice* 3, 2 [June 1962]: 54, reprinted in *The Student Voice*).

21. McComb, *Houston*, 167.

22. Notes, July 28, 1960, Folder 5, "Discrimination, Swimming Pools, 1956–61," Box A111, Series III, NAACP Papers. African Americans had been attempting to swim in Charlotte's white pools since 1958.

23. "Integrate Southern Facilities," *Amusement Business* 73, 37 (September 18, 1961): 18.

24. William Brophy, "Active Acceptance—Active Containment: The Dallas Story," in *Southern Businessmen and Desegregation*, ed. Elizabeth Jacoway and David R. Colburn (Baton Rouge: Louisiana State University Press, 1982), 149.

25. "Brown v. City of Atlanta," *Race Relations Law Reporter* 7, 2 (Summer 1962): 884–85; Kevin Kruse, *White Flight: Atlanta and the Making of Modern Conservatism* (Princeton, N.J.: Princeton University Press, 2005), 123–25.

26. "Some Wild Segregation Ideas in Nashville," *Chicago Defender*, April 8, 1963, 13.

27. "Wood, et al. v. Vaughn, et al.," *Race Relations Law Reporter* 7, 3 (Fall 1962): 1184–91.

28. "Watson, et al. v. City of Memphis," *Race Relations Law Reporter* 6, 3 (Fall 1961): 830.

29. "Watson, et al. v. City of Memphis," *Race Relations Law Reporter* 8, 2 (Summer 1963): 384. See also Michael J. Klarman, *From Jim Crow to Civil Rights: The Supreme Court and the Struggle for Racial Equality* (New York: Oxford University Press, 2004), 341.

30. Al Kuettner, "Integration Faces Hardest Going in Recreation Public Facilities," *Chicago Defender*, August 31, 1963, 9; "Memphis Pools Remain Dry," *Amusement Business* 76, 6 (February 15, 1964): 7; "Ky. Blocks Integration Bill," *Amusement Business* 76, 12 (March 28, 1964): 8. City officials

in Lexington, Virginia, closed their pool when local whites dumped two barrels of oil into the water after only a few days of desegregated swimming ("Some Wild Segregation Ideas in Nashville").

31. "Clark v. Thompson," *Race Relations Law Reporter* 7, 2 (Summer 1962): 558.

32. Ibid., 559. The Fifth Circuit of the U.S. Court of Appeals upheld the ruling the following year. See "Clark v. Thompson," *Race Relations Law Reporter* 8, 1 (Spring 1963): 216.

33. Kuettner, "Integration Faces Hardest Going in Recreation Public Facilities." Jackson's mayor, Allen Thompson, threatened to close all public parks and recreational facilities during the 1961 Freedom Rides. See "May Close Jackson Parks," *Amusement Business* 73, 33 (August 21, 1961): 17.

34. "Palmer v. Thompson," *Race Relations Law Reporter* 12, 3 (Fall 1967): 1468. A class-action lawsuit filed in federal district court failed when the court ruled "plaintiffs have no constitutional right to require the city to maintain public pools or rest rooms" (1468).

35. Randy Battle, "The Great Pool Jump: Integrating Tift Park Pool," 2, http://www.crmvet.org/nars/rbpool.htm (accessed April 3, 2008).

36. Ibid. See also the reminiscences of white SNCC worker Peter de Lissovoy, "Returning to Georgia," in *Perspectives on Reporting*, http://reportingcivilrights.loa.org/perspectives/delissovoy.jsp (accessed May 5, 2008); Peter de Lissovoy, "Albany GA in 1963," http://www.crmvet.org/nars/peter3.htm (accessed May 5, 2008); and Peter de Lissovoy, "A Confrontation," http://www.crmvet.org/nars/peter2.htm (accessed May 5, 2008). On SNCC's organizing in Albany, see Clayborne Carson, *In Struggle: SNCC and the Black Awakening of the 1960s* (Cambridge, Mass.: Harvard University Press, 1991), 56–65; David R. Goldfield, *Black, White, and Southern: Race Relations and Southern Culture 1940 to the Present* (Baton Rouge: Louisiana State University Press, 1990), 130–32; and Wesley C. Hogan, *Many Minds, One Heart: SNCC's Dream for a New America* (Chapel Hill: University of North Carolina Press, 2007), 66–77.

37. Quoted in David R. Colburn, *Racial Change and Community Crisis: St. Augustine, Florida, 1877–1980* (New York: Columbia University Press, 1985), 99. This demonstration and the beach wade-in that followed were widely reported in the print press and on television.

38. Quoted in Colburn, *Racial Change and Community Crisis*, 4.

39. Ibid., 4. This was the largest but not the only wade-in that summer. Willie Bolden, a civil rights activist, remembered, "It was a tough city and it was a tough movement. I know because for nineteen days in a row we went to the beach trying to integrate the beach, and for nineteen days in a row we were jumped up and beaten by the Klan." See Willie Bolden interview, March 21, 2006, Atlanta History Center, http://album.atlantahistorycenter.com/92710-willie-bolden-interview-2006-march-21.aspx (accessed March 5, 2011).

40. "Prymus v. High," *Race Relations Law Reporter* 5, 4 (Winter 1960): 1150; Dunn, *Black Miami*, 216.

41. "Barthe v. City of New Orleans," *Race Relations Law Reporter* 8, 3 (Fall 1963): 113–14. African Americans filed a similar lawsuit in 1957. See "Detiege v. New Orleans City Park Improvement Association," *Race Relations Law Reporter* 2, 5 (October 1957): 994–95.

42. "Freeman v. City of Little Rock," *Race Relations Law Reporter* 8, 1 (Spring 1963): 173–75. This injunction did not cover public parks and allowed the city to lease facilities to private groups. John A. Kirk, in *Redefining the Color Line: Black Activism in Little Rock, Arkansas, 1940–70* (Gainesville: University Press of Florida, 2002), points out that the activists "left out a request to desegregate the swimming pools as it touched upon the issue of interracial bathing and the white fears of miscegenation" (158).

43. Kruse, *White Flight*, 106.

44. "Ordinance of the Danville, Virginia City Council," *Race Relations Law Reporter* 5, 2 (Summer 1960): 532.

45. Charles E. Connerly, *"The Most Segregated City in America": City Planning and Civil Rights in Birmingham, 1920–80* (Charlottesville: University of Virginia Press, 2005), 36. The city built no parks for African Americans until 1942.

46. Quoted in Glenn T. Eskew, *But for Birmingham: The Local and National Movements in the Civil Rights Struggle* (Chapel Hill: University of North Carolina Press, 1997), 179.

47. Connerly, *"The Most Segregated City in America,"* 179–200; Robert Corley, "In Search of Racial Harmony: Birmingham Business Leaders and Desegregation, 1950–63," in *Southern Businessmen and Desegregation*, 183–84; "Shuttlesworth v. City of Birmingham," *Race Relations Law Reporter* 5, 4 (Winter 1960): 1142–44; "Shuttlesworth v. Gaylord," *Race Relations Law Reporter* 6, 4 (Winter 1961): 1101–9; "Shuttlesworth v. Gaylord," *Race Relations Law Reporter* 7, 1 (Spring 1962): 204; "Hanes v. Shuttlesworth," *Race Relations Law Reporter* 7, 3 (Fall 1962): 1194–95; "Birmingham Keeps Parks Closed, Defying Court," *Chicago Defender*, March 19, 1962, 5; "Birmingham to Shut Parks," *Amusement Business* 73, 50 (December 18, 1961): 11; Eskew, *But for Birmingham*, 75–76, 147, 178–80.

48. "Integration Battle Looms over S.C. State Parks," *Amusement Business* 73, 30 (July 31, 1961): 17; "Ask South Carolina to Reopen Parks," *Amusement Business* 73, 50 (December 18, 1961): 14; "S.C. Vote on Parks Issue?" *Amusement Business* 75, 43 (October 26, 1963): 12; "S.C. Will Integrate Parks," *Amusement Business* 7, 21 (May 30, 1964): 8; "Brown v. Lee," *Race Relations Law Reporter* 9, 2 (Summer 1964): 878–79.

49. "Hit Ga. Park's Segregation," *Amusement Business* 75, 41 (October 12, 1963): 11.

50. Susan Sessions Rugh, *Are We There Yet? The Golden Age of American Family Vacations* (Lawrence: University Press of Kansas, 2008), 147–52.

51. Ibid., 168.

52. Ibid., 77–78; Cotton Seiler, *Republic of Drivers: A Cultural History of Automobility in America* (Chicago: University of Chicago Press, 2008), 114–25. *Travelguide* also listed civil rights laws and the addresses of NAACP headquarters throughout the country to encourage black travelers to file complaints of discrimination.

53. Benjamin C. Wilson, "Idlewild: A Black Eden in Michigan," *Michigan History* 65, 5 (September/October 1981): 33–37; Rugh, *Are We There Yet?* 167–68.

54. "Hampton v. City of Jacksonville," *Race Relations Law Reporter* 4, 2 (Summer 1959): 339–40; "Hampton v. City of Jacksonville," *Race Relations Law Reporter* 4, 4 (Winter 1959): 973–77; "Hampton v. City of Jacksonville," *Race Relations Law Reporter* 6, 3 (Fall 1961): 850–53; "Hampton v. City of Jacksonville," *Race Relations Law Reporter* 7, 2 (Summer 1962): 536–45; Abel A. Bartley, "The 1960 and 1964 Jacksonville Riots: How Struggle Led to Progress," *Florida Historical Quarterly* 78, 1 (1999): 46–73; "News from the States," *Student Voice* 1, 5 (December 1960): 30, reprinted in *The Student Voice*; Abel A. Bartley, *Keeping the Faith: Race, Politics, and Social Development in Jacksonville* (New York: Greenwood Press, 2000), 64–66.

55. "Cummings v. The City of Charlestown," *Race Relations Law Reporter* 5, 4 (Winter 1960): 1137–39.

56. "Sawyer v. City of Mobile," *Race Relations Law Reporter* 6, 2 (Summer 1961): 484–85. The golfers, who first challenged the city's segregation in 1958, traveled to Pensacola, Florida, and New Orleans to play.

57. "Clark v. Sherman," *Race Relations Law Reporter* 7, 1 (Spring 1962): 308–10.

58. Archie Vernon Huff, *Greenville: The History of the City and County in the South Carolina Piedmont* (Columbia: University of South Carolina Press), 402–3; "Walker v. Shaw," *Race Relations Law Reporter* 7, 3 (Fall 1962): 1195–96.

59. Quoted in Mike Davis, "Wild Streets: American Graffiti versus the Cold War," *International Socialism Journal* 91 (Summer 2001), http://pubs.socialistreviewindex.org.uk/isj91/davis.htm (accessed January 20, 2009).

60. For descriptions of the riot, see Josh Sides, *L.A. City Limits: African American Los Angeles from the Great Depression to the Present* (Berkeley: University of California Press, 2003), 173; "75 Policemen Quell Riot in Griffith Park," *Los Angeles Times*, May 31, 1961, 1; "2 More Suspects Jailed in Riot at Griffith Park," *Los Angeles Times*, June 1, 1961, B1; and "Blame Ala. Riot for Calif. Race

Brawl," *Chicago Defender*, June 3, 1961, 1. Five police officers were hospitalized after the riot, and three African American men were charged with assault. Bizarrely two of the men were charged under the lynch law because they were "taking a prisoner from the officers by force" ("Two Cited Under Lynch Law After Park Riot," *Los Angeles Times*, June 2, 1961, B1). The seventeen-year-old on the merry-go-round escaped into the crowd and was never charged.

61. "Aftermath of 'Freedom Rides,'" *U.S. News & World Report* (June 12, 1961): 4.

62. "No, This Is Not Alabama," *Los Angeles Times*, June 1, 1961, B4.

63. Chicago Commission on Human Relations, "A Report on the Bessemer Park Disturbance, July 25–August 18, 1960," Folder 24, "Chicago Commission on Human Relations—Memoranda and Reports," Stephen S. Bubacz Papers, Daley Library, Special Collections, University of Illinois at Chicago (hereafter Bubacz Papers). On the Bessemer riot, see also Andrew J. Diamond, *Mean Streets: Chicago Youths and the Everyday Struggle for Empowerment in the Multiracial City, 1908–1969* (Berkeley: University of California Press, 2009), 223–24; Arnold R. Hirsch, *Making the Second Ghetto: Race and Housing in Chicago, 1940–1960* (Cambridge: Cambridge University Press, 1983), 65; "3,000 at Swim Pool Race Riot," *Chicago Defender*, July 28, 1960, A2; and "Fine Two over Swim Pool Riot," *Chicago Defender*, August 2, 1960, A3.

64. "Stage Successful Wade-In," *Chicago Defender*, September 6, 1960, 4; "Police Prevent Trouble at Tense Rainbow Beach," *Chicago Defender*, September 6, 1960, 4; "Police Halt Mob of 3000 at Rainbow Beach," *Chicago Defender*, September 7, 1960, A1. For discussions of the Rainbow Beach violence, see Diamond, *Mean Streets*, 228–31; Hirsch, *Making the Second Ghetto*, 65–66; and Amanda J. Seligman, *Block by Block: Neighborhoods and Public Policy on Chicago's West Side* (Chicago: University of Chicago Press, 2005), 107.

65. Quoted in "Police Prevent Trouble at Tense Rainbow Beach."

66. Kenneth C. Field, "Rap Police as White Mob Drives 10 from Beach," *Chicago Defender*, July 5, 1961, 1; "Arrest 22 at Rainbow Beach," *Chicago Defender*, July 10, 1961, 1; "NOW-Chicago's Summer of Decision," 1961, p. 2, Folder 24, Bubacz Papers.

67. Adolph J. Slaughter, "Blonde Rioter Draws $200 Fine for Sand Kicking Act," *Chicago Defender*, July 13, 1961, 1.

68. Adolph J. Slaughter, "'Freedom Ride,' Even to Race Tense Beach Is Frightening Experience," *Chicago Defender*, July 19, 1961, 4.

69. Adolph J. Slaughter, "Rioting Fades, Police Get Tough, Arrest 10 at Beach," *Chicago Defender*, July 10, 1961, 1; "Arrest Two Servicemen at Rainbow Beach Wade-In," *Chicago Defender*, July 17, 1961, 3; "Arrest 11 on Beach on Sunday," *Chicago Defender*, July 17, 1961, 1; "Arrest Four in Westside 'Clash' Zone," *Chicago Defender*, July 18, 1961, 18; "Police Brass Backs Move to Mix All-White Beach," *Chicago Defender*, July 18, 1961, 1; "Rainbow Beach Strife Eases as Wade-Inners Demonstrate," *Chicago Defender*, August 1, 1961, 23; Robert T. Loughran, "Crude Racial Sign Greets 'Wade-Ins' as They Integrate Rainbow Beach," *Chicago Defender*, August 1, 1961, 3; memorandum, Stephen S. Bubacz to Tony Sorrentino, "Rainbow Beach Wade-In," July 25, 1961, Folder 24, Bubacz Papers.

70. "Police Patrol Mixed Beach," *Cleveland Call and Post*, July 21, 1962, 1C; "Map Action for Beach Integration," *Chicago Defender*, July 12, 1962, 3.

71. Diamond, *Mean Streets*, 231.

72. Hirsch, *Making the Second Ghetto*, 65.

73. "Negro Shoots Niagara Falls with Aim of Integrating Cataract," *Louisville Courier Journal*, July 16, 1961, 1.

74. On the resurgence of northern CORE chapters during this period, see Sugrue, *Sweet Land of Liberty*, 280–82; and Meier and Rudwick, *CORE*, 182–210.

75. "Summary of Contacts, July–November 1959," undated, c. 1959, p. 6, Folder 3, Box 9, Urban League of Greater Cincinnati Papers, Cincinnati Historical Society Library, Cincinnati, Ohio.

76. On the prom, see "News Release," May 9, 1961, microfilm, Reel 42, Series 5, CORE Papers; Cincinnati CORE to C. A. Harrell, May 9, 1961, ibid.; and "CORE Protest Junior Prom, Coney Is-

land," *Cincinnati Herald*, May 19, 1961, 1. In 1960 the NAACP had convinced local parochial schools to not hold their annual outing at Coney Island. See "Coney Island Report," July 6, 1961, Folder 14, Box 5, NAACP Cincinnati Chapter Papers, Cincinnati Historical Society Library, Cincinnati, Ohio.

77. Minutes of the Mayor's Friendly Relations Committee, May 24, 1961, Folder 6, Box 26, Papers of the Jewish Community Relations Council, American Jewish Archives, Cincinnati, Ohio; "Coney Island Report," July 6, 1961; "Summary of Contacts," 1961, Folder 3, Box 9, Urban League of Greater Cincinnati Papers; Charles J. Jacques, Jr., *Cincinnati's Coney Island: America's Finest Amusement Park* (Jefferson, Ohio: Amusement Park Journal, 2002), 158–59. Police arrested twenty-seven activists during the demonstrations.

CORE also targeted LeSourdsville, a nearby amusement park. After an interracial group failed to gain admittance, CORE negotiated with the park's owner and obtained an agreement to desegregate on July 7, 1961. See "Application for Affiliation," p. 2, microfilm, Reel 42, Series 5, CORE Papers; and "The Freedom Line," CORE newsletter, undated, Folder 4, Box 9, Urban League of Greater Cincinnati Papers.

78. "NAACP, CORE, Win Coney Island Fight," *Cincinnati Herald*, June 2, 1961, 2.

79. Al Roman, "Listening Post," *Cincinnati Herald*, June 9, 1961, 4.

80. "Don't Abuse Privilege," *Cincinnati Herald*, June 2, 1961, 4.

81. "Summary of Contacts," 1961.

82. Ibid.

83. William F. Bowen, president of local NAACP, to Bud Boskins, president of Bowling Proprietors Association, July 2, 1962, Folder 8, "Discrimination: 1960–64," Box 16, Papers of the Jewish Community Relations Council; Ohio Civil Rights Commission, "A Report by the Ohio Civil Rights Commission: Discrimination in Public Accommodations in Ohio," December 1960, pp. 23–24, Folder 8, "Discrimination: 1960–64," Box 16, Papers of the Jewish Community Relations Council.

84. Marshall Bragdon, Executive Director's Report for May 1961, p. 4, Folder 5, "Mayor's Friendly Relations Committee, 1959–64," Box 26, Papers of the Jewish Community Relations Council.

85. "Annual Report of Branch Activities, 1961," p. 3, Folder 17, Box 5, NAACP Cincinnati Chapter Papers.

86. George C. Wright, *Life Behind a Veil: Blacks in Louisville, Kentucky, 1865–1930* (Baton Rouge: Louisiana State University Press, 1985), 279.

87. George C. Wright, "Desegregation of Public Accommodations in Louisville," in *Southern Businessmen and Desegregation*, 191–210. See also Wright, *Life Behind a Veil*; Tracy E. K'Meyer, *Civil Rights in the Gateway to the South: Louisville, Kentucky, 1945–1980* (Lexington: University Press of Kentucky, 2009), 94–98; and Luther Adams, *Way Up North in Louisville: African American Migration in the Urban South, 1930–70* (Chapel Hill: University of North Carolina Press, 2010), 123–48.

88. "Memories of Fontaine Ferry Park," http://www.fontaineferrypark.com/ffhistory.html (accessed May 10, 2008). The park was named after the plantation founded in the late eighteenth century by Captain Aaron Fontaine and was often known as "Fountain" Ferry Park.

89. Anne Braden, *The Wall Between* (Knoxville: University of Tennessee Press, 1999), 7–8.

90. "28 Are Arrested at Louisville Park," *Washington Post*, June 17, 1961, A4; "28 Arrested in Stand-In at Fontaine Ferry Park," *Louisville Courier Journal*, June 16, 1961, 1; Wright, "Desegregation of Public Accommodations in Louisville," 200.

91. "Negroes Seek Integration Law," *Louisville Courier Journal*, May 18, 1961, 1; "Hoblitzell Won't Force Integration," *Louisville Courier Journal*, May 25, 1961, 1; "Integrationists to March to Aldermen's Meeting," *Louisville Courier Journal*, June 3, 1961, 1; Wright, "Desegregation of Public Accommodations in Louisville," 195–201.

92. "Negro Group to Ask Removal of Judge," *Louisville Courier Journal*, June 16, 1961, 1; "County Judge Backs Triplett in Stand-Ins," *Louisville Courier Journal*, June 19, 1961, 1; K'Meyer, *Civil Rights in the Gateway to the South*, 97.

93. Quoted in "Judge Curbs Picketing at Fontaine Ferry," *Louisville Courier Journal*, June 21, 1961, 1.

94. "'Private Pool' Operators, Mayor to Attempt to Reach Agreement," *Louisville Defender*, June 4, 1964, 1, 7; "Racial Pressure at Pools," *Amusement Business* 76, 23 (June 13, 1964): 14; "Despite Anti-Bias Code, Won't Serve 2," *Chicago Defender*, September 17, 1963, A10; "Integrate Ky. Park, Ban Negro Swimmers," *Chicago Defender*, June 4, 1964, 5. In addition to targeting Fontaine Ferry, the activists demonstrated at Dub's Fried Oysters Restaurant and Hasenour's Dining Room. See "Demonstrations Hit Louisville as 'Long Hot Summer' Begins," *Louisville Defender*, June 11, 1964, 1, 6.

95. "An Old Ruse," *Louisville Defender*, June 4, 1964, 6.

96. "Okla. City Integrates Fun," *Amusement Business* 76, 24 (June 20, 1964): 14; "Race Issues at Park Pools; Some Close, Some Integrate," *Amusement Business* 76, 26 (July 4, 1964): 5–6; "Commission Rules Against Biased Fontaine Ferry Pool," *Louisville Defender*, June 25, 1964, 1, 5; "'Private Pool' Operators, Mayor to Attempt to Reach Agreement," 1; "Human Relations Commission Sets Public Hearings on Fontaine Ferry Pool Status," *Louisville Defender*, June 18, 1964, 1; "Commission Rules Against Biased Fontaine Ferry Pool," *Louisville Defender*, June 25, 1964, 1; "There Can Be No Doubt," editorial, *Louisville Defender*, June 25, 1964, 4; "Court Bars 'Rabble Rousers' from Funpark at Louisville," *Amusement Business* 76, 28 (July 18, 1964): 14, 15.

97. "Dady Charged with Violating Restraining Order at Park," *Louisville Defender*, July 16, 1964, 1; "Pool Ruled Public Facility," *Louisville Defender*, September 10, 1964, 1; "Funspot Integration Views," *Amusement Business* 76, 31 (August 8, 1964): 6.

98. Telegram, undated, Folder, "Discrimination: Parks and Playgrounds, 1956–65," Box A110, Series 3, NAACP Papers; "Negro Picketing Leader Is Ousted by Followers," *Washington Post*, August 21, 1960; "Glen Echo Park Holds Steadfastly to Jim Crow," *Washington Afro-American*, May 28, 1957; Kenneth Weiss and Willard Clopton, "2 Arrested in Tussle at Glen Echo," *Washington Post*, July 4, 1960, 1; "Five Arrested in Glen Echo Sitdown," *Washington Post*, July 1, 1960, A1; Brigid Schulte, "Protest on a Sculpted Horse," *Washington Post*, June 29, 2004, B1; "Tireless Negro Demonstrators Aim to End Racial Discrimination in Area," *Washington Post*, August 8, 1960, A1; "Six Negroes Sue for Injunction to Prevent Glen Echo Segregation," *Washington Post*, July 9, 1960, A1; "State Reports," *Student Voice* 1, 2 (August 1960): 10, reprinted in *The Student Voice*.

99. "Pickets and Trespassers," *Washington Post*, July 8, 1960, 16.

100. "Legal Spotlight on a Playground," *Washington Post*, July 10, 1960, E3; "Griffin v. Collins," *Race Relations Law Reporter* 5, 3 (Fall 1960): 825–29; "Griffin v. State of Maryland," *Race Relations Law Reporter* 6, 3 (Fall 1961): 853–57; "Griffin v. State of Maryland," *Race Relations Law Reporter* 9, 2 (Summer 1964): 504–7; "Enforcing Discrimination with Agent of State Is Key to Glen Echo Decision," *Washington Post*, June 24, 1964, B14.

101. "Glen Echo Hints Admission Fee," *Washington Post*, March 18, 1961, C1. See also Schulte, "Protest on a Sculpted Horse"; "Glen Echo Park to Open Its Doors to Negroes After Year of Protest," *Washington Post*, March 15, 1961, A1; and "Glen Park Opens on Desegregated Basis," *Washington Post*, April 1, 1961, D2. There is some evidence that attorney general Robert Kennedy pressured Glen Echo Park's owners to desegregate.

102. Alan L. Dessoff, "Desegregation Finds Glen Echo Peaceful," *Washington Post*, July 25, 1961, B1; "Race Blend No Obstacle for Glen Echo," *Amusement Business* 73, 31 (August 7, 1961): 10.

103. George Lardner, Jr., "Gwynn Oak Could Follow Glen Echo," *Washington Post*, July 14, 1963, A9.

104. Peck, *Cracking the Color Line*, 11; James Peck, "Waiting Line Technique Used on 'All Nations Day,'" *CORE-lator*, fall 1958, p. 3, microfilm, Reel 13, EIII, CORE Papers, Addendum; Meier and Rudwick, *CORE*, 74. There is much contradiction in the secondary sources as to when the demonstrations began. But the CORE Papers indicate that it was 1955.

105. Quoted in "Drews v. State of Maryland," *Race Relations Law Reporter* 6, 1 (Spring 1961): 254. See also "Drews v. State of Maryland," *Race Relations Law Reporter* 5, 2 (Summer 1960): 469–72;

and "Drews v. State of Maryland," *Race Relations Law Reporter* 10, 2 (Summer 1965): 484–89. The case against the demonstrators went to the Supreme Court, which refused to hear the case. Two justices, Warren and Douglas, dissented, writing: "Juretha Joyner, a Negro, went with some friends to celebrate 'All Nations Day' at Gwynn Oak Park. Despite the fact that she behaved with complete order and dignity, and that her right to be at the park is protected by federal law, she was asked to leave, solely because of her race. She refused and, upon being handcuffed, displayed some reluctance (though no active resistance) to being pulled through an actively hostile mob. For this she was convicted of 'acting in a disorderly manner, to the disturbance of the public peace.' Today the Court declines to review her conviction, and the convictions of her three companions" (489).

106. "Activists Braved Arrests Hecklers to Integrate Amusement Park," *Afro-American Star*, October 13–19, 2007, 23; Kenneth D. Durr, *Behind the Backlash: White Working-Class Politics in Baltimore, 1940–80* (Chapel Hill: University of North Carolina Press, 2003), 118.

107. For descriptions of the 1963 demonstrations, see "Head of Church Is Arrested in Race March," *Chicago Tribune*, July 5, 1963, 1; "March on Gwynn Oak Park," *Time*, July 12, 1963; Ben A. Franklin, "99 Seized in New Demonstration at Segregated Maryland Resort," *New York Times*, July 8, 1963, 1; "Gwynn Oak Could Follow Glen Echo"; Meier and Rudwick, *CORE*, 223; C. Fraser Smith, *Here Lies Jim Crow: Civil Rights in Maryland* (Baltimore: Johns Hopkins University Press, 2008), 189–97; Durr, *Behind the Backlash*, 117–19; and Todd Gitlin, *The Sixties: Years of Hope, Days of Rage* (New York: Bantam Books, 1987), 132–33. Gitlin downplays the struggle at Gwynn Oak, calling it "a weak echo of the bloody movement down South."

108. "99 Seized in New Demonstration at Segregated Maryland Resort"; Smith, *Here Lies Jim Crow*, 194–95.

109. Quoted in "7 Whites Picket Baltimore Park," *New York Times*, July 21, 1963, 43.

110. "Park at Baltimore Integrates Quietly," *New York Times*, August 29, 1963, 14; Smith, *Here Lies Jim Crow*, 197.

111. "Dance Boycott," *Cleveland Call and Post*, June 1, 1957, 2A. The dance hall was open to blacks one night per week by 1957. In 1955 the park barred two young African American boys who were scheduled to participate in an Amateur Athletic Union swim meet. A lawsuit claiming Peony Park was in violation of Nebraska's civil rights law was successful. But the park owners simply paid the fifty-dollar fine and continued to discriminate. See "State of Nebraska v. Peony Park," *Race Relations Law Reporter* 1, 2 (April 1956): 366. On Peony Park's attractions, see Carl D. Jennings, *Omaha's Peony Park: An American Legend* (New York: Arcadia Publishing, 2001).

112. Quoted in David L. Bristow, "We Just Wanted to Swim, Sir," *Omaha Reader*, February 5, 2009, http://www.thereader.com/cover.php?subaction=showfull&id=1233874358&archive=&start_from=&ucat=5& (accessed October 15, 2007).

113. Ibid.; "Omaha Park Closes," *New York Times*, July 17, 1963, 14; "Cambridge Protests Off While Lawyers Mediate," *Norfolk Journal and Guide*, July 20, 1963, C2.

114. "End 36 Years Mo. Pool Jim Crow," *Chicago Daily Defender*, August 5, 1963, A6.

115. Tanyanika Samuels, "Activists from 50s and 60s Recall Work to Dismantle Segregation," *Kansas City Star*, January 14, 2001; Tracy Allen, "Celebration Will Commemorate Passage of Accommodations Law, Transformation of Amusement Site," *The Call*, July 26, 2002; "Summary of K.C. CORE's Activities Since March 19, 1961," *The Freedom Line*, Folder 4, Box 9, Cincinnati Urban League Papers, Cincinnati Historical Library.

116. "Kansas City Anti-Bias Vote Affects 'Private' Fun Parks," *Amusement Business* 76, 15 (April 18, 1964): 10.

117. "New York State Commission Against Discrimination for an Order Pursuant to Section 298," *Race Relations Law Reporter* 4, 2 (Summer 1959): 358–61.

118. "Opinion No. 59/174," *Race Relations Law Reporter* 4, 4 (Winter 1959): 1085–86.

119. "Lackey v. Sacoolas and Maple Grove Recreation Association," *Race Relations Law Reporter* 8, 2 (Summer 1963): 632–34. Similarly, when a small amusement park in Pennsylvania attempted

to privatize its pool in 1959 to prevent desegregation, an interracial group of activists immediately challenged the management. Under pressure from the ACLU, the state sued the park's owners and prevented the discriminatory club from being incorporated. See "Commonwealth of Pennsylvania v. John V. Gibney," *Race Relations Law Reporter* 5, 2 (Summer 1960): 475–83.

120. "Win Beach Club Case," *CORE-lator*, March 1961, p. 4, microfilm, Reel 13, Series 3, CORE Papers.

121. Caroline Watson to Thurgood Marshall, August 17, 1961, Folder 5, "Discrimination, Swimming Pools, 1956–61," Box A111, Series III, NAACP Papers.

122. "Stand-In at Pool," *CORE-lator*, August 1961, p. 2, microfilm, Reel 13, Series 3, CORE Papers; "Close Troubled Detroit Pool," *Amusement Business* 73, 36 (September 11, 1961): 10.

123. Jan Peterson Roddy, ed., *Let My People Go: Cairo, Illinois, 1967–1973* (Carbondale: Southern Illinois University Press, 1996), xvi.

124. "Cairo Mayor, Students to Huddle on Bias Charges," *Chicago Defender*, July 2, 1962, 2; "Cairo Tense; 5 Barred from Swimming Pool," *Chicago Defender*, July 5, 1962, 2; "Cairo Youth Continue Protests Despite Arrest of 23 Sit-Ins," *Chicago Daily Defender*, July 16, 1962, 2; Paul Good, *Cairo, Illinois: Racism at Floodtide* (Washington, D.C.: U.S. Commission on Civil Rights, 1972), 12. Cairo, Illinois, which was on the border of Missouri, had become notorious for its racism before the 1962 demonstrations. One scholar described it as being known for its "social disorganization and a tradition of general lawlessness" (June Shagaloff, "A Study of Community Acceptance of Desegregation in Two Selected Areas," *Journal of Negro Education* 23, 3 [Summer 1954]: 332–34). For a discussion of Cairo's 1952 campaign to desegregate the city's schools, see Sugrue, *Sweet Land of Liberty*, 458.

125. "Postpone Cairo Sit-In Trials," *Chicago Daily Defender*, July 18, 1962, 1; Kenneth Field, "Convict 17 Kids in Cairo Protests," *Chicago Defender*, July 21, 1962, 1; "New Effort to Integrate," *Chicago Defender*, July 26, 1962, 3; Edward P. Morgan, "Comments on the Racial Problem in Albany and Cairo," *Chicago Defender*, August 4, 1962, 10; "8-Week Anti-Bias Drive in Cairo Shows Progress," *Chicago Defender*, August 18, 1962, 1.

126. Kenneth C. Fields, "Demand Kerner Act in Cairo Race Riots," *Chicago Defender*, August 20, 1962, 1; "Cairo Probe Pledged by Gov. Kerner," *Chicago Defender*, August 21, 1962, 1; "The Fight for Justice in Cairo," *Chicago Defender*, October 13, 1962, 8. African Americans often pointed out the frequency with which black children drowned when excluded from white pools. Although whites viewed desegregation as potentially exposing their children to violence, the fate of young black children swimming in natural waters was rarely a concern for the white public.

127. Quoted in Fields, "Cairo Probe Pledged by Governor Kerner," 2.

128. "Racial Pressure at Pools," *Amusement Business* 76, 23 (June 13, 1964): 14; Good, *Cairo, Illinois*, 12; Roddy, *Let My People Go*, xvi–xvii.

129. "Skate-In Victory KOs Jim Crow," *Daily Worker*, May 7, 1961, Schomburg Clipping File, microfiche.

130. "Stage 'Sit-In' at Michigan Rink," *Chicago Defender*, January 11, 1961, 2.

131. "Indiana Group Rules Against Manager of Rink," *Chicago Defender*, May 22, 1962, 5.

132. "In the Matter of the Rollercade Skating Rink," *Race Relations Law Reporter* 7, 2 (Summer 1962): 985–88.

133. Quoted in Hogan, *Many Minds, One Heart*, 118. See also memorandum, Phillip Savage to news media, "NAACP Official Charges Discrimination at Skating Rink," April 4, 1962, Folder, "Discrimination: Skating Rinks, 1956, 1962," Box A110, Series III, NAACP Papers.

134. Hogan, *Many Minds, One Heart*, 120–25; Smith, *Here Lies Jim Crow*, 197–211; Peter B. Levy, *Civil War on Race Street: The Civil Rights Movement in Cambridge, Maryland* (Gainesville: University Press of Florida, 2003), 34–103.

135. Cleveland Sellers, *The River of No Return: The Autobiography of a Black Militant and the Life and Death of SNCC* (Jackson: University Press of Mississippi, 1990), 67–70; Levy, *Civil War on Race Street*, 107–9.

136. "Williams v. Rescue Fire Company, Inc.," *Race Relations Law Reporter* 11, 3 (Fall 1966): 1446–53. The case was not settled until 1966.

Chapter 6

1. Dick West, "Methods to Halt Teens' Madness," *Chicago Defender*, April 26, 1966, 12.

2. While in the 1950s and early 1960s there were numerous scholarly studies and congressional investigations on juvenile delinquency, by the late 1960s the focus had shifted to the study of violence. See, for example, Louis H. Masotti and Don R. Bowen, *Riots and Rebellion: Civil Violence in the Urban Community* (Beverly Hills, Calif.: Sage Publications, 1968); Saul Bernstein, *Alternatives to Violence: Alienated Youth and Riots, Race, and Poverty* (New York: National Board of Young Men's Christian Associations, 1967); Allen D. Grimshaw, ed., *Racial Violence in the United States* (Chicago: Aldine Publishing Company, 1969); Richard Hofstader and Michael Wallace, eds., *American Violence: A Documentary History* (New York: Alfred A. Knopf, 1970); Robert M. Fogelson, *Violence as Protest: A Study of Riots and Ghettos* (Garden City, N.Y.: Doubleday, 1971); Kerner Commission, *Report of the National Commission on Civil Disorders* (Washington, D.C.: GPO, 1968); and National Commission on the Causes and Prevention of Violence, *To Establish Justice, to Insure Domestic Tranquility* (New York: Praeger Publishers, 1970).

3. National Commission on the Causes and Prevention of Violence, *To Establish Justice, to Insure Domestic Tranquility*, 15. Richard Hofstader discusses this amnesia at length in his 1970 essay "Reflections on Violence in the United States," in *American Violence*, 3–43.

4. Michael W. Flamm, *Law and Order: Street Crime, Civil Unrest, and the Crisis of Liberalism in the 1960s* (New York: Columbia University Press, 2005), 19.

5. Quoted in ibid., 31.

6. Rick Perlstein, *Nixonland: The Rise of a President and the Fracturing of America* (New York: Scribner, 2008), 238.

7. Heather Ann Thompson, "Why Mass Incarceration Matters: Rethinking Crisis, Decline, and Transformation in Postwar American History," *Journal of American History* 97, 3 (December 2010): 703–34. Thompson suggests that Flamm and other scholars have "missed the extent to which mass incarceration, rather than crime, undergirded the Right's rise to power in the later postwar period" (727).

8. For an analysis of competing narratives of urban decline, see S. Paul O'Hara, "'The Very Model of Modern Urban Decay': Outsiders' Narratives of Industry and Urban Decline in Gary, Indiana," *Journal of Urban History* 37, 2 (2011): 135–54. O'Hara notes, "Race not only became the meta-language of Gary but it also reduced the possible declensions of Gary into a single storyline; the moment Gary became a black city" (142).

9. For histories of the Civil Rights Act, see Charles and Barbara Whalen, *The Longest Debate: A Legislative History of the 1964 Civil Rights Act* (Washington, D.C.: Seven Locks Press, 1985); Robert D. Loevy, *To End All Segregation: The Politics of the Passage of the Civil Rights Act of 1964* (New York: University Press of America, 1990); Robert D. Loevy, ed., *The Civil Rights Act of 1964: The Passage of the Law That Ended Segregation* (Albany: State University of New York Press, 1997); Richard C. Cortner, *Civil Rights and Public Accommodations: The Heart of Atlanta Motel and McClung Cases* (Lawrence: University Press of Kansas, 2001); and Susan Sessions Rugh, *Are We There Yet? The Golden Age of American Family Vacations* (Lawrence: University Press of Kansas, 2008), 88–91.

10. Kevin Kruse, *White Flight: Atlanta and the Making of Modern Conservatism* (Princeton, N.J.: Princeton University Press, 2005), 207. Kruse argues, "The rise of southern Republicanism . . . was largely due to the white backlash against the Civil Rights Act" (231). Restaurant owner Lester Maddox, for example, was elected governor of Georgia after refusing to comply with the Civil Rights Act. On the significance of resistance to the Civil Rights Act, see also Nancy MacLean, *Freedom Is Not Enough: The Opening of the American Workplace* (Cambridge, Mass.: Harvard University Press,

2008), 73; and Thomas Sugrue, *Sweet Land of Liberty: The Forgotten Struggle for Civil Rights in the North* (New York: Random House, 2008), 361–62.

11. The question of what facilities were covered under civil rights legislation had long been debated on the state level. Often a state law's wording reflected the popularity of particular amusements at that historical moment. In 1951, for example, the Pennsylvania Senate considered a legislation guaranteeing access to "bath houses, swimming pools, airdromes, race courses, skating rinks, recreation parks, fairs, bowling alleys and shooting galleries" ("Discrimination Law Weighed by Pa. Senate," *Billboard* 3 [February 1951]: 44).

12. *Heart of Atlanta Motel Inc. v. United States* 379 U.S. 241 (1964). For a detailed analysis of the case, see Cortner, *Civil Rights and Public Accommodations*. The use of the commerce clause bypassed the 1883 civil rights cases. See also Kruse, *White Flight*, 220–29; and A. K. Sandoval-Strausz, *Hotel: An American History* (New Haven, Conn.: Yale University Press, 2007), 308–9.

13. "Miller v. Amusement Enterprises," *Race Relations Law Reporter* 12, 3 (Fall 1967): 1505–15; "U.S. Court Upholds Fun Park's Ban on Negroes," *New York Times*, September 7, 1967, 33; "Judges Limit Power of 1964 Civil Rights Act," *Los Angeles Times*, September 7, 1967, 8.

14. "Miller v. Amusement Enterprises," 1507. The court also argued that bowling alleys and skating rinks were not "places of entertainment" (1508).

15. *Miller v. Amusement Enterprises, Inc.* 394 F. 2d 342 (5th Circuit, 1968). The Fifth Circuit upheld the initial ruling in 1967 but reversed this decision after rehearing the case in 1968. See also "Rights Ruling," *Washington Post*, April 10, 1968, A25.

16. "Adams v. Fazzio Real Estate Co.," *Race Relations Law Reporter* 12, 4 (Winter 1967): 2132–39.

17. Joan Garden, "The Private Club Exemption to the Civil Rights Act of 1964" 8 Urb. L. Ann. 333 (1974): 333–41; Marc Rohr, "Association, Privacy and the Private Club: The Constitutional Conflict," Harv. C.R.-C.L. Rev. 5, 460 (1970): 460–71; Joseph William Singer, "No Right to Exclude: Public Accommodations and Private Property," *Northwestern Law Review* 90, 4 (Summer 1996): 1283–1497. Randall Kennedy argues that the "Courts have applied the private club exception with rigorous strictness, permitting only associations that are 'truly private' to escape Title II's antidiscrimination mandate" ("The Struggle for Racial Equality in Public Accommodations," in *Legacies of the 1964 Civil Rights Act*, ed. Bernard Grofman [Charlottesville: University Press of Virginia, 2000], 160). Strict scrutiny of the "private club exception," however, depended on individuals' efforts to challenge private clubs and evolved over time.

18. "Clover Hill Swimming Club, Inc. v. Goldsboro," *Race Relations Law Reporter* 11, 3 (Fall 1966): 1516. Robert Goldsboro filed his complaint with the New Jersey Division on Civil Rights based on the state's antidiscrimination law passed as a direct result of the Palisades Park demonstrations.

19. "Kyles v. Paul, Jr.," *Race Relations Law Reporter* 12, 2 (Summer 1967): 1002–8.

20. "White v. City of Edwards," *Race Relations Law Reporter* 11, 4 (Winter 1966): 1994–96.

21. "Sullivan v. Little Hunting Park, Inc.," *Race Relations Law Reporter* 12, 2 (Summer 1967): 1008–9.

22. "Memphis Park 'Private Club,'" *Amusement Business* 76, 28 (July 18, 1964), 7.

23. "Parks, Pool React to Law: Integrate or Close Doors," *Amusement Business* 76, 29 (July 25, 1964): 5–6.

24. Jimmie Lewis Franklin, *Journey Toward Hope: A History of Blacks in Oklahoma* (Norman: University of Oklahoma Press, 1971), 191; "Oklahoma Protest March," *New York Times*, June 16, 1966, 35; "800 Rights Marchers Periled by Gunman," *Chicago Tribune*, June 18, 1966, A6; "Oklahoma Marchers End Swimming Pool Protest," *New York Times*, June 19, 1966, 66; "Burning Cross Greets March in Mississippi," *Chicago Tribune*, June 19, 1966, 5; "Oklahoma NAACP Youth March on City for Rights," *Chicago Defender*, June 25, 1966, 39; "38 Held at Amusement Park in Anti-Segregation Rally," *New York Times*, July 5, 1966, 22; "52 Oklahoma Demonstrators Jailed," *Chicago Defender*, July 6, 1966, 4; "Lawton, Okla., Bars Rights Aides' Bill," *New York Times*, July 6, 1966, 19; "Negroes Score Antibias Bill," *New York Times*, August 17, 1966, 18; Michael Kimball, "42 Years

Ago Today, a March Toward Equal Opportunities," *NewsOk*, http://newsok.com/article/3265789 (accessed July 4, 2008).

25. "N.C. City Quits Swim Pools," *Amusement Business* 76, 41 (October 17, 1964): 10. The city intended to try to sell the pools to a private enterprise.

26. "Race Issues at Park Pools; Some Close, Some Integrate," *Amusement Business* 76, 26 (July 4, 1964): 5–6; "Court Bars 'Rabble Rousers' from Funpark at Louisville," *Amusement Business* 76, 28 (July 18, 1964): 14–15; "Parks, Pool React to Law: Integrate or Close Doors," *Amusement Business* 76, 29 (July 25, 1964): 5–6. When the American Legion Post in Little Rock attempted to reopen the pools as private segregated facilities in 1965 the NAACP exposed the ruse and forced them to abandon their plans ("NAACP Foils Attempt to Reopen Segregated Pools," press release, May 7, 1965, Folder 7, "Discrimination, Parks & Playgrounds, 1956–65," Box A110, Series III, NAACP Papers, Library of Congress, Washington, D.C.).

27. "Parks, Pool React to Law."

28. Paul Y. Burns, Baton Rouge Council on Human Relations, to Edward C. Crafts, director of the U.S. Bureau of Outdoor Recreation, February 17, 1966, Louisiana State University Special Collections Library, http://louisdl.louislibraries.org/u?/LSU_SCE,206 (accessed January 2011).

29. Timothy B. Tyson, *Blood Done Sign My Name: A True Story* (New York: Crown Publishers, 2004), 18–19.

30. Andrew W. Kahrl, "On the Beach: Race and Leisure in the Jim Crow South" (Ph.D. diss., Indiana University, 2008), 289–95, 345–47.

31. Denise Trowbridge, "Back to the Beach: Pontchartrain Beach Is Still Part of Locals' Lives 20 Years After Closing Its Doors," *Liquid Weekly*, September 2001, http://www.denisetrowbridge.com/portfolio/stories/pontchartrainbeach.html (accessed September 8, 2008).

32. "LaGarde v. Recreation and Park Commission for Parish of East Baton Rouge," *Race Relations Law Reporter* 9, 2 (Summer 1964): 883. In the case of *United States of America v. Galiney* the federal district court required Miracle Lanes Bowling Center, a Portsmouth, Virginia, bowling alley, to abide by Title II of the Civil Rights Act. See *Race Relations Law Reporter* 12, 2 (Summer 1967): 999–1001.

33. Ohio Civil Rights Commission, "In the Matter of Holiday Sands, Inc.," *Race Relations Law Reporter* 9, 4 (Winter 1964): 2025–33.

34. "Little v. The Sedgefield Inn," *Race Relations Law Reporter* 11, 3 (Fall 1966): 1495–96; "Evans v. Laurel Links," *Race Relations Law Reporter* 11, 3 (Fall 1966): 1496–99.

35. "Anti-Discrimination Ordinance, Maryland," *Race Relations Law Reporter* 9, 3 (Fall 1964): 1503–8.

36. "Okla. City Integrates Fun," *Amusement Business* 76, 24 (June 20, 1964): 14.

37. Quoted in "Kansas City Anti-Bias Vote Affects 'Private' Fun Parks," *Amusement Business* 76, 15 (April 18, 1964): 10.

38. Lawrence R. Samuel, *The End of Innocence: The 1964–1965 New York World's Fair* (Syracuse, N.Y.: Syracuse University Press, 2007), 27.

39. Quoted in ibid., 34.

40. For descriptions of the New York World's Fair protest, see ibid., 26–28, 33–37; Brian Purnell, "'Drive Awhile for Freedom': Brooklyn CORE's 1964 Stall-In and Public Discourses on Protest Violence," in *Groundwork: Local Black Freedom Movements in America*, ed. Jeanne F. Theoharis and Komozi Woodward (New York: New York University Press, 2005), 45–76; Craig Steven Wilder, *A Covenant with Color: Race and Social Power in Brooklyn* (New York: Columbia University Press, 2000), 235–40; and Loevy, *To End All Segregation*, 206–10. Purnell disputes the characterization of the stall-in as a failure, noting that it demonstrated "the power of ordinary people to influence and alter business as usual by merely threatening to shut down the city" (48).

41. Ella Baker, "Bigger than a Hamburger," *Southern Patriot* (May 1960): 4. Baker wrote, "Whatever may be the difference in approach to their goal, the Negro and white students, North and

South, are seeking to rid America of the scourge of racial segregation and discrimination—not only at lunch counters, but in every aspect of life."

42. Bayard Rustin, "From Protest to Politics," *Commentary* 39 (February 1965): 25–31.

43. Nikhil Pal Singh, *Black Is a Country: Race and the Unfinished Struggle for Democracy* (Cambridge, Mass.: Harvard University Press, 2004), 223.

44. Sugrue, *Sweet Land of Liberty*, 362.

45. Alan A. Siegel, *Smile: A Picture History of Olympic Park, 1887–1965* (Irvington, N.J.: Irvington Historical Society, 1983), 145; David Nasaw, *Going Out: The Rise and Fall of Public Amusements* (New York: Basic Books, 1993), 243.

46. Quoted in "The Day the Park Opened," *Star Ledger*, May 3, 1965, 1.

47. For descriptions of the Olympic Park riot, see Nasaw, *Going Out*, 253; John Hannigan, *Fantasy City: Pleasure and Profit in the Postmodern Metropolis* (New York: Routledge, 1998), 46–47; Judith A. Adams, *The American Amusement Park Industry: A History of Technology and Thrills* (Boston: Twayne Publishers, 1991), 68–71; Siegel, *Smile*, 163; "Rampaging Youths Stone Cars, Stores Near Jersey Park," *New York Times*, May 2, 1965, 61; "The Day the Park Opened"; and "1,000 Youths Riot, Loot Essex Stores," *Star Ledger*, May 2, 1965, 1.

48. "Amusement Park in Jersey Denied License Renewal," *New York Times*, May 13, 1965, 11.

49. "Amusement Park in Jersey Gets Reprieve in License," *New York Times*, May 16, 1965, 46; "Expect Olympic License Renewal Tomorrow Night," *Star Ledger*, May 13, 1965, 17; "Permit Granted Olympic Park," *Star Ledger*, May 15, 1965, 2.

50. Adams, *The American Amusement Park Industry*, 71; "Disney Attractions," http://disneyworld.disney.go.com/parks/magic-kingdom/attractions/cinderellas-golden-carrousel/ (accessed March 10, 2008).

51. "Citizens' Group Reports on Easter Monday Outbreak," *New York Times*, May 5, 1966, 41.

52. "Thousands of Teen-Agers Riot in a Park Outside the Capital," *New York Times*, April 12, 1966, 29. See also "Youth Role Is Asked in Park Policy," *Washington Post*, April 19, 1966, B4; "Youth Workers Call Riot Spontaneous," *Washington Post*, April 14, 1966, D1; "Washington, D.C. Teen Riot Planned, Officials Charge," *Chicago Defender*, April 13, 1966, 4; "Park Is Blamed in Capital Riot," *New York Times*, May 5, 1966, 41; "D.C. Buses Pulled Off During Riot," *Washington Post*, April 19, 1966, A1.

53. Arthur Krock, "In the Nation: The Washington Riot," *New York Times*, April 14, 1966, 38. See also Krock, "In the Nation: The White House Conference," *New York Times*, June 2, 1966, 42.

54. "D.C. Summer Won't Be Long, Hot, Say Officials," *Chicago Defender*, April 16, 1966, 31; "D.C. Transit Asks End to Cabin John Shuttle," *Washington Post*, April 22, 1966, B2; Brooks McNamara, "Come on Over: The Rise and Fall of the American Amusement Park," *Theatre Crafts* 11, 9 (September 1977): 86; Al Griffin, *"Step Right Up Folks!"* (Chicago: Henry Regnery Company, 1974), 21–22.

55. Quoted in Kirk Scharfenberg, "Laughter Dies at Glen Echo," *Washington Post*, April 2, 1969, C1.

56. Sharon Zukin, "From Coney Island to Las Vegas in the Urban Imaginary: Discursive Practices of Growth and Decline," *Urban Affairs Review* 33, 5 (May 1998): 637; Gary S. Cross and John K. Walton, *The Playful Crowd: Pleasure Places in the Twentieth Century* (New York: Columbia University Press, 2005), 149.

57. "Coney Island Slump Grows Worse," *New York Times*, July 2, 1964, 33. The concessionaires also cited inadequate parking, bad weather, and competition from the world's fair as reasons for the park's decline.

58. Quoted in Martin Arnold, "Subway Ride from Coney Island Can Be Long, Lonely, Fearful," *New York Times*, June 8, 1964, 32.

59. Zukin, "From Coney Island to Las Vegas," 635–45; Michael Immerso, *Coney Island: The People's Playground* (New Brunswick, N.J.: Rutgers University Press, 2002), 158, 167, 169–71; Cross and Walton, *The Playful Crowd*, 148–50; Paul Hoffman, "Coney Island's Slums and Tidy Homes

Reflect Big-City Problems," *New York Times*, July 24, 1967, 28. The African American and Puerto Rican communities were concentrated in the West End of Coney Island, which was declared a "poverty zone" in 1967. In contrast, Seagate, at the tip of Brooklyn, was a largely white, middle-class neighborhood with a private police force and a twelve-foot fence separating it from Coney Island.

60. Quoted in Cross and Walton, *The Playful Crowd*, 149.

61. "4,000 Teen-Agers Brawl at Coney," *New York Times*, May 31, 1966, 28. There were also incidents of "unruly bands of teen-agers" at both Orchard Beach and Rockaway Beach that same day.

62. Bernard Weinraub, "Holiday Patrols Set Up by Police," *New York Times*, July 6, 1966, p. 69.

63. Ibid.

64. "Mayor Blames Transit Authority Planning for Coney Island Disorders," *New York Times*, April 16, 1968, 28: "Mayor Blasts TA Brass on Coney Island Debacle," *New York Amsterdam News*, April 20, 1968, 25; Bernard L. Collier, "Coney Islanders Anticipate Flare-Ups," *New York Times*, April 22, 1968, 36; "Postpone Trial of 11 in Coney Riot Charge," *New York Amsterdam News*, April 27, 1968, 25.

65. Quoted in "Mayor Blasts TA Brass on Coney Island Debacle."

66. "Nazi War Camp Tactics Laid to TA," *New York Amsterdam News*, April 27, 1968, p. 25.

67. Hoffman, "Coney Island's Slums and Tidy Homes Reflect Big-City Problems."

68. Judith Adams views Cedar Point's remote location as the central reason for its continued prosperity after World War II. The park excluded African Americans from its hotels until the NAACP filed a complaint in 1961. Adams, *The American Amusement Park Industry*, 78–83.

69. Quoted in Rick Shale and Charles J. Jacques, Jr., *Idora Park: The Last Ride of Summer* (Jefferson, Ohio: Amusement Park Journal, 1999), 104. For descriptions of the 1967 arrests, see Shale and Jacques, *Idora Park*, 99–100; and Sherry Lee Linkon and John Russo, *Steeltown U.S.A.: Work and Memory in Youngstown* (Lawrence: University Press of Kansas, 2002), 43.

70. "Disturbance," *Chicago Defender*, October 10, 1967, 5.

71. William Boone, "Springlake Park: An Oklahoma City Playground Remembered," *Chronicles of Oklahoma* 69, 1 (1991): 20–21; Jimmie Lewis Franklin, *Journey Toward Hope: A History of Blacks in Oklahoma* (Norman: University of Oklahoma Press, 1971), 191. Wedgewood Amusement Park in Oklahoma City allowed African Americans into the park one day per week.

72. Boone, "Springlake Park," 20.

73. Ibid., 20–24; "Thirty Arrested, Scores in 3-Hour Riot Started at City Amusement Park," *Daily Oklahoman*, April 12, 1971, 1; Douglas Loudenback, *Springlake Amusement Park* (Chicago: Arcadia Publishing, 2008), 10–11, 121–22. After years of decline the park closed in 1981.

74. "Witnesses Say Disorder Was Sparked by Rumor," *Louisville Courier Journal*, May 28, 1968, 11; "Guard Ordered to Riot Duty as West End Looting Flares," *Louisville Courier Journal*, May 28, 1968, 1; "Riots Flare Anew in Louisville's West End," *Louisville Courier Journal*, May 29, 1968, 1; "17 Treated at Hospital, 4 with Gunshot Wounds," *Louisville Courier Journal*, May 29, 1968, 7; "Remove the Causes of Violence," *Louisville Defender*, May 30, 1968, 6; "Guard Leaves Trouble Area," *Louisville Courier Journal*, May 30, 1968, 1; "Mother of Slain Boy Asks End to Violence," *Louisville Courier Journal*, May 31, 1968, 1.

75. "Sunday Rampage Shuts Fontaine Ferry—Permanently," *Louisville Courier Journal*, May 6, 1969, B1, B24.

76. "Fontaine Ferry Park," http://www.fontaineferrypark.com/ffhistory.html (accessed July 1, 2007).

77. Cross and Walton, *The Playful Crowd*, 149.

78. Adams, *The American Amusement Park Industry*, 71.

79. Kerner Commission, *Report of the National Commission on Civil Disorders*, 1.

80. Education was tied with recreation on the list of grievances. The top three were police practices, unemployment, and housing. Kerner Commission, *Report of the National Commission on Civil Disorders*, 4. The authors noted, "Grievances concerning municipal recreation programs

were found in a large majority of the 20 cities and appeared to be one of the most serious complaints in almost half. Inadequate recreational facilities in the ghetto and the lack of organized programs were common complaints" (81).

81. Kerner Commission, *Report of the National Commission on Civil Disorders*, 26, 29.

82. Works on King's time in Chicago include James R. Ralph, Jr., *Northern Protest: Martin Luther King, Jr., Chicago, and the Civil Rights Movement* (Cambridge, Mass.: Harvard University Press, 1993); Alan B. Anderson and George W. Pickering, *Confronting the Color Line: The Broken Promise of the Civil Rights Movement in Chicago* (Athens: University of Georgia Press, 1986), 160–280; and Sugrue, *Sweet Land of Liberty*, 416–20.

83. For descriptions of the riot, see Kerner Commission, *Report of the National Commission on Civil Disorders*, 2; Anderson and Pickering, *Confronting the Color Line*, 210–15; Amanda Seligman, *Block by Block: Neighborhoods and Public Policy on Chicago's West Side* (Chicago: University of Chicago Press, 2005), 217–18; Andrew J. Diamond, *Mean Streets: Chicago Youths and the Everyday Struggle for Empowerment in the Multiracial City, 1908–1969* (Berkeley: University of California Press, 2009), 269–70; Ralph, *Northern Protest*, 109–12; Mike Royko, *Boss: Richard J. Daley of Chicago* (New York: E. P. Dutton, 1971), 147–52; and Jeff Wiltse, *Contested Waters: A Social History of Swimming Pools in America* (Chapel Hill: University of North Carolina Press, 2007), 185–87.

84. Anderson and Pickering, *Confronting the Color Line*, 214.

85. Royko, *Boss*, 151.

86. Martin Luther King, Jr., to Friend, July 1966, Folder 6, Box 51, McCrackin Papers, Cincinnati Historical Society, Cincinnati, Ohio. In *Contested Waters*, Jeff Wiltse notes that cities built many pools during the late 1960s using War on Poverty money in an effort to appease demands for equal recreation. This national "pool-building spree" was sparked, in part, by the fire hydrant riot (184–89).

87. Anderson and Pickering, *Confronting the Color Line*, 220–21.

88. Ibid., 224.

89. Royko, *Boss*, 153.

90. Quoted in ibid., 160

91. Thomas J. Sugrue and Andre P. Goodman, "Plainfield Burning: Black Rebellion in the Suburban North," *Journal of Urban History* 33, 4 (May 2007): 580.

92. For descriptions of the riot, see ibid., 568–601; and Kerner Commission, *Report of the National Commission on Civil Disorders*, 41–45.

93. Sugrue and Goodman, "Plainfield Burning," 592. New Brunswick, New Jersey, also received five portable swimming pools after a race riot there in 1967 (86).

94. See, for example, "Michigan Civil Rights Commission Complaint against Orchard Lanes," *Race Relations Law Reporter* 10, 4 (Winter 1965): 1856–57; "Shields v. Midtown Bowling Lanes, Georgia," *Race Relations Law Reporter* 11, 3 (Fall 1966): 1492–95; "United States of America v. Francis Galiney, Virginia," *Race Relations Law Reporter* 12, 2 (Summer 1967): 999–1001; and "Adams v. Fazzio Real Estate Co., Louisiana."

95. Jack Nelson and Jack Bass, *The Orangeburg Massacre* (New York: World Publishing Company, 1970), 3, 18–31.

96. Cleveland Sellers, *The River of No Return: The Autobiography of a Black Militant and the Life and Death of SNCC* (Jackson: University Press of Mississippi, 1990), 209. Sellers organized the Black Awareness Coordinating Committee (BACC) in Orangeburg. The members of this group agreed that they should not "get involved" in the bowling alley issue.

97. Quoted in Nelson and Bass, *The Orangeburg Massacre*, 50. For descriptions of the February 8 events, see ibid., 34–39; and Mike Davis, "General State of Disorder," *Afro-American*, February 10, 1968, 1.

98. Nelson and Bass, *The Orangeburg Massacre*, 80.

99. For descriptions of the massacre, see Nelson and Bass, *The Orangeburg Massacre*, 67–98;

Davis, "General State of Disorder"; Mike Davis, "Three Dead, Fifty Shot on S.C. Campus," *Afro-American*, February 10, 1968, 1; Robert M. Ford, "Three Students Killed, Thirty Seven Hurt in Uprising," *Atlanta Daily World*, February 10, 1968, 1; "Terror Wave Hits South," *Pittsburgh Courier*, February 21, 1968, 1; "Student Slayings Arouse Nation," *Pittsburgh Courier*, February 17, 1968, 1; Perlstein, *Nixonland*, 237; and Sellers, *The River of No Return*, 209–19. See also the film *Scarred Justice: The Orangeburg Massacre, 1968* (California Newsreel, 2010).

100. Ford, "Three Students Killed, Thirty Seven Hurt in Uprising." Sellers spent seven months in jail after his conviction. Upon his release he earned a master's degree in education from Harvard University and a Ph.D. in history from the University of North Carolina at Greensboro.

101. Quoted in "Dr. King Demands U.S. Action in Student Killing at College," *Atlanta Daily World*, February 15, 1968, 1.

102. Quoted in "Rights Suit Filed in Carolina Riots," *New York Times*, February 11, 1968, 37. The suit was based on the interstate commerce clause as the alley incorporated a snack bar that served interstate travelers and bought supplies from out-of-state businesses. The Justice Department also filed a suit demanding that the Orangeburg Hospital desegregate. The hospital had resisted integration, even after the Department of Health, Education and Welfare threatened to cut off federal aid, including the recently enacted Medicare and Medicaid programs. All of the wounded students were treated in segregated facilities. See "Hospital Target in Carolina Suit," *New York Times*, February 14, 1968, 20.

103. "Rights Suit Fought," *New York Times*, February 16, 1968, 16; "Judge Orders Curb on Bowling Center," *New York Times*, February 24, 1968, 14.

104. "Two Negroes Bowl," *New York Times*, February 27, 1968, 31; Nelson and Bass, *The Orangeburg Massacre*, 118.

105. Martin Luther King, Jr., *Where Do We Go from Here: Chaos or Community?* (New York: Harper and Row, 1967), 13.

106. Sugrue, *Sweet Land of Liberty*, 350.

107. Alison Isenberg, *Downtown America: A History of the Place and the People Who Made It* (Chicago: University of Chicago Press, 2004), 231–33. Isenberg points out that some contemporary observers used "exploitation theory" to explain the riots, which they saw as the outcome of the exploitation of black consumers by white retailers. See also Regina Austin, "'A Nation of Thieves': Consumption, Commerce, and the Black Public Sphere," *Public Culture* 7 (1994): 225–48; and Kevin Mumford, "Harvesting the Crisis: The Newark Uprising, the Kerner Commission, and Writings on Riots," in *African American Urban History Since World War II*, ed. Kenneth L. Kusmer and Joe W. Trotter (Chicago: University of Chicago Press, 2009), 203–18.

108. Isenberg, *Downtown America*, 254.

109. Wesley G. Skogan, "Crime in Contemporary America," in *Violence in America: Historical and Comparative Perspectives*, ed. Hugh Davis Graham and Robert Gurr (Beverly Hills, Calif.: Sage Publications, 1970), 375.

110. Scott Newman, "Riverview Park," 5, http://chicago.urban-history.org/sites/parks/rivervie.htm (accessed October 10, 2007). The one consistent exception was the annual Bud Billiken Parade, which began in 1929 and was sponsored by the *Chicago Defender*. Bud Billiken was a fictional character created by the editor of the paper in 1928 in order to promote the newspaper among young people. See "Bud Billiken Parade," in *Encyclopedia of Chicago*, http://encyclopedia.chicagohistory.org/pages/175.html (accessed October 15, 2007).

111. On the African Dip, see Newman, "Riverview Park," 5; Stan Barker, "Paradises Lost," *Chicago History* 22 (March 1993): 29, 48; Nasaw, *Going Out*, 93–94; Chuck Wlodarczyk, *Riverview: Gone But Not Forgotten, 1904–1967* (Park Ridge, Ill.: Riverview Publications, 1977), 53; Dolores Haugh, *Riverview Amusement Park* (Chicago: Arcadia Publishing, 2004), 118; Jerome Watson, "It Was a Paper Palace, Full of Fun and Thrills," *Chicago Sun-Times*, October 4, 1967, 12; Henry T. Sampson, *The Ghost Walks: A Chronological History of Blacks in Show Business, 1865–1910* (Metuchen, N.J.:

Scarecrow Press, 1988), 237; Mike Royko, "The Dip Gets 'The Business' at Riverview," *Chicago Daily News*, May 21, 1964, 16; and Cross and Walton, *The Playful Crowd*, 54. In some versions of the African Dip (also known as the "African Dodger," "Hit the Nigger," or "Coontown Plunges") white patrons threw balls directly at the heads of blacks. Blacks in Chicago were protesting the African Dip as early as 1912. See "Men in Stature; Babies in Courage," *Chicago Defender*, July 27, 1912, 1; "Will Amusement Parks Continue to Draw Color Line," *Chicago Defender*, March 28, 1914, 1; "Riverview Park Exhibit Disgusting," *Chicago Defender*, July 1, 1944, 12; "Protests Riverview 'Dip,'" *Chicago Defender*, July 6, 1946, 14; "Rap Riverview Park," *Chicago Defender*, July 8, 1950, 6; and "Humor or Ridicule," *Chicago Defender*, December 19, 1953, 11.

112. Newman, "Riverview Park"; Adams, *The American Amusement Park Industry*, 73; Nasaw, *Going Out*, 253–54; "Chicago's Amusement Gap," *Chicago Daily News*, October 5, 1967, 10; William Spencer, "Riverview—Suddenly It's History!" *Chicago's American*, October 4, 1967, 36; "Riverview: The Long, Joyful Ride Ends," *Chicago Daily News*, October 4, 1967, 20.

113. Helen FitzMaurice, "To Riverview, with Love," *Chicago's American Magazine*, April 27, 1969, 14.

114. Gary Cooper, "The World That Was at Belmont and Western," *Chicago Tribune Magazine*, May 16, 1976, 26.

115. "Era Ends, River View to Be Razed," *Chicago Tribune*, October 4, 1967, 1. The local police commander, John Fahey, reported, "It was always a tension spot, but it was not as bad as you might suppose." Quoted in "Riverview—Only a Memory Now," *Northwest Times*, October 11, 1967, 4. Eric Avila, in *Popular Culture in the Age of White Flight: Fear and Fantasy in Suburban Los Angeles* (Berkeley: University of California Press, 2004), repeats the popular idea that "Riverview began a rapid decline as the park became the grounds for racial and gang violence" (1).

116. "Inquiring Photographer," *Chicago Defender*, October 9, 1967, 13. A group of people were asked the question, "How do you feel about Riverview Park being torn down?" See a similar column on Riverview, "Inquiring Photographer," *Chicago Defender*, October 16, 1967, 13.

117. Adams, *The American Amusement Park Industry*, 113.

118. Ernie Waits, Sr., quoted in Lew Moores, "Coney Island Segregation Ended 40 Years Ago," *Cincinnati Enquirer*, May 27, 2001.

119. Dale Samuelson, *The American Amusement Park* (St. Paul, Minn.: MBI Publishing, 2001), 114–15; Charles Jacques, *Cincinnati's Coney Island: America's Finest Amusement Park* (Jefferson, Ohio: Amusement Park Journal, 2002), 189–214. See also Raymond M. Weinstein, "Disneyland and Coney Island: Reflections on the Evolution of the Modern Amusement Park," *Journal of Popular Culture* 26, 1 (1992): 131–64. Taft Broadcasting purchased Coney Island in 1969. Because the huge Sunlite Pool could not be transported, the owner of Kings Island kept it in operation at the old site of the park.

120. Leo O. Bush, "Euclid Beach Park . . . More than Special," *Amusement Park Journal* 5, 2+3 (1983): 32.

121. Adams, *The American Amusement Park*, 81; Samuelson, *The American Amusement Park*, 119. Scholars have used these popular histories to draw similar conclusions. For example, John Hannigan states that Euclid Beach closed because of "juvenile gangs" (*Fantasy City*, 46).

122. Amusement Park Books, *Euclid Beach Park Is Closed for the Season* (Fairview Park, Ohio, 1977), 198. This event was sponsored by the Cleveland Federation of Labor and attracted 51,000 to the park.

123. Quoted in Cyril Dostal, "Paradise Misplaced," *Cleveland Magazine* (September 1977): 128–29.

124. Ibid., 129.

125. Amusement Park Books, *Euclid Beach Park Is Closed for the Season*, 266.

126. Mark Surface, "Recollections of Pacific Ocean Park," *Amusement Park Journal* 5, 1 (1983): 43; Hannigan, *Fantasy City*, 47. Pacific Ocean Park opened in 1958 to compete with the nearby

Disneyland, but its urban location made it vulnerable to the racial antagonisms that would doom older amusement parks.

127. David G. Vanderstal and Connie Zeigler, "Riverside Park," in *The Encyclopedia of Indianapolis* (Bloomington: Indiana University Press, 1994), 1197–98.

128. McNamara, "Come on Over," 83–84.

129. Donna M. DeBlasio, "The Immigrant and the Trolley Park in Youngstown, Ohio, 1899–1945," *Rethinking History* 5, 1 (2001): 88.

130. Adams, *The American Amusement Park Industry*, 76–77.

131. Nasaw, *Going Out*, 254. A number of traditional parks near Denver, Colorado, also remain open today, including Lakeside Amusement Park. Jim Futrell, historian of the National Amusement Park Historical Association, states that there are eleven trolley parks still in operation. "Last of the Trolley Parks," *Buffalo News*, August 1, 2010, F14.

132. Cross and Walton, *The Playful Crowd*, 190, 252.

Conclusion

1. Gary S. Cross, and John K. Walton, *The Playful Crowd: Pleasure Places in the Twentieth Century* (New York: Columbia University Press, 2005), 193–94. John M. Findlay, in *Magic Lands: Western Cityscapes and American Culture After 1940* (Berkeley: University of California Press, 1992), points out that "In spatial terms, Disneyland had to remain a suburban enclave even as it became urbanized" (62). By the late 1990s it was clear this fiction could not be entirely maintained.

2. Quoted in Michael Sorkin, ed., *Variations on a Theme Park: The New American City and the End of Public Space* (New York: Hill and Wang, 1992), 231. For discussions of Disney World, see Cross and Walton, *The Playful Crowd*, 194–202; Scott A. Lukas, *Theme Park* (London: Reaktion Books, 2008), 180–200; Sharon Zukin, *The Culture of Cities* (Oxford: Blackwell, 1995), 49–77; Margaret J. King, "Disneyland and Walt Disney World: Traditional Values in Futuristic Form," *Journal of Popular Culture* 15 (Summer 1981): 116–39; Richard Schickel, *The Disney Version: The Life, Times, Art and Commerce of Walt Disney* (Chicago: Ivan R. Dee, 1997); The Disney Project, *Inside the Mouse: Work and Play at Disney* (Durham, N.C.: Duke University Press, 1995); Richard E. Foglesong, *Married to the Mouse: Walt Disney World and Orlando* (New Haven, Conn.: Yale University Press, 2000); Chad Denver Emerson, *Project Future: The Inside Story Behind the Creation of Disney World* (New York: Ayefour Publishing, 2010); and Sharon Zukin, *Landscapes of Power: From Detroit to Disneyworld* (Berkeley: University of California Press, 1991).

3. The term "Disneyfication" has become commonplace. For a relatively early usage, see Zukin, *The Culture of Cities*. See also Alan E. Bryman, *The Disneyization of Society* (London: Sage Publications, 2004), for a similar analysis. For a discussion of theming, see Mark Gottdiener, *The Theming of America: American Dreams, Media Fantasies, and Themed Environments* (New York: Westview Press, 2001); and John Hannigan, *Fantasy City: Pleasure and Profit in the Postmodern Metropolis* (New York: Routledge, 1998).

4. Sorkin, *Variations on a Theme Park*. See also James Howard Kunstler, *The Geography of Nowhere: The Rise and Decline of America's Man-Made Landscape* (New York: Simon and Schuster, 1993); and Henry A. Giroux, *The Mouse That Roared: Disney and the End of Innocence* (New York: Rowman and Littlefield, 2010).

5. Bryant Simon, *Boardwalk Dreams: Atlantic City and the Fate of Urban America* (New York: Oxford University Press, 2004), 17. Alison Isenberg, in *Downtown America: A History of the Place and the People Who Made It* (Chicago: University of Chicago Press, 2004), makes a similar argument about the nostalgia for downtowns.

6. There is a growing literature on historical memory. See, for example, Renee C. Romano and Leigh Raiford, eds., *The Civil Rights Movement in American Memory* (Athens: University of Georgia Press, 2006); Michael Kammen, *Mystic Chords of Memory* (New York: Knopf, 1991); Roy Rosensz-

weig and David Thelen, *The Presence of the Past* (New York: Columbia University Press, 2000); Michael Wallace, *Mickey Mouse History and Other Essays on American Memory* (Philadelphia: Temple University Press, 1996); David W. Blight, *Race and Reunion: The Civil War in American Memory* (Cambridge, Mass.: Harvard University Press, 2002); and George Lipsitz, *Time Passages: Collective Memory and American Popular Culture* (Minneapolis: University of Minnesota Press, 2001).

7. Arcadia Publishing titles include: *Conneaut Lake Park, Dorney Park, Early Amusement Parks of Orange County, Greetings from Bertrand Island Amusement Park, Hershey Park, Indian Trail and Edgemont Amusement Parks, Kennywood, Lake Pontchartrain, Maryland's Amusement Parks, Lakewood Park, Palisades Park, Ohio's Amusement Parks,* and *Riverview Amusement Park.*

8. *Things That Aren't There Anymore* (WNED, 1994). Other documentaries of Crystal Beach include *I Remember Crystal Beach* (Wex Studio, 1988—A Timothy Wagner film); *The Life and Times of Crystal Beach* (Pacific Productions, 1994); *The Comet Shines Again* (Wex Studio, 1999); *The Canadiana and Crystal Beach* (Wex Studio, 1999); *One Last Ride: Crystal Beach Amusement Park* (Last Ride Productions, 2000); *Thanks for the Memories* (RDPK Productions, 2006); *Remembering Crystal Beach Park* (WNED TV, 2008); and *Crystal Beach Amusement Park: Then and Now* (Seventy Seven Publishing, 2007).

9. Erno Rossi, *Crystal Beach: The Good Old Days* (Port Colborne, Ontario: Seventy Seven Publishing, 2005); Verlyn Klinkenborg, *The Last Fine Time* (New York: Alfred A. Knopf, 1991). For similar titles, see George Kunz, *Buffalo Memories: Gone But Not Forgotten* (Buffalo: Canisius College Press, 2002); and Rose Ann Jankowiak-Hirsch, *Crystal Memories: 101 Years of Fun at Crystal Beach Park* (Palmyra, N.Y.: R. A. Jankowiak-Hirsch, 2004).

10. Kunz, *Buffalo Memories*, 278. The Crystal Beach Candy Company is still in operation and sells the suckers and sugar waffles the park was known for.

11. Quoted in Catherine Fosl and Tracy E. K'Meyer, *Freedom on the Border: An Oral History of the Civil Rights Movement in Kentucky* (Lexington: University Press of Kentucky, 2009), 17.

12. John Green quoted in John C. Pillow, "Shawnee Farms of the 1800s Gave Way to Park and Dignified Homes: Racial Makeup Has Changed," http://www.fontaineferrypark.com/ffarticles.html (accessed October 10, 2005).

13. "Memories," http://www.fontaineferrypark.com/memories/ffmemories6.html (accessed October 9, 2005).

14. Steve Ammon, "Memories," http://www.fontaineferrypark.com/memories/ffmemories8.html (accessed October 9, 2005).

15. Ronna Adkins, "Memories," http://www.fontaineferrypark.com/memories/ffmemories6.html (accessed October 9, 2005).

16. "Memories," http://www.fontaineferrypark.com/memories/ffmemories4.html (accessed October 9, 2005). This was posted by the granddaughter of the majority owners of the park in its later years, Alfred and Emelie Doerr of St. Louis.

17. See George Lipsitz, *How Racism Takes Place* (Philadelphia: Temple University Press, 2011), 31–32; and Evan McKenzie, *Privatopia: Homeowner Associations and the Rise of Residential Private Government* (New Haven, Conn.: Yale University Press, 1996), 22–23. As Lipsitz notes, "At a time when Black activists and their allies of all races were being arrested, mobbed, and beaten for trying to desegregate swimming pools and other venues purportedly open to the public, the FHA argued that public ownership of pools, parks, and playgrounds near new planned unit developments would have to be open to the public at large if general tax revenues paid for them" (31). Both Lipsitz and McKenzie quote former labor secretary Robert Reich, who has argued, "In many cities and towns, the wealthy have in effect withdrawn their dollars from the support of public services and institutions shared by all and dedicated the savings to their own private services" (quoted in Lipsitz, *How Racism Takes Place*, 40 and McKenzie, *Privatopia*, 23). On privatization of public services, see Edward J. Blakely, *Fortress America: Gated Communities in the United States* (Washington, D.C.: Brookings Institution Press, 1999).

18. On the decline of municipal pools, see Jeff Wiltse, *Contested Waters: A Social History of Swimming Pools in America* (Chapel Hill: University of North Carolina Press, 2007), 189–93.

19. Jeffrey Collins, "Public Pools Closing Across Country as Cities Struggle with Budget Cuts," *Huffington Post*, http://www.huffingtonpost.com/2011/05/30/public-pools-closing-acro_n_868753 (accessed May 30, 2011). See also "Looking for a Pool and Coming Up Dry as Cities Shave Budgets," *New York Times*, July 7, 2011, A13. The recent cutbacks in funding for municipal recreation are in direct contrast to the many pools built during the Great Depression, a fact noted by Collins, "Public Pools Closing Across Country."

20. The park is adjacent to the powerful Niagara River and therefore the pond has a strong underlying current. Nine-year-old Joel Rama, an immigrant from Burundi, drowned in the pond in June 2011. The summer before, Diquan Warren, a sixteen-year-old public housing resident, drowned in another pond at the same park. Buffalo does not open its few public pools until July. See Lou Michel and Gene Warner, "Drownings Point to Need for Caution," *Buffalo News*, June 2, 2010; "Unseen Peril of 'Live' Pond Spells Death for Boy," *Buffalo News*, June 7, 2011; and Don Esmonde, "Refugees Find High Risks on Squaw Island," *Buffalo News*, June 24, 2011.

21. Michelle R. Boyd, *Jim Crow Nostalgia: Reconstructing Race in Bronzeville* (Minneapolis: University of Minnesota Press, 2008), xiii.

22. Ibid., xv.

23. Peter M. Kusiak, "Oral History Interview with Dr. Dudley Cooper," November 30, 1978, p. 3, Oral Histories in the Perry Library, Old Dominion University, Norfolk, Va. For a description of Sea View Beach, see "Seaview Beach," *Amusement Business* 73, 37 (September 18, 1961): 27.

24. "Close La. Negro Fun Park," *Amusement Business* 76, 33 (August 22, 1964): 13. For an extensive discussion of Lincoln Beach, see Andrew W. Kahrl, "On the Beach: Race and Leisure in the Jim Crow South" (Ph.D. diss., Indiana University, 2008), chap. 5.

25. Quoted in William H. Chafe, Raymond Gavins, and Robert Korstad, eds., *Remembering Jim Crow: African Americans Tell About Life in the Segregated South* (New York: The New Press, 2001), 166.

26. James Baldwin, *The Fire Next Time* (New York: Vintage 1992), 22.

27. Anders Walker, *The Ghost of Jim Crow: How Southern Moderates Used Brown v. Board of Education to Stall Civil Rights* (New York: Oxford University Press, 2009). Walker focuses on education in his work but extends his analysis to public accommodations.

28. Ibid., 5.

29. Ted Gup, "Skating Rink Bias Splits Fauquier," *Washington Post*, November 10, 1978, B1; "Club in Philadelphia Suburb Faces Accusations of Racism," *New York Times*, July 10, 2009, A11.

30. "'Gang Attire' Ejections Prompt Suit Against Park," *San Francisco Chronicle*, July 3, 1991, A20; Erin Ailworth, "Six Flags Agrees to Settle Discrimination Suit," *Los Angeles Times*, May 14, 2004. In both these cases civil rights lawsuits successfully ended the screening.

31. The memories of those fears linger, as suggested in the South Park episode "Pee" when the character of Cartman sings the memorable lyric, "There are too many minorities in my water park." "Not My Waterpark," http://www.southparkstudios.com/clips/256710/not-my-waterpark (accessed July 18, 2011).

32. Quoted in Brian Livingston, "Pool Resurrected from History," *Meridian Star*, September 2, 2007. See also Adam Nossiter, "Unearthing a Town Pool, and Not for Whites Only," *New York Times*, September 18, 2006; and Wally Northway, "Development Project Giving Old Mill Town of Stonewall New Life," *Mississippi Business Journal*, August 13, 2007. Nossiter reports that Carmichael was a racial moderate who ran for the U.S. Senate and for governor as a Republican in the 1970s.

Index

Acknowledgments

This book commenced a decade ago when I began researching a 1956 riot at Crystal Beach amusement park while teaching at Saint Bonaventure University in western New York. At that time I had no idea I would uncover so many similar incidents throughout the country and compile a national study tracing a movement for racial equality that has been largely overlooked. I could not have done this work without the cooperation and support of many individuals and institutions. Because this project has been an act of recovery, I am particularly indebted to the archivists who helped me locate valuable sources. For example, when I arrived at the Cincinnati Historical Society Library, I found a table with stacks of files laid out in waiting. I will always be grateful to the archivists there for their generous response to my inquiries about their local amusement park. The American Jewish Archives in Cincinnati were also enormously helpful in writing the history of Coney Island. Other archives that aided my research include the Library of Congress, the Moorland Springarn Research Center at Howard University, the Swarthmore Peace Collection, and the Special Collections at the Daley Library at the University of Illinois. In my hometown of Buffalo I received much assistance from the archivists at the Butler Library at Buffalo State College, the Buffalo Historical Society, and the Buffalo Public Library. Across the border the Fort Erie Public Library staff proved invaluable in providing local history sources. A special thanks must go to the intrepid Interlibrary Loan staff at the University of Rochester who agreed to order multiple volumes of *Billboard* for me. Given that these are now digitized on Google books, their labor is particularly appreciated.

The bulk of the time I spent researching and writing this book I was at the University of Rochester. There I was pleased to work with three exceptional undergraduate research assistants, Maya Dukmasova, Emily Meyers, and Caitlin Meives. They spent hours going over newspaper microfilm reels to help locate the dramatic stories of protest in this book. I also worked with a group of graduate students at Rochester who inspired me to push my analysis as they developed their own work. I am particularly indebted to Kathleen Casey, Jamie Saucier, Emily Morry, Michelle Finn, and Jeremy Saucier for their friendship and intellectual companionship. A number of History Department colleagues offered their camaraderie and support throughout my time at Rochester. In particular, Joan Rubin, Mike Jarvis, Lynn Gordon, Stewart Weaver, Daniel Borus, and Matthew Lenoe were supportive and engaged colleagues. The Frederick Douglass Institute for African and African American History was a vibrant and exciting intellectual home for me during my time at Rochester. I would particularly like to thank institute faculty who cheered my research efforts and supported me during my tenure as interim director in 2010–11. Larry Hudson, Joan Saab, Sharon Willis, John Michael, Jeffrey Tucker, Stephani Li, Valeria Sinclair-Chapman, Cilas Kemedjio, and Elias Mandala offered their advice and companionship throughout my time at the Frederick Douglass Institute.

Drafts of chapters were read by a number of extraordinarily generous historians. In particular, the participants of Rochester Area U.S. Historians gave me invaluable feedback on two draft chapters. Alison Parker, who leads this group, is a much-valued colleague and friend. Others who read portions of the manuscript or offered responses to conference papers include Carl Nightingale, Andrew Kahrl, Angel David Nieves, Achva Benzinberg Stein, Marta Gutman, David Nord, David Nasaw, William Graebner, and Nancy MacLean. In 2004 a remarkable group of scholars agreed to join me at the University of Rochester for a conference, "Northern Struggles: New Paradigms in Civil Rights." Our conversations during those two days deeply shaped my work. I owe a debt of gratitude to Thomas Sugrue, Beth Tompkins Bates, Steven Ward, Ula Taylor, Robert Self, and Martha Biondi for traveling to Rochester and participating in a lively set of conversations. I have also had numerous discussions and exchanges with both Kevin Kruse and Matthew Lassiter that have shaped my perspective on the history of racial segregation. For her friendship, intelligence, and conference companionship I also want to thank Georgina Hickey. Back in Buffalo Susan Varney and Elizabeth Peña were wonderful, supportive friends during the years of drafting and revising the manuscript.

A number of Buffalonians—Barbara Seals Nevergold, Sandra Walker, Cathy Herbert, and Vincent Paladino—shared their memories of Crystal Beach with me, for which I am deeply grateful. William Graebner gave me the great gift of his own oral histories of the Crystal Beach riot, as well as a much-redacted FBI file. His generosity will not be soon forgotten. Another group of Buffalonians, my new colleagues at the University at Buffalo, have welcomed me with great goodwill and provided valuable feedback on the manuscript. I am looking forward to working with them in the years ahead. Looking toward the future has also made me reflect on the past. Three extraordinary scholars who trained me at the University of Michigan when I was a graduate student still deeply influence my work and my respect for the craft of history. Robin D. G. Kelly, Earl Lewis, and Elsa Barkely Brown taught me the power that social history has to reshape our understanding of the past. Their belief in my ability to do this work has bolstered me throughout the years.

My experience working with Robert Lockhart at the University of Pennsylvania Press has restored my faith in academic publishing. He is a careful and thoughtful editor, generous with his time and considerable intellectual energy. I am also indebted to Erica Ginsburg, associate managing editor, and a talented copyeditor, Jennifer Backer, for safely steering the book toward publication. Portions of Chapter 4 draw from my previously published article, "Recreation and Race in the Postwar City: Buffalo's 1956 Crystal Beach Riot," *Journal of American History* (June 2006): 63–90, published by Oxford University Press. I also owe a debt of gratitude to the anonymous outside reader for the manuscript, who pointed to crucial revisions. Alison Isenberg provided detailed comments on the entire manuscript. Her reading of my work has proved vital to my revisions, and I am very grateful for her time and level of engagement.

My extended family is spread out far and wide, but they have always supported and applauded my efforts. Thanks go to all my siblings—Joel, Jennie, and Lauren—as well as their partners and children. My parents—Peter, Ilene, Nancy, and Jeff—have stood by me through the years. In particular my mother, Nancy Wolcott, raised me to be attentive to inequality and to value social justice, qualities I try to bring to my academic work. My inlaws, Ray and Gail Seeman, have showered me with affection and support from the day I entered their family. I am deeply grateful for their generosity toward me. My two girls, Nora and Maya, grew up with this book. They would tell their friends, "My dad studies death, and my mom studies amusement parks." They have kept me grounded and at peace, and their love always lifts me up. One new colleague at the University at Buffalo, Erik Seeman, is particularly dear to my heart. This book is dedicated to him for a multitude of reasons. He is the best first reader any writer could hope for, offering insightful criticisms and occasionally correcting lapses in grammar. His own work is a model of history research and writing. He is intellectually curious and a wonderful travel companion. But above all Erik is an extraordinary life partner. Our household sometimes feels like a small utopian experiment in egalitarian living. This book is for him, and for our life together.